INVENTING THE "GREAT AWAKENING"

INVENTING THE
"GREAT AWAKENING"

Frank Lambert

PRINCETON UNIVERSITY PRESS   PRINCETON, NEW JERSEY

Lambert, Frank, 1943–
Inventing the "great awakening" / Frank Lambert.
    p.   cm.
Includes bibliographical references and index.
ISBN 0-691-04379-5 (cloth : alk. paper)
1. Great Awakening.   2. Revivals—New England—History—18th
century.   3. Revivals—New Jersey—History—18th century.
I. Title.
BR520.L36   1999
277.3′07—dc21   98-26646

This book has been composed in Baskerville

For Beth

Contents

Illustrations

Tables

Acknowledgments

FROM the initial musings that inspired the writing of this book, many people have made invaluable contributions to its conceptualization and execution. Tim Breen, my mentor at Northwestern and now my friend, provided much encouragement for my considering the Great Awakening in its intercolonial and transatlantic sweep. While my research has led me down unanticipated interpretive paths, and perhaps some he would not have taken, I owe much to him for suggesting a point of departure.

Throughout the process of researching and writing, I benefited from others. Purdue University provided both funds and time off for research. William M. Fowler, Jr., Editor of the *New England Quarterly*, granted me an opportunity to test my thesis in that journal. He and Coeditor Linda Smith Rhoads have granted permission to reprint portions of my article, "The First Great Awakening: Whose Interpretive Fiction?" *New England Quarterly* 68 (December 1995): 650–659.

At times humbling, occasionally painful, but always instructive, the vetting process contributed greatly to my work, forcing me to justify assumptions, reexamine evidence, clarify arguments, and rethink conclusions. Without doubt, this book is better for the careful, critical scrutiny of outside readers. I am indebted to Virginia Anderson (Colorado), John Murrin (Princeton), and Mark Noll (Wheaton) for their probing questions and trenchant insights.

I also owe much to Brigitta van Rheinberg, Editor of History and Classics at Princeton University Press. Repeatedly, she demonstrated the value of a good editor. In guiding the project from first draft to publication, she pushed for broader, clearer conceptualization while providing encouragement and reassurance. And, because of the superb professional skills of text editor Lauren Lepow, the final version exhibits greater clarity and grace. I, however, take responsibility for any remaining textual or factual errors.

Finally, I owe a special debt to my family, my wife, Beth, and sons, Talley and William. They were gracious, and often critical, listeners to far too lengthy discussions of various arguments and pieces of evidence. They bore it with good humor and steadfast support, proving that familial love can endure all.

INVENTING THE "GREAT AWAKENING"

FOR a brief time in the early 1740s, religious events dominated the news in colonial America. Prime newspaper space usually devoted to matters emanating from statehouses contained the latest developments from meetinghouses. Weeklies from Boston to Charleston reported the huge crowds, often numbering in the thousands, that gathered at outdoor preaching services. Observers at those meetings described bizarre behavior including "Out-Cries, Faintings and Fits" as men and women reacted to frightening depictions of eternal damnation. Reporters noted the presence of persons who had theretofore rarely attended Christian churches. Joseph Park, minister at Westerly, Rhode Island, recorded that while "there were not above *ten or twelve* Indians that used to come to Meeting at all, . . . there is now *near an Hundred* that come very constantly." Others, who had formerly attended worship but paid little attention to sermons, suddenly began to take heed. John Tennent, pastor at Freehold, New Jersey, indicated that many who had previously gone to church "for their Diversion, viz. To hear News or speak to their Trades-Men," now "were taken in the Gospel Net." And concern about religion spread into regions once considered barren of spiritual sensitivities. Samuel Blair of New Londonderry, Pennsylvania, offered a joyful, though chauvinistic, portrayal of religious changes occurring in neighboring Maryland: "Several even in *Baltimore*. . . who were bro't up almost in a State of Heathenism . . . afford very satisfying Evidences of being brought to a saving Acquaintance with God in Jesus Christ."[1]

What was going on is a question that elicited much comment from contemporaries and continues to intrigue historians. Extensive coverage suggests that men and women of the time regarded these unusual occurrences as a major event in mid-eighteenth-century colonial America. Even after war erupted in 1739 between England and Spain, with fighting raging in the Americas, religious news remained on the front pages of colonial newspapers. But the reportage alone fails to provide a clear, unambiguous account of what exactly was happening, and what was behind it. Commentators soon emerged, however, to offer answers. Seizing the initiative was one group of evangelicals, hereafter referred to as revivalists. They offered their explanation of the event through a series of interpretive narratives that appeared in print almost as quickly as the events that inspired them unfolded. They claimed to discover in the scores of reported incidents a single event, one they called *the* "remarkable Revival of Religion." Moreover, these writers insisted that what they described was an *extraordinary* "Work of God." Though God was always at work redeeming fallen humankind, they contended that on rare occasions he dispensed his mercy in unusual outpourings. These narrators, primarily ministers, heralded the "great awakening" they were witnessing as one of those special moments previously seen only at Pentecost and during the Protestant Reformation. Sensitive to suggestions that human actions instead of divine inspiration lay behind the revival, they insisted that they were discoverers, not architects, of the events they reported.

American evangelicals had witnessed revivals before, but they proclaimed this one to be different. William Cooper, a Boston minister and revival promoter, differentiated between what he witnessed in the 1740s and previous local awakenings. Scope was one distinction. Unlike earlier local awakenings, this revival was, according to Cooper, "truly extraordinary in respect of the extent of it." While New England had witnessed the outpouring of God's spirit before, this manifestation was "more or less on the several provinces [of British North America] that measure many hundred miles on this continent."[2] In other words, he regarded this "great awakening" as intercolonial, an American revival before there was an American nation. And he found noteworthy "the uniformity of the work." He concluded from testimonies in "letters, and conversation with ministers and others who live in different parts of the land where this work is going on, [that] it is the same work that is carried on in one place and another."[3] Local circumstances were as varied as in previous revivals, but revivalists saw unity in awakenings occurring in diverse communities separated from each other by great distances. They witnessed the same Spirit at work, the same sudden outburst of awakening, the same rapid spread of the revival, and the same effects on people.[4]

Not everyone agreed with Cooper that the unusual religious occurrences added up to a "Work of God." Nor did they view revivalist narrators as passive discoverers of the events they reported. Charles Chauncy, also a Boston minister, saw a huge gap between events and interpretation, between what actually took place in meetinghouses across the land and how zealous revivalists reported those happenings. He characterized the relation between revival narratives and true revival as much "Noise and little Connection." Referring to one revivalist's claim that colonists were witnessing a mighty work of God, Chauncy rejoined that not "*near* so much hath been done, as to warrant this Gentleman's *high* Encomium upon this Work." It was not the work but the gloss on the work, that troubled Chauncy. He concluded that if thoughtful people separated from the so-called revival all the "enthusiastic Impulses, and such-like Concomitants, . . . [they would] reduce it to a small Thing, that is, in Compare with what it is *made to be* by some who have wrote upon it."[5]

Until recently, most historians disagreed with Chauncy's contention that the revival was a "small Thing." Since the 1840s when minister-historian Joseph Tracy first applied the term *The Great Awakening* to the colonial revivals, scholars have considered the awakenings as a single, grand movement on an intercolonial scale. Many viewed it as the biggest event in British North America before the War for Independence. Then in his 1982 revisionist article, Jon Butler tilted toward Chauncy's position, arguing that the evidence did not add up to something that warranted such an imposing label as *The* Great Awakening. He rejected the assertion that a cohesive revival "swept" through the colonies, and deemed unwarranted the assessment of the Awakening as "the greatest event in the history of religion in eighteenth-century America." Instead, Butler saw a number of heterogeneous, scattered, local awakenings spread over a thirty-year period. The most he was willing to concede was that "the Great Awakening" was "a short-lived Calvinist revival in New England during the 1740s." He accounted for the gap between historians' enthusiasm and historical evidence by insisting that the former was based on an "interpretative fiction" invented by Tracy and read back into the eighteenth century. Following Tracy's lead, historians have, according to Butler, perpetuated an interpretation that "does serious injustice to the minutiae it orders."[6]

More recently, Joseph Conforti concurred with Butler that the Great Awakening was an invention, but he identified different inventors. He argued that *nineteenth-century* revival promoters found in colonial history a useful past: a precedent for an extraordinary effusion of God's grace throughout British North America. In Conforti's words, "the notion of the 'great' colonial awakening that has become almost universally accepted by scholars was a reification that served the cultural and polemical needs of the leaders of the *Second* Great Awakening," the designation most historians use for a series of revivals that flourished in the 1830s.[7] Thus, at a time of social transformation in the early republic, a specific discourse community created or invented *The* eighteenth-century Great Awakening by collecting writings of Jonathan Edwards and other revivalists and weaving them into a coherent narrative. By that construction, nineteenth-century revival promoters could present the current awakening as a continuation or renewal of a mighty and extraordinary Work of God in America.

This study makes an argument similar to those of Butler and Conforti: the colonial "great awakening" was an invention. But it differs by contending that colonial revivalists themselves constructed The Great Awakening—not the term, but the idea of a coherent, intercolonial revival. It explores how American evangelicals expected, perceived, promoted, explained, and debated the revival. It traces the process of invention from small, scattered local "great awakenings" beginning in the Connecticut and Raritan Valleys in the mid-1730s to the interconnected revivals of the 1740s known to contemporaries as "the remarkable Revival of Religion" and to most historians as the Great Awakening.

Revivals are not timeless universals; they are historically contingent. They are cultural formations constructed by persons who believe in and expect periodical outpourings of divine grace that supersede the ordinary means of salvation found in the Christian church. The eighteenth-century Great Awakening was the creation of a particular group of evangelicals who viewed themselves as, first, discoverers of a "Work of God" and, second, instruments in promoting that work. They preached with fervor and prayed with expectation for an effusion of God's Spirit. When scores of men and women came under "conviction" for their sins and seemed to undergo "conversion," the revivalists declared the existence of revival. Then, they spread the news of local awakenings from community to community inspiring similar occurrences throughout America. By the early 1740s, the revivalists, viewing events from the inside—that is, as active participants within a revival culture—declared that an extraordinary Work of God had overspread America.

Promoters found in events of the period 1735–1745 what they considered to be indisputable evidence of revival, and presented "facts" that added up to the long-awaited Revival of Religion. The facts they found and offered as proof of the "great and general Awakening" were what Clifford Geertz calls "facts from the religious perspective." Religious facts, moving "beyond the realities of everyday life to wider ones which correct and complete them," are different from commonsensical facts. And they differ from the "institutionalized skepticism" and "probabilistic hypotheses" of scientific facts by expressing what religious people take to be "wide, nonhypothetical truths." In short, the religious perspective "deepens the concern with fact and seeks to create an aura of utter actuality," or, in Geertz's words, what is "really real."[8]

The facts from which revival promoters constructed the Great Awakening were, to them, "really real" and utterly convincing. First, they cited the huge crowds attending revival services as evidence of an extraordinary outpouring of God's grace. They reported crowds of at least 1,000 on more than sixty occasions, including estimates of 20,000 gathered to hear George Whitefield preach in Boston and Philadelphia. Second, revival pastors attested to genuine conversion experiences by scores and hundreds of their parishioners. Upon close questioning of the converts, ministers certified that their experiences were authentic and conformed to scriptural standards.

Critics, however, demurred, giving no credence to promoters' "facts." Opponents argued that the so-called facts were mere partisan judgments, not observable occurrences. As "outsiders"—that is, persons outside the revival tradition—antirevivalists insisted on assessing the "revival" on verifiable facts. They concluded that awakenings occurred only in a few scattered and highly publicized congregations. Moreover, they claimed that the promoters' own evidence did not sustain the idea of a general awakening. For instance, revivalists had proudly announced in 1743 that 111 New England ministers had attested to "the happy Revival of Religion." Antirevivalists were unimpressed with the number. They expressed surprise that the figure was not considerably higher, considering "all the Art and Pains used" to solicit attestations. They pointed out that the 111 pastors represented "little more than one Quarter Part of the Whole Number of Congregational Ministers in New England," the so-called revival's epicenter.[9] In their view, an awakening was neither great nor general where 75 percent of the ministers in the revival belt refused to testify to its existence.

This book investigates the "facts" of the Great Awakening: how they were generated and the events that inspired them, how they were narrated in published accounts, and how they were contested between those inside and those outside the revival. A useful tool for this examination is the idea of invention, a term revivalists and their opponents employed, usually in attacks on each other's "facts." One opponent, for instance, warned that revival promoters substituted their own "*new inventions*" for religion grounded in Scripture and reason.[10] A leading revivalist, on the other hand, accused opposers of working overtime in fabricating distortions to discredit the awakening. Jonathan Edwards said that critics "put their inventions upon the rack to find out torments that should be cruel enough; and yet, after all, never seem to be satisfied."[11]

By tracing the process of how revivalists fashioned the awakening, one confronts the central complexities that face any student of the period, including the challenge of exploring the boundaries between event and interpretation, between the religious activities of the mid-1700s and the meanings contemporaries assigned them. By examining revivalists' and antirevivalists' inventions one can approach such issues as the relative contributions of itinerants and settled ministers in promoting revival; the role of the spoken and printed word in announcing and propagating the awakening; the importance of lay men and women as active participants in the invention; and the relation between local revivals in the colonies and a global awakening throughout the British Atlantic.

To validate a focus on invention as a vehicle for exploring the revival, we must address several important questions. What did the term "invention" mean in the eighteenth century, and how could its meaning apply to the actions of revivalists? What was invented, who invented it, and for what purpose? What was the process of invention? And, if invention occurred, what counterinventions did opponents fashion in order to fight back?

In the eighteenth century, "invention" had two meanings, both of which applied to the awakeners' understanding of their mission. First, it meant "the discovery of a thing hidden."[12] The revivalists were evangelicals who were looking for a revival of "true religion," and they found it—uncovered or invented it—in the events of the 1730s and 1740s. Guided by "clear marks" outlined in the New Testament, they pronounced the extraordinary religious occurrences a "Work of God." The revivalists insisted that the revival was of divine origin and existed apart from human agency. Their role was primarily that of messengers who faithfully pointed to the extraordinary display of God's grace.

The second meaning of invention was that of fabricating or designing something new, and it too applied to the revivalists. While recognizing that genuine revival of religion was God's work, revivalists believed that human "means" were conduits of divine outpourings of grace. Further, they thought that extraordinary dispensations called for extraordinary measures, and therefore the awakeners employed a cluster of methods, some old, some new, designed to arouse men and women to a sense of the deplorable state of their religious lives and the necessity of the "one thing needful," a spiritual New Birth. In addition to using means to revive sleeping Christians and souls dead to Christ, revivalists developed innovative ways to promote the spread of the revival. Thus they designed a revival program aimed at promoting a spiritual awakening and encouraging its spread; in that sense, the promoters themselves were instrumental in producing the evidence they discovered. They preached "searching" or evangelistic sermons aimed at getting people to acknowledge their sinful condition and turn to God, whose grace alone could save them from eternal damnation. They conducted services almost daily for weeks and invited guest evangelists to preach some of the sermons. They involved the laity in organizing prayer meetings in their homes to pray for and promote the evangelistic effort. However, when signs of revival appeared, the revivalists hastened to explain that the awakening was God's work and not the result of human activity. The large numbers of people attracted to preaching services, the suddenness with which the revival sprang up, the rapidity with which it spread throughout the Atlantic world, and the intensity of its effects upon men and women all suggested to the vigilant evangelists that they had discovered a powerful outpouring of divine grace.

The awakeners also invented the revival by constructing and publishing a series of narratives to interpret the events they witnessed and encouraged. From earliest revival stirrings in western Massachusetts in the early 1730s, revivalists published accounts which made ever-widening connections that ultimately joined events scattered throughout the Atlantic world into one great and general awakening. Jonathan Edwards, pastor at Northampton, began the process by writing *A Faithful Narrative* (1737), relating how hundreds of sinners in that small town found spiritual salvation, and interpreting the dramatic events as an extraordinary work of God, a revival. That publication instituted a new genre and provided a model script for similar accounts that followed, describing awakenings in other communities throughout New England and the Middle Colonies. Then, in 1743, Thomas Prince of Boston began publishing those narratives in a single periodical, the revival magazine *Christian History*, that linked the local accounts into a larger story: a single intercolonial revival. When he reprinted revival narratives published in Great Britain alongside those from the colonies, Prince created an even larger narrative, that of a transatlantic revival. Finally, in 1754, after the revival had ended, John Gillies published *Historical Collections*, wherein the Great Awakening became the latest chapter in the great drama of salvation history whose fountainhead was the first mass revival, which occurred on the day of Pentecost as described in the Acts of the Apostles.

Opponents of the Great Awakening certainly considered the revival to be an invention, but according to the term's negative connotation, that of fabrication of a falsehood. They charged revival promoters with, at best, gross exaggeration and enthusiastic excess in their published accounts of events, and, at worst, with lies and deceits aimed at discrediting nonrevivalist ministers and currying popular favor. They questioned the evidence revivalists cited for claiming that a "Work of God" was under way. And they emphasized the editorial work of zealous promoters who, they argued, created a widespread, unified revival on paper when none had existed in fact. In challenging the revivalists, critics constructed counterinventions that told a very different story, one of "errors and disorders," not a "work of God."

The Great Awakening, then, is also about contestation, a sustained, intensive struggle over meaning that may be termed an early American cultural war. The exchange reflected the colonies' great social and ethnic diversity and religious pluralism as the revival exacerbated deep divisions and sparked acrimonious debate. Viewing events through their disparate cultural lenses, the two factions assigned very different meanings to the same words. For instance, to revivalists itinerancy meant obedience to the biblical commission of carrying the gospel to every corner of the earth. To antirevivalists, itinerancy meant invasion of parish boundaries resulting in disorder and confusion. And opponents disagreed over how to describe what was happening in colonial religion. Revivalists called the event a "great awakening" to suggest its intensity in arousing people to a sense of their need of God's grace. Antirevivalists called it a "great ado" to underscore the emotional tumult and social disorder accompanying hellfire preaching at mass outdoor meetings. The vigor with which the debate proceeded suggests that both sides considered the stakes to be high. Especially in colonies with no establishment laws, or weak ones, religious debate took place in a relatively free, competitive marketplace of ideas. Furthermore, the savage attacks revivalists and antirevivalists launched at each other indicated that they believed the contest was a zero-sum game: converts to one cause meant losses to the other.

When criticizing each other, revivalists and antirevivalists alike demanded that their opponents adhere to standards of evidence insisted on by seventeenth-century Enlightenment thinkers. Frequently, however, polemicists on each side ignored those stringent norms in crafting their own arguments. When directing attention to their critics, awakeners and their opposers embraced the view John Locke enunciated in the late 1600s: "He that is strongly of any opinion, must suppose . . . that his persuasion is built upon good grounds, and that his assent is no greater than what the evidence of the truth he holds forces him to." Locke added that the person whose argument is "well fenced with evidence" need not fear open debate.[13] In the Great Awakening, each side accused the other of advancing propositions through assertion only, instead of supporting claims with solid evidence. Yet, while each regarded their critics' claims as matters of evidence, revivalists and antirevivalists alike elevated their own views to the status of unassailable matters of faith.

The story of the Great Awakening and its invention began in late 1733 in a small community on the Connecticut River, a hundred miles inland from Boston. An awakening at Northampton, Massachusetts, was the opening occasion of a series of events that revivalists would come to interpret as a single work. Pastor Jonathan Edwards described the Northampton revival in *A Faithful Narrative*, first published by John Guyse and Isaac Watts in London in 1737. Upon reading this account, revivalists in America and Great Britain heralded events in western Massachusetts as ushering in what they hailed as another Reformation. Ironically, to Edwards the revival in Northampton was hardly unusual or noteworthy. He could recall six earlier instances when his congregation had experienced "revivals" of similar intensity. What was different was not so much the event but the extensive publicity surrounding it.

This book explores how a rather ordinary occurrence in an obscure corner of colonial America grew into the Great Awakening. In tracing that remarkable evolution, the book examines it as a cultural formation: how a group of evangelicals perceived, reported, and memorialized what they referred to as "the Work of God." This study looks at familiar documents from a new perspective to illuminate the relationship between events as they were discovered and events as they were told and retold. The production of Jonathan Edwards's *Faithful Narrative* illustrates the point. That volume describes events unfolding over a two-year period in the Northampton, Massachusetts, congregation where Edwards was pastor. The publication of the book was itself another two years in the making. In its published form, the event took on much larger meaning and, indeed, became an important first link in a series of connections promoters on both sides of the Atlantic forged in inventing the Great Awakening.

Edwards's *Faithful Narrative* did more than delight evangelicals who had long awaited an extraordinary display of God's grace. It also inspired ministers and laypersons in communities throughout the colonies to stage and report similar revivals. By the early 1740s, revivalists reported local awakenings in scores of congregations. In publicizing those events, promoters interpreted them as a single intercolonial occurrence. Revivalist Jonathan Dickinson, pastor at Elizabeth-Town, New Jersey, referred to the awakening as "the Work of God . . . so remarkably of late began and going on in these American Parts." While writing as a local Presbyterian minister, he wrote about the revival "not only among ourselves, but in several Parts of the Country." He believed that because "this blessed Work has spread so extensively, far and near," it "certainly . . . [was] the Lord's Doing." Giving additional intercolonial color to Dickinson's narrative was its publication in Boston. In a recommendatory preface, a group of New England divines underscored the revival's extensive scope: "He must be a Stranger in Israel," they wrote, "who has not heard of the uncommon religious Appearances in the several Parts of this Land among Persons of all Ages and Characters."[14]

Boston minister and publisher Thomas Prince made connections that extended beyond Dickinson's intercolonial perspective. Prince saw the American awakening as part of an international event that originated in Germany and then spread throughout Great Britain. He solicited and collected revival narratives, publishing them in the *Christian History*, that bore witness to "*the* Revival of Religion [in] Great-Britain and America." In addition to place-names of local revivals, Prince listed transatlantic sites where *the* "Work of God" was evident. Alongside names of American towns are names of towns in England, Wales, Scotland, and Germany. Prince explained that his revival magazine contained accounts of two different sorts of revival: "1. Some *Instances of the transient* REVIVAL *of Religion* in some *particular Places* . . . And then 2. The *more surprizing and more extensive* REVIVALS . . . in the present Day."[15] In other words, in the 1740s, something was going on in the North Atlantic that was far bigger than local awakenings. It was, in the taxonomy of eighteenth-century revivalists, a "General" revival that was a much broader outpouring of God's grace than that witnessed in a "Particular" or local revival.

In interpreting events that they themselves shaped, revivalists engaged in a process of synthesis, and this book is a study of that synthesis. It attempts to follow the process promoters employed to portray local and regional awakenings as an intercolonial and even transatlantic revival. In recent years, historians have become more reflective on their own interpretive writing, how they are guided in constructing syntheses. Most recognize how elusive objectivity is in their scholarship. They know that the strategies they select to tell their stories of the past shape their selection and arrangement of evidence—"facts."[16] Similarly, historical actors arranged the "facts" they chose in order to tell a particular story, a story with a specific plot such as that of triumph or tragedy. When eighteenth-century revivalists reviewed the data that they regarded as self-evident and divinely inspired, they narrated them much in the style of the New Testament Acts of the Apostles, as drama of divine salvation.

This study is not, however, a synthesis in the sense of a weaving together of the works of historians into a single interpretation. Though enriched by the efforts of many scholars, it is not a historiographical essay. It does not, for instance, engage in such important and lively debates as that over causes of the Great Awakening. The goal is more modest: to address how revivalists themselves wove their own web of meaning which convinced them and thousands of others that they were participating in a glorious "Work of God."

That the Great Awakening may be understood as an invention does not mean that cunning promoters somehow foisted an unwelcome religious "product" on passive audiences. While promoters invented revival, thousands of men and women, acting individually and collectively, assigned their own meanings to the invention, often in ways promoters never considered and even opposed. And, in a real sense, people exerted their sovereignty by making certain revivalists popular.[17] By attending services in large numbers and making revival books and pamphlets best-sellers, lay men and women validated the promoters' claims of revival. In market terms, promoters shaped the "supply" of religion—how it was packaged and delivered—but lay people determined "demand." To understand the "great awakening," one must consider the interaction between revival producers and consumers. Evangelists engineered revival crusades, reported them as authentic works of God, and publicized them to distant audiences. Lay men and women accepted or rejected revivalists' claims, supported them with attendance and donations, and decided what awakening meant in their individual lives and communities.

Moreover, revivalists did not constitute a monolithic group. They came from different denominations, primarily Congregationalists in New England and Presbyterians in the Middle Colonies. They were men and women—and gender made a difference, insofar as there were separate religious societies organized for promoting practical piety. They were free and unfree, with slaves sometimes appropriating revival ideas and language of redemption in ways that their owners did not intend. Perhaps the most contested division within the revival culture was that of moderates and radicals. Moderates like Jonathan Edwards and Jonathan Dickinson emphasized the importance of individuals' "trying" their experiences against rational and scriptural standards. They denounced such radical practices as allowing uneducated laymen to preach and encouraging converted persons to leave their churches and form separate congregations. Radicals such as Andrew Croswell, pastor at Groton, Connecticut, countered that the moderates were more concerned with external matters such as doctrine and ecclesiology than with internal operations of the Holy Spirit within individual lives. Croswell, for instance, defended the itinerant James Davenport, who publicly burned books, clothing, and other worldly goods as a dramatic denunciation of "the world."

The story of inventing the Great Awakening unfolds in three parts: "Opening Events," "Wider Connections," and "Contested Inventions." Chapter 1 provides context. It begins by examining the perceptions and expectations of some early-eighteenth-century evangelicals on both sides of the Atlantic. It explores how they perceived the state of religion to be deplorable, a sad declension from what Thomas Prince called "the purer Part . . . of the Reformation."[18] A cause of particular alarm was the growing popularity of rationalist interpretations of the gospel. But the sad state of affairs did not lead to despair, as ministers declared that when religion seemed to be in its darkest hour, God provided deliverance through an extraordinary outpouring of grace. Moreover, the New Testament contained clear indicators of when such a divine event was under way. Through much of the first twenty years of the 1700s, evangelical Protestants in Germany, Britain, and America corresponded with each other, exchanging sightings of signs that a great revival was indeed about to begin, and sharing strategies for how to pray it down and preach it up.

Chapter 2 examines two colonial revivals of the mid-1730s. It concentrates on the Middle Colonies and New England, the two regions where local communities periodically experienced awakenings. This chapter looks at similarities and differences between regional manifestations, and explores interregional awareness and communication. It also explores how the narrative of the Northampton, Massachusetts, revival became published, a cultural production that played a central role in convincing believers on both sides of the Atlantic that an extraordinary Work of God was indeed under way.

Part Two shifts from the local revivals of Massachusetts and New Jersey to the intercolonial awakening historians call the Great Awakening. It tells the story of how revivalists made connections among scattered events to weave a coherent pattern. Chapter 3 begins the exploration of linkages by viewing the revival George Whitefield inspired from the perspective of colonial revival promoters. For months they followed newspaper accounts of remarkable crowds drawn by the young evangelist. Then they received word that he was planning a preaching trip to America. He arrived in October 1739, bringing what antirevivalists called an "imported divinity." This chapter asks, Why 1739? That is, why was it in that

year and not earlier that local revivals became intercolonial? It examines
the rise in population and, in particular, the growth of cities that became
central to mass evangelism. It also looks at the key role of newspapers
in publicizing the revivals throughout the colonies and keeping evangelicals in one region involved even as the awakening's center shifted elsewhere. Finally, this chapter probes the various regions to explain why
some areas were more receptive to the revival than others.

Chapter 4 again focuses on local revivals, this time considering them
within the post-1739 context of an intercolonial and transatlantic movement. It explores the various circumstances and dimensions of particular
awakenings within specific communities, looking especially at how local
revivals were influenced by and influenced the wider revival. How news
of other awakenings figured in a particular congregation raises the notion of the scripted nature of the Great Awakening, as accounts from
different times and places contain strikingly similar language and ideas.
The chapter also describes a new intercolonial linkage, that between
revival promoters in the Middle Colonies and a small group of evangelicals in Virginia's Piedmont.

Chapter 5 traces transatlantic connections between the intercolonial
Great Awakening and the evangelical revivals occurring in Britain. In
particular, it looks at the exchange and circulation of revival news
through a series of interrelated revival magazines. Through those periodicals, men and women in Scotland or England read about the details of
a local awakening in Pennsylvania, for instance, and saw within the
account reflections of their own experiences. The strongest tie, linking
New England and Scotland, is examined most closely.

Part Three explores the Great Awakening as a contested event: promoters and opponents traded charges that the other side invented its account
of what transpired in the 1740s. It investigates the major controversies
and polemics that characterized the struggle between revivalists and
antirevivalists over what the movement meant. Chapter 6 reviews attacks
leveled at the awakeners. Antirevivalists claimed that the evidence revealed no revival; that whatever happened was man-made, not divine;
that revivalists introduced dangerous innovations rather than ancient
gospel principles; that the so-called revival was not as great as its promoters claimed, especially in effecting lasting behavioral change; that
it was not as general as its leaders boasted; and that it ignored sound
tenets grounded in reason and Scripture, preying instead on the emotions of the unthinking masses. Moreover, the chapter looks at how

nonevangelicals viewed the state of the church and insisted that their own rationalist ideas for reform were preferable to the enthusiastic braying of evangelists.

Chapter 7 takes up the revivalist interpretation. It follows the arguments of those who declared a revival, insisted that it was a work of God, proclaimed it to be the revival of true religion—that is, religion of the heart—asserted that it was "great" and that it became "general," and vowed that its propagation was evangelism, not enthusiasm.

The book closes with an epilogue that considers the revival's decline and legacy. An analysis of why the movement ended, and why promoters ceased to declare and publicize an awakening, sheds light on the limits of both event and invention. Revival in America did not end in 1745; but an awakening promoted as intercolonial did cease to exist in that year. The 1760s and 1770s were decades of revival in Virginia, as successive waves of Presbyterians, Baptists, and Methodists offered an alternative to the colony's established Anglicanism. But those revivals shared the characteristics of local revivals that had occurred elsewhere before the Great Awakening: limited geographic extent, little publicity outside the region, few ties with evangelicals elsewhere, and minimum influence on other colonies. Such a return to local revivalism highlights what preceded: that remarkable period of the 1740s when partisans promoted and contested the intercolonial awakening. The epilogue ends by noting that inventing the revival was an ongoing process, as evangelicals in the late eighteenth- and early-nineteenth-centuries reinvented the Great Awakening for their own purposes.

Part One

OPENING EVENTS:
THE "GREAT AWAKENINGS" OF
THE 1730s

IN THE mid-1730s, colonial revivalists surveyed the religious landscape around them and found it to be in a deplorable state. They saw men and women attending worship services, but they witnessed little practice of genuine piety. They feared that, for many, faith had been reduced to an intellectual acceptance of certain propositions rather than a life-changing conversion experience. Rather than despairing, the awakeners took hope in the midst of spiritual decline. Their reading of the Scriptures convinced them that when spiritual light is almost extinguished, God sends an extraordinary effusion of his spirit to arouse his people in a mighty awakening.

The first great revival in Christian history had occurred in the first century A.D. on the day of Pentecost under the apostle Peter's preaching, and the second was the Protestant Reformation of the sixteenth century. Both epochal events produced thousands of converts who experienced salvation by faith. And, for evangelicals of subsequent generations, those glorious occasions represented hope that God would once again dispense his grace in an extraordinary way. During the first third of the eighteenth century, two groups of hopeful colonial revivalists—several New England Congregationalists and a few Middle Colony Presbyterians—began praying for a great awakening and initiated special preaching emphases on the necessity of regeneration or, as they called it, the New Birth. Unusual numbers of men, women, and children came under conviction of their sins, and many experienced conversion. The expectant revivalists, ever alert to signs of God's grace, declared the events to be the work of God. While this was not the first revival in the colonies, what separated it from earlier awakenings, however, is that it became widely known outside the remote corners of America where it occurred. Through a carefully constructed narrative, a published account reached like-minded evangelicals in Britain who concurred that this indeed was a genuine work of God and, they hoped, the beginning of a revival that would spread throughout the Atlantic world. Thus the "great awakening" in Northampton, Massachusetts, became the "first fruits" of what would come to be known as The Great Awakening.

"... that Religion may revive in this Land"

THE GEOGRAPHY of the "great awakenings" in colonial America during the 1730s and 1740s follows a checkerboard pattern. While revival fire burned brightly in the Connecticut River Valley, for example, it was barely discernible along the Hudson River Valley. At a time when Massachusetts and Connecticut witnessed huge crowds at preaching services and reported thousands undergoing a New Birth, New York displayed little evidence of interest in the awakening outside initial curiosity over novel religious practices and venues. Similarly, throngs of men and women followed itinerant preachers in Pennsylvania and Delaware, but in neighboring Maryland the same men delivering the same sermons with the same fervor attracted only tiny gatherings of people who greeted them with a restrained, polite reception.

The uneven pattern of revival enthusiasm suggests the importance of context in any attempt to explain events of the Great Awakening. Certainly revival promoters worked to spread the awakening into every corner of the colonies, sending itinerant evangelists walking and riding on preaching tours that spanned hundreds of miles. Ministers and laymen alike distributed tracts, broadsides, and pamphlets across New York and Maryland as well as Connecticut and Pennsylvania. Scores of titles proclaimed unfolding religious events to be a new Reformation. But responses differed greatly from colony to colony and region to region. Why? Surely it was more than geography. There is nothing intrinsic about a provincial boundary or a riverbed to explain why the awakening was "great and general" on one side and barely visible on the other. What is more plausible is a more impervious divide that separated colonies: religious culture—the web of expectations, beliefs, values, traditions, and ideas through which people in a given province or community made sense of their lives and events that occurred around them. Events are not self-explanatory. People name them and give them meaning. In the 1730s and 1740s some people in some parts of colonial America reflected on the religious happenings and called them a revival. Others saw evi-

dence of disorder. This chapter examines why some persons could see
revival so clearly while others could not.

To see revival in the events of 1735–1745, someone or some group
had to discern a pattern called "revival," adduce convincing evidence
of its reality, and convey that evidence to an audience whose experiences
made the interpretation plausible. In other words, revival as an explanation for the "present Work"—the term contemporaries preferred—was
an invention, especially in the eighteenth-century sense of something
uncovered or found. It was a patterned response to events whose meaning
was not self-evident.

To some evangelicals in Britain and America, there was never any
doubt that the "Work" was God's extraordinary outpouring of grace.
For the loose-knit transatlantic evangelical community that had been
exchanging news about the gospel's progress for decades, the Work was
clearly the long-awaited religious revival. To them it was a revival in two
respects. First, it was an awakening of individuals to what was variously
called "vital" religion as opposed to a dead faith, "experimental" Christianity that one experienced instead of contemplated, and "practical
piety" that transformed how persons spent their time and money. That
kind of revival was God's work. But the Work turned into revival in
another sense. It became an organized strategy or program (present-
day revivalists call it a "crusade"), consisting of meetings and publications that promoted awakenings. While its proponents always identified
the revival as a work of God, they also believed in human agency: men
and women assisting God in promoting revivalism. Thus revival was both
spiritual awakening itself and the instrumentalities that promoted it.

Revivals are extraordinary religious events, and to flourish they require
a particular context. First, they originate where there is a *culture* that
expects a periodic showering of God's grace and recognizes the signs
of a genuine revival when it appears. Second, they occur when people
within that culture perceive a *need* for revival, a time when the state of
religion is thought to have sunk to a low point. And third, revivals result
when ministers and laypersons employ *means* designed to prepare men
and women for a special outpouring of divine mercy. For revival to
emerge, all these factors must converge. For example, revival is unlikely
in a culture without a perceived need for a spiritual awakening. And
revival is improbable if a need is recognized but means are not employed.

In the mid-1730s, all the necessary factors converged in parts of colonial America to spark evangelical revivals. Awakenings emanated from
two geographic centers steeped in rich revival traditions: one in New
England and the other in Pennsylvania and New Jersey (see table 1.1).

TABLE 1.1
Revival Geography: Colonial America, 1739–1745
Place-Names Prominent in the Great Awakening
Listed by Revival Center

Revival Center	City or Town	No. within Colony	Pct. of Total within Colony
New England—		**50**	**63.3**
Centered at Boston and			
Northampton:			
Massachusetts	Attleborough, Berkly, Boston,	34	43.0
	Bridgewater, Brookline,		
	Cambridge, Concord, Dedham,		
	Gloucester, Hallifax, Hampshire		
	County, Harvard, Ipswich, Martha's		
	Vineyard, Marblehead, Medfield,		
	Medway, Middleborough, Natick,		
	Northampton, Norton, Plymouth,		
	Raynham, Reading, Roxbury,		
	Salem, Sherbourne, Somers,		
	Sudbury, Suffield, Sutton,		
	Taunton, Worcester, Wrentham		
Connecticut	Groton, Hartford, Lyme,	9	11.4
	Middletown, New London, New		
	Salem, Norwich, Stonington,		
	Wallingford		
Rhode Island	Charles-Town, Westerly	2	2.5
New Hampshire	Gosport, Hampton, Newcastle,	5	6.3
	Portsmouth, York		

Continued on next page

Each of these districts was heavily populated with men and women who rejoiced in those thrilling moments of salvation history when God had poured out his grace in extraordinary ways. Pentecost was the first of those great events: three thousand souls were added to God's kingdom in a single day. The Protestant Reformation was another, when hundreds of thousands of Christians reaffirmed the biblical truth that salvation comes by faith alone and not through works or institutions or sacraments. To evangelicals in the Connecticut Valley of western Massachusetts and in the Raritan Valley of East Jersey, revival was more than something they read about in the remote past. Each region had periodically experienced awakenings under the leadership of dynamic preachers who knew how to "preach up" a revival: Solomon Stoddard and Jonathan Edwards in

Table 1.1, Cont.

Revival Center	City or Town	No. within Colony	Pct. of Total within Colony
Middle Colonies—		**25**	**31.6**
Centered at Neshaminy,			
Pennsylvania			
New Jersey	Amwell, Basinridge, Cohansie, Elizabeth-Town, Freehold, Hopewell, Maidenhead, Neward, New Brunswick, Salem, Woodbridge	11	13.9
Pennsylvania	Abingdon, Chester, Derby, Fogs Mannor, German Town, Neshaminy, New Londonberry, Nottingham, Philadelphia, Whitely Creek, Whitemarsh	11	13.9
Delaware	Christian Bridge, Newcastle, Wilmington	3	3.8
Colonies outside		**4**	**5.1**
Revival Centers:			
New York	New York City, Staten Island	2	2.5
Maryland	Bohemia	1	1.3
Virginia	None	0	0.0
North Carolina	None	0	0.0
South Carolina	Charleston	1	1.3
Georgia	None	0	0.0
Total		**79**	**100%**

Sources: Place-names are cited in the two works that best describe the geographic sweep of the American revival: the *Christian History* and *Whitefield's Journals.* Names from the former include all listed in an index of place-names; those from the latter are restricted to those sites where crowds of at least 1,000 assembled.

the former and Theodore Frelinghuysen and Gilbert Tennent in the latter. But evangelistic preaching alone is an insufficient explanation for the areas' revivals. In both, revivalist traditions predisposed men and women to expect periodic awakenings and alerted them to the signs of an extraordinary outpouring of God's Spirit.

Outside those revival regions, the awakening found few followers and fewer leaders. Only an occasional congregation expected extraordinary effusions of God's grace. Most believed that the Almighty worked in a more predictable way, through the ordinary means of regular church services and sacraments. In their interpretation of Scripture and their reading of church history, ministers found nothing suggesting that revivals were anything other than human enthusiasm. Thus they and their parishioners perceived no need for an awakening; nothing vital was asleep.

The story was different in the revival regions. There, the idea of "great awakening" made sense only in the wake of decline. In other words, as they saw it, something once vital must be deemed lifeless if there is to be revival. To eighteenth-century revivalists, Protestantism in the late 1700s and early 1800s was in trouble, weakened by indifference and apathy, and assaulted by heterodoxy. Wherever they turned, concerned evangelicals saw decay in the practice of piety. Culprits abounded: rationalism that elevated human reason above divine revelation; commercialism that beckoned people to countinghouses instead of meetinghouses; formalism that reduced religion to ecclesiastical observances rather than spiritual experiences. By any measure, most settled ministers, revivalists contended, failed to propagate the gospel to the masses because of vapid, ineffectual messages and methods.

The solution was both backward-looking and forward-thinking. Revivalists wanted to return to the gospel message and convey it through means such as the powerful preaching of the apostle Peter at Pentecost and John Calvin during the Reformation. They wanted to confront men and women with the necessity of a spiritual new birth, or conversion experience, as the only means of salvation. While advocating an old message, they embraced innovative methods to convey it. That meant new messengers, or at least ones who could demonstrate that they themselves had undergone a new birth and could preach with conviction to others. It also meant strategies designed to reach audiences far beyond parish, provincial, and even national boundaries.

REVIVAL TRADITIONS

The roots of colonial revival traditions reached deep into English and Scottish Protestant history and beyond, originating in Calvin's Geneva. Indeed, eighteenth-century revivalists in colonial America's "great awakening" considered themselves Calvinists. In general, this meant that they embraced the theological tenets set forth by John Calvin and subscribed to the fundamental beliefs of one of the Reformed Protestant traditions,

including such churches as the English Puritan (referred to as Independent in seventeenth-century England, Congregational in America), Scottish Presbyterian, German Reformed, or Dutch Reformed. More specifically, it meant the acceptance of unconditional predestination whereby
God, before all time, predestined some persons to salvation and others
to damnation. The grace of God alone determined the election of some
and the rejection of others. Moreover, contrary to the teachings of
Arminians and others who introduced human agency into the drama
of salvation, Calvinists believed that the merit of an individual's good
works, no matter how pure and noble the conduct, played no role
whatever in one's redemption.

The place of evangelism within a Calvinist tradition is puzzling for
many, given the doctrine of predestination. Why preach the good news
of Christ's sacrificial death to all if God, before human existence, predestined some to salvation and others to damnation? Calvin's answer was
that the gospel must be preached to all persons everywhere because the
visible church could not distinguish between saint and sinner. Moreover,
while the church could not guarantee salvation for anyone, it was, in
Calvin's theology, "the only route to grace." Unlike some of the eighteenth-century revivalists, Calvin taught that regeneration was a lifelong
process rather than a sudden, wrenching "new birth." Growth in grace
rested on "a rational understanding of [God's] word as well as on
illumination by the Spirit." And the Christian in his or her daily behavior
was to strive always for the elusive goal of moral perfection, believing
that a life of disciplined faith was a clear indication that he or she was
numbered among the elect.[1] It was evangelism that informed men and
women of the possibilities of divine election and the means of affirming
it in their lives.

English Puritans were largely responsible for giving Calvinism an evangelical bent. As Puritan divines considered the central question, "Am I
saved?" controversies arose over the nature and timing of conversion.
One group insisted that the New Birth occurred at a precise moment
as God's Spirit entered an individual's heart, and that true converts could
state the exact moment of their conversion. Moreover, this interpretation
held that conversion followed a normative pattern and that men and
women moved through set stages. Subscribers to this view, such as William Perkins, identified the event of conversion as an "experience of the
heart" rather than rational awareness. He believed that "fiery sermons"
"ripped up" the heart, a necessary antecedent for receiving God's Spirit.
Others, such as Richard Sibbes, insisted that no human preparation

was necessary for the "inner witness of the Spirit." Whether preparationist or nonpreparationist, this "conversionist evangelism" was concerned about the specific moment when divine election became actual within an individual, and for its adherents, it provided a clear means of dividing sinners and saints within the Church of England.[2] According to at least one scholar, Puritans like Perkins had pushed Calvinism into something its Genevan founder would have disowned: a theology wherein human as well as divine will participated in the drama of salvation.[3]

Influenced by seventeenth-century English Puritans, colonial revivalists were Calvinists of the evangelical stripe. More difficult to define, and subject to a wide range of interpretations, evangelicals—in the sense claimed by eighteenth-century revivalists—expressed a "consistent pattern of convictions and attitudes." According to one scholar, British evangelicalism emerged in the early 1700s with four central tenets: "biblicism (a reliance on the Bible as ultimate religious authority), conversionism (a stress on the New Birth), activism (an energetic, individualistic approach to religious duties and social involvement), and crucicentrism (a focus on Christ's redeeming work as the heart of essential Christianity)."[4] By contrast, state churches such as the Church of England tended to emphasize tradition as well as Scripture as the basis of belief and practice, and they stressed corporate worship in conformity to a formal, prescribed liturgy over individual acts of faith as the central expression of Christian obedience.

Just as all Calvinists were not evangelicals, not all evangelicals were revivalists. What distinguished revivalists was their belief in periodic extraordinary outpourings of God's grace. Though they accepted that most of the time God's work was performed through such ordinary means as preaching, praying, and bible reading, they also believed in seasons of unusually powerful redemptive showers. At those times, thousands of persons suddenly find themselves convicted of their sins and turn to God as their only hope of salvation. Rarity and power were the hallmarks of revivals. Awakeners could point to only two truly extraordinary Works of God: Pentecost and the Protestant Reformation. Eighteenth-century revivalists expected an extraordinary outpouring of God's Spirit in their day and, beginning in the 1730s, believed that they detected signs of its arrival.

Other English Puritans, however, believed that conversionist evangelism was too rigid and disallowed the Spirit's freedom of dealing with different people in various ways. Richard Baxter was one who "could

not distinctly trace the workings of the Spirit" within his heart, nor
could he state exactly when his conversion occurred. This disturbing
tension between what persons actually experienced and the so-called
normative pattern of conversion led Baxter and others to question the
assumptions of conversion-minded theologians. Rejecting the idea that
God redeems sinners only through an "agonizing, datable 'new birth,' "
Baxter and others in the seventeenth century concluded that "Education
is God's ordinary way for the Conveyance of his Grace."[5] Advocates of
this "sacramental evangelism" and "nurturing education" insisted that
salvation came through regular attendance at divine services, family
devotion, prayer, bible reading, and the sacraments of baptism and the
Lord's Supper.

Puritans who settled New England carried with them both conversionist and sacramental strands of evangelism. According to one historian, the first generation made "the experience of conversion the focus
of religious life." They insisted that church membership be restricted
to those who could give a precise account of when God's Spirit entered
their lives. Second-generation ministers, however, witnessed a decline
in the number of conversions, and thus a drop in the number of saints,
as fewer and fewer people could meet the exacting standards of conversionist evangelism. Consequently, some pastors began to emphasize sacramental themes, stressing "nurture as the way to grace, the slow enlargement of seeds implanted at the time of baptism." Others attempted to
combine elements of conversionist and sacramentalist perspectives by
holding fast to the former ideal while criticizing its harsher features by
quoting liberally from Baxter.[6]

Immigration patterns as well as generational preferences help explain
New Englanders' differences regarding evangelism. According to one
study of the English backgrounds of New England's revival leaders,
seventeenth-century religious culture in Britain was manifested diversely
in two geographic sectors: the Southeast and the Northwest. Defined by
a line from the Wash to Bristol and extended beyond in a southwesterly
direction to a point just west of Exeter, the two sections contained very
different perspectives and practices regarding evangelism. The Southeast
was the seat of Ramist Puritanism, which contained the "seeds of rationalism." Most of those who went to New England during the Great Migration
of 1630–1640 came from this region and transplanted a religious culture
that tended to be "theological and orthodox." By contrast, the Northwest
was a region noted for its pietism and evangelism, the birthplace of

Quakerism and Methodism, and emigrants to New England carried with them a religion more devotional and evangelical than that of their compatriots from the Southeast.[7]

New Englanders who supported the Great Awakening traced their roots to the British Northwest seedbed of evangelism. Those most likely to respond to "calls for a New Birth" during the revival descended from the 25 percent who had emigrated from the Northwest and the 10–15 percent who hailed from the Southeast but bore Northwest surnames. Seventy-five percent of New Light, or revivalist, ministers had Northwest origins. And their church members came from the Northwest, with its strong evangelical tradition wherein ministers sought converts by "emphasizing the New Birth, downplaying theological complexities and relying less on the printed word." They, therefore, naturally were inclined toward awakeners who embraced the same emphases. On the other hand, by the late 1600s, Puritans in the Southeast had become more latitudinarian in their religious orientation, in part a reaction to the enthusiasm of the Commonwealth era. To their descendants in New England, the revivalists represented a return to excess and sectarianism.[8]

While English Puritan traditions informed New England revivalism, those of the Church of Scotland influenced that of the Middle Colonies. As Presbyterian immigrants from Scotland and Ulster poured into New Jersey and Pennsylvania in the late seventeenth and early eighteenth centuries, they brought with them strong ideas of evangelism in general and special seasons of grace in particular. Indeed, some observed an annual or semiannual tradition known as the "Communion Season." Following the practice of Scottish "Holy Fairs," Presbyterians would assemble at a church for several days once or twice a year to celebrate communion in a series of services designed to revive and strengthen the faith of communicants and bear witness to noncommunicants of their unworthiness to participate in the Lord's Supper. In a sense, the communion season was a revival season, a time when the faithful expected a great outpouring of God's grace.[9]

While obscure in origin, the term "Holy Fairs" to designate Scottish revivals or sacramental seasons is quite descriptive and fitting. Writing as a religious outsider—that is, one outside the revival tradition—Robert Burns in the 1780s penned a poem entitled "Holy Fairs," biting satire deriding what he considered to be a "popular spectacle." From his Enlightenment perspective he poked fun at the evangelist whose preaching stirred his listeners:

> Hear how he clears the points o' Faith
> Wi' rattlin' an' thumpin!
> Now meekly calm, now wild in wrath,
> He's stampan an' he's jumpan!

To "pious communicants and devout hearers," however, the occasion had a very different meaning. Accustomed to "fair-days" when merchants and farmers bought and sold various goods, evangelicals thought it only proper that they hold "fair-days of the gospel." If persons were willing to establish special seasons for trading goods that would soon perish, surely believers should reserve periods expressly for renewing their commitment to the gospel.[10]

In rural New Jersey and Pennsylvania, families would walk sometimes ten to fifteen miles to attend a "season" that began on a Thursday or Friday and continued through Monday. They would either camp near the church or lodge with other church members in order to attend daily services conducted by the pastor with assistance from ministers of neighboring congregations. The opening day was set aside as a time of "fasting, humiliation, and worship." Then on Saturday, men and women would gather for a "preparatory service . . . with preaching and praying" designed to promote self-examination and encourage reflection on Christ's sacrifice. At that time, the pastor distributed communion tokens to "those whom he deemed penitent and worthy to receive the sacrament." The tokens were reminders to holders to "seek with renewed earnestness the inward tokens of [their] being members of the Church invisible." Moreover, the tokens were symbols of "redeeming love . . . given and sealed to God's children . . . at this sacred feast by the Spirit of God."[11] The promise and expectation was that during the communion season, God was present in an extraordinary way, and those in attendance would be revived and renewed.

The main attraction was the Lord's Supper on Sunday with communicants seated together at tables often placed on the church grounds if weather permitted. As further preparation to receive the bread and wine, the pastor delivered an "action sermon" that was "long and full of the marrow of the gospel." Following the discourse, which often lasted an hour, the minister turned to the solemn sacrament. He began by "fencing the Tables," a process aimed at debarring the "ignorant, unbelieving, and profane" from partaking of the holy meal. Communicants then "surrendered" their tokens and participated in the Lord's Supper. On

TABLE 1.2
American Revivals before Whitefield's
Arrival September 1739

Date	Location
1679	Northampton, Mass.
ca. 1680	New England
1683	Northampton
1696	Northampton
ca. 1705	Taunton, Mass.
1712	Northampton
1718	Northampton
ca. 1720	New Jersey
1721	Windham, Conn.
1727	New England
ca. 1730	Freehold, N.J.
1733	Northampton

Source: Gillies, *Historical Collections,* 279–292.

Monday, the communion season concluded with a worship service of thanksgiving for spiritual blessings received during the past several days.[12] Communicants returned home revived, and noncommunicants left having been reminded of their need for converting grace.

Both New England and New Jersey revivalists, then, emerged from traditions where revivals were an accepted and integral part of their religious experience. Those traditions furnished awakeners with intellectual scaffolding sufficient to support the promise of new revivals. Their theology promised them that God would from time to time pour out his grace in unusual showers. And their "Evangelicall History" chronicled numerous instances of such refreshing outpouring.[13] Thus tradition explains in large part why the Great Awakening originated and enjoyed its greatest reception in those two regions. (For pre-1740s revivals, see table 1.2.) At the same time, the lack of revival tradition helps account for the revival's weakness in New York, Maryland, Virginia, and the

Carolinas. Few in those colonies had experienced a "great awakening," expected one in their midst, or were disposed to look for signs of an extraordinary display of God's grace.

"IN SUCH AN AGE AS THIS"

By definition, revival follows decline. The fact that people call for revival means that they believe something lofty and good has been lost or diminished, perhaps purity of faith or fervency of piety. New England revivalists remembered, no doubt through rose-colored lenses, that their forefathers had dedicated themselves to "making the visible church"— all persons professing belief in Christianity—a "closer and closer approximation of the invisible" church, which included only those "whom God had predestined for salvation." The Puritan founders had insisted on close examination of all applicants for admission to a congregation, with only those whose lives and testimony bore witness to their salvation granted full membership. Though admitted to communion, visible saints were anxious saints because they could not know for certain if they were of God's elect. Their uncertainty motivated them to greater heights of piety that included intense self-examination, diligent Bible study, and searching prayer.[14]

But, alas, subsequent generations found the demands of faith too great. Churches accommodated by lowering the standards for membership. In the so-called Half-Way Covenant of 1662, men and women could join a congregation by merely "owning the covenant"—that is, giving assent to articles of faith. Granted, these new saints did not enjoy full membership, but nevertheless they were within the visible church. Moreover, embarrassed by what they considered to be too much emphasis on evangelism, some congregations moved closer to a "sacramental theology" wherein the sacraments of baptism and the Lord's Supper, as well as subscription to the covenant, gave assurance of salvation.[15] The result was fewer anxious saints and more secure ones. That is, more people found solace in the observance of rites than suffered through inner struggles with sin and doubt. Thus, in the 1730s, revivalists in New England and New Jersey, where similar trends had occurred, lamented the growing gap between the visible and invisible churches.

American evangelicals had long measured religious decay against an exacting standard of faith and works. In his 1710 essay *Bonifacius*, Cotton Mather argued that the first step toward becoming a true Christian was for unregenerate men and women to "acknowledge the necessity of their turning to God." Only through the working of God's grace within them can they "with *quickened* Souls, *plead* the *sacrifice* and *righteousness* of a glorious Christ for their happy reconciliation to God" and begin lives of "*obedience* to God, and *serious religion.*" In other words, people must experience a spiritual new birth. But the faith Mather described went beyond conversion; it embraced practical piety. He declared that a "workless faith [was] a worthless faith." Opportunities abound in one's secular calling to do good, and Mather urged his readers to be as inventive in discovering benevolent projects as they were in advancing their own interests. While reminding Christians that "the ONE thing, that is *needful,* is, a glorious work of GRACE on the soul," Mather identified ways the faithful could bring "religion into the marketplace."[16] What he and other evangelicals held forth in the early eighteenth century was a lofty goal indeed: that of becoming a newborn person pursuing good works in every walk of life.

Theodorus Frelinghuysen used the biblical metaphor of the "broad way" and the "narrow way" to illustrate options available to men and women. The Dutch Reformed minister whose preaching triggered revival in New Jersey in the 1720s told his audience that the broad way was an attractive one, "whereon you can live at ease, to your Mind, Desire and Lust, and keep your self imploy'd in things of this World, and Use them as you please." He reminded his hearers that while such a life of self-indulgence appealed to the vast majority of people, "The End of that Way is eternal Death and Perdition." The narrow way is the path of self-denial, "wherein you must deny your self, your own Understanding, own Righteousness, own Will and Mind, own Worthiness and Power, wherein you must depart from your loving Sins, and from the Vanities of this World." Though it is difficult to "live a precise and holy Life, [and] follow the Footsteps and Virtues of Christ," the end is "Eternal Life, everlasting Glory, everlasting Joy and Salvation."[17]

While preaching the New Birth and practical piety, evangelicals such as Mather and Frelinghuysen saw decline at every turn in the America of the first third of the eighteenth century. They held a very specific notion of religion, what William James called religion of the "twice-born." They brooded over the condition of life in general and themselves in particular. In his *Pilgrim's Progress,* a classic in evangelical literature widely read by eighteenth-century revivalists, John Bunyan presented himself as one "beset by doubts, fears, and insistent ideas." Frequently he expressed his self-contempt and despair: "Nay, thought I," he wrote, "now I grow worse and worse; now I am farther from conversion than ever I was before. If now I should have burned at the stake, I could not believe that Christ had love for me." Henry Alline, a devoted revivalist preacher in eighteenth-century Nova Scotia, echoed Bunyan's melancholy: "Everything I saw seemed to be a burden to me; the earth seemed accursed for my sake: all trees, plants, rocks, hills, and vales seemed to be dressed in mourning and groaning, under the weight of the curse."[18] If struggling, seeking sinners like Bunyan and Alline populated churches, then revivalists found fertile ground for their message of original sin and the necessity for a new birth. Sick souls sought solace in being "twice-born."

Others, however, had a different assessment of American religion, one far more sanguine than that of the revivalists. They proceeded from the perspective of what James called religion of the "once-born," seeing God "not as a strict Judge, not as a Glorious Potentate; but as the animating Spirit of a beautiful harmonious world." Such a conception of divinity leads to an equally cheerful view of humanity. The once-born "are not distressed by their own imperfections . . . [and do] not shrink from God." These attitudes characterized the latitudinarians of the eighteenth-century Anglican Church that John and Charles Wesley and George Whitefield criticized. Religion was a reasonable proposition aimed toward the happiness of men and women. Children learned from the earliest age that they were God's offspring, and adults clung to that belief. Original sin and a morbid preoccupation with sin had no place in rational expressions of Christianity.[19] Hence healthy-minded clergymen and churchgoers—or, as eighteenth-century revivalists termed them, the "secure"—were generally content with their religion and saw no need for revival.

Not all evangelicals who promoted revival viewed the preawakening state of religion as uniformly gloomy. One of England's leading dissenters, Isaac Watts, offered a balanced response to the question of religious decline in the 1730s and 1740s. Unlike assessments that saw Protestantism retreating on a broad front, his analysis resulted in a more textured portrayal. He wrote that "so far as I have searched into the Matter, I have been informed that whatsoever Decrease may have appeared in some Places, there have been sensible Advances in others."[20] Boston minister and leading revivalist Thomas Prince also testified to religious growth and vitality in the late 1730s. He recorded in his diary of 1737 that he gave his blessing to a new congregation gathered in the "Westerly Part" of Boston and praised it as a "true Church of CHRIST."[21]

Because of different contemporary assessments by the "once-born" and the "twice-born," historians face the problem of differentiating between the actual and the publicized state of religion on the eve of the revival. Some scholars subscribe to a declension thesis wherein second-generation and subsequent New Englanders failed to practice the piety insisted on by their spiritual founding fathers. Fewer and fewer people could own the covenant that bound "visible saints" together. Accommodations such as the halfway covenant were admissions of declining faith. Church membership could be attained by kinship rather than experience. By the late seventeenth and early eighteenth centuries, "owning the covenant," once a profoundly personal commitment following months of self-examination, had become a "communal rite" as entire congregations assented to a written agreement of faith and practice. In this view, the great awakening is an effort to return to individual conversion rather than communal assent.[22]

The view of religious declension in New England rested primarily on jeremiads, sermons lamenting the waning of piety. In a typical expression of this genre, popular in the last half of the seventeenth century, Samuel Danforth asked "Whether we have not in a great measure forgotten our Errand into the Wilderness." The Roxbury pastor reminded his listeners in the 1670 Election Day sermon that the first settlers had crossed the "vast Ocean into this waste and howling Wilderness . . . to walk in the Faith of the Gospel." By contrast, he continued, "Pride, Contention, Worldliness, Covetousness, Luxury, Drunkeness and Uncleanness break in" upon the current generation. No longer content to "sit at Christ's feet and hear his Word," New Englanders had chosen the "Honours, Pleasures and Profits of the world."[23] After reading scores of similar lamentations, one can hardly be surprised that historians have portrayed such a gloomy view of Puritan religion over time.

Others have challenged the declension thesis. One revision of revivalists' gloomy assessments demonstrates that "the slightest shift of perspective" reveals a much more positive view of eighteenth-century colonial religious life. Moving beyond the jeremiad's lament, they point out that many New England men and women "gathered spontaneously for informal services before ministers became available to serve them." While leaders of established churches denounced such lay independence as undermining discipline, the resulting spread of denominational pluralism "promoted competition and sharpened loyalties." Evidence also suggests religious vitality on the frontier, belying that region's depiction as "the receptacle of all sorts of riff-raff people," and "nothing else than the sewer (latrina) of New England." And backcountry settlements in the Middle Colonies often consisted of Scots-Irish or Germans who "promptly reconstituted their churches in the wilderness."[24]

Revisionists have also questioned the bleak view of religion in the southern colonies, where, according to the traditional perspective, church adherence was the weakest. Relying on the Anglican survey of 1724, the most complete census of colonial churches, researchers found that the percentage of adult parishioners attending church regularly ranged from 56 to 61 percent. They discovered that a median of 26 percent of the auditors partook of communion; thus about 15 percent of adult Anglicans were communicants. This compares with evidence from eighteenth-century English parishes, where communicants represented between 5 and 30 percent of the parishioners. "While one could hardly claim that the Anglican church in the southern colonies was as actively supported as the church at home," they concluded, "the 1724 survey gives no reason to suppose that it was sunk in lethargy."[25]

Whatever historians have concluded about the state of colonial religion, most revivalists saw unrelieved declension on the eve of the awakening, and their perceptions became the "facts" upon which they operated. They could hardly have found anything else. As Charles Finney declared a century later, "a 'Revival of Religion' presupposes a declension."[26] Dissenting ministers had long lamented the deplorable state of religion. Frequently cited reasons for decline included the absence of sufficient numbers of trained ministers, especially in the southern colonies; the lack of religious establishment in almost half the colonies; a population scattered over a wide geographic region; ecclesiastical disorder created by competing sects, particularly in the Middle Colonies; and the growing attraction of rationalism and commercialism. In every region, ministers lamented the "indifferency, carelessness, [and] unconcernedness" of parishioners.[27] When revivalists like Whitefield observed that colonial religion had "waxed cold" and was "at a very low ebb," they merely echoed clerical depictions of the previous sixty or seventy years.[28]

Jonathan Edwards provided for eighteenth-century revivalists a model of declension in his *Faithful Narrative*. In the preface to his description of the Northampton revival, Edwards gave a view of the state of religion in his parish that many dissenters found accurate. Edwards reported that after the last revival before the one beginning in 1733, there "came a far more degenerate time . . . than ever before." Most of the congregation "seemed to be at that time very insensible of the things of religion, and engaged in other cares and pursuits." It seemed to be a time of "extraordinary dullness in religion: licentiousness for some years greatly prevailed among the youth of the town; they were many of them very much addicted to night-walking, and frequenting the tavern, and lewd practices." The absence of religious concern affected more than just the youth and church affairs; it spread to the entire town, heightening political as well as religious strife. Edwards noted that "there had also long prevailed in the town a spirit of contention" between proprietors and nonproprietors over who controlled the right to allot undivided land. Avarice flourished in the absence of practical piety.[29]

Edwards's judgment that true religion languished was a theological assessment. He analyzed the state of religion in Northampton on the basis of observed behavior, assuming that external acts mirrored one's internal condition of grace. The kind of spirit that controls one's inner being is revealed in outward pursuits. Satan prompts people to seek "the Pleasures, Profits and Honors of the World," while God inspires them to pursue "the Kingdom of God and his Righteousness."[30] Viewing Northampton through his particular theological lens, he found the state of religion in the early 1730s lamentable indeed.

The South Carolina evangelical Josiah Smith joined Edwards in painting preawakening colonial religion in the darkest hues. In a 1740 pamphlet, Smith wrote, "Now we are none of us ignorant, how far the primitive Spirit of Christianity has sunk into a mere Form of godliness. Irreligion has been rushing in, even upon the Protestant World, like a Flood: The dearest and most obvious Doctrines of the bible have fallen into low Contempt; the Principles and Systems of our good and pious Fathers have been more and more exploded." To him, itinerant evangelists were divine instruments to reverse the decline: "And now behold! God seems to have revived the ancient Spirit and Doctrines. He is raising up of our young Men, with Zeal and Courage, to stem the Torrent."[31]

In the sparsely settled Carolinas, revivalists and antirevivalists alike bewailed the absence rather than the decline of religion. Hardly an unbiased observer, Virginia planter William Byrd II nevertheless captured the raw, rough life in Edenton, North Carolina, in the 1720s. "I believe this is the only metropolis in the Christian or Mahometan world," he wrote in his *History of the Dividing Line* (1728), "where there is neither church, chapel, mosque, synagogue, or any other place of any sect or religion whatsoever." He refused to accept the local explanation that Edentonians preferred private devotion to "priest-ridden" public worship. "One thing [that] may be said for the inhabitants of [this] province," he concluded, "[is] that they are not troubled with any religious fumes. . . . What little devotion there may happen to be is much more private than their vices."[32] Passing through North Carolina ten years later, George Whitefield echoed Byrd's lament. "In North Carolina there is scarcely so much as the form of religion," he noted in his *Journal.* He learned that "two churches were begun, some time since, but neither is finished."[33]

The problem in Virginia was not the lack of religion but the absence of orthodoxy. Without a resident bishop or at least a local church assembly, individual Church of England parishes were permeated with all sorts of teachings. Reverend Hugh Jones reported in 1741 that he found within the church a broad spectrum of heterodoxy: "enthusiasm, deism, and libertism." According to one historian, Virginians "were members of a catholic church": "catholic" not in the sense that it possessed a dogma for all men (for its dogma was vague and inarticulate), but in the sense that all, excepting only fanatics and agitators, could live within it while holding their own private dogmas.[34]

From Anglican missionary Charles Woodmason's perspective, the state of religion on the frontier was chaotic, in large part because of enthusiastic teachings and behavior that had infiltrated the region. The Anglican itinerant lamented what he called a "Medley of Religions" in the backcountry. Moreover, he claimed that among the diverse denominations and sects, "True Genuine Christianity is not to be found." His bias as a Church of England minister who adhered to a prescribed liturgy and time-honored articles of faith led him to see religious anarchy in the backcountry. A seemingly endless number of uneducated itinerant preachers passed through frontier communities preaching all sorts of messages that confused ignorant men and women, who lurched toward first one position and then another.[35]

To Gilbert Tennent in New Jersey any explanation for its decline must begin with the church itself. To him the decay was evident among members who for various reasons no longer practiced the piety they had once professed. Rather than being the core of one's life that gave meaning and direction, faith for many had grown formal and lifeless. In a sermon at Perth Amboy on June 29, 1735, Tennent indicted his auditors according to a taxonomy of transgressors that included the "Secure," "Apostates," "Formalists," "Prophane People," "Covetous, Idolatrous Worldlings," and "Filthy Hypocrites." The secure were those "who have never been so much as convinc'd thoroughly of their damnable Condition." They saw no need for personal salvation because they did not consider themselves to be condemned sinners. Apostates had once been convinced of their damnation but had drawn "back to Perdition." Formalists were people who "content themselves with a dead Form of Religion." They attended only to the outer forms of religion, paying no attention to the necessity of a spiritual new birth. The profane were the irreligious who showed no regard for God's commandments. Tennent listed in this category "Drunkards, Swearers, Whoremongers, Adulterers, Sabbath-Breakers, Thieves." Regarding them he asked, "Don't all these storm Hell, and endeavour to take Damnation by Violence, out of the Hands of the Devil?" Worldings put their souls in danger by being more concerned about temporal than eternal security. Both buying and selling could result in sin if the motive was vanity and greed. He singled out consumers who indulged their "pamper'd Bodies," and merchants who, like rooks, tore property "out of the Hands of its just Owner." Hypocrites were the "Stage Players of Religion." Their "double Tongues and divided Hearts" led them to an outward profession of faith while they pursued "Covetousness and other Lusts."[36]

Pondering how church members had descended to such a sorry state led evangelical ministers to examine their own preaching. Jonathan Edwards's grandfather and predecessor at Northampton, Solomon Stoddard, blamed pastors for not making their congregations aware of the eternal peril they faced as a result of sin. "The misery of many Men is," he proclaimed in a 1713 sermon, "that they do not fear Hell, they are not sensible of the dreadfulness or danger of Damnation, and so they take a great liberty to Sin." In short, he added, "if they were afraid of Hell, they would be afraid of Sin." Only when men and women confronted the awful reality of their sinful lives, and only when they ceased to be secure in their current state, would churches stem the tide of decline.[37]

In addition to shortcomings in preaching, ministers had failed to provide fervent leadership in evangelism. Stoddard found it damning that while "this Work of Reformation has been mightily clogged" throughout the land, "the Countrey has been prosperous in other Designs." Citing examples, he noted that "there has been an indeavour to promote Cloathing, and it hath been prospered." Also, there was a "design to promote Learning and Merchandize, and there hath been Success." But efforts to "promote Reformation," including the enactment of laws governing morality, the preaching of sermons, and the making of covenants, had "miscarried." Stoddard feared that too many pastors depended on governments to promote piety, and he warned that laws punishing "gross iniquities" would not "make the Land Reform." The only solution he saw was for ministers to provide energetic, purposeful leadership in preaching the "Fear of Hell to restrain [people] from Sin."[38]

While self-examination led evangelicals to lament the inefficacy of their own preaching and leadership, they attacked nonevangelicals who were making direct assaults against the very foundation of Christian faith: biblical revelation. Stoddard and other evangelicals believed that Enlightenment ideas, in particular, undermined the gospel as revealed truth. While acknowledging God as creator, some Enlightenment thinkers virtually ignored God as redeemer who intervened in history to save wayward humans. According to their perspective, God, as architect of a mechanistic universe, was content to allow it to operate according to immutable laws. Moreover, in this view, humans assumed new importance because of their ability to understand that universe. Indeed, according to some devotees, perfection was within human reach. Men and women could save themselves by discovering divinely inscribed natural, social, and moral laws—a far cry from the biblical portrayal of natural man condemned by his own sin. Perhaps most dangerous to evangelicals was the belief that human reason, not divine revelation, became the path to enlightenment. That meant that the Bible as revealed truth must be interpreted before the bar of reason, and unreasonable sections must be disregarded or explained as myth. Such a position led a later disciple, Thomas Jefferson, to reduce the Bible to a few score pages of moral teachings attributed to Jesus, and to discard the rest as superstition.[39]

Revivalists singled out Deism, a term that contemporaries identified with a host of attacks on orthodoxy, as a dangerous set of propositions circulating in the eighteenth-century marketplace of ideas. Relying on human reason's direct grasp of "natural religion," Deism was "an attempt fundamentally to simplify traditional theology, distinguishing the major items of belief held in common between all religions and deriving a flexible ... piety from the evidence of creation rather than from specific disclosures to mankind in revelation." Deists conceived of God as a "Creator or First Cause who subsequently stood aside from his creation to allow it to run according to its own rules." They rejected or at least called into question such Christian tenets as original sin and the belief in a future life. Given indirect support by the publication of John Locke's *Essay on Human Understanding* (1690) and *The Reasonableness of Christianity as Delivered in the Scriptures* (1695), Deism attracted interest among the learned members of Anglo-American society.[40]

To evangelicals, a far more insidious enemy of Reformed theology came in the cloak of moderate churchmen like Archbishop John Tillotson. In emphasizing the reasonableness of Christianity, he and other latitudinarians, according to their critics, "at least played into the hands of the Deists."[41] Tillotson's printed sermons circulated widely in eighteenth-century America, especially among the "better sorts" in colonial society. Some leading Puritan divines applauded the "'tolerant and enlarged Catholic Spirit,' typified by the enormously popular sermons of Archbishop Tillotson." Increase Mather reportedly said that if old England had always had ecclesiastical leaders like Tillotson, "New England had never been."[42] Benjamin Colman, pastor of Boston's Brattle Street Church and a promoter of the Great Awakening, gushed in praise of Tillotson, nominating him among "the most venerable Men in the Church of England for Learning, Piety, Labours, Usefulness, Prudence, Meekness and Humility, insulted and outraged while they lived . . . for their Spirit of Moderation, and faithful Services to the Church."[43] One of the most often cited indications of Tillotson's place in the colonies is Virginia planter William Byrd's comment that he often read one of the archbishop's sermons in lieu of attending services at the parish church.[44]

Other Americans, including many who played key roles in the revivals, were less charitable in assessing Tillotson's contributions. To them, his latitudinarian and reasonable approach to Christianity had enervated Calvinist theology. Stressing God's mercy rather than his wrath, Tillotson conceived of the deity in natural terms, invoking a father's love for his children. From that perspective the archbishop found no place for such doctrines as that of predestination, whereby some were relegated to hell by an inscrutable god:

> I am as certain that this doctrine cannot be of God as I am sure that God is good and just, because this [doctrine] grates upon the notion that mankind have of goodness and justice. This is that which no man would do, and therefore cannot be believed of infinite Goodness. If an apostle, or an angel from heaven, teach any doctrine which plainly overthrows the goodness and justice of God, let him be accursed. For every man hath a greater assurance that God is good and just than he can have of any subtle speculations about predestination and the decrees of God.[45]

Revivalists feared that such soothing notions of God's goodness lulled sinners into a false sense of security. Awakeners charged Tillotson with making hell seem benign.

In a 1690 sermon on the eternity of hell that continued to draw praise and fury in America during the 1730s and 1740s, Tillotson advanced a view of damnation that upheld the notion of punishment for sins while softening divine decrees regarding hell. In explaining his position concerning sin and punishment, Tillotson attacked three orthodox views. First, he assaulted the certainty of eternal punishment by asserting that while God in the Scriptures *threatened* eternal punishment, the Almighty was not "obliged to follow through on this threat in every case of mortal sin." Second, he answered the orthodox claim that all sins were "infinite" because they were offenses against an infinite being. Tillotson argued that such a position was "palpably absurd" insofar as it relied on the same reasoning that supported the view that all punishment meted out by God, an infinite being, was infinite. Finally, Tillotson dismissed the idea that all sins were equal in God's sight, maintaining that offenses must be differentiated much as transgressions in an earthly kingdom are classified on the basis of their perpetrator and object. Treason is worse than petty larceny because it is aimed against the prince. By that logic, atheism is far more serious than telling a harmless lie. In secular law, stealing to feed one's family is less of an offense than betraying one's country for riches and glory. Likewise, Tillotson contended, "justice requires the weakness of the sinners to be consider'd, as well as the person again[st] whom the sin is committed."[46] In his scheme, God's view of transgressions took on human tones.

Reaching a broader segment of American society with a message similar to Tillotson's was the popular seventeenth-century handbook on Christian morality and devotions *The Whole Duty of Man* (1658), attributed to Richard Allestree. A subtitle indicates that the author intended the work for a wide audience because it was "*Laid down in a plain and Familiar Way for the Use of All, but especially the Meanest Reader.*" One study of personal libraries in eighteenth-century southern colonies found the frequency of the volume's presence second only to that of the Bible. SPG (Society for the Propagation of the Gospel in Foreign Parts) missionaries distributed hundreds of copies, and the Williamsburg printer William Parks reprinted the London edition for Virginia readers.[47]

Evangelicals opposed *The Whole Duty of Man* because of its teachings as well as its popularity. In its preface, the author stated his intention for the book: "to be a short plain Direction to the very meanest Readers, to behave themselves so in this World, that they may be happy for ever in the next." The emphasis on human endeavors, "good works," violated the basic tenet of Calvinism that God alone worked salvation sufficient for the next life. Moreover, the writer assured readers that they did not need learned ministers, Calvinist or otherwise, to instruct them on how to take care of their souls: it "needs no deep Learning or extraordinary Parts, the simplest Man living . . . hath Understanding enough for it, if he will but act in this by the same Rules of common Reason whereby he proceeds in his worldly Business."[48]

Like evangelicals, Allestree sought to awaken readers to the true condition of their souls and alert them to what must be done for salvation. Unlike evangelicals, the writer presented a kind and benevolent God who guided wayward men and women with the gentle hand of reason as opposed to preordaining some to salvation and others to damnation. Because of Adam's sin, people lost the full knowledge of their duty toward God and themselves and the power to perform it. But rather than condemning humans for their failure to obey divine laws, God sent Christ to "enable us to do what God requires of us." One way Christ assisted men and women was by "taking off from the Law given to Adam, which was, never to commit the least Sin, upon Pain of Damnation, and requiring of us only a honest and hearty Endeavour to do what we are able, and where we fail, accepting of sincerely Repentance." In other words, God realized that the terms of the first covenant were too harsh, and he replaced it with a second, easily attainable with a good-faith effort. Once people realize that God has freed them from an impossible law, enlightened their understandings, and strengthened their wills, they are enabled to "bestow a little Care" on their own souls and work out their salvation.[49] Propagating teachings antithetical to Calvinist notions of the absolute sovereignty of God and the total depravity of humans, Tillotson's sermons and *The Whole Duty of Man* naturally became targets for revivalist attacks.

DECLARING THE ACCEPTABLE YEAR OF THE LORD

What distinguished eighteenth-century revivalists from other evangelicals was their belief that God periodically pours out his grace in an extraordinary way to redeem a sinful people, *and* that they were participating in one of those unusual outpourings. They found biblical authority for their beliefs in the Old and New Testaments, citing numerous promises of enlarged dispensations of divine deliverance to wayward men and women. Moreover, those passages identified certain signs pointing to such a gracious revival. In the events of the 1730s and 1740s in the North Atlantic world, revivalists found unmistakable evidence of an unusual showering of God's saving favor.

The fact that many other evangelicals did not recognize and acknowledge a revival suggests that extraordinary dispensations were not self-evident and were indeed human inventions. Many opponents of the so-called great awakenings made just that charge. Like revivalists, these antirevivalists believed that God was the central actor in the drama of salvation. And they preached the gospel of Christ's redemptive love. Many even affirmed their belief in special outpourings of divine grace such as that witnessed on the day of Pentecost. However, they did not see revival in mid-eighteenth-century Anglo-America.

Understanding how some evangelicals proclaimed revival while others did not begins with an examination of how revivalists read the Bible, followed by an exploration of how they interpreted events of their own day. Awakeners, like the Puritan divines who inspired their preaching, believed that "the content of a sermon should be discovered by invention." They applied Ramist "laws of invention" to biblical texts in order to extract arguments. In that usage, "invention" meant discovering, "opening" a passage and find its true meaning. Ramist rules of interpretation rested on the assumption that Scripture contained truth, and the job of the reader was to uncover it. In no sense did the exegetical scheme allow for the interpreter to create new meaning by reading artful notions into the text. God stamped his patterns onto Holy Writ, and the faithful preacher lifts those eternal truths and explains them to others. Eighteenth-century revivalists came from a long line of preachers who found the promise of revival in God's Word.

For revivalists the outpouring of God's Spirit at Pentecost fulfilled Old Testament promises and gave hope for future dispensations. The account in the Acts of the Apostles described how the Holy Ghost filled Peter and the other disciples with unusual power that enabled them to preach with extraordinary success, resulting in thousands' being converted. Witnessing the unparalleled work of grace, the author declared that the day of Pentecost fulfilled Old Testament prophecies, citing in particular that found in Joel 2:28–32. In that passage God declared that "in the last days . . . I will pour out my Spirit upon all flesh" and give to men and women powers of prophecy. Moreover, the Lord foretold how on that day "whoever calls on the name of the Lord shall be saved." The three thousand souls that experienced the spiritual new birth on Pentecost bore witness to the fulfillment of that promise.[50]

Eighteenth-century revivalists fully expected another outpouring of God's Spirit. As they assessed the state of religion in late-seventeenth- and early-eighteenth-century Anglo-America, they saw disturbing paral-

lels with the sin and degradation described in Joel. Because of the Jews'
turning away from God, they faced divine wrath and destruction. God
instructed Joel to warn his people of the coming judgment before it was
too late: "Awake, you drunkards, and weep." The prophet described
what was in store for a nation that had turned away from God: "The
cereal offering and the drink offering are cut off from the house of the
Lord. The priests mourn, the ministers of the Lord. The fields are laid
waste, the ground mourns; because the grain is destroyed, the wine fails,
the oil languishes." The only way of salvation was for the people to
repent and "return to the Lord, your God, for he is gracious, and
merciful." He will hear his people and pour out his Spirit on them.
Everywhere they turned in Britain and British America, revivalists saw
men and women turning against revealed religion, relying on themselves
rather than God. In the awakeners' view, such behavior would surely
lead to calamities similar to those foretold in Joel. But the revivalists
were just as certain that, once again, God would reform his people
through an extraordinary outpouring of his grace.[51] Some, such as
Thomas Prince, longed for a return to "ye old ways of N[ew] E[ngland],"
when truly pious men and women were ever vigilant for another display
of divine mercy.[52]

   Though spiritual awakenings came from God, evangelicals in revival
traditions believed that they had an active role to play in preparing
themselves and others to receive God's outpouring. What, then, could
men and women do in promoting revival? Christians should, first, recognize that the church of God is "subject to great Change." During times
when Christianity is not flourishing, the faithful should realize that such
a condition may not continue, that the "withering" will pass. Second,
believers should pray or, more specifically, "beg of God, that Religion
may revive in the Land." Stoddard made clear that people "shold not
pray for this in a formal way, . . . but with Groanings that cannot be
uttered." Though God is the lone actor in the work of grace, he "delights
to hear such Prayers." The Bible attests to the Almighty's responses: "He
hath in many times revived his Work in *Israel* formerly." During the third
of five revivals spanning his long pastorate at Northampton, Stoddard
reminded his readers that "we should take Notice of God's Mercy to
our selves, once and again, and now a third Time." Finally, Christians
can promote revival by avoiding those things that "quench the Spirit,"
such as paying undue attention to the new "Commodities that are in
Demand" and tend to detract from the work of grace.[53] In other words, by
allowing matters of the marketplace to overshadow God's work, Christian

men and women unwittingly thwart the stirrings of revival, making it difficult for others to receive a special outpouring of grace.

Increase Mather called on Christians to pray for an imminent effusion of God's spirit resulting in the conversion of thousands of men and women throughout the world. He exhorted the faithful to "Pray that there may be a plentiful Effusion of the Holy Spirit on the world. Then will Converting work go forward among the Nations, and the Glorious Kingdom of Christ will fill the Earth."[54] Mather was confident that those prayers would be answered, expressing in 1719 his belief that "there are some here living [who] will see the beginning of those glorious days" when God's grace washes over the land.[55]

Cotton Mather also viewed prayer as essential in preparation for revival. In a 1724 publication, he extolled the virtues of religious societies for "the Revival of Dying Religion." Under his proposal, inspired in part by his correspondence with the German Pietist August Hermann Francke, Mather urged men and women to unite in small voluntary groups for prayer, exhortation, and singing. Such gatherings would be "strong Engines to uphold the Power of Godliness" and would reverse the "visible Decay of Godliness." While encouraging other forms of worship, Mather above all called on society members to pray, recognizing that "Prayer of such well disposed Societies may fetch down marvellous Favours from Heaven."[56] During the Great Awakening, revival promoters repeated Mather's call for prayer. Jonathan Edwards sounded the theme in a treatise urging evangelicals to engage in "Extraordinary Prayer for the Revival of Religion and the Advancement of Christ's kingdom on earth."[57]

While acknowledging that God alone brought revival, and that Christians should "fetch down" awakening through prayer, Solomon Stoddard also recognized the importance of effective preaching in the promotion of a religious revival. Those faithful to the mysteries of God's dispensing grace knew that revivals result as much from believers' *preaching them up* as *praying them down*. For Stoddard the beginning point in good preaching was to scare the hell out of people—that is, to convince men and women that their sins would result in eternal damnation, and that they were powerless to save themselves. Sinners must see that they are totally dependent upon a merciful God for their salvation. Moreover, God dispensed his grace in a seasonal and arbitrary manner. "God is very Arbitrary in this Matter," Stoddard wrote; "God takes his own time to Refresh their Hearts." It was incumbent upon ministers, therefore, to recognize the signs of those "special seasons wherein God doth in a remarkable Manner revive Religion among his People." When they see such times, pastors must "preach the acceptable Year of the Lord," "give Notice" to men and women of God's extraordinary effusion of grace. Stoddard admonished his fellow ministers to be ever vigilant because "God doth not always carry on his Work in the Church in the same Proportion." Like the rhythms of nature, there are "great Vicissitudes" in the movement of God's grace; it "waxes and wanes" and "ebbs and flows."[58]

In a popular handbook on how to promote revival through preaching, Isaac Watts stressed both style and substance. He urged pastors to employ "the Arts of *Method* and *Oratory* . . . to set the Things of God before Men in the plainest, the most conspicuous and convincing Light." An awakening sermon must engage all of the human faculties: understanding, reason, memory, conscience, will, and affections. While advocating sound reason and tight logic, he argued that revivalist preaching must exert power over the "*Fancy or Imagination.*" Watts instructed preachers to practice "all Methods to rouse and awaken the cold, the stupid, the sleepy Race of Sinners." Certain topics, he declared, were more "suited to do good to Souls . . . for the Conviction of the Stupid and Ignorant." He suggested that orators should fill their discourses with stories of how God has awakened sinners by some "special and awful Providence" such as earthquakes or shipwrecks. The idea was to produce inward "Terrors of Mind" and trigger "Fears of the Wrath of God."[59]

Like Stoddard and Watts, Gilbert Tennent of New Jersey knew how to preach up revival. In particular he directed sermons toward those who evidenced the least concern about the need for a spiritual awakening: the secure, whom he described as those "who have never been so much as convinc'd thoroughly of their damnable Condition."[60] Secure sinners failed to "consider what their Case is, and what is like to be the End of their present Course." Because of a false sense of security bred of confidence in their abilities to save themselves, secure sinners "seldom enquire what their present state is or consider what will be the End of their Way; they are secure, Thoughtless and Indolent about everlasting concerns." To Tennent, the first step in revival preaching was to awaken men and women by calling on them to consider or ponder the gravity of their plight. He, therefore, warned them that "serious and speedy Consideration is so necessary a Mean to prevent the Sinners utter Destruction."[61]

Once sinners consider the gravity of their true spiritual condition, they are ready to accept God's grace. However, like Edwards and New England revivalists, Tennent believed that God poured out his mercy more fully at specific times, during seasons of revival. Tennent believed that such a time existed in New Jersey and New York in the mid-1730s. He urged sinners to seize the moment and to move quickly to claim God's gift. To delay meant risking eternal abandonment. In a sermon preached at New York in March 1735, Tennent made his case: "That while God is upon a Treaty with Sinners, there is yet a Door of Mercy opened; and therefore that it highly concerns those whose [*sic*] have hitherto forgotten God, in Regard of Knowledge, Dependance and Service, that they would now, without further Delay, consider and lay to Heart their present Danger and Misery, while they have the Offer of Mercy, lest they be forever deprived thereof and exposed to the Stroaks of his avenging Severity."[62] Failure to accept God's grace while it is extended may mean that an individual will never again have such an offer.

Tennent believed that good revival preaching depended on the right messenger as well as the right message. Like many of his fellow revivalists, he thought that true religion was experiential, and that those who had themselves undergone a spiritual new birth were best suited to preach conversion to sinners. On the other hand, he compared most American ministers with the Pharisees whose legalistic religion Jesus blasted. Although the "modern Pharisees have learned to prate a little more orthodoxy about the New Birth than their Predecessor[s]," he wrote, "they are "as great Strangers to the feeling Experience of it." Because they have not experienced conversion, their discourses were "cold and sapless." Tennent reasoned that "a dead Man [was not] fit to bring Others to Life." That being the case, "it is both lawful and expedient" for their parishioners "to go from them to hear Godly Persons." Tennent asked, "If God's People . . . should go a few Miles farther than ordinary to enjoy those which they profit most by, who do they wrong?"[63]

Tennent suggested that parishioners should exercise choice in regard to ministers. He explained that an individual has a "choice . . . of Sermons and Preachers; seeing at one time we cannot hear all, neither doth the Explication and Application of all, equally suit such a Person, in such a Time, or Condition, or equally quicken and subserve the Encrease of Knowledge." On the one hand, "the Carnality of the [settled] Ministry [had] spread Arminianism, Socinianism, Arianism, and Deism." To Tennent, those were bad options. On the other hand, parishioners could make good selections. He urged that congregations with vacant ministries "take due Care in the Choice of their Ministers," testing prospects "by their Manner of Praying, Preaching, and Living."[64]

Revivalists believed that special "seasons of grace" occurred from time to time, were recognizable by those with eyes to see, and were particularly propitious times for conversions. During those periods great numbers of men and women underwent spiritual new births. Thus when evangelists detected the extraordinary work of God, they were to confront persons with one simple message: salvation comes only through a conversion experience within each individual—in their words, the new birth was "the one thing needful." Revival was not about correct theology but about a life-changing experience.

By focusing on a simple message, revivalists followed the lead suggested by Cotton Mather earlier in the eighteenth century. Mather advocated a return to a "few distilled Gospel principles of vital piety" that had been diluted by constant squabbles among various Protestant sects. In 1715, he published *Religion of the Everlasting Maxims*, which reduced Christianity to fourteen "unshakable maxims on which Christians throughout the world of whatever sect ... would agree." Hoping, as Luther had hoped of his own pamphleteering, that the pamphlet would become a "Little Engine of Piety," he aimed to send copies wherever missionaries labored from Malabar to Scotland. By 1717, he had reduced the number of maxims to three: "belief in the Trinity, utter reliance on Christ for salvation, and love of neighbor out of respect for Christ." "Real and vital Piety," he wrote, consists of "Fearing of God, and in Prizing of His Christ, and in Doing of Good unto Men." The awakeners of the mid–eighteenth century similarly represented Christianity as a few essential beliefs and practices, dispensing with all questions of polity and "External Rites and Forms."[65]

At the center of the awakener's message was the necessity of a new birth, also known as the doctrine of regeneration. To John Wesley and George Whitefield the new birth was "the very hinge on which the salvation of each of us turns, and a point too in which all sincere Christians, of whatever denomination agree." If that was the case, why was a religious revival necessary? The answer was that while churches agreed on the doctrine, few people, including ministers, had actually undergone genuine conversion. In other words, though many understood the concept of a spiritual rebirth, most had never experienced regeneration. To Whitefield, new birth was "so seldom considered and so little experimentally understood by the generality of professors that, were we to judge of the truth of it by the experience of most who call themselves Christians, we should be apt to imagine they had 'not so much as heard' whether there be any such thing as regeneration or no."[66]

The defining notion behind the new birth was that of "experimental religion," a term evangelicals applied to a personal salvation experience. They drew distinctions between religion of the heart and mere "head-knowledge." The latter was derided as shallow or barren, the product of rationalists who reduced Christian faith to the affirmation of certain reasonable propositions. Objects of revivalist polemics included latitudinarians, whose broad construction of theology embraced a wide range of positions, and rationalists such as Arminians, Arians, Socinians, and Deists. To evangelicals, all of those reversed the proper roles in salvation by suggesting that men and women worked out their own redemption, rather than understanding redemption to be exclusively the work of a preordaining God.

By establishing the new birth as inward change rather than outward profession, the evangelical revivalists broadened their audience to include men and women within churches as well as those without. They rejected as "notoriously false" the idea that "'everyone that names the name of Christ' or is baptized into His invisible church would be a new creature." They believed that neither church membership nor baptism captured the scriptural sense of regeneration. Revivalists understood the new birth in a "second and closer signification," in which the Holy Spirit works an inward change whereby individuals are "so altered as to the qualities and tempers of [their] minds that [they] must entirely forget what manner of persons [they] once were." Such a mystical transformation can occur only through "a true and lively faith" infused by divine grace. After conversion, the indwelling Holy Spirit becomes a boundless supply of "spiritual virtue" enabling the Christian to bear the true fruits of salvation—faith, hope, and love.[67]

The inward nature of conversion presented revivalists with a challenging problem: how to publicize an event that occurred within an individual's heart, one that only God could authenticate. The solution lay in a device long favored by evangelicals, the conversion narrative wherein the newborn related his or her account of the indwelling Spirit. Through the reduction of such a narrative to print, a personal, subjective experience could circulate as objective fact.

Revival promoters solicited conversion narratives and published collections as evidence of God's grace at work. William McCullough, pastor at Cambuslang, Scotland, compiled the most extensive set of conversion narratives. Recording the majority during the two years following the 1742 Cambuslang revival, he transcribed the testimonies of 106 converts, noting especially the "Place of Abode, Time and Manner of their being seiz'd." Other pastors kept similar records for publication. James Robe of Kilsyth, Scotland, maintained "with the most scrupulous Niceness . . . a JOURNAL of what was most observable in the Case of many in the Congregation; who have applied to me from Time to Time, for Instruction and Direction under their spiritual Distress."[68]

American revivalists also solicited, produced, and disseminated conversion narratives. During the New England awakenings instigated by the 1727 earthquake, ministers recorded personal accounts of God's redemptive work within individuals. Then in the Great Awakening, Jonathan Edwards and other American awakeners frequently included conversion narratives in their accounts of community revivals. The Northampton pastor concluded his revival narrative with two extensive conversion narratives, accounts of an adult, Abigail Hutchison, and a four-year-old child, Phoebe Bartlett.[69]

The revivalists directed their message toward the individual. Their concern was narrow: had the person experienced the new birth? If the answer was no, then they sought to convince him or her of the necessity of conversion. Toward that end, they first attempted to confront the sinner with the horrible consequences that surely awaited the unconverted. If the answer was yes, then the revivalists exhorted him or her to a life of greater practical piety.

While aiming their message at each person individually, the revivalists sought to convey the gospel to all. That meant devising a strategy for evangelizing the "whole world." In pursuing their ambitious mission, they knew that their greatest challenge was gaining the attention of a mass audience. The cultural marketplace of the day gave rise to a cacophony of voices: publishers, entertainers, quack doctors. Evangelists thus entered a crowded arena with intense competition. However, revivalists turned to their own advantage many of the recent innovations that made the marketplace of culture both an object of their criticism and a powerful vehicle for reaching vast numbers of men and women. They expanded their vision of their "market" or audience, transcending traditional parish lines and reaching beyond even national boundaries. They also employed some of the new strategies that merchants like Josiah Wedgwood used to revolutionize consumer marketing.[70] The revivalists advertised their services as aggressively as Wedgwood did his new products, and their techniques included the "puffing" of their successes through testimonials by "disinterested" third parties.[71]

Once they had employed all the means at their disposal to prepare men and women for a great awakening, revivalists then shifted their focus to vigilance, ever watchful for signs that an extraordinary effusion of grace was becoming evident. The question they posed was, How could one know "when Religion is revived"? Stoddard cited three manifestations. First, "Saints are quickened," meaning that those who have already experienced the New Birth feel God's Spirit working within them in an unusual manner. Second, sinners are converted in an extraordinary way. "There is a mighty Change wrought in a little Time," Stoddard wrote; "The Number of Saints is greatly multiplyed." Third, even the unconverted "become more religious" during a revival and "reform their evil Manners, and engage in Religious Duties."[72] Evangelical Christians have an obligation to be ever vigilant for signs of "the acceptable Year of the Lord" that they may "give Notice" of it to others.

In the mid-1730s the stage was set in both colonial revival districts for the proclamation that a "mighty Work of God" had begun. Predisposed to look for God to send extraordinary grace at the darkest hour, revivalists proclaimed the times to be the "Midnight of the Church." Expectant parishioners responded to special series of sermons, hellfire in both message and tone, as if they were God's own warning. And when persons outside the tradition scoffed at claims that God was behind the intensified religious activity, revivalists interpreted their opposition as another sure sign that a revival of true religion was under way.

What revivalists did not know at the first stirrings of a spiritual awakening was what kind of revival was unfolding. Solomon Stoddard explained that revival comes in two distinct expressions: "sometimes more General and sometimes more Particular." "It is more General," he observed, "when it is throughout a Country, when in all Parts of a Land there is turning to God." The only historical example of a general awakening that he cited was "about Luther's time, when some Nations broke off from Popery, and imbraced the Gospel." However, just as an entire nation can experience revival, "sometimes the Country doth generally Decline." Writing early in the eighteenth century, Stoddard lamented that the American colonies were currently in such a state. Not all revivals were extensive; in fact, most were not. "Sometimes this reviving is more Particular," he stated, "when in some particular Towns Religion doth revive and flourish." The New Testament described local awakenings at Sardis and Laodicea. And, referring to the revival then under way in Northampton as he wrote, Stoddard added, "So it is in this Case."[73]

Revivals can be classified by temporal as well as spatial dimensions. "This reviving [of God's grace]," Stoddard continued, "is sometimes of longer, and sometimes of shorter Continuance." On occasion, revivals last for "a great many Years together." He noted that in the days of

Hezekiah, a revival spanned twenty-nine years. Another began with the preaching of John the Baptist and continued "several Years after the Death of Christ." However, often awakenings are of shorter duration. The apostle Paul described one of just one and one-half years. "Sometimes it is not so long," Stoddard pointed out; "There is a great stirring for a little time, and then it fails. Though the same outward Means continue, yet there is not that Blessing going along with them."[74] Whether "particular" or "general," of short or long duration, revivals disguised themselves in their beginnings. Only after they had run their courses could labels be applied.

When revival broke out in Northampton, Massachusetts, and Freehold, New Jersey, in the mid-1730s, the beginning was perceptible to only a small number of America's approximately 750,000 inhabitants. Almost no one outside the two tiny, remote communities noticed anything unusual. Within the revival districts themselves, nobody could have known that the "seasons of grace" that were astir would turn out to be the "first fruits" of the biggest religious awakening since the Protestant Reformation.

"the *first fruits* of this extraordinary and mighty Work of God's Special Grace"

IN THE mid-1730s, two occurrences triggered the chain of events that American revivalists in the 1740s would call "*the* Revival of Religion." First, local awakenings took place, one in the Raritan Valley of East Jersey and the other in the Connecticut Valley of western New England. While participants attributed them to a special effusion of God's Spirit, each revival manifested human actions specifically designed to produce a spiritual awakening: small groups of laypersons meeting to "pray down" God's Spirit and ministers delivering evangelistic sermons designed to "preach up" the necessity of individual conversion—in believers' language, a New Birth. Although led by young ministers, the revivals took place among congregations with rich and long-standing revival traditions. Indeed, both river valleys had been the scenes of many previous awakenings.

The second occurrence in the mid-1730s, however, distinguished the revivals from each other and from earlier awakenings. In addition to implementing strategies to produce revival, promoters publicized the Northampton awakening to a transatlantic audience, and in the telling and retelling, the local event assumed much wider significance. Previous revivals in the two regions had gone unnoticed outside their respective valleys. But this time the collaborative efforts of Jonathan Edwards, minister at Northampton, Massachusetts, Benjamin Colman, a Boston evangelical, and John Guyse and Isaac Watts, London dissenting ministers, resulted in an extensive published account of the New England awakening that became a best-seller among evangelicals in England, Scotland, and America. First published in London in 1737, the *Faithful Narrative* convinced revivalists that what happened in remote American communities was the beginning of a "great and general awakening" on the order of that witnessed by Saint Peter and Martin Luther. By the early 1740s when the revival had spread throughout the Atlantic world, one revivalist proclaimed that the Northampton awakening had borne "the *first fruits* of this extraordinary and mighty Work of God's Special Grace."[1]

This chapter explores the awakenings in New England and New Jersey, first, as they unfolded, and second, as the former was publicized. It traces the beginnings of revival in small, remote communities located in the hinterlands of British North America, places hitherto unknown to most outsiders. It examines the respective revival traditions and experiences in the Connecticut and Raritan Valleys that made particular congregations predisposed to periodic awakenings. It describes strategies that ministers devised to promote revivals: targeting specific groups, preaching special sermon series, conducting home prayer meetings, counseling persons "under conviction," and sharing news of awakenings in other communities. This chapter also follows the implementation of revival strategies and their results: growing crowds, altered conversation and behavior, increased numbers of conversions, and new awakenings in surrounding congregations. It, finally, analyzes the invention of the revivals in the sense that events were declared to be a genuine work of God as authenticated by Scripture.

The chapter's last section shifts from the events as they occurred to the process by which revivalists constructed a narrative for publication. Though the revival itself occurred in a remote frontier community, publication decisions centered largely in Boston and London, the respective print capitals of the colonies and England itself. The events described in the *Faithful Narrative* occurred over roughly a two-year period ending in 1736. The writing, editing, and publishing of the revival account itself also took a little more than two years. On May 30, 1735, Jonathan Edwards responded to Benjamin Colman's request for a "Particular account of the Present Extraordinary circumstances . . . with Respect to Religion" in the Connecticut Valley. Edwards's reply was an eight-page letter describing the awakening. In late 1737, the first edition of the *Faithful Narrative* appeared in London bookstalls. During the intervening period, Edwards's private letter had been transformed into a 132-page book. This chapter tells the story of that transformation.

REVIVAL IN NEW JERSEY

Ironically, a New Englander introduced Anglo-Americans to New Jersey's revival. In the mid-1730s, Jonathan Edwards learned of an awakening in "some parts of the Jerseys." William Tennent, a Presbyterian minister at Freehold, New Jersey, told Edwards of "a very great awakening of many in a place called The Mountains, under the ministry of one Mr. [Robert] Cross." Moreover, Tennent described also a "very considerable revival of religion" at New Brunswick, where his brother, Gilbert, was the pastor. When Edwards described the New Jersey awakenings in *A Faithful Narrative*, he considered them to be part of the same "shower of divine blessing" manifested in western Massachusetts and cited them as evidence that the revival was growing "yet more extensive."[2]

Evidence supports Edwards's pronouncement that the local revivals in New England and the Middle Colonies were of the same work. Both occurred in communities with rich revival traditions, featured dynamic preaching that emphasized conversion, and witnessed increased numbers of men and women testifying to a New Birth. But there were differences as well. The New Jersey work took place primarily among men and women with a Scottish Presbyterian heritage instead of an English Independent background. However, the most striking distinction between the two in terms of the invention of the great awakening was the fact that the Northampton work became widely publicized. Only after George Whitefield's arrival in 1739 triggered a more general revival did the Freehold awakening become familiar to evangelicals outside the region.

Well before the mid-1730s, New Jersey, like New England, had experienced evangelical revivals. And, in another irony, while they occurred primarily among emigrants from Northern Ireland, they were led by a Dutch preacher. In 1721, Theodore Frelinghuysen began preaching "soul-searching sermons" in the Raritan Valley of New Jersey that resulted in both conflict and revival. A recent immigrant from Holland, Frelinghuysen had been influenced by a group of German Protestants known as Pietists who believed that most Christians had grown flaccid in practicing their faith. Their solution was twofold: evangelistic preaching and the enactment of piety. The former meant an emphasis on the necessity of regeneration, defined as a "thoroughgoing conversion." The latter meant a disciplined life of worship and service, including the relief of others' physical and spiritual suffering. Some of Frelinghuysen's fellow churchmen in the Dutch Reformed tradition found his definition of regeneration too narrow and his regime of pious practice too harsh. Yet lay men and women responded to his fresh message, and his "emotionally-powerful preaching brought an increasing number of new converts" into the churches.[3]

Frelinghuysen's influence was uneven among New Jersey congregations. At New Brunswick, his labors were "much blessed." Yet he had no positive effect on the congregation at nearby Freehold. According to William Tennent, "the doctrine of the new-birth, when clearly explained, and powerfully pressed upon [the people of Freehold], as absolutely necessary to salvation (by that faithful preacher of God's word, Mr. Theodorus Jacobus Frelinghousa, a Dutch minister, and some other English ministers, who were occasionally here) was made a common game of; so that not only the preachers but professors of that truth were called in derision new-born, and looked upon as holders forth of some new and false doctrine."[4] Clearly revivals derived from something more than dynamic preaching. They required congregations that expected "seasons of grace" and were capable of recognizing their presence. A decade later, the people of Freehold were ready for revival, and they then experienced a great awakening.

No name was more closely associated with New Jersey awakenings than that of Tennent. Gilbert, John, and William, Jr., were Presbyterian evangelicals whose preaching was instrumental in starting revivals in their respective congregations at New Brunswick, Hopewell, and Freehold. Beginning in 1740, Gilbert played a major role in spreading the revival throughout the Middle Colonies and connecting that awakening with the New England revival. Behind the Tennent influence was the patriarch, William, Sr. Born in Ulster, he left the Anglican Church and became a dissenting Presbyterian minister before arriving in Philadelphia in 1718. The synod at Philadelphia examined the elder Tennent in the year of his arrival and questioned him at length about his reasons for leaving the Church of England. His responses reveal much about his theological views and those of the so-called Log College he established in 1725 at Neshaminy, Pennsylvania, to train evangelical ministers.

Tennent defended his decision to leave the established church because he believed that its structure, discipline, and theology departed from biblical truth. To him, episcopal government was "wholly un-scriptural"; ecclesiastical courts had no "foundation in the word of God"; and the office of diocesan bishop is without support "anywhere . . . in the word of God, and so is a mere human invention." In other words, Tennent rejected any ecclesiastical organization or practice for which he could not find scriptural authorization. Similarly, he measured theological matters against a biblical standard and found that Calvinism most closely conformed to divine revelation. On the other hand, he found the Church of England "conniving at the practice of Arminian doctrines inconsistent with the eternal purpose of God, and an encouragement of vice."[5] He and his sons not only subscribed to a Calvinist interpretation of the Bible but adhered to the more evangelistic expression found in parts of the Church of Scotland.

William Tennent's evangelism pervaded all his preaching and teaching but was particularly evident during the traditional Scottish church communion season. In a sermon he first preached in county Derry and repeated at his church in Westchester County, New York, Tennent underscored his view that the one thing needful was the new birth, a spiritual regeneration worked by God's Spirit. As he addressed his congregation before administering the Lord's Supper, he distinguished between those members who "only ate the bread of the Lord" and those who partook of "*the bread the Lord.*" The former he numbered among the "many [who] come to this Royal Supper, and go away unreformed, untouched, and unconcerned." They have "no sense of the design Christ had in instituting this sacrament" because they have not rejected the "pomp and grandeur of the world." On the other hand, those who participate in the "scriptural sense" have their priorities straight. They place at the center of their lives the redemptive work of the Lord, and therefore they "eat with a relishing of Christ's death and passion."[6]

For Tennent, the communion season was a time of revival when Christians examined themselves and reflected upon Christ's redeeming work. Like his Scottish counterparts at the Holy Fairs, he stressed the Christian's need for preparation before coming to the Lord's Table. First, the communicant must ask himself or herself: "what have I done,—what sins are those I am apt to lodge in my bosom?" But the scrutiny must go beyond a review of conduct and intentions; it must include beliefs: "what evil doctrines [am I] ready to entertain?" Good works were important in Tennent's view of the Christian faith only if they followed right belief. At the center of correct doctrine was divine regeneration. Thus a second component of preparation is "contemplating what God hath done for us in Christ Jesus; how God was in Christ reconciling the world unto himself, not imputing their trespasses to them."[7] While the experience of the new birth was central to Tennent's conception of salvation, the rational consideration of what God had done within the individual was an important part of that experience.

In the 1720s, William Tennent was concerned that for many men and women the communion season was not a time of revival and regeneration, but instead of blaming them, he blamed their pastors. In sentiments that his son Gilbert would echo in his famous 1741 sermon on unconverted ministers, William charged that some pastors came to the Lord's Table "only of a sense of duty or official obligation." Like a layperson, a "minister or clergyman may come to the Lord's Supper, and yet not eat the Lord's Supper. He may celebrate it as a minister, and yet not eat it as a sincere Christian."[8] To ensure that churches would be supplied with converted, orthodox, evangelical ministers, he organized a seminary in 1725 whose graduates would provide much of the leadership for revival in the Middle Colonies.

Antirevivalists derided William Tennent's evangelical seminary as the "Log College," drawing attention to the construction of the tiny school located on Neshaminy Creek just north of Philadelphia. Critics within the Presbyterian Church found the brand of religion Tennent taught there to be too enthusiastic for their sensibilities, and, as his graduates gained a large popular following, synod leaders viewed the Log College ministers as a threat to their control of the synod. Despite the opposition, the seminary influenced American revivalism far beyond what its humble campus would suggest possible. Consisting of a single log house, twenty feet on a side, the school provided theological training for only about twenty students in its brief existence. William Tennent made certain that his charges learned Hebrew, Greek, Latin, logic, philosophy, and theology. More important, he saw to it that his graduates learned how to construct and deliver powerful evangelical sermons complete with careful biblical exegesis and sound doctrine. In addition to his two sons, Gilbert and William, Jr., graduates who became giants in the Great Awakening included Samuel Blair and Samuel Finley.[9]

Gilbert Tennent proved to be the most dynamic and influential revival leader among the Log College graduates. Born in Northern Ireland into the Church of England, he began at the age of fourteen to study divinity, but he soon decided against entering the ministry because he believed that his spiritual state was "bad." He then shifted his academic focus to medicine. However, after one year, he underwent a cataclysmic conversion experience in which, in the language of evangelicals, he "was satisfied as to his interest in the divine favor." At the age of fifteen, Gilbert emigrated with his parents to America where he began anew his preparation for the ministry, this time within the Presbyterian Church following his father, who had left the Church of England. He received his theological education at the Log College under the tutelage of his father and became the new seminary's first graduate. He must have received a thorough grounding in doctrine and biblical languages: he met the qualifications of the Philadelphia presbytery, dominated by ministers educated at British universities or at Harvard or Yale. After being licensed to preach in 1725, he appears to have spent some time studying at Yale, although the details are unclear. Having received an honorary degree of A.M. from the New Haven college in 1726, he became the pastor at

New Brunswick, New Jersey, where he soon became known as a rousing preacher—a reputation that eventually earned him the epithet "Son of Thunder."[10]

Gilbert's father and Theodorus Frelinghuysen influenced the younger man's ministry through diverse, though related, emphases. While coming from very different ethnic and denominational backgrounds, the two mentors shared similar beliefs: opposition to "the idea that one's childhood training, ethnic origin, or theological acumen assured salvation," and stress on "the internal state of the individual over external observance of liturgical rites, and . . . the need for repentance, conversion, and a sincere practice of piety." But each contributed to Gilbert something unique. Frelinghuysen focused primarily on conversion as the central event in the Christian experience. His father, on the other hand, acknowledged the importance of conversion but gave precedence to right doctrine. Conversion was but the beginning in a life that must grow in grace, and it was the growth that William Tennent stressed. Both influences are evident in Gilbert's sermons, although his insistence on the necessity of the new birth suggests that Frelinghuysen's may have predominated.[11]

In 1734, Gilbert Tennent offered a series of proposals involving clergymen and their parishioners to stem "the declining power of godliness" in Presbyterian congregations. First, ministers should "make it their awful, constant, and diligent care, to approve themselves to God, to their own consciences, and to their hearers, [as] serious faithful stewards of the mysteries of god, and of holy exemplary conversions." In other words, pastors should make certain that they themselves had experienced the New Birth before preaching conversion to their people. Second, pastors should search for evidence of the grace of God before admitting anyone to the communion table. With those propositions, Tennent began to develop a revival program designed to promote an awakening among laity and clergy alike. The key was the "diligent use of those means necessary to obtain the sanctifying influences of the Spirit of God." Effective means included catechetical instruction and family training for the young people, home visitation and close examination of adults to test their experimental knowledge of grace, and oversight of ministerial candidates to make certain that they lived exemplary lives and understood the "normal workings of the Holy Spirit in the sinful world."[12]

One study of the New Jersey revivals suggests that the Tennents' revival program flourished because of the ethnic composition of congregations experiencing awakenings. Noting that "revival movements often occur as the result of the meeting of different cultural groups," Ned Landsman found in his study of the congregation at Freehold that the awakening in the early 1730s first served to strengthen the members' Scottish identity. Indeed, at least initially, what took place at Freehold reflected many of the characteristics of what anthropologists call a " 'nativistic revival,' one that emphasized not the integration of diverse persons, customs, or values, but their separation or elimination from view."[13] In other words, the revival underscored the congregation's Scottish heritage, which heightened differences between the participants and their English and Dutch neighbors.

While the Tennents shared much with English Puritans, they led the East Jersey awakenings in the distinctive Scottish revivalist style. Nowhere was that more evident than in their conception of the conversion experience. In the Scottish tradition, the New Birth was a time-consuming process that often occurred over a period of years under the close supervision of a minister. The Tennents reported that most of the first wave of conversions were not completed at Freehold until 1733, three years after the revival began. They were wary of instantaneous conversions expressed with great emotion but little understanding. Accordingly, they followed a process of first preaching "conviction and conversion" sermons aimed at making their listeners realize their sinful state and their utter inability to save themselves. After perhaps months of convincing men and women of the necessity of regeneration, the Tennents would shift their sermonic emphasis to "laying open the way of recovery." Converts under such preaching still faced months of instruction on religious doctrine, questioning about their conversion experiences, and testing of their answers. Gilbert Tennent explained that he visited parishioners in their homes, "examining them one by one as to their experiences, and telling natural people the dangers of their state . . . and those that were convinced, to seek Jesus."[14]

Though the Freehold revival was decidedly Scottish in the years after 1730, it became less ethnic and more ecumenical after George Whitefield's arrival in 1739. In the early period, the awakening unified the Scots of East Jersey by providing parishioners with a revival experience rooted in homeland tradition. Even as the revival strengthened ethnic bonds, it also built bridges to other evangelicals who believed that a mighty work of God was extending across national and denominational boundaries. In the Middle Colonies, "what had started out as a Scottish religious movement became a Presbyterian movement that attracted members of several ethnic groups." Acceptance of "Scottish-style evangelism, rather than actual Scottish descent" became the "principal criterion for inclusion in the religious community."[15] In 1740–1741, Gilbert Tennent demonstrated his primary concern for winning souls rather than promoting Scottish tradition by preaching for months in Puritan New England. The warm reception he received there indicated that his evangelism spanned regional and ethnic differences.

AWAKENING IN THE CONNECTICUT VALLEY

It might be said that Jonathan Edwards was predestined to become a revivalist. Born in East Windsor, Connecticut, in 1703, the same year Gilbert Tennent was born, Edwards grew up in a family steeped in the evangelical Puritan tradition. His father, Timothy, was a pastor, and his mother, Esther, was a daughter of Solomon Stoddard. The fifth of eleven children and the only male, Jonathan pursued an education that would equip him to follow in his father's and grandfather's footsteps. He graduated from Yale at the age of seventeen, a typical age for eighteenth-century college graduates. He remained at Yale, earning a master of arts degree in 1723, which qualified him to become a tutor at the New Haven institution. After three years of preparing others for the ministry, he joined his grandfather in Northampton as associate pastor and heir apparent. No one could match Solomon Stoddard as a revivalist. The "harvests" of 1679, 1683, 1696, 1712, and 1718 attest to the effectiveness of his evangelistic preaching. Edwards arrived in time to participate in one last revival under Stoddard's leadership, an awakening in 1727 triggered by an earthquake. Edwards, then, was well equipped to continue the revival tradition when he assumed the pastorate upon his grandfather's death in 1729.[16]

In 1731, Edwards made his Boston debut. He preached at a public lecture, a forum enabling senior ministers to take the full measure of Stoddard's grandson. Jonathan did not disappoint them. His sermon, *God Glorified in the Work of Redemption,* sounded evangelistic themes his grandfather had popularized, and was accorded the high compliment of being published, Edwards's first publication. Thomas Prince and William Cooper, two of Boston's most revered pastors, expressed their "Joy and Thankfulness, that the great Head of the Church is pleas'd still to raise up from among the Children of his People, for the Supply of His Churches, those who assert and maintain these Evangelical Principles."

Their praise of Edwards's sermon reflected well on the church at Northampton, which "has for so many Lustres of Years flourished under the Influence of such Pious Doctrines."[17] Young Edwards returned to western Massachusetts to labor at the ongoing and arduous task of helping his congregation live the principles he had propounded in Boston.

When Edwards surveyed the state of religion in Northampton in the early 1730s, he reflected on the community's history of revivals, but he also recognized the persistence of sin that, despite periodic awakenings, ate away at spiritual commitment and practical piety until the resulting decay necessitated another awakening. He knew especially that for faith to remain vital and active, each new generation must experience first-hand the conviction of their dependence on God and the liberation that comes only through accepting his grace. Edwards was also aware that just as evil knew no generational boundaries, it also ignored geographic distances. Though located far from Boston's vices and temptations, Northampton was vulnerable to insidious sin. Even if distance reduced exposure to sinful imports from Boston, locals proved capable of manufacturing enough of their own worldliness to plunge Northampton into a steep spiritual declension. In the mid-1730s, Edwards concluded that the town witnessed "a far more degenerate time (at least among the young people), I suppose, than ever before."[18]

The town's youth had long served as the community's spiritual barometer. Stoddard had informed Edwards that in each of the revivals, "the bigger part of the young People in the Town seemed to be mainly concerned for their eternal Salvation." And, in times of "extraordinary Dullness in Religion," the youth likewise set the tone. In the early 1730s, they were out of control, if we can believe Edwards: "It was their Manner very frequently to get together in Conventions of both Sexes, for Mirth and Jollity, which they called Frolicks; and they would often spend the greater part of the Night in them, without regard to any Order in the Families they belonged to: and indeed Family-Government did too much fail in the Town."[19] Edwards was not alone in viewing young people as needful of special reform. In a sermon addressing the problem of spiritual decline throughout Massachusetts, Samuel Wigglesworth, pastor at Ipswich, singled out for special attention the "*Pride, Scornfulness and Ungovernableness in Youth.*"[20] For Edwards, young people were the key to revival. Figure out how to get them back into the church, and the rest of society will follow.

Edwards knew how to mount a revival. When he began his ministry, he brought with him an evangelistic model fashioned while he was serving as Stoddard's assistant from late 1726 through early 1729. During that period, beginning in 1727, the Northampton congregation experienced yet another revival, adding a sixth "harvest" to Stoddard's ministry. During the revival of 1734–1735, Edwards recalled that he had observed an earlier awakening and benefited from it. Writing in the *Faithful Narrative*, he reflected on the late 1720s as "a Time where there were no small appearances of a divine Work amongst some, and a considerable Ingathering of Souls, even after I was settled with him [Stoddard] in the Ministry, . . . ; and I have reason to bless God for the great Advantage I had by it."[21] Having experienced a revival up close, Edwards knew how to recognize one when he saw it. Moreover, he knew how to initiate an awakening.

The 1727 revival underscored two convictions that shaped Edwards's view of how awakenings unfolded. First, in a dramatic fashion, the awakening began with a work of God—in this instance, an earthquake. When tremors shook the earth throughout much of New England, pastors were quick to find religious significance. Referring to the shocks, Samuel Wigglesworth wrote, "these notable Works of God do very often betoken his Anger toward Mankind." He noted, however, that it was an earthquake which "occasioned the Jaylor's Conversion," as depicted in Acts 16, when a tremor prompted the guard to ask, "*What must I do to be Saved?*"[22] Second, Edwards learned in 1727 that while God instigates revival, his ministers can and should take action to promote awakening. He and other New England pastors seized the occasion to preach evangelistic sermons calling on their parishioners to repent of their sins in the face of God's obvious displeasure. He discovered how to "preach down" a revival.

In late 1733 and early 1734, Edwards again implemented his evangelistic strategy, this time without an earthquake to set the stage. First, he targeted young people, especially those who were "addicted to nightwalking, and frequenting the tavern, and lewd practices." Frequently, the youth had made the time immediately following the public lecture a regular occasion for "their mirth and company-keeping." Second, Edwards established a new service, again designed particularly for the young people. He inaugurated a sermon *before* the lecture "to shew the evil tendency" of leaving the church for merrymaking, and to persuade them to stop the base practice. Third, Edwards enlisted the help of parents, urging them to keep their children home during times when many had commonly engaged in licentious behavior, and to have them in attendance at services. Fourth, he initiated a series of neighborhood meetings wherein the adults could "know each other's minds" on the proposed reforms. Hence pastor and parents united in a concerted effort to influence the youths' behavior.[23]

Edwards's sermons appealed to the heads and hearts of his audience. He had mastered the rationalist notions of such Enlightenment thinkers as Sir Isaac Newton and John Locke, and applied them to his understanding of grace. While crafting sermons as tightly reasoned discourse, Edwards preached a message that centered on the emotions. He viewed salvation as a thorough change of the heart, "a holy affection at the center of [a person's] being which radiates its transforming power through the whole [person]." His rational defense of emotions had an emotional effect on his listeners as they heard calm, quiet, clear, reasonable sermons setting forth the terrors awaiting the unredeemed in an everlasting hell.[24] Unlike Gilbert Tennent, Edwards was no "Son of Thunder." He belied the notion that all revivalists were hellfire preachers in the sense of possessing booming voices and dramatic pulpit styles. Nevertheless, his message confronted listeners with hell itself, and his eloquent, matter-of-fact depiction seared the hearts of listeners like dry ice.

Through his preaching, Edwards sought not only to scare people out of a future hell but to promote piety in the present. In particular he strove for economic justice. For Edwards, an important aim of a religious awakening was to transform individual lives through genuine conversion experiences that, in turn, would reform community life in its many dimensions, including "all men's common business and employments." As a millennialist, he believed that during Christ's thousand-year reign wealth would be abundant and widespread, and people would live long, prosperous lives. That vision served as an indictment of economic practices in the Connecticut Valley in the mid-1730s. There "river gods" controlled commerce in a way that channeled profits into their hands at the expense of small farmers who depended on the powerful merchants for the financing, marketing, and distribution of their produce. Edwards contrasted what will be when the revivals usher in the millennium with what existed in Northampton: "the art of navigation that is now improved so much in fear, with covetousness and pride, and is used so much by wicked, debauched men, shall be consecrated to God, and improved for holy uses."[25] During the awakening, Edwards "mounted a campaign of practical economic reform that focused on the saints rather than on the whole community."[26] In other words, if church members underwent a spiritual new birth and committed themselves to lives of practical piety, then they could transform Northampton's market-places with values that placed the common good above private gain.

In addition to preaching special sermons that targeted first the young people and then adults, Edwards advertised sensational conversions to promote revival. Believing that news of one conversion often prompted others, he publicized a particularly dramatic new birth. A woman, "one of the greatest Company-Keepers in the whole Town," came to Edwards for counseling. In the process, she underwent a salvation experience. Edwards broadcast throughout Northampton the "Event" of her conversion. He considered the woman's "account [to be] of a glorious Work of God's infinite Power and sovereign Grace; and that God had given her a new Heart." According to Edwards, God made that "Event . . . the greatest occasion of awakening to others, of any thing that ever came to pass in the Town." While crediting the Almighty, Edwards ensured that the episode received the widest coverage. And he reported that "the news of it seemed to be almost like a flash of Lightning, upon the Hearts of young People," and that many seemed to be "greatly awakened" by it.[27]

Edwards's revival strategy worked. The pastor reported that soon after he initiated his program, "the young People declared themselves convinced by what they had heard from the Pulpit, and were willing of themselves to comply with the Counsel that had been given." Results were immediate and dramatic: "there was a thorough Reformation of these Disorders thenceforward." From that beginning, Edwards extended his revival strategy to the entire congregation and to those in surrounding towns with similar success.[28]

Edwards found that news of the Northampton revival was effective in instigating awakenings throughout Hampshire County. Just as reports of the woman's dramatic conversion had stimulated others in town, accounts of revival in Edwards's congregation spawned similar outbreaks in South Hadley, Suffield, Sunderland, Deerfield, Hatfield, West-Spring-field, Long-Meadow, Westfield, Northfield, Windsor, and other locations. Of the power of publicity, Edwards wrote, "what other Towns heard of and found in this, was a great means of awakening them." He acknowledged that he and his parishioners also benefited from news of surrounding revivals: "our hearing of such a swift, and extraordinary Propagation, and Extent of this Work did doubtless for a time serve to uphold the Work amongst us. The continual News kept alive the talk of Religion . . . and much awaken'd those that looked on themselves as still *left behind.*" However, there were limits to the reach of publicity in an area void of newspapers. Edwards later discovered that revivals had occurred beyond the county in other parts of Connecticut, but residents at the time had "no Knowledge of each other's Circumstances."[29]

Bold in conceiving a strategy for initiating and spreading revival, Edwards was effusive in labeling his program and its results. He referred to the event as "this work of God," "this remarkable pouring out of the Spirit of God," "a considerable revival of religion," "this shower of divine blessing," "a very extraordinary dispensation of Providence," "a very general awakening," and "a very great awakening."[30]

Edwards's measurements of revival were quite varied. In his *Faithful Narrative*, Edwards expressed reluctance to estimate the number of converts. Like his grandfather, he believed that the private, inward nature of salvation rendered detection difficult. Nevertheless, he ventured a guess or a hope "that more than 300 Souls were savingly brought home to Christ in this Town in the space of half a Year (how many more I don't guess)."[31] Evidence suggests that Edwards may have exaggerated, perhaps in hopes of inspiring further awakenings. According to one scholar, "he recorded fewer than half that many names in the church membership rolls during that time."[32]

Edwards found the demographics of the new converts as noteworthy as their numbers. Compared to new births recorded during Stoddard's awakenings, those he reported included more males and more adults. About the same number of men as women were converted in 1734–1735, a departure from earlier revivals when "many more Women were converted than Men." As in past revivals, most of the converts were young. However, this time those under "regenerating influences [included] . . . elderly Persons and also those that are very young." In the past, he added, "it has been a thing heretofore rarely to be heard of, that any were converted past middle Age."[33]

Edwards measured the revival's success in behavioral as well as statistical terms. He observed a marked change in his congregation during services. They were "eager to drink in the words of the minister as they came from his mouth," and were frequently moved to "tears while the Word was preached." The transformation extended beyond the meetinghouse. "When once the Spirit of God began to be so wonderfully poured out in a general way through the Town," he wrote, "People had soon done with their old Quarrels, Backbitings, and Intermeddling with other Men's Matters." The greatest visible and perhaps symbolic alteration was that of the townspeople's favorite place to congregate: "it was no longer the Tavern," Edwards exulted, "but the Minister's House, that was thronged far more than ever the Tavern had been wont to be."[34]

While exulting in the number of persons experiencing the new birth and the changes in conduct, Edwards worried that some parishioners were defining the awakening in unscriptural ways. Reflecting on the Northampton revival years after its occurrence, he noted that many lay men and women had established "certain wrong notions and ways in religion." The root of the problem was their misunderstanding of conversion. To some, conversion was limited to the initial sudden indwelling of God's Spirit, something that darted into one's heart in a single memorable moment. While agreeing that salvation could begin suddenly, Edwards fretted that too many stressed "the first work of the Spirit of God on their hearts in their convictions and conversion, and . . . look[ed] but little at the abiding sense and temper of their hearts, and the course of their exercises, and fruits of grace, for evidences of their good estate." Moreover, because the new birth was an inward event, anyone could claim to have experienced it. The problem was how to distinguish what was genuine from what was imagined, delusional, or fraudulent. Edwards found that some people could not "distinguish between impressions on the imagination, and truly spiritual experiences."[35] In other words, laypersons "found"—that is, invented—awakening where their pastor did not believe it existed.

Some parishioners saw the awakening in apocalyptic terms, and they expressed their outlook in bizarre and tragic behavior. Consumed with the conviction that he was a helpless sinner, one Thomas Stebbins, unable to find spiritual comfort, "was harried with violent temptations to cut his own throat, and made an [unsuccessful] attempt." Then Edwards's uncle, Joseph Hawley, also concerned about his spiritual state, put "an end to his own life, by cutting his throat." Stebbins's suicide attempt and Hawley's suicide led Edwards to conclude that Satan was at work subverting the revival because of its great success. Others, however, upon hearing this extraordinary news, "seemed to have it strongly suggested to 'em . . . to do as [Hawley] had done."[36] Edwards began to despair that Satan was getting the upper hand. He sought desperately to get a grip on a revival that seemed to be spinning out of control.

Like his grandfather who preceded him at Northampton, Edwards believed that only the pastor, after much probing and counseling, could determine who had experienced a genuine conversion. Stoddard argued that the pastor alone "is appointed by Christ to baptize and administer the Lord's Supper, and therefore he is made the Judge by God, what persons those ordinances are to be administered to." Edwards concurred: "Without doubt, ministers are to administer the sacraments to Christians, and they are to administer them only to such as they think Christ would have them administer them."[37] Reflecting on events of the mid-1730s, Edwards confessed that he had allowed the revival to get out of hand in the sense that too many unsubstantiated claims and assertions about salvation went unchallenged. He blamed his youth. "Instead of a child," he wrote, "there was want [i.e., need] of [a] giant in judgment and discretion among a people in such an extraordinary state of things."[38] What Edwards failed to understand was that, while he could proclaim and promote revival, he could not control how others interpreted events at Northampton. He soon learned that publishers and readers also developed their own notions about the revival.

A FAITHFUL NARRATIVE: THE NORTHAMPTON REVIVAL AS TOLD . . . AND RETOLD

As revival fervor abated in 1735, Jonathan Edwards returned to his pastoral duties, lamenting the decline of piety but confident of future showers of God's grace. Like his counterparts in New Jersey, Edwards longed for a more general revival that would sweep the world. That the Northampton awakening could have been the beginning of a global revival did not seriously occur to Edwards, and if it had, he felt inadequate to take a leading role in promoting the idea. Indeed, left to Edwards's own initiative, the Northampton story might never have been published. He was a diffident young minister still in his twenties and wished to defer to the judgment of older evangelicals. He also begged off assuming a leadership role in publishing revival news by citing Northampton's remote location, especially its great distance from a press.[39]

Older evangelicals located in Boston and London took over the task of publishing an account of the Northampton revival. They believed that the awakening could signal the beginning of something much bigger. The process of writing, editing, and publishing the narrative was a cooperative, if at times contentious, effort, with Edwards as author, Benjamin Colman as publisher, and Isaac Watts and John Guyse as editors. Table 2.1 summarizes their efforts.

The first published account of the "great awakening" in western Massachusetts appeared in a Boston newspaper. In the waning days of

TABLE 2.1

Events Leading to Publication of the *Faithful Narrative*

Date	Event
Apr. 28, 1735	William Williams, pastor at Hatfield, sent a letter to Colman describing revival in the Connecticut Valley.
May 12, 1735	At Colman's request, Kneeland and Green published excerpts of Williams's letter in the *New England Weekly Journal*
May 30, 1735	Responding to Colman's desire for a fuller account, Jonathan Edwards sent Colman an eight-page narrative of the revival. Colman forwarded it to Isaac Watts and John Guyse in London.
Nov. 6, 1736	At Watts's and Guyse's request, Edwards wrote a greatly expanded account and sent it to Colman.
1736	Colman prepared an abridged version of Edwards's new narrative, and Kneeland and Green published it as an appendix to Williams's sermon, *The Duty and Interest of a People*.
Dec. 17, 1736	Colman sent a copy of the published abridgment to Watts and Guyse.
Feb. 28, 1737	Watts replied to Colman with his view of the narrative, saying that it described a work of God unlike anything "since the Reformation" or perhaps even "the days of the apostles." He expressed his desire to see the narrative "corrected" and published.
Apr. 2, 1737	Watts repeated his willingness to help underwrite publication and requested that Colman send him an unabridged narrative.
May 1737	Colman sent the full narrative to Watts.
Fall 1737	Watts and Guyse published the *Faithful Narrative* in London.

the revival, Colman, dean of Boston's Congregational pastors, became aware of the Northampton awakening. An active participant in a far-flung evangelical letter-writing network, Colman received a letter from Reverend William Williams, pastor at Hatfield, describing the revival that had spread throughout Hampshire County. By printing Williams's account in the *New England Weekly Journal*, Colman introduced a much broader audience to the local event. The first printed report of the awakening informed readers that "there hath been, the latter part of the Winter, at Northampton, and hath now for above a Month reach'd all the Towns in the upper Part of the County & some in the lower, a very general Concern upon the Hearts of all." He noted that changed hearts resulted in altered behavior: "Vain and idle Company is left, and an Air of Seriousness to be Observed; careful Attention to the Word preached; and abundance came to us with that important Question, What must we do to be saved?" Moreover, he added, "Many [were] willing to give up their names to the Lord, and to join in Fellowship with our Churches." Williams concluded that "The thing is Extraordinary, and such as hath not been known in these Parts, before."[40]

More than a passive conduit, Colman concerned himself with telling the Northampton story in a way that would inspire large numbers of evangelicals on both sides of the Atlantic. He was convinced that a true revival had occurred. In his interpretive preface to Williams's letter, he called the Northampton event a "Remarkable Success of the Gospel" and an "Observable Work of God."[41] But he wanted more information and additional testimonies in order to publish a fuller, more convincing account. Through Williams, Colman asked Edwards to send him an expanded narrative.

In response, Edwards forwarded Colman a letter containing what turned out to be the first draft of the *Faithful Narrative*. In an eight-page letter consisting of fourteen paragraphs, Edwards described the awakening's beginning, spread, and effects. Providing little specific information about the revival's onset, the Northampton pastor said that a "remarkable religious concern" had swept over the congregation. He explained that "news of it filled the neighbouring towns," and the revival spread. He reported a great alteration in his parishioners, with many turning from an "inordinate engagedness after the world" to "the other extreme . . . [of] mind[ing] nothing but religion." While offering no precise number of converts, Edwards said the revival was "very extraordinary as to the numbers that are hopefully savingly wrought upon."[42]

Having provided an account of the revival as a community event, Edwards turned to individual responses of the awakened. In writing conversion narratives, he worked in a genre familiar to evangelicals. Accounts of conversions were meant to display God's redemptive work within an individual and to inspire readers to consider the state of their own souls. Edwards introduced the two conversion narratives he included in the *Faithful Narrative* by discussing the morphology of individual conversion. It began with "a sense of their miserable condition by nature, the danger they are in of perishing eternally, and . . . [the] great importance to them that they speedily escape, and get into a better state."

The "awful apprehensions" persons had of their sinful condition varied widely. For some the path to understanding their own insufficiency and God's abundant grace was "ten times as long as" that of others. But sooner or later, all converts come to see the "excellency of God's justice" and accept the "all-sufficiency of the mercy and grace of God." Thus the turmoil of conviction is followed by the calm of conversion.[43]

After discussing the varied manifestations of God's work on individuals' souls, Edwards, "to give a clearer idea of the nature and manner of the operations of God's Spirit . . ., [gave] an account of two particular instances." He chose the experiences of a young adult woman, Abigail Hutchinson, and a four-year-old girl, Phoebe Bartlett. The former centers on the woman's highly emotional expression of grace on her deathbed, where she stated her wish to die that she might be where "strong grace might have more liberty, and be without the clog of a weak body." The latter relates the little girl's utterances as God worked in her heart: "Pray, blessed Lord, give me salvation! I pray, beg, pardon all my sins!" "Yes, I am afraid I shall go to hell!" And finally, "Mother, the kingdom of heaven is come to me!"[44]

When Colman forwarded Edwards's account to Watts and Guyse, the London dissenters replied with unrestrained enthusiasm at what they had read: "never did we hear or read, since the first ages of Christianity, any event of this kind so surprising as the present narrative hath set before us." To them, what had occurred in remote western Massachusetts represented a divine act seldom seen since biblical days. To skeptics who questioned the awakening's importance because of its limited geographic extent, Watts and Guyse replied that "God has seemed to act over again the miracle of Gideon's fleece, which was plentifully watered with the dew of heaven, while the rest of the earth round about it was dry, and had no such remarkable blessing." Moreover, they viewed the Northampton revival as a potential catalyst for promoting a much wider awakening. Believing that evangelicals everywhere would delight in this dramatic evidence of God's grace, they declared that "such an eminent work of God ought not to be concealed from the world."[45] They added that "certainly it becomes us to take notice of such astonishing exercises of his power and mercy, . . . and it gives us further encouragement to pray, and wait, and hope for the like display of his power in the midst of us."[46]

In reaching the conclusion that events at Northampton constituted a genuine work of God, Watts found one act of providence during the revival particularly convincing. Puritans and their ancestors had long pointed to such "remarkable providences" as shipwrecks, earthquakes, and witchcraft as evidence that God was sending a message to his people. In March 1737, a "remarkable providence" occurred during one Sunday service when a balcony collapsed. One eyewitness described the scene: "soon after the beginning of sermon, the whole gallery full of people, with all the seats and timber, suddenly and without any warning sunk, and fell down, with most amazing noise, upon the heads of those that sat under, to the astonishment of the congregation, the house being filled with dolorous shrieking and crying, and nothing else was expected than to find many people dead, and dashed to pieces."[47] But, as Watts noted, no one died and only a few were injured, and those only slightly. While the "unthinking world" may have concluded that the accident resulted from aging timbers' being stressed beyond their capacity, to the London dissenter the incident was a clear signal that God was guiding occurrences in a remote corner of America. More than ever, he believed that Edwards's narrative was "faithful," and that the Almighty was beginning something big.

Watts had very specific criteria for judging a narrative to be faithful to the events described. Five years earlier, he had published a work setting forth what constituted a faithful account of religious occurrences. He began by declaring that any narration is an invention because of the nature of language: "words and names are mere *arbitrary Signs* invented by Men to communicate their Thoughts, or Ideas, to one another." However, writers can narrow the gap between words describing events and the events themselves by taking care in the "Invention of an Argument." Completeness is important, and Watts urged reporters to "see that no important Circumstance be omitted." Accuracy is equally imperative, and he admonished writers to "let your *Enumerations,* your *Divisions* and *Distributions* of things be so accurate, that no needful Part or Idea may be left out." Those reporting religious matters shouldered special responsibilities. Divine revelations and "*supernatural Appearances*" claimed by individuals should be related, but, Watts warned, they must always be confirmed. Reflecting his adherence to Enlightenment tenets for judging the validity of human claims, he cautioned that "divine Appearances or Attestations to Revelation must be either *known to ourselves,* by our own personal Observation of them, or they must be *sufficiently attested by others,* according to the *Principles and Rules* by which Matters of *human Faith* are to be judged."[48]

In judging the *Faithful Narrative,* Watts and Guyse expressed concern about Edwards's relation of Abigail Hutchinson's and Phoebe Bartlett's conversions. The Londoners found the conversion narratives too sensational for their taste. They feared that Edwards might have given too much credence to the converts' descriptions of a spiritual new birth within their souls and not undertaken enough independent observation of changed behavior. And they thought that British audiences would object to Edwards's making the testimonials the centerpiece of his account. However, Watts and Guyse conceded that they "must allow every writer his own way; and must allow him to choose what particular instances he would select, from the numerous cases which came before him."[49] For his part, Edwards resented certain liberties the editors took with his manuscript, but he acquiesced, explaining that he would "willingly submit it to their correction" because he was "sensible there are some things in it that it would not be best to publish in England."[50] Colman was the mediator who kept the project moving toward publication that it might "please God to revive his work throughout this land; and may all the ends of the earth see his salvation!"[51]

To satisfy Watts's and Guyse's desire for a more detailed account of the work of God, Colman solicited from Edwards a much expanded version, the draft that would become the basis for the *Faithful Narrative*. In that much lengthened report, Edwards provided specifics, such as "about 300" for the number of persons converted. And he gave a fuller explanation of how the revival spread, including its manifestation outside New England.

Watts and Guyse expressed one more worry. They were concerned about publishing a description of such a momentous work based solely on Edwards's witness. Seeking broader attestation of the revival, they asked Colman to secure testimonies from ministers of surrounding towns who could "bear eye and ear witness to some of these numerous conversions in the other towns thereabout . . . [and who could] draw up a prudent and judicious account if brief of the work of God in some of those other towns."[52]

Colman secured the desired attestation from six Hampshire County ministers. William Williams of Hatfield, Ebenezer Devotion of Suffield, Stephen Williams of Suffield, Peter Reynolds of Enfield, Nehemiah Bull of Westfield, and Samuel Hopkins of West Springfield drew up a brief statement and forwarded it to Colman. They provided assurance "that the account Mr. Edwards has given in his narrative of our several towns or parishes is true; and that much more of the like nature might have been added with respect to some of them." Satisfied that the Connecticut Valley revival had now been adequately documented, Watts and Guyse affixed the attestation to the 1738 edition of *A Faithful Narrative*.[53]

When the first edition of the *Faithful Narrative* appeared in London in late 1737, it bore the clear stamp of its editors and publishers. First, Watts and Guyse provided the title: *A Faithful Narrative of the Surprizing Work of God in the Conversion of Many Hundred Souls in* Northampton, *and the Neighbouring Towns and Villages of* New-Hampshire *in* New-England. The title reflected the editors' perspective of events and revealed an understanding quite different from that of the author. Part of the difference stemmed from their imperfect knowledge of a distant land. For instance, they mistakenly identified the revivals as occurring in New Hampshire instead of in Hampshire County, Massachusetts. But more important, they lacked Edwards's intimate knowledge of the region's history of revivals. To Edwards, the awakening was remarkable and even extraordinary, but not surprising. Steeped in revival tradition and successor to an evangelistic preacher, he expected periodic, unusual effusions of God's grace. He was well aware that under his predecessor's ministry, the church had experienced revivals from 1679 through 1718. In each of the six awakenings during Solomon Stoddard's pastorate, "the bigger Part of the young People in the Town seemed to be mainly concerned for their eternal Salvation." Edwards was Stoddard's assistant during the sixth revival, the one occasioned by the 1727 earthquake. Having participated in an awakening, he was not surprised when "at the latter end of the year 1733, there appeared a very unusual flexibleness, and yielding to Advice, in our young People." He hoped that the ensuing revival, like those before it, would mean "extraordinary Success . . . in the Conversion of many Souls."[54] What Watts and Guyse described as the "surprizing" work of God looked quite different to someone in a congregation that had experienced seven awakenings in sixty years. For men and women in Northampton who had witnessed previous awakenings and prayed for another, the 1734–1735 awakening was familiar and expected. But to persons at a distance, it was a glorious, new, surprising, and extraordinary event.

In addition to highlighting the revival as a work of God and underscoring the large number of conversions, the editors provided a fourteen-page preface. They attested to the "truth of this narrative," noting that many ministers from surrounding towns affirmed Edwards's account. They summarized their characterization of what had occurred in western Massachusetts by writing that "it pleased God two years ago to display his free and saving mercy in the concern of a great multitude of souls in a short space of time." In other words, the event was God's work, and it was extraordinary. Watts and Guyse questioned parts of the narrative, especially Edwards's choosing the conversion narratives of a woman and

A Faithful

NARRATIVE

OF THE

Surprizing Work of GOD

IN THE

CONVERSION

OF

Many HUNDRED SOULS in *Northampton*, and the Neighbouring Towns and Villages of *New-Hampſhire* in *New-England*.

In a LETTER to the Rev^d. Dr. BENJAMIN COLMAN of *Boſton*.

Written by the Rev^d. Mr. EDWARDS, Miniſter of *Northampton*, on *Nov.* 6. 1736.

And Publiſhed,

With a Large PREFACE,

By Dr. WATTS and Dr. GUYSE.

LONDON;
Printed for JOHN OSWALD, at the *Roſe and Crown*, in the *Poultry*, near *Stocks-Market*. M.DCC.XXXVII.

Price ſtitch'd 1 ſ. Bound in Calf-Leather, 1 ſ. 6 d.

1. Opening declaration of Work of God

a girl to illustrate how God's grace affected individuals. Nevertheless, the publishers expressed their hope that the "account of such an extraordinary illustrious appearance of divine grace" might lead to an "enlargement of the kingdom of Christ" throughout the Atlantic world.[55] The fact that the *Faithful Narrative* appeared in London bookstalls at the same time that George Whitefield was attracting large crowds to hear his revivalistic message must have reinforced Watts's and Guyse's expectation of a widespread awakening.

Not content to allow Edwards's narrative to speak for itself, Watts and Guyse provided readers with eighty marginal glosses to guide persons through the account. Most of the entries were straightforward phrases summarizing paragraph contents. For instance, in the margin of a succession of five paragraphs on "The Special Character of this awakening Work," they added glosses enumerating the revival's distinguishing characteristics: "1. Universal. 2. Efficacious and saving. 3. Among Persons very young, and others elderly. 4. Speedy in its Progress. 5. Remarkable in the Degree of it." In other places, the editors introduced their own interpretation through glosses. For example, in preparing readers for Edwards's account of the conversion experience, marginalia said of converts that they receive "a Sense of that new Light in which Experience shews them divine Things." Edwards had great misgivings about converts' relying too much on "new Light" rooted in inner experience and not enough on an expression of God's work in their lives firmly planted in Scripture and reason.[56] Clearly the published account of the Northampton revival was a collaborative, transatlantic work and contained some views that diverged from the author's.

With its London publication, the transformation of Edwards's revival narrative was complete. The first published account consisted of a single paragraph inserted in the *Boston Weekly News-Letter* describing "a very *general Concern* upon the Hearts of all . . . for Christ and Salvation; and a great *visible Change* . . . every where to be seen." After two years of expanding, editing, and revising, revivalists published a 132-page book in London, Boston, and Glasgow, interpreting events in Hampshire County as a "Surprizing Work of God" and a "General Awakening."[57]

When he published Williams's letter in April 1735, Colman initiated the process that linked two powerful forces operating in the mid–eighteenth century: evangelical revivalism and a "consumer revolution." Residing in the commercial center of Boston, he was well situated to appropriate trading metaphors and strategies for religious ends. Addressing a "trading Town" in a sermon published in 1736, Colman compared Boston to the great ancient Mediterranean trading centers of Tyre and Sidon. He selected as his text Isa. 23:18: "And her merchandise and her hire shall be holiness to the Lord." After reminding his audience that God eventually destroyed Tyre at the hands of Nebuchadnezzar because of the city's "inordinate lust after riches," Colman noted that "trading places by their merchandise and commerce have advantages in propagating the Gospel." First, commerce puts traders "in the way of the knowledge of God." Tyrians traded in Jerusalem and heard there of the "true God," and Jews traded in Tyre and spoke of the "true God." Throughout its history, Christianity has traveled along trade routes. "Christianity has been greatly serv'd by trade and merchandise," Colman wrote, "by means whereof a great part of the world has been gospelized."[58]

Colman especially recognized the power of print to reach a mass audience. Just as merchants in his Brattle Street congregation advertised their wares in Boston's five newspapers, he saw the press's potential for publicizing the Northampton revival. Hence, upon hearing about an unusual stirring of the Holy Spirit in the Connecticut Valley, he began to solicit information, corresponding first with William Williams and then directly with Edwards. Although the initial reports were brief and sketchy, Colman made them public. He was at home in Boston's publishing community. A prolific author himself, he had seen seventy-one of his sermons published between 1702 and 1736, a number surpassed by only Increase and Cotton Mather. In 1735, he determined to exploit the press on both sides of the Atlantic hoping that "the publishing [of the Northampton revival narrative] may be of great use and benefit to souls" throughout the British Atlantic world.[59]

The Northampton narrative succeeded in inspiring English evangelicals such as John Wesley and George Whitefield to promote a religious revival that by the early 1740s had become transatlantic in scope. As the awakening spread, however, detractors placed their own construction on events. To one group of Massachusetts ministers, religious disorder and confusion, not revivalism, best described what had transpired. Rather than divine inspiration, human artifice, such as Whitefield's frequently publicizing his accomplishments, lay behind the so-called revival. His opponents resented how the evangelist, with "uncommon Pride and Arrogance, and vanity of Mind, [engaged in] very liberal boasting . . . [of] his great Success."[60] As the attacks intensified, evangelicals sought a vehicle that would authenticate the awakening as the revival of true religion. They found their solution in Thomas Prince's *Christian History*, a weekly magazine that solicited and published accounts of awakenings from pastors all over the British Atlantic.[61] In that publication, Northampton became a prologue to the much more extensive revival following Whitefield's American debut. And Edwards's narrative served as a model for more than two dozen similar accounts in communities scattered over the Middle Colonies and New England. Reports from Britain indicated that narratives of colonial revivals had inspired awakenings in England, Scotland, and Wales, which, in turn, generated yet more material for Prince's magazine. When collected into a two-volume work, the *Christian History*'s 104 issues reflect a great and general awakening stretching from Northampton to Cambuslang, Scotland. The events at Northampton were no longer a local matter confined to one of the "remote corners of the earth" but the opening act in a transatlantic revival.[62]

Among evangelicals and their historians, the Northampton story does not end with the great awakening. In one more invention, it assumed its place within salvation history, memorialized in the work of the Scottish revivalist John Gillies. Beginning with the Acts of the Apostles, Gillies's *Historical Collections* traced revivalism through the ages. In his construction, the eighteenth-century awakening was nothing less than the latest of God's "extraordinary dispensations of grace."[63] As part of that divine outpouring, Northampton had undergone yet another interpretation. In its telling and retelling, Northampton emerged as an important "interpretive fiction" evangelicals constructed to assert, inspire, promote, and defend evangelical revivalism. However, when Edwards, Colman, Watts, and Guyse published their account of the Northampton revival in the mid-1730s, they were unaware that an obscure Anglican minister was about to recast the meaning of revival.

Through correspondence with dissenters, Colman learned how the Northampton account played in England. A letter-writer, one R. Pearsall from Warminster, informed Colman that it was at John Guyse's house that he had "had the first account of the Great & Wonderful Operation of divine Grace in new Hampshire [*sic*], from the abstract then publish'd by you at the end of a larger Book publish'd at Boston."[64] He added that "since that time we have had the fuller account from Mr. Edwards Publish'd & recommended by Revd. Drs. Watts and Guise." He reported that the "account has occasioned many thanksgivings & much Joy & enlargedness of Heart in the People of God on this Side the Atlantic Ocean." Pearsall noted also that, because of the *Faithful Narrative*, "great Bickerings have broke forth from the Breasts of many, as this very History has confronted their darling Opinions and opened those Errors of which they have been as fond as every indulgent mother was fond of a distem-pered & distorted Child." He related how some had sought to discredit the publication by claiming that "the account was false & that Dr. Watts was ashamed of the Publication of it." Pearsall assured Colman that "the latter point I have had well contradict'd." As to the former, Colman's own extensive "Examination . . . into that important Event" confirmed its authenticity.[65]

Ironically, the London publication of his narrative disturbed Edwards. He was uneasy about the widening gap that was developing between the revival being experienced in Northampton and the revival being re-ported in England. He expressed great pleasure upon hearing how English evangelicals rejoiced in news of the Connecticut Valley awaken-ing. But a lessening of the revival spirit at home disheartened him. "It is refreshing to hear of the notice that God's servants abroad take of the great things god has done for us," he wrote in a letter to Benjamin Colman. But, he added, "at the same time it is a great damp to that joy to consider how we decline, and what decays that lively spirit in religion suffers amongst us; while others are rejoicing and praising God for us."[66] Just as men and women in Britain and other parts of America were about to learn of "The Surprising Work of God in the Conversion of Many Hundred Souls in *Northampton*," Edwards reported that "we are sensibly by little and little, more and more declining" and witnessing "a return to ways of lewdness and sensuality, among young and old." He knew that "others afar off are rejoicing in, and praising God for" what God had done in his congregation. He concluded by hoping that he had "by no means represent[ed] us better than we are."[67]

Despite Edwards's misgivings, within a few years many English evangeli-cals regarded the Northampton revival as the "*first fruits*" of a long-expected revival. Edwards's *Faithful Narrative* conveyed an inspiring mes-sage: first, Northampton had to be the work of God because such surpris-ing results in a remote American frontier town could come only from divine inspiration; and, second, the beginnings of awakenings in Britain, in part encouraged by Northampton, indicated that a more general Work of God was under way. British evangelicals eagerly bought copies of the sensational revival account, and Northampton became a familiar name to hopeful revivalists even if they were ignorant as to its precise geographic location.

On the other hand, Freehold, whose revival had been as dramatic as that in Northampton, remained unknown to the British, whose awareness of a New Jersey awakening was confined to Edwards's passing reference.

The difference between the two local revivals lay not in the events them-selves but in the publicity of those events. During the period of the revivals' occurrence in the early 1730s, few outside the areas surrounding Northampton and Freehold were aware of these awakenings.[68] Indeed, as they unfolded, the revivals more closely fit Stoddard's description of local or "particular" awakenings, occasional outpourings confined to specific areas with little impact beyond, rather than more global or "general" revivals. However, by 1737–1738, the Northampton revival was a well-known event publicized throughout Britain and America. Moreover, it was heralded not just as another local awakening but as the beginning of an extraordinary outpouring with signs of becoming a much bigger revival that would sweep the Christian world much as the Protestant Reformation had done. Clearly in the telling and retelling, the Northampton revival assumed much greater significance than its participants and leaders could have foreseen.

Why the 1734–1735 Northampton revival became the almost exclusive center of attention in virtually every contemporary and historical account of the Great Awakening is somewhat puzzling. Why, for example, does the 1727 revival that spread throughout New England not qualify as the point of departure for discussions of the Great Awakening? Or, why did not one of Stoddard's five "harvests" launch a more general revival? Given the strong similarities between the Freehold and Northampton awakenings, why does the former not share equal billing with the latter? The answers lie in the fact that the Northampton story, unlike its New Jersey counterpart, became known to a transatlantic evangelical audi-ence through a remarkable cultural construction crafted under the guidance of an eminent Boston minister and two London dissenting pastors. Both Northampton and Freehold bore revival fruit, but the *Faithful Narrative* was the vessel that carried the spore of a great awaken-ing from America to Britain in 1737. Quite fortuitously, that same year a young English evangelist, George Whitefield, would plant another "gospel seed" that would grow into a "great tree . . . [with] Multitudes both in England, Scotland, Wales, Ireland, and various parts of North America . . . lodg[ing] under the branches of it."[69]

Part Two

WIDER CONNECTIONS:
AN INTERCOLONIAL GREAT AND
GENERAL AWAKENING
1739–1745

WITHOUT wider connections, local revivals in Freehold and Northampton would have remained "great awakenings" but would not have been heralded as the opening movement of the intercolonial and transatlantic "general awakening" of 1739–1742. When British revivalists received news of the Northampton revival, it was just one of the several pieces of evidence that, together, convinced them that God was beginning an extraordinary work. From Germany came reports that a particular group of evangelicals called Pietists were having great success in their missionary initiatives around the world. Through a young Anglican clergyman named John Wesley, Pietist ideas, methods, and institutions found their most influential expression in England. Beginning with a few Oxford students, Wesley embarked on a lifetime task of organizing Christians from the bottom up, banding small groups of Christians together in religious societies for the purpose of deepening their faith and then putting it into action through charities and evangelism.

One member of his Oxford group, George Whitefield, concentrated on a single aspect of Pietism: evangelism in the form of exhortation as to the necessity of the one thing needful, the New Birth. Through a dramatic preaching style and an innovative use of print publicity, Whitefield developed a revival campaign, completely packaged and portable. He took his revival over much of the southern half of England and Wales in the late 1730s, attracting enormous crowds and widespread publicity that reached as far as the American colonies. When in 1739 he announced his intentions of traveling to America, colonial revivalists awaited him with great anticipation. His arrival in America in late October triggered an intercolonial awakening promulgated by much-publicized preaching tours that spanned the length of the Atlantic seaboard. The result was a new kind of invention, what colonial promoters referred to as a "general" awakening that gathered up local or "particular" awakenings into a cohesive revival. Part Two explores the ligatures of the intercolonial revival: ties that bound local revivals into a larger movement, both interregional connections and links between the colonial awakening and the evangelical revival in Britain.

"imported Divinity"

IN THEIR preface to Edwards's *Faithful Narrative*, Isaac Watts and John Guyse expressed the delight evangelicals found in exchanging revival news across the Atlantic. "The friendly Correspondence which we maintain with our Brethren of New England," they wrote, "gives us now and then the Pleasure of hearing some remarkable Instances of divine Grace in the Conversion of Sinners, and some eminent Examples of Piety in the *American* Part of the World." They attached particular importance to what they learned from Benjamin Colman about events in the Connecticut Valley in the mid-1730s. "Never did we hear or read," they avowed, "any Event of this Kind so surprizing as the present Narrative hath set before us." Scots reacted in a similar way. After reading the *Narrative*, a Glasgow correspondent indicated in a letter to Boston ministers that "the Friends of serious Religion here were much refreshed with a printed Account of the extraordinary Success of the Gospel, of late, in some Parts of New England."[1]

Revival news across the Atlantic was reciprocal. While accounts of the awakening in western Massachusetts inspired British revivalists, reports of evangelistic successes from England in the late 1730s heartened their American counterparts, who hoped that Northampton and Freehold were more than isolated, local events. At the same time that Watts and Guyse published the *Faithful Narrative* in England, Americans began to hear about extraordinary developments among London evangelicals. In late 1737, a small band of Oxford graduates arrived in the city and preached at every opportunity, including at fund-raising services designed to raise awareness and money for charity schools across England. Among those men was George Whitefield, whose dramatic style attracted huge crowds and the attention of London's newspapers. As British evangelicals delighted in reading about God's surprising work in a remote corner of America, Americans exulted in news of a work stirring in England's great metropolis. Indeed, news from each side of the Atlantic was influential in spreading revival on the other.

As colonists followed the extensive news about the English revival, many became convinced that they were reading about a mighty work of

God as foretold in Scripture. Ever alert to events signifying that approaching work, revivalists read about the unusual occurrences in England with great hope. With each report reprinted from London newspapers, American readers grew in confidence that the biblical promise was being realized.

To the Boston revivalist Thomas Foxcroft, George Whitefield's arrival in late 1739 fulfilled Cotton Mather's prophecy in the early 1700s that a great Work of God would overspread America. Mather had foretold that the "Lord will order that *good Seed* ere long be cast upon the fertile Regions of America, and it shall here find *a good Ground*." Writing during the revival in 1743, Foxcroft proclaimed that the prophesied time had arrived: "the blessed God has by surprizing Ways begun among us, in almost all Parts of this Land . . . a most signal Reviving of his Work." Foxcroft further noted that the revival had come as Mather had predicted: from abroad. "By Navigation there will be brought the Word of a glorious Christ," Mather had written, "unto a Multitude afar off: and as the *Ships cover the Sea*, the Earth (and thou America too) shall be filled with the Knowledge of the glorious God." Foxcroft asked, "Has not 'the Word of a glorious Christ, brought by Navigation to a Multitude afar off' . . . [become] as 'good Seed sown in good Ground, and bringing forth Fruit?'" He added that revival opponents wittily called the religion Whitefield brought "your imported Divinity."[2]

Critics' characterization of the American revival as "imported Divinity" is apt in many ways. While local revivals were indigenous to parts of New England and the Middle Colonies, a general awakening spanning much of British North America began only with Whitefield's arrival. Through itinerant preaching, the "Pedlar in Divinity" spanned regional and denominational boundaries and brought a certain degree of uniformity to the revival. His extensive publicity campaign prepared men and women for his arrival in their communities much as advertisements for consumer goods announced the "latest fashions from London." But if one takes seriously the notion of an imported revival, then one must consider as well the American market that awaited Whitefield. Clearly it was a market of uneven demand, with some regions predisposed to buy what Benjamin Colman called "Holy Merchandize," and other areas indifferent or even hostile.

Americans had never before seen anything quite like the noise generated by Whitefield's arrival, and to many evangelicals it was a welcome change in what they considered a torpid state of religion. In 1700, Boston minister and Harvard vice president Samuel Willard preached a sermon lamenting "that there is so little Success of the Gospel." The signs of spiritual decay were clear to him: there was no "*outward Conversion,*" which meant to him a change in behavior indicating "*inward*" regeneration. He explained that for some people, the converting work of God "is wrought without a noise," but he added that when the gospel stirs the souls of most men and women, there is attendant noise as they "cry out for help and direction."[3] With the exception of occasional local revivals scattered among colonial congregations, Willard and other ministers heard little "noise" among the "dry bones" that inhabited their communities.

Forty years later Boston and much of the rest of America were filled with extraordinary religious noise, exceeding in intensity and extent anything witnessed before. While Willard no doubt would have welcomed the ado, eyewitnesses assigned different meanings to it. In his assessment of the revivals in New England, Boston antirevivalist Charles Chauncy highlighted the commotion that George Whitefield, Gilbert Tennent, James Davenport, and other itinerants created in the region. Their preaching, Chauncy charged, was "in the extemporaneous Way, with much Noise and little Connection." Wherever they went, the itinerants generated "much Noise in the Country." By preaching every day in the week, and often two or even three times a day, the roaming evangelists captured popular attention. "The grand Subject of Conversation was Mr. Whitefield," Chauncy lamented, "and the whole Business of the Town [was] to run, from Place to Place, to hear him preach." Not only did itinerants create much noise, Chauncy claimed that they effectively silenced those who disliked the revival; opponents "were stigmatised as Enemies of God and true Religion . . . [and] were openly represented, both from the Pulpit and the Press, as in danger of committing the Sin against the Holy Ghost."[4]

Revivalists defended their noisemaking. Edwards argued that the "work of the Spirit of God . . . [generates] *a great deal of Noise about Religion.*" This was true in the apostles' days, when Christ's presence "occasioned a great Stir and Ado everywhere." Then, as now, Edwards noted, there appeared a "mighty Opposition . . . on occasion of that great Effusion of the Spirit." Moreover, he wrote, "the Affair filled the World with Noise, and gave Occasion to some to say of the Apostles, *that they had turned the World upside down.*" Christ's return will also be a noisy affair. Edwards proclaimed that when the Messiah comes to set up his kingdom, the event will "be open and publick in the Sight of the whole World, with clear Manifestation, like Lightning that can't be hid, but glares in everyone's Eyes, and shines from one Side of Heaven to the other."[5] Therefore, one should not wonder at a great noise during what Edwards considered to be nothing less than an outpouring of God's Spirit in a second Reformation.

Whitefield's long-anticipated arrival in fall 1739 was indeed a noisy affair. By late afternoon, November 8, 1739, hordes of Philadelphians had converged on the city center. Seldom if ever had so many men and women crowded into the town of twelve thousand. Throughout that cold Thursday word circulated that George Whitefield, a young Anglican preacher, would preach that evening. Too big to assemble in one of the city's nine or ten churches, the throng stood quietly before the evangelist as he mounted the courthouse steps. Benjamin Franklin's *Pennsylvania Gazette* reported a crowd estimated at six thousand.[6]

At first glance, the scene had an air of spontaneity as people appeared from all parts of the city. However, upon closer examination one finds that those men and women were assembling to witness a long-awaited event. No doubt they gathered at the courthouse hoping to see Whitefield stage an outdoor sermon similar to the London assemblies they had read about in the *Gazette* and the *American Mercury Weekly*. Over the previous six months, Whitefield's "press agent" had supplied Philadelphia's newspapers with regular reports on the revivalist's exploits in England. Careful planning and organization had also gone into the day's events, as riders fanned out in the city drumming up a crowd, tacking up broadsides along the way. Most of what occurred that day, including the sermon itself, had been rehearsed over the previous year in England. What Philadelphians witnessed that Thursday evening was the beginning of the "Whitefieldian" revival in America. Like much of mid-eighteenth-century colonial culture, it was a prepackaged, well-publicized import.

While the Northampton revival had been the seventh awakening in that town, the Whitefieldian awakening was an original: the first intercolonial religious movement. Compared to the Northampton revival, which was a quiet affair until Colman lifted it from obscurity, the Whitefieldian awakening was noisy from the beginning, with advance publicity and frequent reports that filled newspapers on both sides of the Atlantic. Never before, with the possible exception of the Reformation, had a particular expression or "brand" of Protestantism been disseminated as quickly and efficiently to a mass audience over such a broad region. Seizing opportunities made available by advances in commerce and print, Whitefield developed the necessary machinery to orchestrate large-scale revivals. During the first six months of 1739 in England and Wales, he experimented with many of his evangelistic strategies, constructing a style and approach that made his awakening unique and remarkable.

The scope of the Whitefieldian revival also distinguished it from the Northampton and other local awakenings. Speaking of the intercolonial revival Whitefield sparked, William Cooper, a revivalist minister in Boston, wrote, "This work is truly extraordinary in respect of the extent of it." He observed that it had "entered and spread in some of the most populous Towns, the chief Places of Concourse and Business." By the time Whitefield returned to England in early 1741, it was "more or less on the several Provinces that measure many hundred Miles on this Continent." Cooper commented on its human as well as geographic reach, viewing the revival as "extraordinary . . . with respect to the Numbers that have been the Subjects of this Operation." He reported that "Stupid Sinners have been awakened by Hundreds . . . [and] some Thousands [were] under religious Impressions as they never felt before."[7]

The Whitefieldian revival differed most visibly from earlier colonial awakenings in the "new measures" the evangelist introduced to propagate his brand of the gospel. Having worked out in England a set of techniques and strategies to promote revival, Whitefield introduced them to Americans. And he exploited the colonial press as he had the English print trade to publicize his successes and prime distant audiences to expect similar experiences when he preached among them. The huge crowd gathered in Philadelphia on November 8 attests to the effectiveness of Whitefield's campaign for organizing and promoting a revival.

As an innovator of revival techniques, Whitefield stands in a long line of evangelicals who preceded and followed him. His brand of mass revivalism flowed from the same tradition of renewal that characterized the Protestant Reformation and Scottish "Holy Fairs." And the "new measures" he employed such as open-air services, extemporaneous exhortation, and daily itinerant preaching became standard fare in the so-called Second Great Awakening of the nineteenth century. The Whitefieldian revival emphasized newness—the New Birth delivered through new measures in a New World. Whitefield and other evangelicals practiced the formula for novelty enunciated by revivalists of succeeding generations. "The object of our measures is to gain attention," nineteenth-century evangelist Charles Grandison Finney wrote in his *Lectures on Revivals of Religion* (1835), and to do that, "you must have something new." Later in the nineteenth century, Dwight Moody, another dynamic preacher, stated the issue more bluntly: "If one method don't wake them up, let us try another."[8] A century earlier, Whitefield constructed a revival from a similar willingness to experiment.

With the Whitefieldian revival, the great awakening assumed a new character. The evangelist arrived as a long-expected, fashionable import, and colonists eagerly anticipated his coming much the way late-twentieth-century Americans await the latest rock star. Immediately, the Whitefieldian revival became front-page news as newspapers followed his every move and reported on public opinion, both favorable and unfavorable. No longer were revivals local, isolated awakenings; they became linked into a single movement that supporters regarded as a genuine work of God and opponents considered shameless self-promotion. Not all evangelicals or even revivalists embraced the Whitefieldian revival. But all were shaped by it, whether their assessments led to acceptance, modification, or rejection.

GEORGE WHITEFIELD AND REVIVALISM IN ENGLAND

Beginning in late 1737 and early 1738, American revivalists were delighted to read about a young Anglican evangelist who was taking London by storm in a series of preaching services that attracted enormous crowds. Now Edwards and the Tennents and Colman and others could be inspired by a dramatic awakening in a distant land just as British evangelicals had delighted in learning about the revival at Northampton. Colonial newspapers in all parts of America, within and without the two major revival districts, introduced Americans to George Whitefield, the preacher who was making headlines in London with his fiery sermons delivered to packed churches. Even in Virginia, where few dissenters resided, the *Virginia Gazette* kept people informed of developments. Publisher William Parks first reported events by reprinting in late 1737 a London account of Whitefield's inaugural sermon in the metropolis. Then in 1738, the newspaper told of the young evangelist's plans to embark for Georgia to become pastor in Savannah and assess the feasibility of erecting an orphanage in that poor, struggling colony. After Whitefield returned to England late that year following a brief trip to Georgia, Parks accelerated his coverage of the evangelist's activities. Whitefield had become far more popular and much more controversial. His preaching took on an accusatory edge as he charged Anglican ministers with preaching a dry, lifeless message because many of them had not personally experienced the New Birth. Denied access to their pulpits, Whitefield began preaching in parks and fields, and huge crowds assembled to hear him. Through thirteen different reports beginning in June 1739, Parks notified his readers of crowds and controversies gathering around Whitefield and of the evangelist's plans to come to America for a second visit, this time on a preaching mission throughout the colonies.

The principal figure in the newspaper stories was a twenty-three-year-old Anglican evangelist whose rapid advance to the center of public attention resulted from the combination of a dramatic conversion experience with uncommon zeal for preaching the gospel, extraordinary oratorical talents, and masterful self-promotion. Born in 1714 into a middling family in Gloucester, George Whitefield worked as a young boy in his father's inn and wineshop. Like his older brother, James, who became a successful Bristol merchant, George envisioned a life in commerce. As a schoolboy, however, he showed a flair for public speaking and acting, won some drama and speech competitions in his school at St. Mary de Crypt, and convinced his family and friends that he was destined for something bigger. With financial support from James and others, George matriculated at Pembroke College, Oxford, in 1732. To help pay for his education, he worked as a servitor or attendant to students of more noble breeding: polishing their shoes, cleaning their clothes, running endless errands.[9] It was in that humble, and to him demeaning, capacity that he fell in with a group of evangelicals who would embark him on the course that made him headline news.

While a member of the "Holy Club," the derisive name other students gave to the the small religious society, Whitefield underwent a wrenching conversion experience.[10] Under the guidance of the group's leaders, John and Charles Wesley, George read such Puritan classics as Henry Scougal's *The Life of God in the Soul of Man* (1677). While reading that particular work, he was struck by the words: "true religion was union of the soul with God, and Christ formed within us." Realizing that he had not experienced that kind of religion, Whitefield entered into a period of intense self-abasement during which he believed himself to be the worst of sinners, deserving of eternal punishment in hell. He fasted for weeks until his weakened body succumbed to illness, and he had to go home to recuperate. He wore nothing but the meanest apparel and thought it "unbecoming of a penitent to have his hair powdered." Finally, after months in this state of self-emptying, he suddenly awakened to the realization that God's unmerited grace extended to him was unconditional and sufficient to transform his life despite his inadequacies.[11]

Whitefield then threw himself into the work of the Holy Club with all the zeal of a recent convert determined to make up for years wasted. The students had two goals: first, to practice piety by ordering their lives according to a disciplined method of daily prayer, self-examination, mutual encouragement, and godly conversation; and second, to minister to the physical and spiritual needs of those who had never experienced "true" religion. They found plenty of distressed souls in Oxford's poorhouse and jail. Upon graduation, the students continued their regimen on a much larger scale. The Wesleys went to America's newest colony to preach the gospel to Georgians freshly arrived from England and to natives of the region. Thomas Broughton joined the Society for Promoting Christian Knowledge, whose mission was to spread the good news through publishing moral and religious books and pamphlets to millions throughout the British Empire. Whitefield discovered, or rediscovered, his gift of oratory and became a spellbinding evangelist.

How Whitefield transformed himself into a popular, exportable commodity is worthy of investigation. During 1739, when the Wesleys returned to England and began laying the foundation for a disciplined, permanent organization for promoting the practice of piety, Whitefield tacked in another direction, following the Welsh model of itinerant field-preaching with astounding success. Indeed, John Wesley and George Whitefield had different conceptions of their ministries: Whitefield saw his role as "sowing" gospel seeds, while Wesley viewed his as "reaping" the gospel harvest. Of his work in building societies and purging them of weak members, Wesley wrote his brother, Charles, in early 1741, "I must go round gleaning after George Whitefield. . . . The bands and society are my first care. The bands are purged; the society is purging." He first gained control over societies in Bristol and London, purged them of persons who could not subject themselves to Methodist discipline, and issued "tickets" to those remaining as marks of membership. His entire organization formed a hierarchy of divisions and subdivisions designed to promote the pursuit of faith and good works. By 1744, the nested structure started with the smallest group, the class-meeting, and extended in ascending order through bands and societies to an overall organization known as the Conferences.[12] While Wesley expanded his network of religious societies, George Whitefield emerged as the more flamboyant, popular public figure whose dramatic preaching style excited enormous crowds throughout spring and summer 1739.

Whitefield's mentor John Wesley had encouraged members of the Holy Club to be innovative in conveying the gospel to persons within and without the church. But by the late 1730s, the student had become far bolder than his teacher. The most radical step Whitefield took was to ignore existing ecclesiastical structures, such as parish boundaries, and to preach whenever and wherever he wished to whoever would listen. The Wesleys, whose father Samuel was an Anglican priest, were reluctant to trample on church tradition. However, inspired by George's success, both John and Charles ventured into the unfamiliar practice of itinerant preaching in the public parks of London and the open fields of the English countryside. John Wesley defended his actions against accusations that he was "invading" other ministers' parishes. "God in Scripture commands me," he retorted, "according to my power to instruct the ignorant, reform the wicked, confirm the virtuous. Man forbids me to do this in another's parish: that is, in effect to do it at all, seeing I have now no parish of my own, nor probably shall ever have." He expressed far more concern about disobeying God's commandment to declare the good news to all people than about violating human conventions. "Woe is me," he wrote, "if I preach not the gospel."[13]

In his bold new way of preaching, John Wesley came to a much broader definition of his audience. "I look upon all the world as my parish," he declared in a phrase Whitefield would echo, "and am bounden duty to declare unto all that are willing to hear the glad tidings of salvation." Whitefield developed a similar perspective and, like his mentor, explored new measures to attract sinners. He introduced many of the innovative evangelistic methods that later revivalists would adopt. Novelty was his greatest asset. In his handbook on how to promote a revival, Charles Grandison Finney, as previously noted, underscored the importance of innovation: "The object of our measures is to gain attention, and you must have something new. You need not make innovations in every thing. But whenever the state of things is such that any thing more is needed, it must be something *new*, otherwise it will fail."[14] Finney placed more emphasis on novelty than on the specific nature of the measures. He saw no "*particular system of measures*" mandated in the biblical commission to preach the gospel. Effective evangelists from Paul and Silas to Finney himself employed "*a succession of New Measures.*"[15]

Whitefield's critics and admirers linked his success to innovative measures. Samuel Johnson attributed the evangelist's acclaimed effectiveness to his novel means of preaching. "His popularity," said Johnson, "is chiefly owing to the peculiarity of his manner. He would be followed by crowds were he to wear a nightcap in the pulpit, or were he to preach from a tree."[16] Later, Finney acknowledged his forerunner as an experimenter, writing, "Whitefield was . . . like Wesley . . . an innovator." So bold were Whitefield's new measures that he encountered bitter opposition in the American colonies. Finney explained: "The General Association of Connecticut refused to countenance Whitefield, he was such an innovator. 'Why, he will preach out of doors and any where!' Awful! What a terrible thing, that a man should preach in the fields or in the streets. Cast him out." Citing resistance to religious innovation in Whitefield's time as well as in his own, Finney wrote, "A letter was published . . . by a minister against Whitefield, which brought up the same objections against innovations that we hear now."[17]

During spring 1739, Whitefield pieced together his revival style, element by element. Upon returning to London from Georgia in December 1738, Whitefield had alienated many clergymen because of his attacks on their lassitude in preaching and practicing the gospel. Consequently, five pastors announced they would no longer allow him to preach in their pulpits. Forced from churches, he preached outdoors. The first occurrence was in Kingswood near Bristol, where he viewed the "poor colliers, who are very numerous, . . . as sheep having no shepherd." He then "went upon a mount, and spake to as many people as came unto me. They were upwards of two hundred." He reflected on the event's significance to him and to his ministry in a journal entry. "Blessed be God that I have now broken the ice!" he exclaimed; "I believe I never was more acceptable to my Master than when I was standing to teach those hearers in the open fields."[18] Future entries alluded to crowds numbering in the thousands and tens of thousands.

Whitefield's success as a preacher depended on more than his willingness to preach in open fields. By all accounts, he was a peerless orator. He could stir mass audiences to outbursts of emotions or render them silent. Benjamin Franklin witnessed firsthand the "extraordinary influence of his oratory on his hearers," noting that "his eloquence had a wonderful power over the hearts and purses of his hearers"—a reference to the evangelist's remarkable ability to raise large sums for charities. Part of the explanation for his success in the pulpit was his powerful, at times almost hypnotic, voice. Again Franklin is our reporter: "He had a loud and clear voice, and articulated his words and sentences so perfectly, that he might be heard and understood at a great distance, especially as his auditories, however numerous, observed the most exact silence." Franklin thought that much of his success derived from his being an itinerant rather than a stationary preacher, a case of practice's making for perfection. The printer could easily distinguish between the revivalist's newly composed discourses and those he delivered frequently. "His delivery of the latter," Franklin wrote, "was so improved by frequent repetitions that every accent, every emphasis, every modulation of voice, was so perfectly well turned and well placed that, without being interested in the subject, one could not help being pleased with the discourse; a pleasure of much the same kind with that received from an excellent piece of music."[19]

Whitefield's audience appeal consisted of more than a "booming voice [and] charismatic presence." He ushered in what one scholar has called a new communications style, "a rhetoric of persuasion that was strange to the American ear." Through his extemporaneous sermons delivered in everyday language to mass audiences, the itinerant "sought to transcend both the rational manner of polite Liberal preaching and the plain style of orthodox preaching in order to speak directly to the people-at-large." Before the revivals New England Puritans and Chesapeake Anglicans, while differing in style and substance, "believed traditionally with Samuel Willard that God did 'Ordain Orders of Superiority and Inferiority among men.'" That hierarchical view of society was reinforced every time congregations met, manifested in "forms of attire, the seating of public meetings, and patterns of speech." Prerevival worship services served to sustain the prevailing social organization, and in that context, speaker and audience assumed socially constructed positions, "constantly reminded of their places in the community."[20] Whitefield, as outsider and stranger, spoke to huge audiences with persons of every order intermixed.

Whitefield was a consummate actor in the pulpit. One biographer views him as a "Divine Dramatist" and places at the center of his development his youthful "immersion in theater." In his autobiography, Whitefield recalled how "during the time of my being at school, I was very fond of reading plays, and have kept from school for days together to prepare myself for acting in them." Although we know little about the direct influence of the eighteenth-century expansion of theater on the growing middle class, we have Whitefield's own witness as to his taste for plays. His dramatic style of preaching suggests that he was also familiar with actors' manuals of the day. One manual, Aaron Hill's *The Art of Acting*, contains insights Whitefield expressed: "the passions men are actuated by, must be the Objects they are most familiar with."[21] He became a master at preaching extemporaneous sermons on familiar topics: current events, local circumstances, and fleeting fads.

As Whitefield preached to vast throngs in London's public parks, he competed with other performers seeking the crowd's attention. Patent medicine salesmen, strolling actors, and pugilists were ubiquitous figures in Hyde Park, Moorfields, and Kennington Common. All were gifted at attracting people, hoping to extract a few pence for their efforts. Whitefield had no choice but to present his message with a colorful delivery that could transfix his audience's attention. In his popular sermon "The Eternity of Hell's-Torments," he re-created in gripping drama the scene of a sinner's arrival at the gates of hell:

> O wretched Man that I am, who shall deliver me from the Body of Death! Are all the Grand Deceiver's inviting Promises come to this? O Damned Apostate! Oh that I had never hearkened to his beguiling Insinuations! Oh that I had rejected his very first Suggestions with the utmost Detestation and Abhorrence! Oh that I had taken up my cross and followed Christ! But alas! These reflections come now too late. But must I live for ever tormented in these Flames? Oh, Eternity! That thought fills me with Despair. I cannot, will not, yet I must be miserable for ever.[22]

Such passionate portrayals were intended to transport listeners to the brink of hell itself, and the shouts and cries of some auditors indicated that they succeeded.

Whitefield's dramatic preaching style and revolutionary meeting format constituted but half of his "preach and print" strategy. The other was a promotional effort whereby the printed word served to publicize and reinforce the preached word. In exploiting the power of print to reach a mass audience, Whitefield stood squarely in the center of Reformation tradition. As one historian observed, the Reformation represented "for the first time in history . . . a propaganda campaign conducted through the medium of the press." While denying that the book caused the Reformation, Lucien Febvre and Henri-Jean Martin concluded that it was a powerful force for change. "If it does not succeed in convincing," they wrote, "the printed book is at least tangible evidence of convictions held because it embodies and symbolizes them; it furnishes arguments to those who are already converts, lets them develop and refine their faith, offers them points which will help them to triumph in debate, and encourages the hesitant. For all these reasons books played a critical part in the development of Protestantism in the 16th century."[23] John Gillies was less reserved in his assessment of print's impact. He saw the press as a powerful new tool capable of extending the gospel far beyond the reach of tongue or pen. Through print, "the Bible, which had for so many ages been shut up, [could now] be universally spread, and thus made accessible for the poorest boy or maid's having familiar converse therewith, and to have it at the easiest rate." Presses brought forth "to the world, in defence of the truth, and promoting of the knowledge of Jesus Christ, which no pen could have reached without the advantage of such a singular means given of the Lord for his Church's use."[24]

John Wesley realized that preaching alone could not reach the multitudes who needed to hear the gospel. Accordingly, he began to publish inexpensive works designed specifically for a mass audience. Like Whitefield and others from the Holy Club, he printed his own sermons. His discourse on salvation by faith, first published in 1738, was what one historian has termed "the first trumpet-call of the Evangelical Revival." Wesley and other revival promoters went beyond publishing their own works. They also made available the "choicest Pieces of Practical Divinity which have been published in the English Tongue." Culling extracts and abridgments from a "prodigious number of books," Wesley eventually published fifty volumes that constituted a *Reader's Digest* of theology for the masses. While reprints of theological works were commonplace in mid-eighteenth-century England, never before had anyone attempted on such a grand scale to acquaint men and women in the lower and middling social orders with "a galaxy of the noblest men the Christian church had ever had." To make the volumes more accessible to persons of limited education, Wesley omitted what he thought was "objectionable or unimportant in sentiment and superfluous language." He sought to "divest practical theology from logical technicalities and unnecessary digressions."[25] Through the preached or printed word, Wesley and his band of promoters proclaimed in everyday language the revival of practical piety.

Whitefield's exploitation of newspapers to publicize his ministry represents his most original contribution to print as an evangelistic tool. While reformers used broadsheets and handbills to announce meetings and report news of their activities, Whitefield tapped the most powerful of all printed ephemera, the newspaper. By the 1730s, newspapers had proliferated, first in London and then in the provinces and the American colonies. As the number of dailies and weeklies rose, the price plummeted, making newspapers affordable to the middling as well as better sorts. Moreover, public houses made newspapers available to their patrons, extending their readership even further. Samuel Johnson complained that "the common newspapers are more eagerly snatched in the public coffee-houses than my essays."[26] And, although rising literacy in many parts of the British Atlantic meant that a growing number of persons could read the papers, even the illiterate often followed newspaper accounts by hearing others read aloud. Coached by William Seward, a shrewd stockjobber turned zealot convert, Whitefield learned how to turn the newspaper into a powerful engine of self-promotion.

During the three months prior to their departure for America in August 1739, Seward and Whitefield fully exploited the newspaper. Consider their exposure in the London *Daily Advertiser*. From May through July Whitefield spent thirty-nine days in London and managed to generate newspaper publicity on thirty-two of them. Three-fourths of the items consisted of announcements of upcoming revival services and reports of previous ones. Eager for news of broad interest, the publisher was more than willing to devote space to Seward's florid accounts, especially since Seward paid for them. With no apparent editorial restraints, Seward exercised full license as Whitefield's public relations agent. In reporting crowd sizes, sometimes Seward simply copied the figures Whitefield had entered in his *Journals*. For example, Seward reported that 20,000 people had attended Whitefield's service at Kennington Common on May 5, the same estimate the evangelist recorded. On other occasions, Seward changed the numbers; sometimes perhaps to make them more credible. While Whitefield claimed that 80,000 had congregated in Hyde Park on June 1 to hear him preach, Seward cited 50,000 in his newspaper account. Apparently he liked that figure, because he repeated it two days later at Kennington although Whitefield offered only his impression that the crowd was "the most numerous . . . I ever saw in that place."[27] Regardless of the actual attendance, Seward and Whitefield were creating a public perception of unprecedented interest in experimental religion.

In Seward, Whitefield had a skilled and aggressive publicist. Before his conversion and decision to assist Whitefield and the Wesleys, Seward was a stockjobber in London whose advertisements bore the same hyperbolic stamp as those he placed for Whitefield. In the early eighteenth century, many deplored stockjobbing, calling it a "pernicious art." The fact is, as one scholar observed, brokers were "fine fellows when things were going well, but instantly became scapegoats when anything went wrong."[28] Though controversial, brokers were at times regarded as super-salesmen capable of selling what amounted to little more than blue sky.

Investors still blamed jobbers for the South Sea Bubble of 1722, a stock market crash that ruined many, including a considerable number of small, first-time shareholders who had risked their life savings on the speculative venture. But Seward knew how to sell, and when he applied his salesmanship to Whitefield and the evangelical revival, he made certain that Whitefield's name became a household word in a transatlantic market.

Having read Edwards's *Faithful Narrative*, Whitefield believed that the great crowds he attracted in England were suffused with the same divine inspiration that informed the revival in western Massachusetts. Through print as well as preaching, he linked his ministry with the Northampton "great awakening." He made a clear connection by echoing the title of Edwards's revival account in that of his autobiography, published in 1739 as *A Faithful Narrative of the Life and Character of the Reverend Mr. Whitefield*.[29] The subtitle provided another tie between the Work of God in England and that in America as it announced Whitefield's intention to travel to Georgia later in the year.

As his popularity increased, Whitefield assumed mythic proportions in print. He appeared larger than life in yet another *Faithful Narrative*, this time a largely fictive biography published by an ardent supporter in 1739. Having accused Whitefield's detractors of showing their "Wit and Invention" in turning the preacher into a "mercenary knave," the biographer proceeded to weave a few inventions of his own. He started by presenting Whitefield as a man of rather noble origins, born to wealth and provided with "an education suitable to his Fortune." No mention here of his entering Oxford as a servitor, forced to polish classmates' shoes to pay his room and board. Moreover, in this account, it was Whitefield, not John Wesley, who formed the Holy Club, "where he instructed with his Method of expounding the Holy Scripture."[30] Another writer responded to such effusive praise by chastising the biographer for "blowing up [Whitefield's] Character to an undue Size," fearing that some "giddy Folks" would be unable to separate fact from fiction.[31]

To the bishop of London Edmund Gibson, Whitefield's and his followers' use of print amounted to shameless self-promotion. He believed that revivalists' publications were no more than "pompous accounts of their labours and the success of them, with mutual commendations in no low strains." In particular he singled out Whitefield's popular *Journals* and printed letters as unrestrained puff.[32] Another opponent worried that uncritical readers would conclude of Whitefield's publications, "It's true because it's printed!" The critic found a financial motive behind the revivalist practice of reading aloud letters reporting revival successes "from distant lands." He cynically claimed that reports on "how fast their numbers do increase" were directly related to "how free the contributions flow."[33]

To American revivalists, however, such criticisms authenticated the Whitefieldian revival as a work of God. Just as detractors had tried to discredit the awakening at Northampton, English antirevivalists sought to undermine the popular evangelical revival afoot among their own countrymen. Scripture taught colonial awakeners to expect increased criticism during seasons of extraordinary grace. They eagerly followed news of the progress of the gospel in general and the ministry of Whitefield in particular.

"WE HEAR FROM ABROAD": NEWS OF THE
ENGLISH EVANGELICAL REVIVAL

Ever vigilant for signs of an extraordinary outpouring of God's grace, American revivalists eagerly sought reports of any evidence that such a moment was at hand anywhere in the world. They relied on two principal means for gathering religious news: correspondence with fellow evangelicals around the globe and newspaper stories. In the late 1730s, they learned about the evangelical awakening in England first from British correspondents. For decades, colonial divines had exchanged evangelical news with their English brethren through "the Old Dissenting network—a network with its roots in the seventeenth-century Puritan 'community of saints.'" It was through that medium that Benjamin Colman had communicated news of the Northampton awakening to Isaac Watts and John Guyse. Now promoters on both sides of the Atlantic converted the letter-writing network into an important channel of revival news and information. Through an active and prolific exchange of correspondence, they narrated revivals as they occurred in various local communities, shared techniques that proved successful as "means to grace," and related conversion experiences to prove that the awakenings were authentic works of God's Spirit within the lives of individuals.[34] It was through this revival network that Americans learned of an extraordinary development in evangelism emanating from England.

In spring 1739, Colman received a letter from the same Reverend Pearsall of Warminster who had informed him of English reaction to the account of revival in western Massachusetts. Pearsall reported that "what has employ'd tho't, Pens, and Tongues of many of late has been the Rise of (as they are commonly call'd) the New Methodists." He indicated that "they are run down by many, but God seems to be raising them (especially Mr. Whitefield) for very important Ends." He explained that to some "they are look'd upon as Enthusiasts . . ., I suppose chiefly because they very much insist upon the Doctrines of *Faith* & the Necessity of a *New Birth*." Pearsall wrote that Whitefield preached "to the most crowded Auditories in London and Bristol, [that his Anglican opponents] excluded him [from] all the Churches in the latter Place, [and] . . . oblig'd him to retire to the Villages & Fields adjoining, where he has been preaching to Thousands." He told Colman that audiences had been "deeply impressed" under the Methodists' preaching and that "indeed there seems in many Places to be a great Noise among the dry Bones." One sign of evangelistic success was intense opposition. "The carnal World is up in Arms," he explained, "but in spight of all our glorious Lord seems to be getting himself a Wonderful Victory." Moreover, the revival was spreading: "In parts of Wales the face of Things seems to be changed from Profaneness to Piety."[35]

Pearsall's report spoke of revival news beyond that unfolding in England. He related an account of revival on the Continent, especially in parts of Germany. "What has surpriz'd and rejoiced the Souls of some in the Highest Degrees," he exulted to Colman, "has been the Narrative of the Planting of the Moravian Church at Hernhout & the uncommon Operation of divine Grace upon the Heart of Count [Nicholas] Zinzendorff." The significance of Zinzendorff's involvement to Pearsall was that the revival reached beyond the Anglo-American world and attracted persons of noble as well as mean birth. "A prime Minister [Zinzendorff] turning his Back upon a luxurious Court, where he shone & presided," Pearsall wrote, had taken up "with an Handful of despised poor Refugees, who had nothing to recommend them, but that they belong'd to Christ."[36]

In concluding his letter to Colman, Pearsall interpreted its contents as signs of an authentic and extensive revival. The Northampton account, reports of the New Methodists in England, and the Moravian narrative equaled in his mind a wonderful, extraordinary work of God. "The more I think of it," he mused, "the more I am led to admire the Strangeness of the Change & adore the Author of it." Common to all the evangelical events was the hand of God. "Methinks the Spirit of Moses is revived," he concluded, referring to the awakenings as a new spiritual deliverance, "and God is showing how great is the Power of his Grace."[37]

Colonial revivalists also received revival accounts through reading newspapers. From early in his ministry, Jonathan Edwards had combed newspapers for any news of the spread of Christianity. He recorded in his diary the joy that a favorable report brought him. His January 12, 1723, entry reads, "If I heard the least hint of any thing that happened, in any part of the world, that appeared, in some respect or other, to have a favorable aspect on the interests of Christ's kingdom, my soul eagerly catched at it; and it would much animate and refresh me." He searched for good news wherever he could find it, including colonial newspapers, whose news was predominantly English and European in origin. "I used to be eager to read public news letters," Edwards wrote, "to see if I could not find some news favorable to the interest of religion in the world."[38] During his tenure as pastor at Northampton, Edwards continued to be an avid reader of the Boston newspapers. On occasion a news item inspired a sermon idea, which he would develop on the spot, sometimes scratching out in the paper's margins the outlines of a discourse he planned to deliver from his pulpit.[39]

Edwards was not alone in scanning newspapers for inspiring religious news. Wherever evangelicals looked for signs of revival, they stayed abreast of reports from abroad that might signal the beginning of a general awakening. Fortunately for them, their interests coincided with newspaper publishers' desire to print or—as was most often the case among colonial printers—to *reprint* any newsworthy story emanating from England or Europe that would edify or amuse their subscribers. By 1739, George Whitefield and the evangelical revival he popularized were major stories in English newspapers and, as such, soon received extensive coverage in colonial weeklies.

If one learned of the evangelical revival only through colonial newspapers, he or she would conclude that the major story line was that of George Whitefield and the huge crowds he attracted. While historians know that the revival comprised far more than Whitefield's activities, contemporary American revivalists received a highly filtered and thereby restricted version. Though John Wesley was building from the ground up the organization that would eventually become the Methodist Church, colonists learned almost nothing of Wesley's efforts. And they read little about the many dissenting pastors throughout England and Wales instrumental in preaching the necessity of the New Birth. Part of the reason is that Whitefield dominated newspaper coverage. He was also particularly appealing to colonial revivalists. His Calvinism linked him theologically to New England Congregationalists and Middle Colony Presbyterians. His public challenge of Anglican clergy played well in colonial regions where dissenting traditions were established. And his work across class lines in England found favor in America's loose and fluid society.

Whitefield was quickly identified with big numbers, and statistics played a large role in the reporting of revival news and were meaningful to supporters of the awakenings. Quantitative measurement had long been important in economic enterprises. By the mid–eighteenth century, Anglo-American culture had become numerate as more and more people became enmeshed in market exchanges and had to reckon with prices, weights, costs, and wages. Numeracy, "the ability to use written symbols for concepts of number," was essential in commercial capitalism; thus from the time of their earliest settlement British North Americans were a calculating people, whether surveying land in order to make "profits in the wilderness" or keeping track of prices in buying and selling tobacco on international markets.[40] To figure gain, one had to manipulate revenues and costs. One way that revivalists conceived of their efforts was to "make merchandize for the Lord." To measure their success, they reported numbers: crowds at preaching services, persons converted, amounts collected.

In spring 1739, colonial newspapers began reporting on the Methodist itinerancies. New England and Middle Colony papers provided readers with accounts stressing the large crowds that gathered to hear George Whitefield and John Wesley preach and the unusual settings in which the services took place. The May 22 issue of the *New England Weekly Journal* noted that Whitefield preached "from a Mount at Rose Green amongst the Kingswood Colliers, to a prodigious Multitude, computed at 10,000 Souls." The June 19 edition indicated that 20,000 gathered at Moorfields in London and 30,000 at Kennington Common. Benjamin Franklin's *Pennsylvania Gazette* conveyed similar coverage to readers in the Middle Colonies, emphasizing the huge crowds.[41]

In addition to being newsworthy, the large crowds reported in colonial newspapers sparked controversy. Some marveled at estimates that reached 50,000, while others disputed the numbers, suggesting that 5,000 was closer to reality. To quell such skepticism, one believer sent the editor of the *New England Weekly Journal* an account of an experiment recently conducted in London and reported in the August 1739 edition of the *Gentleman's Magazine*. In the account, the London experimenter, writing as *Thoninonca*, described his measurement:

On the 29th of July in the Morning, being the last time Mr. Whitefield preach'd in *Moorfields*, before he dismiss'd his Audience, I made several Marks where the outermost of them stood, and the next Morning found the Distance of the farthest Mark from the Rostrum to be 32 Yards, and that of the nearest to it 28. Of the intermediate Distance, I took that which was 30 Yards, and made it the Semidiameter of a Circle, which Circle must be nearly equal to the Space taken up by the standing Congregation, and contains 2827 square Yards. In a square Yard I have found that 9 Persons may easily stand; and therefore 2827 Yards square must contain 25,443 People.[42]

The person conducting the measurement asserted that "so great a Number . . . none but the pious Mr. Whitefield ever preach to." His bias in favor of the evangelist contributed to assumptions designed to yield the highest numbers. Nine persons in a square yard assumes uniformly small people pressed close together. And nine people in *every* square yard allows virtually no space for movement.[43]

Persons opposing the revival contested *Thoninonca*'s calculation. In an editorial following the original report in the *Gentleman's Magazine*, editor Sylvanus Urban printed the following: "Soldiers in close Order stand but 4 in a Yard Square, at which Rate the Circle will contain but 11,388, (perhaps 12,000) Persons." Whatever the final number, the conclusion was the same: "Our Correspondent's Computation is too High."[44]

The revivalist deemed the matter too important, however, to allow the challenge to stand. In the next issue of the magazine, *Thoninonca* defended his calculations. He argued that nine persons per square yard was justified because people "stand as close together as they possibly can . . . to hear [Whitefield] distinctly." He added a personal testimony, explaining that "I have been so press'd, when near 30 Yards Distance from him, that I have not been able to stir." Turning to the objector's military analogy, *Thoninonca* stipulated that the average person had a shoulder span of about three feet. He then conceded that "if 3 Men . . . standing Side by Side, should somewhat exceed a Yard; 3 Men standing before one another, would fall as much short of it." In closing he invited all doubters to test his assumptions by "drawing a Square Yard upon the Floor, and placing 9 Persons of the above-mentioned Size in it."[45] The lengths to which the disputants went to prove their points did not settle the issue, but they do illustrate the intensity of the controversy and the significance revivalists and antirevivalists attached to fixing their respective numbers on public opinion. It is also noteworthy that the revivalist publishers of the Boston newspaper that reprinted *Thoninonca*'s original estimate did not reprint the challenge to his numbers.

To revivalists, calculating crowd sizes and numbers converted was far more than an academic exercise. For a religious event to qualify as a revival, it must produce unusually large numbers. Those reporting on the events of Pentecost, the New Testament paradigm for an extraordinary outpouring of God's Spirit, indicated that "there were added that day about three thousand souls." In 1738, Watts and Guyse had cited as clear evidence of a "surprizing Work of God" in Northampton the conversion of "many hundred Souls." Indeed, Jonathan Edwards in identifying a revival's distinguishing marks, emphasized the role of numbers. One can be certain that a religious movement is a genuine work of God "when it is observed in a great multitude of people."[46] Thus, to expectant colonial evangelists looking for signs of an extraordinary outpouring of grace, the reports of huge crowds in England were telling evidence.

American revivalists had no doubt that reports arriving from England signaled an extraordinary outpouring of God's Spirit. Five years after the reports, Thomas Prince of Boston reflected on the significance of the accounts of Whitefield's preaching that had arrived in America. To him the "surprizing Power and Success" of the evangelist's preaching indicated that God had raised up "in the Spirit of the *Reformers*" a new instrument for awakening slumbering Christians and converting the unsaved.[47]

Even as they published the accounts in 1739, the revivalists of the *New England Weekly Journal* invested the London reports with local meaning. Not only did Samuel Kneeland and Timothy Green believe that they were reporting news of a general revival, they viewed events in England as the continuation and growth of the awakenings five years earlier in the Connecticut Valley. In a telling juxtaposition on the advertisement page of the November 27 issue, the editors listed three documents that would enable readers to make connections between Northampton and Moorfields. Listed first was a sermon by William Williams of Hatfield, *Directions How to Obtain a True Conversion Unto God*. A note explained that this sermon was delivered at a "Time of General Awakenings." Next appeared an ad for Jonathan Edwards's *Account of the late Surprizing Work of God . . . at Northampton*. Last was a sermon by George Whitefield, billed as "an excellent Sermon on Regeneration" preached to a large audience. The layout of the advertisements was itself a sermon, one proclaiming that the great work of God begun in Northampton in 1735 had spread and grown in England in 1739 and was on its way back to America later that year in the person of Whitefield.[48]

Before the Whitefieldian revival reached New England, local pastors stayed abreast of revival news in Britain and other parts of America. In addition to hearing about the spreading awakening through newspaper reports and the evangelical letter-writing network, ministers learned of developments from each other. On May 28, 1740, a convention of pastors met at Boston in their annual conference and shared news of the progress of gospel propagation. Ebenezer Parkman, pastor at Westboro, Massachusetts, recorded the proceeding's highlights in his diary. What he remembered most was Benjamin Colman's communicating "several Things relating to the Spreading the Success of the Kingdom of Christ." He recorded specifically Colman's mentioning the evangelism of Count Zinzendorf, the Moravian leader in Germany.[49]

Ministers made certain that revival news spread far beyond their convention meetings and diary entries. Following the convention, lay men and women read in the *New England Weekly Journal* an account of the proceedings. They learned that Thomas Prince had preached the convention sermon at the Old South Meeting House, choosing as his text a portion of Isa. 9:7, which the newspaper report highlighted: *"Of the Increase of his Government—there shall be no End."* The account concluded by noting that the ministers had made a contribution of almost two hundred pounds for the "Propagation of the Gospel."[50] On the same page of the newspaper was an extensive report from Pennsylvania of Whitefield's preaching to large crowds, a report that seemed to bear out hopes expressed at the convention.

Evangelical pastors greatly expanded the reach of newspaper reports by reading extracts to their congregations. Ministers routinely kept laypersons informed of revival news through regular reports from the pulpit as well as prayers for continued blessings on evangelistic undertakings. In a letter to Whitefield, Colman assured him that "we have prayed for you in Public." Gilbert Tennent indicated that from his pulpit he routinely mentioned by name those preachers who were leading the revival in Britain.[51] Thus, long before Whitefield's arrival in America triggered a general awakening in the northern colonies, evangelical men and women knew firsthand of the British revival and had prayed for a similar outpouring of God's grace in the colonies.

Benjamin Colman was more guarded in his initial reactions to revival news from England, expressing cautious optimism about this "new Thing in our Day" being reported from abroad. Whether it was a genuine revival that would be "eventually [a] Mercy or . . . Judgment with respect to the Nation" remained to be seen. He was encouraged by two signs that the Methodists' evangelism was part of a work of God: the "abundant Rewards of [their] Labours" and the "Reviling and Abuses of many." The Boston minister compared the present work with previous awakenings and concluded that something unusual was occurring. In a letter to Whitefield concerning reports of the Methodist revival in England, he wrote that he had not "seen the like in our *New-England* Churches, altho' there have been, at times, uncommon Operations of the holy Spirit on the Souls of many under the Ministry of the Word . . .; but I do indeed account for the Impressions from God upon the *Methodists* . . . to be something very extraordinary."[52]

Gilbert Tennent's first assessment of the current revival being imported from England was positive. Basing his evaluation on New Jersey's revival tradition, he compared Whitefield's sermons with those of Frelinghuysen and his own father and concluded that the Methodist's "Sermons have much confirmed the Truths of Christ which have been preach'd here for many Years in the *Dutch* and *English* Language." As he learned of the awakening's progress in Britain and observed its beginnings in his own community, he expressed his hope that this was indeed an extensive work of God: "I have seen hopeful Appearances of Concern amongst a pretty many in the Places I belong to. It seems as if *Emanual*, to whom a Bow, a Crown is given, wou'd ride upon the Steed of his Gospel, to the Spreading of his gracious Conquests over stubborn Sinners through the Nations." Tennent's vision was global: he believed that he was linked with evangelicals on the other side of the Atlantic in promoting this wonderful outpouring of grace. He wrote in 1739 that "[I] make frequent Mention of those Worthies in England, Wales, and Scotland, who are imbark'd with us in the same blessed Cause of God."[53]

While hearing from England a favorable report written and interpreted by revival promoters, Americans also received unfavorable accounts written by opponents. To critics, the events being described represented no revival at all but "enthusiasm," a pejorative term suggesting that the religious notions being propagated flowed from the overheated imagination of self-promoting evangelists. One commentator to the London magazine *Common Sense* asserted that "False Notions and Schemes of Religion deserve to be expos'd in your Paper, no less than wrong Management and Corruptions in Government. The Propagators of both are equal Offenders against Common Sense, and, upon that Account, should be equally stigmatiz'd by it." The writer claimed that the "bad

Effects of an enthusiastick Spirit" exceed those of libertinism in undermining true religion. He explained that the libertine generally "acts upon no Principles, or else upon very unsettled ones, [but] may, as the Heat of Youth goes off, and after a Fatigue of sensual Pleasures, arrive at his right Mind and a true Notion of Things." By contrast, the enthusiast, such as a Methodist evangelist, "acts upon Notions, wild as they are, which to him appear as certain as Revelations from the Deity, nay, which he oftentimes is positively persuaded in himself are Revelations."[54] The warning was clear: though they claim to be bearing witness to a great Work of God, revivalists are promoting with great certitude their own enthusiastic fancies.

Thus on the eve of Whitefield's arrival in the colonies, Americans awaited him as either the instrument God had chosen for a great awakening or the harbinger of malevolence threatening social, economic, and political order. Which interpretation gained favor in a given community rested in large part on the religious tradition that prevailed there. Thousands in New England and the Middle Colonies were predisposed to welcome him, having read in the events reported from England clear signs that his was a work of God. Thousands of others in those regions as well as the Anglican South gave more credence to the notion that the Methodists had invented a movement for their own gain and masked their venal goals behind pious utterances.

WHY 1739?

Eighteen months before arriving at Philadelphia, when he was yet little known to most Americans, George Whitefield had made a brief visit to the colonies, restricting his stay to Georgia and South Carolina. On May 7, 1738, he disembarked at Savannah. Few colonial newspapers mentioned his coming because he was not yet newsworthy; he had not developed the reputation that would make his name familiar to people throughout the Atlantic world. His inaugural sermon attracted a "crowd" of forty-two people, seventeen adults and twenty-five children. No press agent had prepared advance publicity, and none reported on Whitefield's performance that day. What we know about the occasion comes from the evangelist himself, an account published well after the fact. Whitefield had not come as an evangelist but as John Wesley's replacement at the Anglican church in Savannah. The young deacon of the Church of England did not linger long in Georgia. After assessing the colony's spiritual and humanitarian needs, he returned to England for ordination, vowing to return to relieve the suffering settlers, especially orphans.[55]

Whitefield returned to America in late October 1739; and this time it seemed that all colonists took note of the celebrated young preacher's arrival. His return to the colonies was much expected and reported in the town's two newspapers. Before he reached the city, in the smallest hamlets along his route to Philadelphia, men and women hailed him as a well-known public figure. People in the city poured out to see the person who had caused such a stir in England. The thousands who gathered at his first Philadelphia sermon bore witness to their anticipation of his arrival. He came not as an obscure pastor but as a popular revivalist, and he brought with him a fully developed revival program consisting of what he referred to as a "cargo of heavenly wares."[56]

During the time between his first two American trips, Whitefield had developed in England an exportable revival.[57] The program he fashioned consisted of a series of preaching meetings crafted in a distinctive style and a publicity campaign modeled after innovative advertising programs employed by forward-thinking merchants. His "preach and print" approach to evangelism included itinerant preaching and newspaper publicity, a combination that attracted huge outdoor crowds. The result was revival as a crusade to promote the spread of awakening within the hearts of men and women. His was a specific revival: the Whitefieldian revival.

In spring 1739, Americans learned that Whitefield was bringing his revival to the colonies. The great anticipation colonists expressed as they awaited his arrival stood in stark contrast to the general silence and indifference that had marked his first trip. Colonial newspapers had announced his 1738 trip in small notices tucked away on interior pages.[58] That was before his preaching in London became front-page news in Britain and America. Now, in 1739, newspapers reported his every move from the announcement of his American trip to his departure. Colonial revivalists expressed great disappointment when they learned that his trip was delayed because of an embargo. Then their hopes revived with news that he had embarked on his transatlantic journey.

By summer 1739, all elements of the Whitefieldian revival were in place. Whitefield and Seward had woven them into a whole that had been thoroughly tested in western England, southern Wales, and the city of London. Now they were ready to export it to British America.

In the revivalists' view, the religious market on both sides of the Atlantic had too long been overregulated, dominated by principles other than those of experimental religion. Therefore, it must be challenged. According to John Gillies, religious ideas operated in a market similar to that of fashion. He observed that on the eve of the evangelical revival, "serious and practical christianity in England was in a very low condition; scriptural, experimental religion (which in the last century had been the subject of the sermons and writings of the clergy) had become quite unfashionable."[59] The revivalists' goal was to make it fashionable once more, and colonial revivalists eagerly awaited the arrival of this latest fashion from London.

Whitefield's arrival triggered an intercolonial revival that swept through much of the northern provinces, from Pennsylvania's Lower Counties to Maine, and in pockets of the southern colonies. Unlike previous outpourings, this "general awakening" spanned denominational and provincial boundaries. When earthquakes shook New England in 1727, revivals had broken out in many communities as ministers preached sermons asking men and women to seek causes for God's anger and ask for a renewal of his grace. But the awakenings were confined to the region and failed to spark similar occurrences even in the Middle Colonies' revival belts.

The question of why a general awakening occurred in 1739 and not earlier leads one first to examine structural changes within colonial America that may have contributed to an intercolonial movement. By the time Whitefield arrived, British North America could well support the evangelist's "preach and print" strategy. Tremendous population growth played an important role, enabling itinerants to attract huge crowds often numbering in the thousands, a characteristic distinguishing the Great Awakening from previous revivals. In the period 1700–1740, the estimated population of the American colonies grew from about 250,000 to approximately 905,000, an increase of 260 percent. In the previous forty-year period (1660–1770), the growth rate was 233 percent, and in the following (1740–1780), 200 percent. During the years leading to the intercolonial revival, churches failed to accommodate the expanding population, providing awakeners with a field "white for the harvesting."[60]

In addition to population growth, the increase in the number and size of towns and cities contributed to the early phase of the Great Awakening, which centered on urban communities. The English revival that colonists had followed in newspapers had featured London and Bristol, with their huge outdoor audiences gathered in public parks and churchyards to hear Whitefield. By 1739, America boasted just four cities: Boston, New York, Philadelphia, and Charleston. The first three numbered between 10,000 and 15,000 people, the last, about 6,000–7,000 souls. While in America, Whitefield conducted three preaching tours, the first two organized around Philadelphia, and the third around Boston. In each of those cities he reported crowds of 20,000, a figure he compared favorably to London gatherings.

While most of the population growth resulted from natural increase, large numbers of immigrants also poured into the colonies. Noteworthy for an understanding of the Great Awakening were the large groups of Irish, Scots, and Germans, many of whom came from rich revival traditions and were predisposed toward evangelism and special periods of praying down and preaching up God's grace. From Ulster and Scotland arrived men and women accustomed to communion seasons wherein they expected special outpourings of God's grace during preaching services spanning several days. And many of the German newcomers to the Middle Colonies had been exposed to Continental Pietism, with its emphasis on practical piety and evangelism.

In addition to population increase, expansion of the colonial press furnished revival promoters with an important means of both publicizing the movement and connecting awakenings in different regions into a whole. A comparison of the number of print shops in 1700 with that in 1739 reveals the growth. According to Isaiah Thomas, the number of booksellers operating in Massachusetts increased about fourfold in that period. He also noted that "before 1740, more printing was done there [in Massachusetts] than in all the other colonies." But by the time Whitefield arrived, Philadelphia was becoming a major colonial print center, and by 1760, according to Thomas, "the quantum of printing done in Boston and Philadelphia was nearly equal."[61] Printers in those two cities ensured that the revival would be well publicized.

Important to an intercolonial movement were newspapers. The revival was news, and aggressive publicity kept public attention focused on it. The absence of any colonial newspaper before 1704 meant that earlier revivals were likely to remain local in scope. With the publication of the *Boston News-Letter* in that year, subscribers were informed of matters in other colonies as well as in England and Scotland. In the first issue, readers found Queen Anne's speech to Parliament respecting the pretender's sending "popish missionaries from France into Scotland." They also could peruse a few articles "under the Boston head." And those interested in trade discovered in four short paragraphs "marine intelligence from Newyork, Philadelphia, and Newlondon."[62] Reports on merchant vessels in American ports illustrate how a newspaper enabled readers to follow the progress of goods, persons, and ideas moving toward or away from them. In 1739, evangelical readers would track the movement of the revival as it progressed from town to town.

Publishers of colonial newspapers filled them with articles gleaned from London weeklies. But they also sought from their readers and correspondents "Things worthy of reporting in this as well as in other Parts of the World." With no professional staff of reporters, printers relied upon travelers to report on events in other colonies. Thus ships' captains, merchants, itinerants, and military officers, among others, provided intelligence about happenings elsewhere. And publishers solicited and received information through correspondence with persons in other provinces. Frequently, reports were in the form of reprinted letters or were summaries of letters or conversations that began with, "We hear from. . . ." With all the advance publicity of the Methodist revival in England and with Whitefield's attracting huge crowds in the colonies, events of the Great Awakening from the outset qualified as "Things worthy of reporting."[63]

By 1739, revival promoters, eager to send reports on the awakening's progress, had access to a total of twelve colonial newspapers located in six cities (see table 3.1). The Whitefield revival was one of the major news stories in colonial America throughout the evangelist's fifteen-month visit. Publishers eagerly filled their weeklies with accounts of revival events, especially those of an unusual nature, such as the enormous crowds that gathered to hear Whitefield, and the bizarre behavior of some who attended his services. In November 1739, a New Yorker reported that "many Hundreds of People" attended the afternoon service and an estimated 2,000 gathered for the evening sermon. When Whitefield returned to New York the next spring, he preached to crowds of 7,000 and 8,000.[64] Even allowing for inflated estimates, the gatherings during the "Work" far exceeded those assembling each Sunday at parish churches, where the scale of worship was much more intimate. For example, on the eve of the Work, the membership of the First Church of Norwich, Connecticut, totaled only about four hundred, including halfway members—that is, those who had "owned the covenant," or professed their formal beliefs, without professing a conversion experience.[65] And in Woodbury, one of Connecticut's larger towns, a total of 275 men and women had been admitted to church membership in the forty years immediately preceding the Work.[66]

Americans commented at length on the huge crowds gathered to

TABLE 3.1
Colonial Newspapers in Print, 1739

Newspaper	Location	Date Established
Boston Weekly News-Letter	Boston	1704
Boston Gazette	Boston	1719
New England Weekly Journal	Boston	1727
Boston Weekly Post-Boy	Boston	1734
Boston Evening-Post	Boston	1735
New-York Gazette	New York	1725
New-York Weekly Journal	New York	1733
American Weekly Mercury	Philadelphia	1721
Pennsylvania Gazette	Philadelphia	1728
Pennsylvania German Recorder	Germantown	1739
Virginia Gazette	Williamsburg	1736
South Carolina Gazette	Charleston	1734

Source: Isaiah Thomas, *The History of Printing in America*, 2:186–408.

hear revivalists. Although skeptical of some of Whitefield's numbers, opponents agreed with supporters that the gatherings were without precedent. Indeed, throngs of 20,000 or more were unusual under any circumstances in the mid–eighteenth century. Americans certainly were not accustomed to seeing that many people assembled at one place; even armies arrayed for the biggest battles did not match the revivalist crowds in number. During the French and Indian War, the largest concentration of troops was an estimated 18,000 to 20,000 encamped near Ticonderoga. Eyewitnesses at the bivouac expressed their amazement at "so great" a host.[67] Similarly, colonists paused in wonder before the throngs gathered to hear an evangelist.

Crowd behavior merited much contemporary discussion. Critics denounced as disruptive of good order the shouting, crying, and bodily fits that sometimes accompanied a spiritual new birth. They also opposed such practices as allowing "FEMALE EXHORTERS" to speak in the church, a "plain breach of that commandment of the Lord, . . . Let your WOMEN keep silence in the churches."[68] Revivalist Samuel Blair was also disturbed by emotional outbursts. He observed that "some burst out with an audible Noise into bitter crying," adding that such behavior was "not known in those Parts before." He admonished his listeners "to restrain themselves from making a Noise that would hinder themselves or others from hearing what was spoken."[69]

At times crowd behavior resulted in sensational news stories reported widely throughout the colonies. One such occasion was a tragic accident that occurred on September 22, 1740. At a Boston meetinghouse on that Monday, a huge crowd gathered to hear Whitefield preach. Reporters depicted a packed meetinghouse, filled to overflowing, with hundreds on the outside peering through windows to get a glimpse of the evangelist. The cramped congregation was awaiting his arrival with great anticipation when, suddenly, some persons in the crowded balcony heard what sounded like a cracking timber. Perhaps recalling that the balcony at Northampton had recently crashed, and fearing that this balcony was indeed collapsing, many panicked and leaped from the structure onto the equally crowded first floor. In the pandemonium, five people were trampled to death.[70] Again a comparison with the Northampton incident is instructive. Edwards had interpreted the fact that no one died in his congregation as an act of providence, divine endorsement of the awakening underfoot in western Massachusetts. This time, the focus was not providential protection but the extraordinary divine outpouring of grace that produced numbers greater than buildings could contain.

PROMOTING WHITEFIELD IN THE COLONIES

A glimpse of Whitefield's itinerancies during his fifteen-month American mission from late 1739 through 1740 indicates that he undertook "the work of conversion" with indefatigable zeal. Although his official assignment was that of pastor at the Savannah, Georgia, church, he preached almost 350 public sermons outside his parish in three extended preaching tours (see table 3.2). The first began with his arrival at Lewis Town, Pennsylvania, on October 31, 1739; featured services that attracted large crowds throughout the Middle Colonies; continued with sporadic stops and much smaller assemblies in the Chesapeake and North Carolina; and concluded in Savannah on January 9, 1740. His spring itinerary originated on March 14 in Charleston, South Carolina, whence he departed after about a week for Pennsylvania. Throughout April and May Whitefield preached in the Middle Colonies, again attracting huge crowds. This time, he sailed from Lewis Town directly to Savannah,

TABLE 3.2
George Whitefield's American Preaching Tours, 1739–1741

	Number of Public Sermons		
	First Tour: Oct. 31, 1739– Jan. 9, 1740	Second Tour: Mar. 14– May 25, 1740	Third Tour: Sept. 15– Dec. 10, 1740
New England			
New Hampshire			6
Massachusetts			62
Connecticut			16
Rhode Island			5
Middle Colonies			
New York	8	11	12
New Jersey	10	14	13
Pennsylvania/ Delaware	30	42	24
Chesapeake			
Maryland	5		1
Virginia	1		
Lower South			
North Carolina	4		
South Carolina	3	46	30
Georgia	4		
Totals	65	113	169

Source: Whitefield's Journals, 338–502.

bypassing the Chesapeake and Carolinas. His arrival in Newport, Rhode Island. on September 15 marked the beginning of his third preaching tour. For about seven weeks he preached throughout New England. Then, after five more weeks in the Middle Colonies, Whitefield returned to Savannah.

While Jonathan Edwards's *Faithful Narrative* describes a community revival, Whitefield's *Journals* depict an intercolonial and even transatlantic awakening. Published in seven volumes beginning in summer 1738 and ending in winter 1741, the *Journals* follow the itinerant through England and Wales as well as on his first two American trips. An unpublished diary described the beginning of his third American journey. In the preface to the 1756 edition of the *Journals*, Whitefield reflected on the scope of recorded events: "Glory be to his holy Name! Multitudes both in England, Scotland, Wales, Ireland, and various parts of North America, have been brought to lodge under the branches of it. How far it is yet to spread can be known only to Him with whom the residue of the Spirit is."[71]

Whitefield's *Journals* chart the geographic spread of the Whitefieldian revival by analyzing the colonial sites where the evangelist preached to large groups of men and women. Whitefield recorded the names of towns where he attracted at least one thousand people on each of his three preaching tours. During his first trip, in the period extending from November 7 to December 3, 1739, he reported thirteen crowds exceeding a thousand, all but one of them (North East, Maryland) located in the Middle Colonies of New York, Pennsylvania, New Jersey, and Delaware. During one segment of his second journey—April 14 to May 25, 1740—he estimated congregations of at least one thousand on twenty-four occasions, all of them in the Middle Colonies. On his final preaching tour from September 15 through November 20, 1740, Whitefield again cited two dozen thousand-plus crowds: one in the South, twenty in New England, and three in the Middle Colonies. By his own account, Whitefield's attraction among Americans was limited primarily to the existing revival belts of New England and the Middle Colonies.

The biggest crowds assembled in colonial America's two largest cities, Boston and Philadelphia, each located in a revival region. On each of his three preaching tours, Whitefield made Philadelphia a center for his itinerating. From his first outdoor sermon there, he attracted progressively huger crowds, from the 6,000 who first gathered at the courthouse to hear him, to 8,000, and eventually 10,000 at the farewell sermon ending his first tour. At three subsequent Philadelphia services, Whitefield reported crowds of at least 10,000, and then during spring 1740 they swelled to 15,000 and reached the amazing number of 20,000, a figure that Franklin reported without dispute. Whitefield attracted similar crowds in Boston during the one trip he made there in fall 1740. For his farewell sermon delivered on Boston Common, he reported a gathering of 20,000, but two Boston newspapers estimated that 23,000 attended.[72]

Crowd reports also indicate those areas where Whitefield received a much cooler reception. Though New York City was almost as large as Boston or Philadelphia, it lacked a revival tradition that would have predisposed its population to receive Whitefield as one of their own. The largest crowd he attracted numbered approximately 5,000, far below the numbers in Boston and Philadelphia. Whitefield made hardly a

ripple in his single tour through the Chesapeake and the Carolinas. At
Joppa, Maryland, he reported a crowd that numbered 40. At Annapolis
he took comfort in the fact that the "small" assemblies hearing him
preach were also polite and curious. At Williamsburg, Virginia, "several
gentlemen" attended Whitefield's service. In Virginia and North Carolina, Whitefield repeatedly arrived at the announced preaching site only
to find tiny crowds. He explained the presence of so few by suggesting
that many more would have attended if "proper notice" had been given.
The only place south of Pennsylvania where a crowd of 1,000 or more
gathered was Charleston, South Carolina.[73]

By filling their pages with revival news, colonial newspapers extended
the awakening far beyond the revival districts of Boston and Philadelphia,
contributing to the perception of an event truly intercolonial in scope.
Eighteenth-century printer and historian of American printing Isaiah
Thomas described Whitefield as a hot news item that newspaper publishers covered extensively:

> This celebrated itinerant preacher, when he visited America, like a comet,
> drew the attention of all classes of people. The blaze of his ministration
> was extended through the continent, and he became the common topic
> of conversation from Georgia to Newhampshire. All the newspapers were
> filled with paragraphs of information respecting him, or with pieces of
> animated disputations pro or con; and, the press groaned with pamphlets
> written in favor of, or against, his person and ministry. In short, his early visits
> to America excited a great and general agitation throughout the country.[74]

Boston minister Thomas Prince provided a personal link between
Boston's print trade and the revival. According to Isaiah Thomas, Prince
had taken an "active part" in the publication of the *Weekly Journal* and
for a time "assisted in correcting the press." He was better known,
however, as a historian whose *Chronological History of New England* appeared in 1736. He had loved reading history from boyhood, when his
mother instilled in him "such a View of the Reformation" that he
considered it the most important historical event "next to the Scripture
History." In his chronology, he developed a "Connected *Line of Time*"
that ran from "the Creation to the Birth of Christ" and "From thence
to the Discovery of the New World," and "From thence to the Discovery
of New England."[75]

From Prince's perspective, something great that had been begun in
the New Testament and revived in the Reformation was being perfected
in New England. During the Great Awakening, Prince situated the

evangelical revival within his grand historical scheme primarily through the *Christian History,* a weekly revival magazine modeled on periodicals pioneered by London evangelicals to promote the revivals. Indeed, Prince's publication, which spanned a full two years, may be called America's first successful magazine. Two years earlier, Benjamin Franklin and Andrew Bradford had each started monthly periodicals patterned after the *Gentleman's Monthly,* but neither magazine survived the first six months. Prince succeeded in part by extending circulation throughout the transatlantic revival community. He broadened appeal by soliciting and printing accounts of awakenings in the Middle Colonies as well as New England, and in Scotland and Wales as well as America. He did not, however, escape criticism for his enthusiastic, unabashed support of the revivals. Charles Chauncy said of Prince that he knew of no "one that had more learning among us, except Doct. Cotton Mather." The revival critic added, though, that in covering the so-called great awakening Prince gave "too much credit to surprising stories."[76] However valid Chauncy's observation was, without doubt Prince's tireless, enthusiastic support contributed greatly to Whitefield's popularity in the colonies.

In the Middle Colonies, Whitefield's greatest supporter within the print trade was Benjamin Franklin. Unlike Kneeland and Green, Franklin was not a fervent evangelical who wished to promote the necessity of a new birth. Indeed, he had already turned away from his Presbyterian congregation and had embarked on a program of enlightened self-improvement. He often expressed his lack of interest in Whitefield's message, which Franklin found antirationalist and enthusiastic. However, the Philadelphia printer applauded Whitefield's preaching for its positive effects on the morals of men and women. Moreover, he genuinely liked Whitefield, perhaps seeing parallels between the Englishman and himself: both came from modest beginnings; both were entrepreneurs who had left the establishment and struck out on their own; and both came to Philadelphia as outsiders and took the city by storm. Of course, Franklin, always alert to a new business opportunity, saw Whitefield as a hot commodity whose popularity would sell books and newspapers.[77]

While printers were important in promoting the Great Awakening, American evangelical ministers were indispensable to Whitefield's success. As mediators between the visitor and colonial laypersons, pastors investigated the evangelist, pronounced him theologically sound, and recommended him to their parishioners. In tracking Whitefield's progress in America, one can conclude that, in most cases, strong endorsements by evangelical ministers greatly enhanced the itinerant's reception and effectiveness in a given community.

Within the Middle Colonies, Whitefield found powerful allies and sponsors among evangelical ministers who had been leaders in the region's revivals over the previous two decades. In the 1730s, Gilbert Tennent had led his congregation in a remarkable awakening. Upon meeting, Whitefield and Tennent found each other to be spiritual allies. When some Presbyterians criticized Whitefield's theology as being too Arminian, Tennent published a defense in the *Pennsylvania Gazette*. After reading Tennent's sermon attacking unconverted ministers, Whitefield expressed his view that the piece was "unanswerable." Thus it was not surprising that Whitefield asked Tennent to succeed him in New England, to water the seeds that he had sown.[78]

No one, however, was more aggressive or more effective than Benjamin Colman of Boston. As he had played a major role in telling the Northampton story, he also avidly promoted the Whitefieldian revival. Colman's endorsement and promotion of Whitefield's itinerancy lent instant credibility to the revival. Opponents who depicted followers of revivalists as largely unlettered and weak had difficulties in explaining the support of someone of Colman's erudition and standing. Not only was he a Harvard graduate, he served as a fellow and an overseer of the school and had been offered its presidency. Certainly nobody could accuse him of being a wild-eyed enthusiast. Indeed, by 1735, Colman, aged sixty-two, had established himself as the dean of Boston's ministers. He enjoyed a long pastorate, having served Brattle Street for thirty-six years since its founding in 1699 by many of Boston's leading merchants and civic leaders.

After receiving initial reports on Whitefield's doctrines and conduct in England, Colman corresponded with the evangelical sensation whose activities were already being reported in American newspapers. The Boston pastor noted that long before Whitefield's New England arrival, "some Letters had passed between him and me and my colleague Mr. Cooper. . . ." He wrote, "In mine I had expressed to him my joy that it had pleased the high God to raise up from the Bowels of Oxford a number of young Gentlemen to bear a zealous Testimony to the articles of the Church of England which . . . had for many years been generally [disobeyed?]."[79] Whitefield reciprocated with letters of his own, often enclosing copies of recently published or soon-to-be-published journals or sermons.[80]

Whitefield's writings appealed to Colman primarily for three reasons. First, they were theologically sound. After reading the revivalist's works, Colman expressed his adoration for "the Providence of God which orders this Testimony to the saving Truths of the Gospel and the right

Evangelical Articles of Faith upon which the Church reform'd from popery, as also to vital Religion and practical Godliness. . . ." In other words, Whitefield was reviving the great Reformation doctrines that, in Colman's opinion, had been dormant in too many churches. Second, Whitefield's ecumenical perspective appealed to Colman. Disenchanted with the Mathers' narrow view of the church, at the turn of the seventeenth century Colman had helped establish the Brattle Street Church on a "broad" and "catholick" foundation, incorporating in worship elements from the Anglican as well as the Congregational tradition, while eschewing narrow denominational beliefs and practices. No doubt he applauded Whitefield's refusal to succumb to pressure by dissenters to leave the Church of England and the evangelist's insistence that preaching the necessity of the new birth transcended sectarian distinctions. Whitefield succeeded in New England in part because he was able to revive, at least implicitly, the old belief in nonseparation. His preaching demonstrated that all English Protestants were still part of the same church. A third reason Whitefield's books and pamphlets had made an impression on Colman was precisely that they were the thoughts of an Anglican. The Methodists' critique of Anglicanism came "from the Hearts and Lives of a pious Number of her own Sons, not to be suspected of Prejudice against her by Education, but honour her Hierarchy and Liturgy, and in all Things conformable to her sacred Festivals."[81] Whitefield represented an insider who was leveling the same kinds of criticisms against the established church that dissenters had voiced for years.

While Colman was unclear about the revival's future course, he was certain that Whitefield was ushering in something new. "Whether this new Thing in our Day be eventually in Mercy or in Judgment with Respect to the Nation in general, and to the Church of England in particular, I know not," he wrote. But he knew it was novel. He distinguished between the current transatlantic awakening and such local revivals as the recent instance at Northampton. Colman declared that he had not "seen the like in our New-England Churches, altho' there have been, at Times, uncommon Operations of the holy Spirit on the Souls of many under the Ministry of the Word." Writing to Whitefield, he cited, for example, the awakening in Hampshire County, referring to "the Narrative of which by Mr. Edwards I suppose you may have seen." But he quickly added, "I do account the Impressions from God upon the Methodists (our dear Brethren) . . . to be something very extraordinary."[82]

Acting as Whitefield's press agent, Seward sent Colman a steady supply of the evangelist's latest printed works and newspaper accounts of his progress in other colonies. Colman acknowledged the impact of advance publicity in a sermon to his Brattle Street congregation. "The Fame of a singular servant and holy Youth, an extraordinary Servant and Minister of Jesus Christ . . . had prepar'd you for his Visit," Colman wrote in a sermon delivered after Whitefield's Boston appearance. Although he had been instrumental in promoting the itinerant in the local press, Colman downplayed his own efforts and indicated that "God gave him a wonderful Manner of Entrance among us." He concluded that it was with "raised Expectations we received" Whitefield, predisposed to hear him as the voice of a second Reformation.[83]

Colman was not alone in promoting Whitefield in New England. Jonathan Edwards opened the Connecticut Valley for the Whitefieldian revival. Shortly after the evangelist arrived, Edwards invited him to Northampton. He explained that he had received good reports of Whitefield and had become convinced that the itinerant was "one that has the Blessing of Heaven attending [him] wherever [he goes]." Edwards hoped that "Such a Blessing as attends your Person and Labours may descend on this town." However, Edwards warned Whitefield that New England would present a special challenge. "We who have dwelt in a Land that has been distinguish'd with Light," he wrote, "and have long enjoyed the Gospel, and have been glutted with it . . . are I fear more hardened than most." No doubt thinking of his own encounters with Anglican missionaries encroaching on his parish, Edwards expressed his pleasure that God had "raised up in the Church of England [one] to revive the mysterious Spiritual, despised and exploded Doctrines of the Gospel."[84]

When Whitefield arrived in the Connecticut Valley on October 17, 1740, he found the way well prepared by Edwards. Referring to the awakening of 1734–1735, Whitefield was aware that he was in a "place where a great work was carried on some years ago." In addition to opening his pulpit to Whitefield, Edwards introduced him to persons in surrounding towns such as Hadley, Westfield, and Springfield where he was greeted with large congregations.[85] While revival was familiar to evangelicals in the Connecticut River Valley, they for the first time eagerly embraced one who brought an "imported Divinity." To a large extent because of Whitefield's ministry, the "great awakening" begun six years earlier in Northampton had become a "general awakening" spanning the North Atlantic.

Though Whitefield triggered an intercolonial movement, he was only one of many who shaped the Great Awakening. After he departed in January 1741, the revival continued. Colonial ministers who supported the awakening worked hard to reinforce the good work under way, to counsel those who longed for a New Birth experience, to curb the excesses of overzealous preachers and parishioners, and to promote the spread of revival where it had not yet taken root. And lay men and women also contributed to the Great Awakening: they were not merely passive receptors who heard revival messages exactly as they were spoken or printed, and who responded as if scripted. On the contrary, they gave the Great Awakening a rich diversity through thousands of individual expressions, sometimes in ways that Whitefield could not have imagined.

CHAPTER 4

The "Revival at . . ."

THE WHITEFIELDIAN revival casts a huge shadow over the "great awakening." At times the Grand Itinerant, as some referred to George Whitefield, obscures the scores of lesser known evangelicals whose work shaped the transatlantic awakening, and his carefully staged outdoor services divert attention from the meetinghouses where revivals also occurred. As Whitefield moved through the colonies, he indeed attracted huge crowds and captured headlines, but the evangelical awakening was not coextensive with him. Some local revivals had been going on for months prior to his arrival, and many would continue long after his departure. For some communities, the Whitefieldian influence was strong, specific, and direct. Indeed, some revival leaders credited a Whitefield visit with igniting the local awakening.

In other places, however, the sway was more general and indirect. Of a Whitefield sermon in one community, the local pastor wrote that he "could observe no further influence upon our people by that address, than a general thoughtfulness about religion." The evangelist's presence did not trigger a revival. However, the minister did acknowledge that Whitefield's "extraordinary zeal and diligence" had made the gospel "the common and turning topic of [his parishioners'] conversation."[1] Elsewhere, parish ministers accorded even less credit to itinerants, including Whitefield, for promoting revival. "It is . . . very evident that this general Awakening was not from the Influence of travelling Ministers," reported the pastors of the two congregations in Wrentham, Massachusetts. They explained that "there was but one Sermon preached in the Town in such a Way, and that to a small Auditory." They too were careful not to minimize itinerants' activities in other churches, adding that they were "satisfied God has made Use of some of them for the revival of Religion in many Places."[2]

With or without help from itinerants, throughout the revival districts of New England and parts of New Jersey and Pennsylvania, communities created or invented their own awakenings during the late 1730s and early 1740s. This chapter focuses on those local revivals. It explores how ministers and laypersons promoted awakenings. And it examines the many varieties of revival as men and women considered afresh the old message of the new birth, looking at it always through local circumstances. In making their own awakenings, congregations drew upon revival traditions that predated Whitefield's ministry. Most followed strong pastors whose evangelistic preaching had effects on their congregations similar to those Whitefield's had on large outdoor crowds.

Preaching and other means of awakening sinners produced a wide variety of responses. In every community, residents filtered revival experiences through local social, cultural, economic, and demographic circumstances. Sometimes pro- and antirevival factions followed deeply etched social divisions deriving from long-remembered quarrels, such as bitter political struggles. One makes generalizations about socioeconomic causes of revivals at his or her own peril. Through case studies of individual congregations, historians have found, for example, that men and women embraced local revivals during both economic upswings and downturns. In some communities, prosperity produced guilt that only a revival castigating greedy sinners could assuage. But in other places a bleak economic future created despair that could be relieved only by spiritual rebirth. Hence local people did not refer to *the* Great Awakening but to *a* "great awakening" in their hometowns.

Local revivals, however, felt the influence of the larger awakening going on throughout the colonies. In some towns, itinerants or perhaps a visiting preacher on a pulpit exchange delivered a series of sermons that ignited sparks in an expectant church. John Cotton recalled that it was the outsider Eleazar Wheelock's sermon at Plymouth that produced "the first instance of any crying out among us." And, on occasion, ministers from New England or the Middle Colonies invited revivalist preachers from the other region to visit their congregations. Ebenezer Pemberton, Presbyterian minister in New York City, responded to one such invitation and preached a series of sermons in Boston during summer 1740, before Whitefield's first New England preaching tour. Though addressing primarily Congregational audiences, he sounded familiar themes such as the "Nature and Necessity of Conversion."[3] One of the Neshaminy Log College graduates, Samuel Finley, made an extensive trip through Connecticut preaching the necessity of the New Birth. Reciprocally, Congregationalist Daniel Rogers of Ipswich traveled from Massachusetts down into New York, New Jersey, and Pennsylvania, preaching mainly to receptive Presbyterians.

In addition to visiting preachers, news of awakenings elsewhere stimulated interest within a congregation. John Cotton observed that, even before Wheelock's sermon, the first steps toward revival occurred at a private meeting at his home, when people first learned of the Connecticut Valley awakening as Cotton "read to them Mr Edward's Narrative."[4] Revival publications wove scattered, local revivals into a seamless web. Printed sermons and apologies circulated in all the colonies and thus represented a powerful medium for linking the regional revivals into a whole. They constituted a common text that gave readers a shared vocabulary for describing and understanding their revival experiences. Works of revivalists in one region circulated in another, adding to the sense of a single Work of God. Jonathan Edwards's works enjoyed wide distribution and readership in the Middle Colonies, as did Jonathan Dickinson's in New England. Readers of each discovered that their messages were very similar, as if springing from a common source. And through newspaper reports and accounts reprinted in the *Christian History*, a steady supply of revival news, promoters kept subscribers in one region informed of events in other areas.

The Northampton account served as a blueprint for numerous congregations to stage and report their own awakenings.[5] This chapter examines how local revivals, despite their differences, assumed a certain sameness—especially in the telling, as revivalists constructed accounts of community awakenings through revival narratives, a new genre invented by eighteenth-century promoters. In a circular letter of spring 1743, Thomas Prince, Boston minister and historian, solicited revival narratives from pastors of congregations experiencing awakenings. In that request he expressed his belief that "*particular Accounts of the Revival of Religion in every Town*, in this remarkable Day of Grace, . . . would greatly tend to the glory of our Redeemer, and the Increase of his Triumphs." Prince included specific instructions and set forth a detailed outline for pastors to follow in composing their submissions. He asked pastors to send him as "*cautious and exact an Account as may be, of the Rise, Progress and Effects of this work among you to the present Day.*"[6] Published in the revival magazine entitled the *Christian History*, revival narratives were one of the important means of connecting local revivals into an intercolonial movement. During 1744 and 1745, Prince published about two dozen accounts of local awakenings, all from New England and the Middle Colonies. Appearing in successive issues, the scripted narratives contributed to the sense of a uniform revival spreading over the land.

LOCAL AND REGIONAL DIMENSIONS

The Whitefieldian revival tends to impose more uniformity on the awakenings occurring throughout the colonies than actually existed. To capture the Great Awakening's many hues, one must analyze it within a regional as well as an intercolonial framework. In the Middle Colonies the awakening was refracted through the region's great religious pluralism, with its myriad Protestant denominations and sects, many of which were avowedly evangelical, viewing the revival from a variety of theological and ethnic perspectives. In New England, where there was greater ecclesiastical uniformity, it was social and economic strain that gave the revival there a particular twist. And in the South, where the revival took root much later than it did in the northern colonies, the Anglican establishment and the "peculiar institution" of slavery gave that region's awakening a distinctive cast.

Middle Colonies

As the revival spread through the mid-Atlantic colonies, the region's religious pluralism was evident. As one scholar described the scene in the 1740s: "an overflow of New England Puritans shared New York with an older immigrant population of Reformed Dutch and French Huguenots. Scottish and Irish Presbyterians lived alongside enclaves of more Dutch in the Raritan valley of New Jersey and coexisted with English Quakers and Anglicans, Swedish and German Lutherans, as well as a variety of German sectarians beside the lower Delaware River and in the city of Philadelphia." As a result of the revival message's being sifted through different social and ethnic matrices, there emerged not one but several awakenings, calling into question the idea of "a single effort between Massachusetts and Georgia."[7]

Ethnicity and tradition played an important part in shaping the awakening experienced by German settlers in the Middle Colonies. Many Pietist emigrants entering the region during the early 1700s were disappointed to find that Old World ecclesiastical institutions had not been successfully transplanted to America. Instead, the diversity and voluntarism that characterized Pennsylvania religion had eroded church discipline and relaxed individual piety. At first, the revivals seemed to promise renewal, and many Germans welcomed the awakening. Although preaching a universal message that transcended ethnic distinctions, the revivals, at least in the short run, intensified German identity. According to one historian, "effective proclamation of the gospel in the German language, under German auspices, enabled the German settlers to retain their ethnic identity." He concluded that while the revival of religion "increased the German colonists' piety [it] also accentuated their group consciousness to such a degree that their religion became an ethnic as well as spiritual refuge."[8] In short, Germans, like the Scots-Irish, invented their own revivals out of beliefs and practices rooted in their European past.

German Pietism emerged from the Thirty Years War as a rejection of the religious certitudes and externalities that characterized both sides of that bloody conflagration. Instead of reasserting their faith in dogmatic creeds, Pietists stressed the inner light of personal spiritual experience, the new birth or conversion that gave rise to vital religion. The reformers "emphasized a return to primitive Christianity and interdenominationalism," rejecting the divisions that warring sects had created in the Christian world. To the Pietist theologian Philip Jacob Spener piety flourished best within individuals who met in small groups for mutual support through Bible study, prayer, and exhortation. Hence the individual, not an institution, again became the center of concern, especially in regard to salvation. However, Spener did not urge his followers to become ascetic hermits; he always thought in terms of individuals living within society. His was a practical Christianity: "He emphasized Bible study, lay participation in church government, and the practical nature of Christianity. Instead of doctrinal refinements, he urged 'practical' preaching and devotion."

Two centers of practical piety emerged within German Pietism. One was at Halle in Westphalia: under the leadership of August Hermann Francke, Halle became known throughout the Protestant world as a place where people practiced their faith daily. There an orphanage housed, educated, and nurtured hundreds of boys and girls. A dispensary sent medicines throughout Germany. And a printing press published tens of thousands of Bibles and devotional works and distributed them as far as India.

Count Nicholas Zinzendorf built a second and rival Pietist center on his estate at Herrnhut in Moravia. Although he had been nurtured and inspired by the believers at Halle, differences between the count and the Hallensians had become irreconcilable by 1734. The conflict involved personalities and principles. Zinzendorf and Francke were strong leaders with bold visions of spreading the practice of piety around Europe and beyond. When Zinzendorf began venturing out on his own in establishing missions, Francke viewed the count's enterprise as competition, as both men would seek donations in what Francke considered to be a fixed "international charity market." Beyond egos and competition, Zinzendorf and Francke held different theological views, especially on the "matter of conversion." Francke and the Hallensians subscribed to the view that salvation was by faith alone, but they also held that the process of redemption extended over a long, sometimes agonizing, period of time, during which believers remained uncertain whether they actually had saving grace. Thus a "time of sifting" preceded the assurance of a spiritual new birth. Zinzendorf and the Moravians believed in the "quick method" of salvation. Christ died for all, and as soon as one received forgiveness for his or her sins, one could in an instant be certain of salvation.[9]

Both Hallensian and Moravian Pietists came to America, and while each proclaimed the message of the "one thing needful," they also continued their squabbling and rivalry. While American revivalists had long followed Continental Pietism with great interest and embraced many of its major tenets, they were wary of some Pietists who arrived seeking converts. In the 1740s the Moravian leader Nicholas Zinzendorf hoped to establish in the Middle Colonies a Pietist movement where spiritual ties would be stronger than sectarian loyalties. He wished to seize upon the interdenominational cooperation already fostered by popular participation in the great awakenings. However, he soon discovered that while those influenced by Pietism shared a common commitment to the new birth and practical piety, they differed radically over ecclesiastical polity, rites, and doctrines. Some sects, such as the Dunkers and Seventh-Day Baptists, separated themselves from other groups in order to create "pure religious communities." Presbyterians and other confessionalists clung steadfastly to the practices and beliefs of their traditions. Thus ecumenists like Zinzendorf and the Moravians faced great opposition from those who refused to ignore "differences of creed or form."[10]

During the 1740s, revival among Lutherans in the Middle Colonies reflected the strong influence of German Pietism. The most direct means by which Continental evangelicalism was transmitted was through German immigrants and missionaries. In 1741, the elders of the Lutheran congregations at New Hannover, Providence, and Philadelphia in Pennsylvania asked Reverend Frederick Michael Zigenhagen, the London-based Hallensian minister and member of the Society for Promoting

Christian Knowledge, to send them an ordained minister. In 1742, Henry Melchior Muhlenberg, a graduate of Göttingen and a teacher sponsored by the Halle Pietists, arrived in Pennsylvania to assume his ministerial responsibilities.[11]

Muhlenberg arrived with characteristic Pietist zeal for missions, but before he could begin his evangelistic work, he confronted a challenge from the Moravian leader, Count Zinzendorf. The count and his lieutenant, Peter Bohler, had established a Lutheran consistory in Philadelphia, drafted articles of church governance, claimed church property, and assumed leadership of congregations, including those that had called Muhlenberg. Some Lutherans followed Zinzendorf, while others rejected him. Thus Muhlenberg found himself embroiled in a controversy between rival evangelical, pietistic groups. Rather than spreading the good news, German evangelicals, at least for the moment, brought chaos to Pennsylvania Lutherans.

In a heated confrontation, Zinzendorf and Muhlenberg laid bare the two expressions of German Pietism. Zinzendorf claimed that he was "inspector of all Lutheran churches in Pennsylvania and Lutheran pastor in Philadelphia," and that he had held synods, installed pastors, and deposed one minister. Muhlenberg denied his authority on the grounds that Zinzendorf was a Reformed preacher and had no standing with Lutherans. Zinzendorf retorted that Muhlenberg was no Lutheran either but a "Hallensian." The name-calling reflected personality and theological differences that had characterized German evangelicalism for years and prevented a united, cooperative evangelistic effort in America.[12] Despite the controversy, Muhlenberg carried out his ministerial duties with energy and purpose, preaching, catechizing, and visiting within his three congregations. He also traveled through Pennsylvania preaching to Lutherans in other locations. But wherever he went, he noticed division. While at Germantown, he observed "a fine group of Lutherans" but added that "the group is divided by factions." At Philadelphia there were many Reformed Germans, but they also were "divided into two parties."[13]

Revival in the Middle Colonies also undid the precarious unity among Presbyterian clergymen. Before the first wave of Ulster immigration in the early 1700s, three presbyteries and the Synod of Philadelphia provided order and discipline for Middle Colony Presbyterians. The presbyteries maintained contact with the brethren through visitations that brought the governing bodies to widely dispersed communities. They exercised "oversight of local congregations and ordained and disciplined the clergy." As the head of the church's supervisory structure, the synod "provided a forum where clerical disputes over church doctrine and governing authority could be resolved." Throughout the 1720s and 1730s the presbyteries and synod were able to mediate disputes, foster harmony, and enforce moral discipline. The key to successful governance was clerical solidarity; as long as the clergy closed ranks, tensions within and between congregations could be suppressed. In 1738, the ministerial ranks split asunder under a "steady assault from an evangelical faction in the church" who insisted on forming their own presbytery to "facilitate the ordination of evangelical preachers." In one historian's words, the "stage was set for a showdown that would shatter ministerial unity, elevate discontent within congregations, and usher in the great awakening."[14]

Although the synod had witnessed ministerial disputations before, the clergy had been able to resolve differences and continue to lead their presbyteries and congregations. However, the 1738 ruling making a university degree the prerequisite for licensure produced an irreconcilable rift. The antirevivalist Old Side faction insisted on a rationalist approach to faith that expressed itself in subscribing to correct doctrine, prompting their opponents to charge them with embracing a lifeless religion of the head. Old Siders advocated a proper university education for all ministers, preferably to be undertaken in English and European institutions where rational thought and pure doctrine prevailed. The revivalist New Side faction opposed rationalist tendencies toward an empty, "ceremonial way of worship" and advocated instead experiential Christianity, or religion of the heart. To their leader, William Tennent, Sr., a genuine conversion experience, not book learning that often produced intellectual conceit, qualified one for the ministry. The two opposing factions reflected differences in taste and style. The Old Side was dominated by older clergymen born in Northern Ireland. The New Side were the younger ministers born, for the most part, in the colonies. The Old Siders preferred traditional worship according to prescriptions set forth in the Westminster Confession. The New Siders were much more receptive to innovation and thus "tended to clothe their appeals in popular dress."[15] The division among the clergy had the unintended consequence of empowering the Presbyterian laity, giving them a choice—a power they exercised with their feet by attending the services of one or the other side, whichever better satisfied their needs. In a real sense, then, the revival in the Middle Colonies represented the "Triumph of the Laity."[16]

Thus the Middle Colonies' religious pluralism was a prism that refracted the Great Awakening into many different hues and shades. And the region's ethnic diversity further expanded the spectrum of revival experience. The result was that the awakening appeared far less united there than it did as it unfolded in the other great revival region to the north.

New England

Though accustomed to "great awakenings," New Englanders experienced something entirely new in the revival of the 1740s. For the first time, ministers from outside the region played major roles. Boston pastor John Webb was clear about the "present Work's" origins: "The Revival of God's Work, after a long time of dead Security, was begun here some Months past," he wrote in 1741, "by the painful and successful Ministry of the Reverend Mr. Whitefield." He added that it was continued by another outsider, Gilbert Tennent, "whose awakening Ministry, God has likewise own'd and succeeded, in a surprizing Manner."[17] In that same year, another Boston pastor, Joseph Sewall, acknowledged the positive influence of revival reports arriving in New England from the Middle Colonies. "As more lately," he wrote, "we have receiv'd *good News* of this Kind from more distant Places on this Continent."[18] Though the great work did not originate in New England, Sewall expressed his thanks that "God hath brought this Work home to our Doors" through print and the preaching of itinerants like Tennent.[19]

Jonathan Edwards differentiated between the Connecticut Valley revivals of 1735–1736 and the intercolonial awakenings of 1739–1745. In the *Faithful Narrative*, he made no connection between the Northampton awakening and the coming millennium. He reminded his readers that the revival had broken out in a "remote part" of one country. To him, such a localized affair was insufficient evidence of a revival powerful enough to usher in the millennium—the last and most glorious revival. In 1739, he continued to resist speculating on when and where the millennium would begin: "We know not where this pouring out of the Spirit shall begin, or whether in *many* places at once, or whether what has already taken place ben't some forerunner and beginning of it." As Whitefield swept through America and Edwards read accounts of gospel successes around the globe, however, doubt turned to hope. Edwards expressed in a 1740 letter to Whitefield his "*hope* [that] this is the dawning of a day of God's mighty power."[20]

In its New England phase, the Great Awakening expressed itself in local revivals in living communities with unique histories and current problems. When an awakening sprang up in a town, whether arriving from the outside via an itinerant like Whitefield or generated from within by the local pastor, men and women responded to it as social beings beset by all sorts of issues including social tensions, economic challenges, and political struggles. Because New England revivals of the 1740s often occurred in a context of controversy and division, local awakenings assumed many different dimensions, shaped by nonreligious as well as religious forces.

Consider the social and political atmosphere that pervaded Massachusetts towns at the revival's outset. As Whitefield toured New England in fall 1740, the Boston press debated a controversial money measure in highly moral terms. At issue was the suspension of Massachusetts currency and two proposals for issuing new credit instruments. One, favored by the wealthiest merchants, would establish a Silver Bank, which would restrict the amount of cash in circulation to the silver supply. The other, advocated by farmers and smaller merchants, called for a Land Bank, whereby landholders would receive legal tender notes with land as security. Supporters of both ideas cast the argument in moral terms.

An advocate of the Land Bank saw the matter as a contest between "good" and "bad" people. In a letter to the *Post-Boy*, the writer praised every farmer who "by his Labour and Industry supply'd us with the Necessaries of Life, without which we could not subsist." Also praiseworthy was the merchant "who takes from the Countryman all his Surplus, he takes his Timber, his Plank, he builds Ships, he loads them with his Grain and all other the Produce of his Ground, (and then on his own Account and Risque, sends them abroad, the Produce is return'd in valuable Commodities and Cash) for all these Things bought of the Countryman he pays his Cash." The cooperative relationship between farmer and merchant had important religious consequences: with cash received from trade, the countryman could "pay his Taxes to his Country and Ministers, with great ease and Pleasure."[21]

But not all merchants pursued the public good. Some "out of mere Principle of Self-Interest, and [with] no View to the Good of the Country, heap upon us Such vast Quantities of Goods, the whole Produce of the Land is not able to repay." One result is a money drainage from New England to Britain. The other is economic dependence. By extending credit and making "Payment so easy," merchants ensnare countrymen in a web of extravagance and dependence. "The Truth is this," the writer explained, "There is Hundreds of honest House-keepers, who, if they were paid in Cash for their Work, would many Times look on their Money before they would give it to buy their Wives and Daughters Velvet Hoods, red Cloaks, or Silk Garments!" The Land Bank proposal would provide cash that would check such "imbounded Extravigancies" and release people from "dependency on greedy Merchants."[22]

Itinerants brought merchants a message that attacked the sources of their guilt directly. First, speaking with extraordinary authority, the revivalists confronted the new traders with their sin of worldliness. As one preacher stated, the business of Christians "is not to hunt for Riches, and Honours, and Pleasures in this World, but to despise them, and deny themselves, and be ready to part with even all the lawful Pleasures and Comforts of the World at any Time." Many responded by admitting their sins, repudiating their worldliness, and "casting off with great relief their guilt-producing ambition." Second, the itinerants provided the means to end the merchants' long struggle with the social order by denying its authority to save. Whitefield and others reminded their listeners that only God's grace was sufficient for salvation. Civil and religious leaders could advocate and even insist upon moral behavior and obedience to law, but they could not save. Thus the new birth cleansed the converts of guilt and implanted within them an internal authority, producing inner peace and confidence. One historian noted that converts expressed their redemption in bold action: "reborn men set out to create a new society compatible with the vision opened in the Great Awakening."[23]

In a study of church records and membership lists of Land and Silver Banks of 1740, one scholar found that "Land Bankers worshiped preponderantly at New Light Congregational churches or at Congregational churches that had both Old Light and New Light elements, [and] Silver Bankers worshipped mostly at Anglican and Old Light Congregational churches."[24] While Whitefield's supporters and opponents did not divide neatly along lines of the currency controversy, they nevertheless interpreted the evangelist's message to defend their positions.

Revivalists in Worcester County, Massachusetts, were united by their adherence to the Land Bank proposal. Five of the New Light ministers were participants in the Land Bank, having mortgaged their properties. Seven of the county's nine New Light congregations were located in towns where Land Bankers were strongly represented. On the other hand, all but two of the sixteen Old Light congregations were situated in towns where only a few Land Bankers resided. Ironically, while the

Great Awakening appealed to many advocating new, more inflationary and democratic monetary proposals, New Lights also responded to the revivalists' call for "submission to traditional, deferential, corporate unity and harmony" rather than religious individualism.[25]

Although socioeconomic issues shaped the contours of local revivals, a focus limited to events external to churches is reductive. In some cases, ministers invented revivals in order to address ecclesiastical, not socioeconomic issues. The pastor of First Church, Norwich, Connecticut, Benjamin Lord, welcomed the Great Awakening to buttress his congregation's membership. From the beginning of his pastorate in 1717 to 1740, only one-fifth of those who became halfway members eventually owned the covenant and became full members. His problem was that "halfway membership was a permanent stopping place for most of those within his church." And because halfway members were not as committed as the visible saints, Lord was unhappy with the spiritual well-being of his flock. Moreover, the creation of four new congregations within Norwich removed taxpayers who had supported First Church. Of particular concern to Lord was the effect of those removals on his annual salary of 100 pounds current money. According to his records, yearly "failure of payment" ranged from 7 pounds, 10 shillings, to 85 pounds, which along with steady inflation, resulted in his falling nearly 1,000 pounds behind the "just amount" due him.[26]

To Lord, the great awakening represented a solution to the First Society's membership problems. He sought to foster revival in his own congregation because "full membership in the church would be increased and halfway members brought to the communion table by the only means conceivable within the covenant theology—a satisfactory conversion experience which could be related to the church." Although Whitefield did not visit Norwich, Lord succeeded in attracting such revivalist preachers as Jonathan Parsons and Eleazar Wheelock, who possessed "ability to rouse the people." The evangelists sparked an awakening unmatched in the church's history. Between 1741 and 1744, ninety-one men and women joined the church in full communion, an annual rate six times higher than that of the previous twenty-three years. And more members meant more funds available for the pastor's salary; "for the first time in Lord's ministry, he was not only paid what he considered was an equitable salary, but was actually overpaid for the years 1742, 1743, and 1744!" Cutting across socioeconomic lines, the awakening at Norwich seems to have been primarily a religious solution to a religious problem.[27]

The experience in Woodbury, Connecticut, was similar. There too the awakening occurred primarily within the church itself, attracting mainly sons and daughters of full communicants. In a case study of the First Church of Woodbury, one historian took seriously the "possibility that the Awakening originated among people attuned to emotional religious stimuli." His analysis of the family background of persons joining the congregation during the revivals found that about 70 percent came from long-resident church members, another 9 percent from long-resident nonmembers, and just 22 percent from families new to the community. In other words, the awakening did not "generate communicants from a large mass of persons basically indifferent to religion or to the church." Nor was the revival a form of social protest by the "economically disadvantaged"; rather, it attracted people from every economic class. Woodbury converts did not fit the stereotype some have suggested: that the "typical convert . . . [was] a man on the make, tormented by his own prosperity." There, most converts were young people still living at home with their parents.[28]

Age was also significant in Andover, Massachusetts. Founded in 1646, the town was almost a century old at the time of the great awakening. For many, Andover was a stable community that offered a comfortable life with prospects for a secure future. But for others, especially younger sons among the fourth generation, partible inheritance worked against them. Possessing acreage only a fraction of that farmed by their fathers and grandfathers, many moved west, south, and north to towns elsewhere in Massachusetts, in Connecticut, and in New Hampshire. After exploring the lives of Andover families over four generations, one scholar speculated that "there might very well be a close connection between their physical mobility, with all that it implies of the uprooting, the dislocations, the anxieties experienced by those who left, and their heightened religious needs and religious experiences." He noted that many of the towns receiving Andover's emigrants "were caught up in the revivals of the 1720's and 1740's." "In contrast," he observed, "many of those who remained behind in Andover failed to be touched by the Awakening, and Andover itself was an Old Light, nonrevivalist town during the 1740's."[29]

Virginia

With the exception of Whitefield's single trip through the southern colonies in 1739, the Chesapeake and Lower South had remained beyond the Great Awakening in the early 1740s. But by 1745 a small group of persons in Virginia's Piedmont had made connections with the larger awakening. The story of how those evangelicals, mainly lay men and women, introduced the revival to Anglican Virginia, with assistance from New Jersey Presbyterians, underscores both its regional distinctiveness and intercolonial connections.

A great awakening came to Virginia's Piedmont in the 1740s during a period of expansion and prosperity. Something of a boom occurred in the western counties of Hanover, Henrico, Louisa, Goochland, and Caroline as a result of population growth and the expansion of the tobacco culture into the region. The problem for Piedmont growers was how to finance and market their leaf in order to compete with that of the more established Tidewater. Virginia law worked against the western-ers. The Tobacco Inspection and Warehouse Act of 1730 "passed with the support of British merchants and Tidewater planters over the objec-tion of farmers outside the Tidewater area." Piedmont growers protested the fact that the law favored established Tidewater warehouses and down-graded tobacco damaged in overland transportation. Dissatisfied with the arrangement, Piedmont farmers, beginning around 1740, turned to Scottish factors, who provided farmers with financial and marketing services that opened European markets to Piedmont tobacco. The Glas-gow agents built warehouses in the western counties along the fall line and, through the direct purchase of tobacco, provided farmers with instant capital. The Scots brought something else to the region: an evangelical tradition and evangelistic desire that had great influence in encouraging revival in the Piedmont.[30]

Established in 1704, St. Paul's Parish in Hanover County had become home to persons with Scottish and Ulster backgrounds from its earliest settlement. Fueled by immigration from Scotland, the region along the Pamunkey River developed a culture tinged with strong Scottish influ-ences. The first public mention of Hanover County in the colony's only newspaper underscored that culture. The October 7, 1737, edition of the *Virginia Gazette* included this announcement: "We have advice from Hanover County that on St. Andrew's Day, being the 30th of November next, there are to be Horse Races and several other Diversion for the Entertainment of the Gentlemen and ladies. . . ." For some Hanoverians, their Scottish heritage involved religious issues and observances far more significant than celebrations inspired by Scotland's patron saint.

In the late 1730s, a small group of Virginians separated from St. Paul's parish in Hanover County. Mostly of Scottish and Ulster descent, the lay men and women had grown "deeply disturbed about the religious condition" in their community and believed that the minister, Patrick Henry, was incapable of providing spiritual sustenance. One of the dissenters, Roger Shackleford, said that Henry was an "unconverted graceless man" who preached "damnable doctrine." Moreover, he expressed his belief that the overseer of American Anglicans, the bishop of London, was also an unconverted man. One of the separatists, Samuel Morris, a bricklayer, was a self-educated Bible student, and "his study of Luther's commentary on Galatians convinced him that [his] need could not be filled in his parish church." Thus Morris and his friends "concerted to disregard the law requiring their attendance at church."[31]

In lieu of worshipping at St. Paul's, Morris and his friends began convening in private homes on Sundays to read sound Reformation doctrine. What they discovered in the few books they possessed were teachings compatible with the religious heritage of their Scottish and Ulster parents and grandparents. Of particular appeal was a book of Whitefield's sermons that they had acquired in 1743 from a "young Scotch gentleman" passing through Hanover County. With Morris acting as their elder, the dissenters organized themselves into a lay-led congregation. Morris built a reading-house on his land to provide a place for the group to meet and read from the Bible and other works. In addition to conducting services at that site, Morris became an itinerant reader in Hanover and surrounding counties, gathering several other reading groups and exhorting people in the necessity of the new birth and the discipline of practical piety. Soon reading-houses abounded: two more in Hanover County, one at David Rise's farm and another at Stephen Leacy's place; one in Henrico Country at Thomas Watkins's; another on the land of Joseph Shelton in Louisa County; one at Tucker Woodson's in Goochland County; and one at John Sutton Needwood's in Caroline County.[32]

The names of those who organized reading groups underscore the dissenters' diverse social backgrounds. While many were of "humble birth," like the bricklayer Morris, others enjoyed social prominence and political influence. Joseph Shelton was a gentleman, "a prosperous planter, an official in local government, and an active dissenter." Another member of the Hanover gentry, Isaac Winston, Sr., was fined for conducting dissenting services in his home in violation of Virginia's Act against Conventicles. Either in deference to Winston's social standing or in sympathy with his religious views, the jury, while finding that "people did assemble at the house of the defendant," concluded that the meeting was not "riotous" and did not violate "the canons of the Church of England." Clearly, dissent in Piedmont Virginia enjoyed support across social lines.[33]

As Virginia's dissenters increased in number, the colony's political leaders grew more concerned about their separation from the established Church of England. Consequently, Governor William Gooch summoned the group's leaders to Williamsburg to explain themselves to the magistrates. Without any formal denominational affiliation, Morris and the other emissaries presented the governor and council with a book that "expressed their views on the doctrines of religion." Of Scottish Presbyterian origin, Gooch recognized the tenets as those of the Presbyterian Church and pronounced the band Presbyterians. Moreover, he concluded that the book was "the Confession of Faith of the Presbyterian Church of Scotland; and that they were not only tolerated but acknowledged as part of the Presbyterian Church of Scotland."[34]

The Virginia dissenters wanted to deepen their faith and desired a minister who could assist them in their spiritual growth and spread the gospel to hungry souls in the Piedmont. With no suitable evangelical clergymen in Virginia, the Hanoverians petitioned the New Light Presbyteries of New Brunswick (New Jersey) and New Castle (Pennsylvania) to send them a minister "to officiate for some time among them." Although in Hanover for only a week, Log College graduate William Robinson accomplished much. He helped the lay dissenters put their church "in regular order" according to New Light beliefs. And through his open-air preaching, he attracted people from all over the region to hear his evangelistic message. When Robinson returned to New Jersey, he left "a General Concern about Religion . . . through the neighborhood, and some hundreds . . . were brought anxiously to enquire what shall we do to be saved?"[35] The strong connection between the presbytery at New Castle and the Virginians persisted. Next, the New Lights sent John Roan, another Log College graduate, who was "instrumental in beginning and promoting the religious concern in several places where there was little appearance of it before." Other mid-Atlantic revivalists who preached in Virginia included William Tennent, Samuel Blair, and Samuel Davies. In 1745, Davies led Virginia Presbyterians in petitioning Governor William Gooch to grant New Light preachers liberty to preach among them.[36]

From the beginning, the Hanover revival displayed a strong Scottish influence. Morris acknowledged the importance of the volume of Whitefield sermons the group had obtained from a Glaswegian gentlemen traveling in Virginia. He added that the sermons had been preached in Glasgow and taken down in shorthand by a Scot. William Robinson had received his theological training at William Tennent's Log College, an institution steeped in Scottish evangelical traditions. Later, Gilbert Tennent and Samuel Davies would also visit the Virginia dissenters. When Davies arrived as the group's first permanent pastor, he instituted "protracted meeting[s] modeled after the Scottish sacramental festivals" that New Light Presbyterians had continued in the Middle Colonies. Morris described the initial sacramental meeting as "the first administration of that heavenly ordinance among us since our dissent from the Church of England," and observed that "the novelty of the mode of administration did peculiarly engage" the Hanoverian dissenters.[37]

For Hanover's New Lights, when Whitefield finally visited western Virginia in 1745, the occasion was memorable. One wrote a lengthy account that was published in the *Virginia Gazette.* What the reporter found noteworthy were the same things that had elicited comment wherever the itinerant preached: his dramatic delivery, the size of the crowd, and the audience's response. The correspondent wrote: "I was present at several of his sermons, which he delivered off hand, with all the graces of action and voice, and with all the success which an easy extempore delivery is apt to have with such as never saw anything like it before. . . . Such was the universal attention, when he preached at church in particular that tho' we were very much throng, there was nothing to interrupt him, but every now and then a groan or sob from his hearers."[38]

When John Gillies published his *Historical Collections* in 1754, he included a section describing the Virginia revival of the 1740s. Relying heavily upon Samuel Davies's account, Gillies captured the local and regional differences that gave the Virginia awakening its distinctive color. But he also saw the Piedmont Work as part of the intercolonial revival, noting in his running account of the Great Awakening that in 1743 "the same Work spreads to Virginia."[39]

While promoters considered the revival that entered Virginia in the mid-1740s to be "the same Work" as that in the northern colonies, Virginia's slave society gave the Great Awakening a dimension not seen in New England and the Middle Colonies. Indeed, one of the reasons for the awakening's remaining localized in the Piedmont, with its relatively low concentration of slaves, was the long-standing fear among Tidewater slaveholders that religion could plant the wrong notions in slaves' heads. Virginia planters had followed with interest and alarm New York's slave conspiracy of 1741 and no doubt believed the speculation that revivalist ideas of redemption had fueled the uprising. They were right. Slaves filtered the revivalists' message through their experience in bondage. According to one historian studying the effects of the "great awakening" on the New York conspiracy, "African-Americans gave their own revolutionary meanings to the [revivals], spreading stubborn rumors that baptism meant freedom." In the words of an Anglican missionary, "the Negroes have this notion, that when they are baptized, they are immediately free from their masters."[40] The precise connection between the awakening and the conspiracy of New York slaves is unclear. To at least one New York clergyman, John Ury, however, the link was direct: "it was through the great encouragement the negroes had from Mr. Whitefield, we had all the disturbance."[41] Whatever the relation between revival and rioting, slaves invented their own notions of what the "new birth" meant. To slaveholders in the Chesapeake, evangelists who ignored such fundamental boundaries as race and servitude could only sow dangerous seeds of social disorder.

Region, as well as race and ethnicity, shaped local responses to the awakening in the Chesapeake and the Carolinas. The greatest disparity is evident between areas dominated by the Church of England and those with strong dissenting traditions. Although the revival came late to Virginia, it challenged the local standing order. The Church of England promoted a highly structured ritual prescribed by the Book of Common Prayer. Lay participation was generally restricted to prayer book reading and rare congregational singing. To many, the predictability and regularity of Anglican worship was comforting, furnishing stability "amid the confusion engendered by new landscapes, new settlements, new elites, new labor, and new forms of government."[42]

But other Virginians longed for a more participatory, emotional worship experience. For them, the evangelical revival liberated the laity from the staid constraints imposed by ancient authors of prayer books. With their denomination's emphasis on congregational singing, extemporaneous lay praying, and voluntary testifying, Baptists afforded a welcomed alternative for many. As one minister reported, even when a preacher could not be present, "our people meet notwithstanding, and spend . . . time in praying, singing, reading, and in religious conversation."[43]

Many laypersons in Virginia responded to the revival by redefining the Christian ordinances of baptism and the Lord's Supper. While ministers continued to administer the rituals, the congregations participated much more fully than in the Anglican tradition. A Baptist minister, Daniel Fristoe, described the spontaneity that characterized one baptismal service. "When I had finished [baptizing]," he wrote, "we went to a field and making a circle in the center, there laid hands on the persons baptized. The multitude stood round weeping, but when we sang *Come we that love the lord* they were so affected that they lifted up their hands and faces towards heaven and discovered such chearful countenances in the midst of flowing tears as I had never seen before."[44] Similarly, revivalist audiences favored a more "open enactment" of communion.

The only other area in the southern colonies where the great awakening had considerable support was Charleston, South Carolina. Despite being the residence of the Anglican commissary, Alexander Garden, one of the revival's severest critics, Charleston had some ardent, confident dissenting ministers with strong ties to New England revivalists. Josiah Smith was one of Whitefield's ablest apologists. He wrote a defense of the itinerant's character and preaching that was published in Boston and Philadelphia. A Harvard graduate, Smith had attracted the attention of Benjamin Colman, William Cooper, and other Boston evangelicals. At Smith's ordination in 1726, Colman said that "no one has risen among us and gone from us so suddenly, with like esteem, affection and applause, as Mr. Smith has done."[45] He commended the young preacher for his sermons on the "blessed and saving Operations" of Christ. Another Charleston dissenter, Isaac Chanler, joined Smith in promoting the revival in South Carolina. Chanler also published proawakening sermons that were published in Boston, and he conducted evangelistic services at a special Wednesday evening lecture set up by Whitefield.[46] While the revival did not spread very deeply in South Carolina culture, Charleston was a bright beacon that reinforced revivalists' convictions that the awakening was indeed intercolonial.

REVIVAL NARRATIVES: A COMMON SCRIPT

Though men and women experienced revivals as local and regional events, and awakenings were as diverse as the communities that gave each its distinctive color and texture, they were connected to a larger, overarching intercolonial revival. Unlike earlier awakenings prior to those of the mid-1730s, local revivals after Northampton and Freehold, and especially after Whitefield's visit, were linked together in a much more far-flung movement. Never before had outside forces and outsiders so influenced religious life within local parishes and communities. Two types of ligatures bound local and regional revivals into the Great Awakening. First, through itinerant preachers traveling from one community to another and pastors exchanging pulpits, men and women participated in a revival whose origins and scope transcended that of a single congregation. Second, through published work, such as newspaper reports, revival narratives, a revival magazine, revival sermons, revivalists' diaries and journals, persons separated by great distances were drawn together into a revivalist "imagined community" by reading about events in remote places that sounded very similar to ones at home.[47] They found in a common body of literature a familiar vocabulary describing familiar experiences.

Of all the revival publications, none fostered a stronger sense of connection among local awakenings than that of revival narratives. This new genre, a creation of the Great Awakening, recast accounts of local awakenings with all their variety into a common format. The result was that, *as reported*, local revivals assumed a greater degree of uniformity than they did *as experienced*. As the revival narratives circulated throughout colonial America, they confirmed for believers their hope that they were partakers of the same divine dispensation. They were aware that as they found the new birth, others in distant locations had similar conversions. Through the efforts of promoters eager to advance not only local but global revival, like-minded persons participated in an awakening that extended far beyond their parish borders. Revival narratives played an important role in depicting local awakenings as being part of the same Work of God and occurring in many congregations throughout the northern provinces. As William Seward—Whitefield's traveling companion, who acted as his press agent—departed for England in spring 1740, he reflected on the colonial revival as a single awakening, calling it "the Work of God in America." He referred to the present as "this Day of God's Visitation" when men and women in "*England* and *America*, hear the *Gospel preached with Power*, and in its *Purity*."[48]

Adding to the sense of a united, intercolonial revival was the fact that the revival narratives were collected and published in the same place, appearing first as serial installments in the *Christian History*, and then bound together in a two-volume work by the same title as a single, unified testimony of revival in colonial America. All of the published accounts of local awakenings follow a similar format, covering the same topics in the same sequence. The reason for this uniformity becomes clear when one looks at the instructions that called them into being in the first place. In early 1743, Thomas Prince, the *Christian History*'s publisher and editor, solicited accounts from pastors through a printed circular letter setting forth a detailed outline of what he wanted. He also indicated that the accounts would appear alongside each other in his revival magazine. His instructions revealed his assumption that the contributors were providing local expressions of a single event. The purpose of the narratives, he wrote, was "To give an Account of the Rise, Progress and effects, of the said Work."[49]

He asked contributors to document details in their communities that pointed to the Work of God. He requested that each write a "*Particular* Account *of the most remarkable Instances* of the Power and Grace of God, both in *convincing* and *converting* Sinners, and in *edifying* Converts in Knowledge, Faith, Holiness, Love to God and their Neighbours, divine Joys, and an answerable Life and Conversation." Further clarifying the scheme he wished each pastor to follow, Prince added,

> And in *convincing* and *converting* Sinners, it is desired you would take an especial Notice of *remarkable Instances* of the Power and Grace of God on these *four Sorts* of People.
>
> 1. *Young* Persons
> 2. *Immoral* Persons
> 3. The *Opposers* of this Work at first
> 4. Those who have been before in Repute for *Morality* and *Religion*.[50]

Aware that the narrators were describing current events, Prince indicated that "*Names* may be omitted; *especially* those *alive*." While interested in protecting the privacy of converts, he was also concerned about the credibility of the accounts. Therefore, he wrote, "We doubt not but you are willing to venture forth *your own Name*, as a *Witness* for our divine Lord who hath so highly favoured you. And it will probably be for his greater Service, if you send such *Attestations* as you may think proper of some *creditable Persons* well acquainted with the Rise, Progress and Effects of the Work among you; either of the *Work* and *Fruits in General*, or of any *remarkable Parts* thereof." Finally, Prince recognized that the revival was ongoing, and that the narratives would probably require updating. He concluded his circular letter by expressing his hope that contributors would "*continue* the like Accounts and *transmit* them from Time to Time, especially when any Thing *remarkable* of this Nature happens."[51]

In a surviving copy of Prince's letter, he assured the recipient that his suggested format was flexible. At the bottom, he added a handwritten note: "The above are Hints; But Please to follow your own Method; and also to give an Account of what you have seen in other Places." Most

Rev & Dear Sir,

IT being earnestly defired by many pious and judicious People, that *particular Accounts* of the *Revival* of *Religion* in *every Town*, in this remarkable Day of Grace, may be taken and publifhed in THE CHRISTIAN HISTORY, judging it would greatly tend to the Glory of our REDEEMER, and the Increafe of his Triumphs; and being informed of the *Revival* of this happy Work in *your Congregation :* This comes therefore to intreat you, *for that Purpofe,* to fend me *as cautious and exact an Account as may be, of the Rife, Progrefs and Effects of this Work among you to the prefent Day ;* as alfo to *excite other fuitable Perfons to do the like :* And to fend the fame, *free of Charge.*

In which it is apprehended advifeable,

I. To give an Account of the Rife, Progrefs and Effects, of the faid Work *in a more General Way ;* and *after that,*

II. A *more Particular* Account of the *moft Remarkable Inftances* of the Power and Grace of GOD, both in *convincing* and *converting* Sinners, and in *edifying* Converts in Knowledge, Faith, Holinefs, Love to GOD and their Neighbours, divine Joys, and an anfwerable Life and Converfation.

And in *convincing* and *converting* Sinners, it is defired you would take an efpecial Notice of *remarkable Inftances* of the Power and Grace of GOD on thefe *four Sorts* of People.

1. *Young* Perfons.
2. *Immoral* Perfons.
3. The *Oppofers* of this Work at firft.
4. Thofe who have been before in Repute for *Morality* and *Religion.*

But *their Names* may be omitted ; *efpecially* thofe *alive.*

We doubt not but you are willing to venture forth *your own Name,* as a *Witnefs* for our divine LORD who hath fo highly favoured you. And it will probably be for his greater Service, if you fend fuch *Atteftations* as you may think proper of fome *creditable Perfons* well acquainted with the Rife, Progrefs and Effects of the Work among you ; either of the *Work* and *Fruits* in *General,* or of any *remarkable Parts* thereof.

And *laftly,* 'tis defired that you would *continue* the like Accounts and *tranfmit* them from Time to Time ; efpecially when any Thing *remarkable* of this Nature happens.

And fo may the GOD of all Light, Power, Grace and Comfort be continually with, direct, affift, blefs and profper you ; is the Prayer of

Your humble Servant,

Bofton, *April. 18. 1743.*   *Thomas Prince*

The above are hints; But pleafe to follow your own method; en alfo to give an account of what you have feen in other places.

2. Thomas Prince's solicitation of revival narratives

pastors who submitted narratives, however, adhered closely to his printed instructions.

While not mentioning the circular letter, historian Michael Crawford's analysis of all the revival narratives uncovered Prince's structure. Each included:

1. a brief history of the town, especially the state of religion before the present pastor's arrival;

2. a statement of spiritual decline manifested usually by "religious formality" and unwholesome behavior, especially such vices as "tavern haunting" among the youth;

3. a description of the revival's origins and spread, with emphasis on the nature and frequency of awakening sermons;

4. a picture of moral reformation often reflecting a switch from tavern haunting to religious meetings;

5. some analysis of the types of people awakened, including age, gender, and spiritual history;

6. an examination of religious experiences, with emphasis on degrees of terror, joy, etc.;

7. a comment on extraordinary "bodily effects";

8. accounts of selected individuals' conversions;

9. assessment of the revival's effects over time, including testimony regarding new convictions and those suggesting backsliding;

10. attestation that the awakening was a "genuine work of God."[52]

Jonathan Edwards's *Faithful Narrative* lies behind Prince's outline, serving as a script upon which other pastors modeled descriptions of local awakenings. Some revival narratives contain clear echoes of Edwards's original. By the time of Whitefield's arrival in 1739, English, Scottish, and American editions of the *Faithful Narrative* had been published and widely read by evangelicals. When Whitefield requested an account of the revival in New Jersey, Robert Cross accommodated with what he described as a work that "directly answered the account given by Mr. Edwards of the work in Northampton." Citing the exact number of conversions Edwards had reported in 1736, Cross said that "three hundred of his congregation, which [was] not a very large one, were brought home to Christ."[53] The pastor at Kilsyth, Scotland, would repeat the same number in his account published in 1742. Indeed, most of the twenty-three revival narratives published between 1741 and 1745 followed the Northampton model.

Sometimes Edwards's *Narrative* was a script both for staging a revival and for reporting it. As Edwards had targeted young people to initiate revival in the 1730s, other pastors likewise singled out the youth for special sermon emphases. Jonathan Dickinson's account of his strategy at Elizabethtown sounds strikingly like that of Edwards. First, he invited young men and women to hear a sermon written specially for them. He then suggested that they meet in private assemblies for mutual admonition and encouragement. The consequences were swift and remarkable. He then reported results that echoed those Edwards described. "From this time," he wrote, "we heard no more of our young People's meeting together for Frolicks and extravagant Diversions, as had been usual among them; but instead thereof, private Meetings for religious Exercises were by them set up in several Parts of the Town."[54]

The revival narratives provide further evidence that the Great Awakening emanated primarily from two centers. Table 4.1 lists the communities that produced revival narratives. When arranged in geographical order, the narratives reflect the clustered nature of the local awakenings. The two major colonial revival regions, rich in evangelistic traditions, produced all the published accounts. Eighteen of the twenty-three emanated from New England, while the remaining five originated within a fifty-mile radius of Neshaminy, Pennsylvania, site of the evangelical Log College. New England's predominance may reflect more the fact that Thomas Prince resided in Boston—whence he solicited, and where he edited and published the narratives—than the region's greater commitment to revivalism.

Abundant evidence suggests that revival narratives' influence reached beyond the communities described in them. As they circulated from town to town, they inspired additional awakenings. Jonathan Parsons, pastor of the West Parish in Lyme, Connecticut, related how he used news to promote revival. He first gathered "a considerable history of the work from many places, attested by credible witnesses." His collection included "Letters from Dr Colman of the wonderful Progress of the Gospel at Boston, and the Towns round about . . . upon the fervent Ministry of Mr Tennent, and their own Pastors." Then he made his revival history the theme of a sermon, which produced the desired effect. "The History and Application of [the revivals] in this Sermon had greater visible Effects upon the Auditory than ever I had seen before in the Course of my Ministry,"[55] he wrote. In concluding his own account of the awakening in Boston, Thomas Prince called his narrative "a grateful publick Testimony of the memorable Work of the Divine Power and Grace among us" and declared his hope that "others may thereby receive

TABLE 4.1
Communities Publishing Revival Narratives, 1741–1745

Community	Pastor/Author
Boston, Mass.	Thomas Prince
Bridgewater, Mass.	John Porter
Brookline, Mass.	James Allen
Charlestown/Westerly, R.I.	Joseph Parks
Freehold, N.J.	William Tennent
Gloucester, Mass.	John White
Hallifax, Mass.	John Cotton
Harvard, Mass.	John Seccomb
Hopewell/Amwell, N.J.	John Rowland
Lyme, Conn. (East Parish)	George Griswold
Lyme, Conn. (West Parish)	Jonathan Parsons
Middleborough, Mass.	Peter Thacher
Newark/Elizabethtown, N.J.	Jonathan Dickinson
New Brunswick, N.J.	Gilbert Tennent
New London, Conn.	George Griswold
New Londonderry, Penn.	Samuel Blair
Northampton, Mass.	Jonathan Edwards
Plymouth, Mass.	Nathaniel Leonard
Portsmouth, N.H.	William Shurtleff
Somers, Mass.	Samuel Allis
Taunton, Mass.	Josiah Crocker
Worcester, Mass.	David Hall
Wrentham, Mass.	Henry Messinger and Elias Haven

Source: Crawford, *Seasons of Grace*, 255–257.

eternal Benefit."[56] Certainly the congregation at Halifax, Massachusetts, received "eternal benefit" from Edwards's Northampton account. As part of his concerted effort to promote revival within his church, pastor John Cotton gathered a small group of devoted followers at his home and read through Edwards's narrative of the Northampton revival.[57] Revival did occur at Halifax, and Cotton wrote a narrative of his own that God may "go on conquering and to conquer, till he has subdued the land."[58]

Others viewed revival narratives primarily as apologies for the awakening. Josiah Crocker expressed the sentiments of many narrators in his desire to defend against "the repeated Misrepresentations which by some seemed to have been devised and industriously spread," depicting the awakenings as enthusiasm. By such reports, men and women "have been prejudiced against, or stumbled at it." He concluded that "these Things oblige me to declare and publish the Conquests and Triumphs of the Almighty Redeemer."[59]

Gilbert Tennent joined Crocker in publishing against those who "so virulently opposed and unjustly aspersed" the revival. "Here we must observe," wrote Tennent and his associates, "that diverse false reports have been invented and spread industriously both by word and writing, in order to blacken the characters of several ministers whom God has been pleased of his pure goodness to honor with success." The attesters therefore lodged their "protest against all those passages in any of the pamphlets which have been published in these parts, which seem to reflect upon the work of Divine power and grace." Their aspirations extended beyond that of setting the record straight. They hoped that their own construction or invention would promote further awakenings by encouraging the "reviving and propagating" of true religion in other locations.[60]

Revival narratives circulated far beyond the American provinces. Prince made the accounts a central feature in his revival magazine, which circulated throughout the Atlantic evangelical community. Similarly, magazines from Scotland and England brought news of British awakenings to the colonies. Thus the revival narratives that helped excite and spread revivalism in British North America contributed to a wider movement, and they contributed further to the revivalists' belief that the extraordinary work they witnessed in local communities was part of a much broader effusion of God's Spirit. Indeed, the same process that linked local and regional revivals into a single intercolonial awakening would weave the American revival into a transatlantic Work of God.

"similar facts . . . are now united": Constructing a Transatlantic Awakening

WHILE American revivalists forged links between local awakenings to create an intercolonial revival, they made connections with their British counterparts who were engaged in similar undertakings in England, Scotland, and Wales. Primarily through letter writing and news exchange, revival promoters on both sides of the Atlantic bore witness to a transatlantic awakening that they compared to the Protestant Reformation. People like Thomas Prince in Boston, James Robe in Edinburgh, William McCullough in Cambuslang, and John Lewis in London compiled accounts of local and regional revivals in their own countries, published them alongside reports of awakenings in other countries, and circulated them among subscribers throughout the Anglo-American world. These revival magazines all bore witness to a single Work of God. And each sounded the same theme: progress. The message they wished to convey was that something big was on the move and that God was behind it.

The transatlantic revival reflected a geographic pattern similar to that in America. While revival activity occurred throughout the British Atlantic, its distribution was uneven, following distinctive regional patterns. Viewed together, table 5.1, showing British revival centers, and table 1.1, depicting American revival centers, reveal the revival's transatlantic scope. They also indicate its regional character on both sides of the Atlantic. Though itinerants traveled the length and breadth of Britain and America, the awakening was particularly intense in certain regions while barely discernible in others. Communities reporting revival clustered around regional epicenters from which revivalists promoted awakenings in surrounding cities and towns.

When the historian focuses on a single country, the revival appears much more regional than national. In each nation the revival emanated from one or more centers where it burned brightest: London and Bristol in England; Trevecca in Wales; Cambuslang and Kilsyth in Scotland; Boston and Northampton in New England, and Neshaminy, Pennsylvania in the Middle Colonies. Although similar activities occurred sporadically elsewhere, awakenings flourished, and revival narratives were inspired,

TABLE 5.1
Revival Geography: Britain, 1739–1745
Place-Names Prominent in the Great Awakening Distributed by Revival Center

Regional Revival Center	Town or City	No. within Region	Pct. of Total within Region
England		**40**	**41.2**
London	Basingstoke, Bedford, Bexley, Bishop Stortford, Blackheath, Blendon, Broad-Oaks, Chatham, Deptford, Dulwich, Gravesend, Hertford, Lewisham, London, Northampton, Olney, Oxford, Saffron Walden, St. Albans, Thaxted, Windsor	21	21.6
Bristol	Abingdon, Bath, Bristol, Chafford, Cheltenham, Circencester, Coleford, Evesham, Gloucester, Hampton Common, Keynsham, Kingswood, New Passage, Old Passage, Painswick, Pershore, Randwick, Salisbury, Stroud, Thornbury	19	19.6
Rest of England	None	0	0.0
Wales		**10**	**10.3**
Trevecca	Abergavenny, Caerleon, Cardiff, Chepstow, Comihoy, Newport, Pontypool, Treleck, Trevecca, Usk	10	10.3
Rest of Wales	None	0	0.0
Scotland		**47**	**48.4**
Cambuslang and Kilsyth	Aberdeen, Auchterarder, Badernoch, Biggar, Bothwell, Caithness, Calder, Cambuslang, Campsie, Carnoch, Coldingham, Craigannatt, Crief, Cumbernauld, Denny, Dundaff, Dundee, Dunnipace, Edinburgh, Fife, Gargunnoch, Glasgow, Irvine, Kilcarn, Kilmarnoch, Kilsyth, Kippen, Kirkintilloch, Larbert, Lang Dregborn, Lochbroom, Monyvard, Murray, Muthel, Nairn, Nigg, Queen's-Ferry, Ross, Ross-keen, Ross-marky, Ross-shire, Sintrie, Southerland, St. Ninians, Torphican, Torryburne	46	47.4
Rest of Scotland	Aberdeen	1	1.0
Total		**97**	**100%**[a]

Sources: Place-names are cited in the two works that best describe the geographic sweep of the revival in Britain, *from the perspective of American revivalists:* the *Christian History* and *Whitefield's Journals.*

[a] Sum of percentages is less than 100 because of rounding.

within a fifty-mile radius of each center.[1] In most cases, each node included a city with sufficient population to support mass evangelism and a print trade that supplied a steady stream of pamphlets and books, as well as newspaper and magazine reports.

The revival's regional pattern raises questions, particularly that of why it was fruitful in some regions and barren in others. Territories outside the clusters barely experienced an awakening at all. English districts beyond the London and Bristol centers were largely untouched by the Whitefieldian revival. A survey of place-names in the Grand Itinerant's *Journals* indicates that he spent little time in the Midlands and the north of England, and newspapers in those regions hardly noted his existence. Those areas of Scotland, Wales, and the American South where the Church of England was strongest managed to turn aside the evangelicals' incursions. Generally, the awakening flourished where dissenters were most influential, and where a revival tradition existed, and faltered where dissenters were weak and no revival tradition fueled expectations.

Besides following a regional geographic pattern, the Anglo-American revivals also reflected regional timetables. In England, the awakening reached its peak in the spring and summer of 1739 as Whitefield and Wesley crisscrossed the district between London and Bristol preaching to enormous crowds and experimented with innovative means of perfecting mass evangelism. Led by Howell Harris, Griffith Jones, and Daniel Rowlands, the revival flourished in Wales at the same time. Whitefield's Philadelphia arrival in October 1739 triggered a revival in the Middle Colonies, and his disembarkation at Newport, Rhode Island, a year later touched off a general awakening in New England. The Scottish revivals, centered at Cambuslang and Kilsyth, reached their peaks in 1742. Table 5.2 provides a revival timetable.

The chronology reveals a notable paucity of temporal interregional overlappings. In America, three years elapsed between the end of the Northampton awakening in 1736 and the beginning of the Whitefieldian revival in 1739. John Wesley and other members of his Oxford society benefited greatly from reading Edwards's *Faithful Narrative*, but when the evangelical revival flourished in England during 1739, there was little evidence that the awakenings had sparked similar stirrings in the colonies before Whitefield's arrival. Then, when the revival spread in America between 1740 and 1742, it waned in England. The strongest temporal connection was that between the Scottish and New England awakenings; the two areas exchanged encouraging news throughout 1742 and 1743.

TABLE 5.2
Revival Timetable, 1735–1745

	England	Wales	America	Scotland
1735			X	
1736			X	
1737	X	X		
1738	X	X		
1739	X	X	X	
1740			X	
1741			X	
1742			X	X
1743			X	X
1744			X	
1745			X	

Although occurring at different times, the various regional revivals manifested similar sequences of events. The revivalists' metaphor of "awakening" is useful in illustrating developmental stages. In each case there was an initial "stirring" from what evangelicals called a deep spiritual sleep. The "surprizing Work of God" in Northampton in 1734–1735 was such a preliminary event. At the same time a similar yet unrelated revival in Freehold, New Jersey, prepared the way for the more extensive awakening that would arrive in that region in 1739. After an initial stirring came a full-blown "awakening" when preaching and printing reached their greatest intensity, and crowds and conversions swelled to their highest numbers. But, as opponents were quick to point out, revivals were short-lived, and as many revivalist pastors lamented, congregations returned to spiritual drowsiness as the special season of grace subsided, and even promoters referred to it as the "late revival." Whitefield explained declension as a natural part of revivalism. Returning to New England in 1744, he found that many who had been awakened under his preaching three years earlier had returned to their former ways. "Some were savingly converted," he wrote in his *Journals,* but "the greater part, as is customary in general awakening, many lost their impressions and have fallen off."[2]

Despite its uneven geographic pattern and asynchronous development, the transatlantic revival was, to its promoters and followers, a single mighty work of God. And while skeptics and critics, then as now, questioned both its extensiveness and its divine inspiration, revivalists celebrated and publicized a movement they saw as sweeping across the world. Revival publications reflected a growing sense of the awakening as something on the march and something global.

William Cooper understood the importance of revivalists' interpreting events as a global revival and not merely a series of widely scattered awakenings. He was, therefore, one of the first to call for a unified account of the revival:

> I can't help expressing my wish, that those who have been conversant in this work, in one place and another, would transmit accounts of it to such a hand as the reverend author of this discourse, [Jonathan Edwards], to be compiled into a narrative like that of the conversions at Northampton which was published a few years ago: that so the world may know this surprising dispensation, in the beginning, progress, and various circumstances of it.[3]

In other words, Cooper called for a publication that would document and publicize the transatlantic revival as Edwards's *Faithful Narrative* had done for the local Northampton awakening.

To Cooper, an account of the global revival would serve two purposes. First, if published while the awakening continued to spread in Anglo-America, it would be a vehicle for promoting revival. He hoped that news of revival success would convince men and women that God's spirit was indeed unusually effusive, extending far beyond individual towns. Second, a complete revival narrative would become an important volume in salvation history. "I can't but think it would be one of the most useful pieces of church history the people of God are blessed with. Perhaps it would come the nearest to *the Acts of the Apostles* of anything extant; and all the histories in the world do not come up to that: there we have something as surprising, as in the *Book of Genesis;* and a new creation, of another kind, seems to open to our view."[4] Thomas Prince and others provided that new creation, the revival magazine, and John Gillies added a revival history. This chapter explores those "new creations," which transmitted the invention to contemporaries and historians alike.

BRITISH-AMERICAN REVIVAL NETWORKS

A survey of the evidence available to John Gillies in 1754 when he compiled his history of the eighteenth-century revival indicates that to a large extent the transatlantic revival was a cultural invention. His documents included 23 published revival narratives from American towns: 13 from Massachusetts, 3 from Connecticut, 1 from Rhode Island, 1 from New Hampshire, 4 from New Jersey, and 1 from Pennsylvania. In addition, he had a lengthy letter written by Samuel Morris describing the beginning of a revival in western Virginia. He possessed no narratives or accounts of revivals from New York, Delaware, Maryland, North Carolina, South Carolina, and Georgia. The revival as reported had occurred in a few "burnt over districts" (regions that had experienced previous awakenings): New England, especially the Connecticut Valley, and parts of New Jersey and Pennsylvania surrounding the evangelistic Log College. In Virginia, the revival, which began a decade after it had waned in the northern colonies, was confined to five frontier counties, bypassing the more populous Tidewater despite Whitefield's preaching there. Nevertheless, Gillies assembled all the accounts under a heading suggesting a much more extensive revival: "THAT EXTRAORDINARY REVIVAL IN THE BRITISH COLONIES IN AMERICA."[5]

Gillies had even less to work with from Britain. In Scotland, he had two revival narratives, one from Cambuslang and the other from Kilsyth. And in England and Wales, he had no published accounts of local awakenings. He relied on the journals of John Wesley, George Whitefield, and Howell Harris. Whitefield's, in particular, were highly self-promotional. When he revised his *Journals* in 1756, Whitefield explained that problems with earlier editions warranted a new publication. In prefatory comments, he acknowledged mistakes caused by youthful exuberance and recommended the new version to readers as one "in which thou wilt find many mistakes rectified; many passages that were justly exceptionable, erased; and the whole abridged."[6]

For the vast majority of evangelical men and women who never crossed the Atlantic in the mid-1740s, letters were the principal means of becoming part of a revival reaching beyond the local parish. While evangelicals had a long and rich epistolary tradition, revival promoters turned that heritage into a powerful means of creating a sense of community. Indeed, letters enabled revivalists to make the awakening "extensive" by linking scattered awakenings into a whole. Transatlantic connections among revival centers were an intrinsic feature in the evangelical culture, encompassing lay men and women as well as ministers. Worship services abounded in reminders that the great awakening spanned the entire British Atlantic. Hymns were commissioned especially for occasions set aside for sharing revival news from home and abroad. At the close of one service held in the London Tabernacle "to celebrate the latest news of religious revival," the congregation sang:

> Great things in England, Wales and Scotland wrought,
> And in America to pass are brought,
> Awaken'd souls, warn'd of the wrath to come
> In Numbers flee to Jesus as their Home....
> What is this News, that flies throughout our Land?[7]

To stay abreast of the revival's progress in distant parts, the Tabernacle's congregation gathered periodically on what were designated Letter Days. Historian Susan O'Brien has described the services, which often lasted for several hours. The assembly "usually began with an exhortation followed by a reading of letters, each of which might be concluded by communal singing of a specially written verse. Another exhortation and prayer rounded off the service." The letters read were of two types. One was the personal letter in which revivalists exchanged revival news. The other was an epistle written for the purpose of being read aloud to an audience. Whitefield periodically wrote a summary account of his American ministry and forwarded it to Howell Harris, who was in charge of the Tabernacle in his absence.[8]

Listening to the letters admitted men and women to the transatlantic community of faith. Nineteen-year-old Elizabeth Jackson of Cambuslang, Scotland, voiced what many thought as they heard ministers read news from revival centers. At one service she "heard Mr. M'cullough [pastor] read some papers concerning the spread of the gospel in foreign parts, which moved [her] greatly." The letters aided Elizabeth in her own search for the new birth, "especially on observing how much good others were getting."[9] After reading accounts of the New England revival, John Willison, a Scottish minister who assisted in the Cambuslang revival, commented on how shared letters contributed toward a common bond. He exulted in "seeing the extraordinary Work there [New England] at present (tho' several Thousands of Miles distant from Scotland) is of the same Kind with that at Cambuslang and other Places about." He noted that American and Scottish audiences responded to revival preaching in similar ways: "there were the very same Appearances accompanying such an Effusion of the Holy Spirit in some of our American Colonies."[10]

The creation of a global revival occurred in a shrinking Atlantic world. During the fifty years prior to the Whitefieldian revival, transatlantic communications had undergone revolutionary changes. The process began in the British commercial and political capital of London. From 1662 to 1695, the Licensing Act had limited to twenty the number of master printers allowed in England. Imposed during the Restoration, the regulation represented a reassertion of executive authority over the presses in an effort to curb the "franker and fuller discussion of political events" of the 1640s. The only official newspaper in the last third of the seventeenth century was the *London Gazette*, although several "very popular manuscript newsletters" provided some competition. The lapsing of the Licensing Act in 1695 opened the floodgates of print in London. Ian Steele described the magnitude of the expansion: "Within days of the expiry of the law, five new newspapers appeared in London. . . . By 1704 there were some 70 printing houses in and around London, and the city had 9 newspapers (including the world's first daily) issuing 27 editions a week. Within another five years there were 55 editions a week of some 19 London papers, almost all of them privately sponsored and presenting some political bias."[11] By the beginning of the evangelical revival in the late 1730s, London printers published approximately 200 more newspapers, magazines, and reviews. In addition to a dramatic increase in their number, the variety of journals increased. While many continued to focus primarily on news, foreign and domestic, others specialized in literature, religion, commerce, theater, history, gardening, etiquette and entertaining, gossip, love and romance, medicine, and law.[12]

The Anglo-American print trade capitalized on the revival's popularity, further illustrating and contributing to its transatlantic scope. Printers on both sides of the Atlantic circulated hundreds of books and pamphlets about the awakening. The monthly "Register of Books" published in the *Gentleman's Magazine* provides some idea of the print trade's interest in works for and against the revival. Table 5.3 shows the total number of new releases featured each month during 1739, when the English phase of the evangelical awakening was at its height. While not a reflection of the English press's entire production nor even a random sample, the lists give some notion of what the editors believed would appeal to their "polite" or "gentlemanly" readership. It certainly shows that the revival received much attention in summer and early fall but waned after Whitefield's departure for America.

Presses published and circulated a variety of revival writings that revivalists eagerly purchased. In her content analysis of the revival publishing network, O'Brien has identified two types of materials: sermons/essays and revival news. Sermons included both exhortatory discourses, such

TABLE 5.3
Revival-Related Publications in England, 1739

Month	Total Titles	Revival Publications	%
Jan.	43	3	6.9
Feb.	54	4	7.4
Mar.	63	0	0
Apr.	56	1	1.7
May	48	2	4.1
June	56	11	19.6
July	51	4	7.8
Aug.	37	10	27.0
Sept.	45	6	13.3
Oct.	32	5	15.6
Nov.	42	1	2.3
Dec.	35	0	0

Source: Data compiled from each issue of *Gentlemen's Magazine* for 1739.

as Samuel Finley's *Christ Triumphant*, and theological treatises, such as Jonathan Edwards's *Religious Affections*. While most exegetical sermons circulated in regional markets, some enjoyed transatlantic exposure. For example, Finley's *Christ Triumphant* and Benjamin Colman's *Souls Flying to Jesus Christ* were originally published in the colonies. The Methodist publisher in London Samuel Mason reprinted both works and then sent fifty copies of each to his Edinburgh bookseller.[13]

Polemical works abounded in the evangelical publishing network. Sometimes they appeared as sermons, sometimes as open letters. In all cases they were intended to counter opponents' "misconstructions" of the revivals. James Robe of Scotland wrote to Jonathan Edwards of antirevivalist literature, originated in New England and circulated in Scotland: "the most unseasonable accounts from America, the most scurrilous and bitter pamphlets, and representations from mistaking brethren, were much and zealously propagated."[14]

Sermons and essays, however, were not the most widely disseminated and read revival literature. That honor belonged to revival news. The reportage of the awakening consisted of "individual testimony, revival narrative, mission journals, printed correspondence, and evangelical magazines."[15] One example will illustrate how news heartened revivalists on each side of the Atlantic. American promoters of the awakening sent copies of the *Christian History* to their counterparts in Britain. One recipient was the distinguished dissenter Isaac Watts. In a letter to William Shurtleff of Portsmouth, New Hampshire, Watts referred to "the Papers which relate to these Matters [i.e., the revival], and have been written in New-England." He added that he took "Pleasure to see and read" about the gospel's success in the colonies. Watts concluded with his opinion that throughout the world "the Work of our Lord Jesus Christ [is] making some Steps toward his glorious Kingdom."[16] Because Watts's letter was published in the colonies, it became a news item for American revivalists. Its appearance in the midst of the ministerial debate between supporters and opposers going on in Boston gave hope to awakeners, who regarded it as a ringing endorsement from an eminent observer viewing developments from afar.

With the *Weekly History* and other evangelical magazines, a publishing network operated alongside the letter-writing network to create a truly transatlantic audience. (See table 5.4 for revival magazines.) Nicholas Gilman, pastor of Durham in New Hampshire, provides one of the best glimpses of how the new periodicals, plus newspapers, kept revivalists informed of distant revival events. Through reading the *Boston Gazette*, Gilman, though living on the periphery of the British Empire, followed the progress of awakenings first in the Middle Colonies and then in New England. In her analysis of Gilman's reading, Susan O'Brien noted that "in January 1740 alone he read George Whitefield's *Journal, Life, Nine Sermons, Answer to the Bishop of London's Pastoral Letter*, and *Account of the Rise of the Methodists at Oxford*." Then, in 1742, when the center of revival activity shifted to Scotland, Gilman kept abreast of the Cambuslang and Kilsyth awakenings through the *Glasgow Weekly History*. In 1743, he acquainted himself with "detailed accounts of awakenings throughout the revival world" by reading copies of the Boston *Christian History* and the Edinburgh *Christian Monthly History*.[17]

Gilman's experience of following a remote revival through the publication network mirrored that of his counterparts on the other side of the Atlantic residing on Britain's perimeter. Henry Davidson, pastor at Galashiels, Scotland, labeled himself an "'omne-gatherum of pamphlets.'" In *Letters to Christian Friends* he described how he kept himself and others in touch with the latest events in America and England as well as Scotland, despite the fact that he was impoverished and isolated.[18]

TABLE 5.4
Revival Magazines

London

The Christian Amusement containing Letters Concerning the Progress of the Gospel both at Home and Abroad etc. Together with an Account of the Waldenses and Albigenses.... Published by John Lewis, Sept. 1740–Mar. 1741.

The Weekly History: Or, An Account of the Most Remarkable Particulars Relating to the Present Progress of the Gospel. By the Encouragement of the Rev. Mr. Whitefield. Published by John Lewis, Ap. 1741–Nov. 1742.

An Account of the Most Remarkable Particulars Relating to the Present Progress of the Gospel. Published by John Lewis, autumn 1742–autumn 1743.

The Christian History or General Account of the Progress of the Gospel in England, Wales, Scotland and America, as far as the Rev. Mr. Whitefield, His Fellow Labourers and Assistants are concerned. Published by John Lewis, Autumn 1743–1748.

Glasgow

The Glasgow-Weekly-History Relating to the Late Progress of the Gospel at Home and Abroad; Being a Collection of Letters partly reprinted from the London-Weekly-History.... Published by William McCullough, Dec. 1741–Dec. 1742.

Edinburgh

The Christian Monthly History or an Account of the Revival and Progress of Religion Abroad and at Home. Published by James Robe, Nov. 1743–Jan. 1746.

Boston

The Christian History, Containing Accounts of the Revival and Propagation of Religion in Great Britain and America. Published by Thomas Prince, Mar. 1743–Feb. 1745.

Source: Durden [O'Brien], "A Study of the First Evangelical Magazines," 257–258.

A closer examination of revivalists' libraries reveals three main types of print material available: revival news, such as that Gilman found in magazines and newspapers, sermons, letters, journals generated in the course of the current revival, and "works from the past in the Reformed and Puritan traditions." For example, Gilman read, along with revival narratives and newly written sermons, works of earlier divines John Flavel, Matthew Henry, Joseph Alleine, Thomas Shepard, William Law, Richard Baxter, and Solomon Stoddard. Booksellers like William McCrea of White Clay Creek in Pennsylvania sold seventeenth-century works such as John Bunyan's *Two Covenants*, Baxter's *A Call to the Unconverted*, and Alleine's *Alarme to the Unconverted*. Ministers testified to the role of the older works in awakening men and women. Samuel Davies reported that in Virginia, "Such were awakened, as they told me, either by their own serious reflections ... or on reading some authors of the last century, such as Boston, Baxter, Flavel, Bunyan etc, and they often wondered if there were such doctrines taught anywhere in the world at present as they found in the writings of these great good men." Colonial printers were quick in responding to the demand for erstwhile best-sellers. Thomas Prince noted in his account of the Boston awakening that "the People seemed to have a renewed Taste for those old Pious and Experimental writers: Mr. Hooker, Mr. Shepard, Guthrie, Alleine. . . . The evangelical writings of these deceased Authors, as well as of others alive, both in England, Scotland, and New England, [are] now read with singular Pleasure: some of them reprinted and in great numbers quickly bought and studied."[19]

In addition to publicizing revival events, printers published and sold scores of sermons, letters, and journals written by revivalists. Consider the Philadelphia print trade. Both Benjamin Franklin's *Pennsylvania Gazette* and Andrew Bradford's *American Weekly Mercury* provided extensive coverage of Whitefield, Tennent, and other awakeners. Franklin also advertised for sale such current works as Samuel Blair's attack against antirevivalists, Ralph Erskine's *Gospel Sonnets*, Samuel Finley's sermons, and William Seward's *Journal*.[20] While Franklin concentrated on publishing new works, his rival, Andrew Bradford, shipped reprints of older works to his customers. For instance, in 1743 William McCrea, a White Clay Creek (Pennsylvania) shopkeeper ordered "30 copies of Bunyan on Two Covenants, 2 dozen 'Sincere Converts,' 11 Alarme's, 8 Baxter's Call," and "many other seventeenth-century works as well as contemporary works by Edwards, Ralph and Ebenezer Erskine, John Willison, and Charles Chauncy."[21]

The strongest cross-cultural link established by the revivalist publishing network was that between New England and Scotland. Thomas Prince and James Robe exchanged revival narratives to reprint in each other's revival magazines. And New England and Scottish newspapers carried full coverage of the awakenings on both sides of the Atlantic. Middle Colony revivalists also stayed abreast of religious events in Scotland. Gilbert Tennent and other Log College preachers included Scots among the "witnesses [God raised up] in diverse Parts of the World to appear for his Cause by publick Attestations and Defences." They cited Robe for his *Narrative* and Alexander Webster for his *Divine Influence: The True Spring of the Extraordinary Work at Cambuslang and other Parts of the West of Scotland*.[22] Accounts of a work similar to that in New Jersey and Pennsylvania authenticated the revival they had witnessed, and strengthened the ministers' view that they were participating in an unusual and widespread showering of God's grace.

Reprints of revival publications provided a direct connection between New England and Scotland. In 1740 Kneeland and Green published an edition of Daniel Campbell's *Sacramental Meditations on the Sufferings and Death of Christ*. A minister in Kilmichael, Campbell first published the work in 1698 in an effort to "codify the practice of piety that accompanied the sacramental occasions," or Holy Fairs, frequently held by Scottish evangelicals. His intention was to prepare men and women by encouraging them in self-examination and reflection.[23] He wanted his readers "to see the Love of Christ that endured such Torments for our Redemption," hoping in the process "to excite our Faith." Writing for a broad audience, Campbell opted to craft a book wherein "the Stile is plain, and the Method obvious."[24] American revivalists thought that New Englanders could benefit from a work that had for decades helped Scottish evangelicals prepare for a special season of God's grace. Like Campbell, they hoped that the volume would enable people to attend services with "a Heart-Melting Frame of Spirit."[25]

James Robe, Alexander Webster, and Ralph and Ebenezer Erskine were other Scottish evangelicals whose works found a receptive market in America. In 1742, Andrew Bradford published Robe's revival magazine, *A Short Narrative of the Extraordinary Work at Cambuslang in Scotland*. Samuel Kneeland and Timothy Green of Boston quickly reprinted it for the New England market. Kneeland and Green also republished Alexander Webster's defense of the Scottish revivals, *Divine Influence: The True Spring of the Extraordinary Work at Cambuslang*. American revivalists welcomed Webster's apology as part of their armament in warding off attacks by opponents. In addition to reading a collection of his sermons, colonial revivalists made Ralph Erskine's *Gospel Sonnets* a best-seller. Franklin introduced the Dunfermline minister's popular collection of spiritual songs in a 1742 Philadelphia edition. Reprints appeared in Boston and Philadelphia in 1743, 1745, and 1749. In a 1743 letter to Robe, Jonathan Edwards reported that Scottish revivalists' "writings, especially Mr. Ralph Erskine's *Gospel Sonnets*, have been in great repute among God's people here."[26]

Scots were eager readers of American revivalists. Jonathan Edwards was arguably their favorite writer. Two reprints of his *Faithful Narrative* appeared in Edinburgh, the first in 1737 and the second the following year. Within the first year of Edwards's *The Distinguishing Marks*, printers in both Glasgow and Edinburgh issued editions. And *Some Thoughts Concerning the Revival* appeared in Edinburgh a year after its first issuance in Boston. Scottish revivalist John Erskine cited, as evidence that the revivals in western Scotland were authentic, reports from elsewhere.

"The Seriousness and Fervency that appears in the Writings of many in that Part of the World [America]," he wrote in 1742, "with the Accounts of their Assiduity and Success, published in the *Weekly Histories* and elsewhere, more than confirm what is here asserted." He interpreted the wide scope of the awakening as fulfilling biblical prophecy of a great outpouring of God's Spirit. As evidence of the revival's great extent, he cited narratives of the Work in America, "whence [we] . . . find that in *America* the Down-pouring of the Spirit is more or less in the several Provinces that measure many Hundred Miles on the Continent; has entered and spread in some of the most populous Towns, the chief Seats of Concourse and Business, and visited their principal Seats of Learning; and in some Places, particularly Boston, Thousands in one Winter were under serious Impressions." The revival's success abroad gave Erskine hope that it would continue to "spread from Kingdom to Kingdom."[27]

In 1744, some Scots recommended that evangelicals on both sides of the Atlantic establish a more formal spiritual community through what they called a "Concert for Prayer." The design was that revivalists in Britain and America would join in prayer "relating to stated times for such exercises; so far as this would not interfere with other duties: particularly a part of Saturday evening, and Sabbath morning every week; and more solemnly of some one of the first days of each of the four great divisions of the year." By appointing a specific prayer time, revivalists would be conscious of a wider "imagined community" all joining in the same activity for the same purpose.[28]

The proposal met with favor in New England, where Jonathan Edwards had made a similar proposal in his work *An humble Attempt to promote explicit Agreement, and visible Union of God's People in extraordinary Prayer.* In a preface by such leading American revivalists as Sewall, Prince, Webb, Foxcroft, and Gee, hope for global revival found expression: "this design we cannot but recommend to all who desire the coming of that blissful kingdom, in its promised extent and glory, in this wretched world."[29]

The Concert was short-lived. One American commentator on its last days recognized that the key to the success of any transatlantic promotion was news of success. Only if participants on both sides of the ocean continued reporting that the awakening proceeded from triumph to triumph could any cooperative effort persist. A New England pastor expressed his hopes and misgivings regarding the Concert in a letter to his Scottish correspondent, dated May 23, 1749. "'Tis matter of great thankfulness and joy," he wrote, "that God puts it into the hearts of so many, in various parts, to unite in extraordinary prayer for the coming of Christ's kingdom: and surely it is a thing that bodes well." Commenting on the specific kind of news that would inspire Americans, he continued, "It would tend to cause this concert to prevail much more here, if we could hear that it was greatly spreading and prevailing on your side of the Atlantick, where it was first begun, and from whence it was first proposed to us." But, he cautioned, "On the contrary, it will undoubtedly be a discouragement to people here, if they hear that the matter decays and languishes, or is come to a stand."[30]

Although not as strong as the New England–Scotland connection, revivalist ties were solid between American promoters and their English counterparts. While traveling with Whitefield in the colonies, William Seward had corresponded with Samuel Mason, a leading publisher of early Methodism in London. Among other things, Mason was the "Friend in London" to whom Whitefield addressed his attack on Archbishop Tillotson. Seward copied that letter and sent it to Mason for publication in England.[31] In 1741, Benjamin Colman sent Mason a copy of his sermon *Souls Flying to Jesus Christ* and included a preface written especially to inform English supporters of the revival of the "great and remarkable success" of the American awakening.[32]

REVIVAL MAGAZINES: "THE PROGRESS OF THE GOSPEL IN ENGLAND, WALES, SCOTLAND, AND AMERICA"

When William Cooper called for a revival magazine, he spoke for many who sought an efficient, dedicated vehicle for circulating revival successes and strategies. Revival magazines would serve a dual purpose. First, they could publicize local and regional awakenings to evangelicals in distant lands and, thus, become instruments in the revival's spread. Second, their cumulative issues would constitute a history of the revival and situate it within a larger, older tradition. Revival magazines fulfilled their advocates' desires. They were indeed vehicles for promoting revivals as they occurred, and means for inventing an interpretation of global awakening. Subsequent histories have relied heavily on the periodicals, largely accepting the notion therein of an extensive revival that spread throughout Anglo-America.

The first magazine, the *Christian's Amusement* (1740), was a miscellany of past and present struggles to spread the gospel. (For a list of revival magazines, see table 5.3 above.) It contained letters and comments on the theological breach between Whitefield and Wesley over the doctrine of Free Grace. In addition, it reprinted letters from various ministers reporting on revival activity in America, England, and Wales. John Lewis also provided exhortations to piety, including a series of his own creation entitled "A History of the Waldenses and Albigens." His purpose was to draw "parallels between persecuted medieval Christians and contemporary Methodists."[33] Poems, hymns, sermon extracts, editorial notes, and advertisements rounded out the periodical's contents.

Despite Lewis's aim to focus on the breadth and unity of Methodism, his magazine acquired a marked parochial and partisan quality. An examination of advertisements reflects social separation, as only persons plying humble trades accepted Lewis's offer of free publicity, including "plumbers, chandlers, tailors, seamstresses, a razor-maker, a glovewasher, a watch-mender." Lewis made free advertising available because he assumed that polite society would not patronize those declared for Methodism. "I shall be willing to advertise for any brother or sister, in this Paper, gratis," he announced, "for if you do but begin to be in earnest about Religion, you will soon find the frowns of an ill natur'd world. And some have lost their Bread for conscience sake."[34]

Unfortunately, the magazine's first issue coincided with the Whitefield-Wesley rift over predestination. "Despite Lewis's proposal to promote peace and charity as much as possible," Susan O'Brien observed, "the paper was clearly anti-Arminian and may have aided the delineation of parties."[35] As Lewis selected letters for reprinting in the *Amusement*, he sided more and more with Whitefield, making increasingly difficult his objective of promoting "unity & brotherly love between the followers of Wesley and Whitefield." A typical partisan selection came from Howell Harris, who stated that "our Brother J. W. is not yet enlightened to see God's Electing Love." He added that until Wesley received sufficient light to embrace the doctrine of Election, "let him not oppose it."[36]

In addition to theological partisanship, Lewis's growing financial difficulties lent a negative tone to his prominent editorial voice. From the outset, he expressed his concern over the magazine's financial performance. He told one well-wisher that the project had suffered from "want of money," and that he had been "a considerable loser by this paper" from the start.[37] His frustrations found expression in the magazine itself as he blamed his woes on a conspiratorial world. "Both Hell and Earth have conspir'd against it [the paper] for if the Common Hawkers are asked for it, some of them do tell their customers that I will not sell it to the Hawkers. . . . And the Printers of News will not advertise this Paper."[38] On the edge of despair in the winter of 1741, he eagerly awaited the arrival of "Mr. Whitefield amongst us, in hopes that he will both advise and assist me therein."[39]

When Whitefield returned to England after an eighteen-month absence, he found that his base of support had dwindled. Some followers had defected to Wesley, others to the Moravians. Along with the latter went his principal London publisher, James Hutton. At a time when he needed a means of communicating and propagating his brand of the revival, differentiating it from that of competitors, Whitefield found himself without his chief printer. The nearly bankrupt Lewis and his moribund magazine suddenly attracted renewed interest. Whitefield decided to assume editorial control over the *Christian's Amusement* and turn it into an exclusive organ for his revival program.

He first determined to change the paper's tone and format. Whitefield opted not to emphasize problems as Lewis had. Instead he focused on the revival's success and the "progress of the Gospel." According to O'Brien, "the paper became more concerned with successes and with creating a feeling of strength among its members than with displaying any weaknesses." She added that the new "note sounded was optimistic, even ecstatic at times.[40]

While the *Christian's Amusement* had contained a few letters describing the revival's progress, the new version, renamed the *Weekly History*, made letters its principal genre. Whitefield had long favored the reprinting of letters praising the revival. While preaching in America, he sent London printer Samuel Mason a packet of letters with instructions: "If some Passages of the Letters were extracted and inserted in the *Daily Advertiser* it might comfort and rejoice God's people."[41] Now he would provide Lewis with a steady supply of epistles from revivalists in England, Scotland, and America. During its twenty-month existence, the *Weekly History* published a total of 232 separate pieces, 198 (85 percent) of them letters. The letters' authors divide into three approximately equal groups: anonymous reporters of local revivals, Whitefield and his closest associates, and more than thirty other writers who wrote one or two apiece. The other 15 percent of the entries fall into two categories: approximately half were nonepistolary reports of awakenings, and the other half were miscellaneous writings including hymns, poems, sermons, and book extracts. Reportage from America arrived primarily in the form of newspaper reprints, while that from England and Scotland consisted of specially written accounts sent directly to Lewis for publication.

Lewis and Whitefield solicited regular reports from itinerant evangelists, and the accounts' positive tone reflected that of the editors.

Whitefield established an ebullient pitch in his frequent letters in the magazine. "This Afternoon we arrived here in the Fullness of the Blazing of the Gospel of Peace," he wrote from Scotland in June 1742. "It would have melted your dear Heart, as it did mine," he continued with unabashed self-promotion, "to see the People run after me with Tears of Joy, blessing God that I was come. Wonderful Things are indeed doing here. The Work of God breaks out in fresh Places."[42] Others imitated his effusive style. Reporting on the Scottish revival in spring 1742, one writer noted, "Since I wrote the inclos'd [referring to a printed piece], more Accounts of Zion's King riding on the White Horse of the Gospel making a triumphant Conquest of many to the Obedience of his Will have come to my knowledge."[43]

Lewis also solicited letters from America, giving the *Weekly History* a transatlantic flavor. In spring 1741, a letter from Gilbert Tennent presented readers with a glowing account of the revival's progress in the colonies. Referring to his New England itinerancy, Tennent reported that he had "met with Success much exceeding my Expectations," adding that "multitudes were awakened." He then surveyed in a summary and rather formulaic way accounts from other itinerants: "My Brother William has had remarkable Success this Winter at Burlington [New Jersey]. . . . Mr. John Cross has had remarkable Success at Stratten [*sic*] Island. . . . Mr. Mills has had remarkable Success in Connecticut. . . . Mr. [Samuel] Blair has had remarkable Success in Pennsylvania."[44]

Lewis and Whitefield filled the *Weekly History* with colorful anecdotes that illustrated how God worked through ordinary human instruments to do extraordinary things. A typical account came from New England. A Boston gentleman, it was reported, stumbled upon his slave one day preaching to an empty room in the style of George Whitefield. Amused at the performance, the slaveholder, who was also an antirevivalist, decided to take advantage of his servant's talents. The next day, the gentleman hosted a dinner and afterwards announced with glee, "I'll entertain you with Mr. Whitefield's preaching; for my Negroe can preach as well as he." Supplying his friends with pipes and glasses all around, he instructed his slave to mount a stool in the center of the room and preach as he had the day before. As he began, the company laughed heartily, but when he warned against blaspheming the Holy Spirit and proclaimed the necessity of a new birth, "the Negro spoke with such Authority that struck the Gentlemen to Heart." To their host's dismay, the men began to listen intently, and many, as a result of that day's "entertainment," became "pious sober Men."[45]

The editor of the *Weekly History* also solicited and reprinted conversion narratives that informed readers of the success of the gospel in individual lives. In one of the magazine's early issues, Lewis published a letter urging readers to submit accounts of their New Births. "I would every [Reader]," the plea began, "for the general good of the Christian Republick, to send you an Account of what they have experienced of the Work of God upon their Souls." The letter-writer urged men and women to lay aside fears of writing for publication and to speak from their hearts. He proposed a format: "The best way . . . is for every person simply to write what he *once was* in a state of nature, how and by what means he came to have the drawings of light and grace upon his soul, and how it has been with him since this time."[46] By including testimonials from throughout the Anglo-American world, the editors suggested that the revival was extensive. And by showing similarity in vocabulary and style, they indicated that the conversions were all of the same origin and nature—that is, genuine rebirths.

Typical of the conversion narratives Lewis published was one by a nine-year-old English girl. In a letter addressed to Whitefield, she informed the evangelist that she had "read one of your Journals, and afterward some Sermons of yours we had got from London." Though but a child she spoke of being a wicked person before her new birth. But, through reflecting on what she read and applying the ideas to her own life, she related triumphantly that she had experienced a "Change of Heart."[47] Evangelical pastors on both sides of the Atlantic supplied Lewis with scores of similar narratives. William McCullough, pastor at Cambuslang, Scotland, solicited conversion accounts from his parishioners, which he forwarded to the *Weekly History* and other revival magazines for publication.

Lewis's initiative inspired the publication of similar magazines in Scotland. When William McCullough of Cambuslang began the *Glasgow Weekly History* in December 1741, he borrowed heavily from Lewis's periodical. With more than thirty issues of the London magazine in print, McCullough had a great deal of material to glean. The format was epistolary, and the source of letters reflected the magazine's transatlantic character. During its first six months, roughly one-quarter of the items came from England, about one-half from America, and the remaining quarter from Scotland. When revival broke out in May 1742, in part because of the *Glasgow Weekly History*, Cambuslang supplied most of the material. However, McCullough continued to show readers how events in Scotland connected with those in New England, "facilitated by theological similarities, and more practically by trade and educational links."[48]

In 1743, James Robe of Kilsyth began publishing Scotland's second revival magazine. While McCullough's periodical had been a "miscellany of contemporary materials ranging from Holland, Wales, England and New England," Robe's provided more historical assessment of the revival. He cited three purposes for publishing another revival magazine. First, he intended it as a history: "Hereby God's wonderful dealings with His Church in this Age shall be propagated to many Ages to come." Second, he sought to encourage a sense of "community of sincere Christians in present times," noting that the periodical was a "choice Means to promote the Communion of Saints upon the Earth." Third, Robe, like so many other revivalists, viewed his magazine as a promotional tool. He hoped that "the good news of a great and effectual door being opened up to the Lord's servant, in any part of the Christian Churches, will excite all who make mention of the name of the Lord to strive . . . That a Door of Utterance may be given to them." Robe, like editors of similar magazines, hoped that it would "make serious Impressions and awaken a concern upon Careless and secure sinners."[49]

Upon learning of spreading New England revivals that bore striking similarities to the ones in Scotland, Robe wrote Jonathan Edwards, urging him to write another narrative that would encompass all the North Atlantic revivals. William Cooper of the Brattle Street Church in Boston made a similar request. He thought it would be well if "those who have been conversant in this work, in one place and another, would transmit accounts of it to such a hand as the revered author of this discourse, [i.e., Edwards], to be compiled into a narrative like that of the conversions at Northampton which was published a few years ago."[50] Both Robe and Cooper desired a narrative linking all the local and regional revivals into one unified account. Thomas Prince met the challenge by undertaking a weekly magazine that would constitute a history of the revival.[51] Publishing his history near the awakening's end, Prince was in a position to make connections that had been less discernible in the midst of the revival.

Prince's *Christian History* was the American magazine dedicated to publicizing awakenings and reporting revival news. Though primarily targeting a local audience, it also emphasized the transatlantic scope and nature of the awakening. Like the Scottish magazines, the *Christian History* was patterned after the *Christian's Amusement*, and it offered its readers an opportunity to follow "the Progress of the Gospel both at Home and Abroad." Prince filled his magazine with new materials, primarily conversion accounts and revival narratives solicited from colonial pastors, and with old items reprinted largely from other magazines.

Prince published the *Christian History* in two formats. He printed it as a weekly magazine of eight pages, usually containing a single revival account from one location. At the end of each of the magazine's two years, he collected that year's issues and published them in a single volume with continuous pagination. The two formats highlight the editor's role in inventing the idea of a transatlantic revival. Each weekly installment had a decided local flavor, reflecting its authorship by a local pastor who described revival in his community. The year-end bound volume had a transatlantic air, reflecting the interleaving of revival accounts from New England, the Middle Colonies, Scotland, and England.

Revival opponents recognized the *Christian History* as one of the most effective means by which the awakening was propagated to a transatlantic audience. One critic viewed it as an "instrument of perpetuating the *evil Spirit*" among men and women. He viewed it as a repeated expression of the "Sentiments of weak enthusiastical Men" but granted its effectiveness, especially among new converts. "It is esteem'd," he wrote, "almost of equal Authority with the inspired Writings! Hence it is, that it is publickly read on the Lord's Day in several Churches." Moreover, the *Christian History* was a most "diffusive Evil," extending the "Spirit of Contention, Division and Separation thro' all the American Provinces, and even beyond the *Atlantic*."[52] Though criticizing the revival magazines' message and influence, the opposer acknowledged its success as a powerful evangelizing component of the transatlantic publishing network.

When viewed separately, the letters that fill the pages of the revival magazines describe a series of local and regional awakenings. A global, unified revival is not self-evident. But when gathered together and placed under headings proclaiming a global revival, they portray a transatlantic revival. To promoters of the American awakening, the periodicals emanating simultaneously from several locations in the British Atlantic world meant that the colonial event was surely part of an extraordinary work of God.

HISTORICAL CONNECTIONS: THE GREAT AWAKENING
IN SALVATION HISTORY

In addition to spanning geographic divides, revival promoters reached across time to place the "present Work" within a larger context. In

THE

Chriſtian Hiſtory,

Saturday MARCH 5. 1743. Nº I.

To be publiſh'd *Weekly*;

Containing Accounts of the Propagation and Revival of Religion; more particularly

I. Authentick Accounts from Miniſters and other creditable Perſons of the Revival of Religion in the ſeveral Parts of NEW ENGLAND.

II. Extracts of the moſt remarkable Pieces in the *weekly Hiſtories* of Religion, and *other Accounts*, PRINTED both in England and Scotland.

III. Extracts of WRITTEN LETTERS both from *England, Scotland, New-York, New-Jerſey, Penſylvania, South-Carolina*, and *Georgia* of a religious Nature, as they ſhall be ſent hither from creditablePerſons and communicated to us.

IV. In Intervals of freſh Occurences, and on other Occaſions, it is propoſed to give theReader the *moſt remarkablePaſſages Hiſtorical* and *Doctrinal*, out of the moſt famous OLD WRITERS both of the Church of *England* and *Scotland* from the Reformation, as alſo the *firſt Settlers* of *New-England* and *their Children* : that we may ſee how far their pious *Principles* and *Spirit* are at this Day revived ; and may alſo guard againſt all Extreams.

Pſal. 26. 7. *That I may* PUBLISH *with the Voice of* THANKSGIVING, *and tell of all* THY WONDROUS WORKS.

BOSTO N,N.E. Printed by KNEELAND & GREEN, 1743. for THOMAS PRINCE, Junr. A. B.

3. Contents of revival magazine

1741, John Webb, senior pastor at Boston's New North Church, used the vehicle of print to link an earlier New England revival with the intercolonial awakening occurring as he wrote. He made his observations in a preface to a second edition of sermons he had first published in 1727 "after the Terrible Earthquake, whereby, the People in New England, were generally very much awakened." Webb thought the reprint appropriate because "the Subject of [the discourses] is of universal infinite Importance." They contained "Some Plain and Necessary Directions to Obtain Eternal Salvation," and thus were as valid in 1741 as in 1727. While arguing that God's outpouring was the same grace at both times, Webb noted some important distinctions. First, the latter revival was much bigger: a "Season, when God is pouring out his Spirit, both here [i.e., New England], and in many other Places." And second, God brought revival to New England this time not by a natural phenomenon but by human instruments, specifically, Whitefield and Tennent.[53]

A second reprint in 1741 linked the "present Work" with great Puritan revivals in seventeenth-century England. New England revival supporter Mather Byles published an extract of one of John Flavel's sermons. Flavel had been one of the leading divines in preaching in a "warm" evangelistic style. Byles introduced the discourse as one "delivered at a Season something like this among ourselves, when there were mighty Impressions from GOD upon the Hearts of Multitudes." He said that Flavel's sermons reach across the ages and speak "immediately to the Heart" and "set the great Doctrines of the Gospel in the most affecting and engaging Lights." Byles provided his readers with another tie between Flavel and revivalists of the 1740s. He quoted from a letter Flavel had sent Increase Mather, Byles's grandfather, in which he enclosed one of his sermons, a "Discourse God hath so signally owned for the Conversion of very many Souls in this Town and Country." Byles concluded his preface by expressing his hope that "the same Almighty Agent may accompany the reading of it in the like Manner." He thought that the republication was "well timed, when such Numbers are awakened, to direct and incourage them in the Way of Salvation."[54]

To narrate the revival as a coherent story linked across temporal as well as spatial boundaries, promoters thought of writing a history. They had made extensive use of print in publicizing and defending the "great awakening," but they recognized the limitations of newspapers and magazines in telling a coherent story of God's extraordinary work. The problem was that periodicals by their nature presented fragmented accounts of the revival, printing reports from scattered regions whenever they arrived. In 1743, some readers of the *Christian History* complained about the lack of continuity in the magazines' reports. One issue might contain a description of current events in Scotland, the next an account of present developments in New England, and the following a historical review of revivals in America. In an apology, Thomas Prince explained: "It is not expected that, in publishing the Accounts successively sent us of Revival in various Parts, we should observe so exact an Order with Respect either to Time or Place, as if we had them all before us at the Beginning."[55]

To best present the revival as an extensive, uniform, coherent event, awakeners turned their attention to writing a narrative history. The historian could do what the periodical publisher could not: collect and arrange information in a way that revealed the spatial and temporal sweep of the awakening. Moreover, he could place the eighteenth-century revivals within the larger story of salvation history. In 1754, nine years after the awakenings had subsided, the Scottish revivalist John Gillies published his history of "Remarkable Periods of the Success of the Gospel," a unified account that began at Pentecost and culminated in the most recent awakenings.[56]

When Gillies undertook the task, the source documents available did not in themselves contain a narrative of an extensive awakening or a special divine dispensation. By themselves or considered one at a time, they did not add up to global revival. Rather, the revival accounts he relied upon described local revivals stretching over several decades and scattered throughout Anglo-America. From the 1740s, he had access to about three dozen accounts of disparate religious awakenings in various parts of England, Scotland, and America. He believed, however, that compiled in one place and viewed together, reports of local revivals would portray a global awakening much more extensive than the individual events suggested. Therefore, through weaving the various accounts into a single "narration of the success of the gospel," Gillies invented something bigger: an extensive, uniform transatlantic revival.[57]

In *Historical Collections*, Gillies displayed his editorial work, gathering source documents and arranging them in a pattern that told a story of widespread revival success. In the preface, he set forth his task and purpose as compiler: "When similar facts, that were so dispersed, and sometimes mixed with other subjects in different books ... are now united, so as to be laid before the reader in one view, and methodized according to the order of time in which the events happened in different places; they may be read and compared with much greater advantage."[58] The whole, if rightly presented, was greater than the sum of its parts.

Gillies wrote from a biblical framework, finding his blueprint in the New Testament. Contending that "a considerable part of [the New Testament] is employed in historical narrations of the success of the Gospel," Gillies found a pattern that explained for him the eighteenth-century evangelical revivals. To him, the spiritual awakenings that occurred throughout the English world were nothing less than the latest instance of "the success of the Gospel." Like his scriptural model, Gillies's history would relate "the numbers that were converted," "the religious instructions that were the means" of conversions, "the providences" that enabled men and women to benefit from those instructions, "the uncommon influences of the Holy Spirit" on prayers for revival, and "the blessed fruits of holiness in the lives of the converts."[59]

In constructing his story of the success of the gospel, Gillies desired to include only what he considered to be the most reliable information. He wished to emulate the apostle Paul who "set us a pattern of seeking information about such facts from men who had access to know them." He was convinced that "when witnesses are sufficient as to their characters, their numbers, and their means of information; their testimony affords a very high degree of moral evidence." Thus, like Colman and Prince before him, he paraded before the reader a succession of witnesses who attested to revivals throughout the ages. He began his history with "the swift progress of the Gospel, in the time of the Apostles" and concluded with the "late extraordinary dispensations of grace, with which the Lord has favoured so many different corners."[60]

Gillies did not write his history as an academic exercise. Rather, he hoped that it would move evangelicals "to continual ardent prayer that the Lord would give more success than ever to his gospel in all parts of the earth." Moreover, he recognized that many "pious persons [were] ... not yet sufficiently informed, and persuaded of several past events, as instances of the success of the Gospel." His task was to convince readers of the authenticity of "these late gracious dispensations." Thus his was a work in "practical religion," an effort to promote future revivals by showing the progress of preceding ones.[61] Gillies hoped that his account of evangelical revivalism would be instrumental in inspiring men and women to experience the new birth themselves and to work on behalf of its propagation.

Although he emphasized the eighteenth-century revivals, Gillies devoted more than half of his history to previous centuries. He desired to place the more recent awakenings within an evangelical tradition with roots in the New Testament. His primary question dealt with the success of the gospel. In examining the success of the gospel from the Apostolic

Age, Gillies followed a strategy that persists throughout the volume. First, he explored some of the "means employed by divine wisdom for promoting" the faith. In particular, he noted the written documents instrumental in shaping and publicizing early Christianity, such as "the apologies for Christianity written by men of learning." Second, he reminded his readers of the persecutions that people of faith face in every age. The main barriers to the gospel's progress in the first three centuries were powerful Roman emperors. But in every age true believers spread the good news despite all obstacles.[62]

Gillies's history is not a narrative of the advance of Christianity in general. Rather, it is an account of a particular type of Protestantism, usually referred to by revivalists as "experimental religion," or "piety," or "practical religion." All of those expressions represented attempts to capture the essence of New Testament and Reformed Christianity. Experimental religion was that experienced firsthand by an individual through conversion, a spiritual new birth. Revivalists insisted that faith mediated by priests and churches and merely assented to by adherents was cold, formal, and without efficacy. Piety suggested a life "more suitable to the principles and spirit of Christianity" than that lived by most avowed Christians.[63] It was an awakened life given more completely to the study and practice of scriptural precepts and less inclined to worldly vanities. Practical religion emphasized an active faith whereby persons devoted their time, talent, and money to spreading the gospel and relieving the suffering of those less fortunate.

The denouement of Gillies's narration presented the evangelical revivals occurring in the British Atlantic world, and especially those in British North America in the eighteenth century; enumerating "instances of success of the gospel" in America, Gillies charted revivals in New England, New Jersey, and Georgia.[64] His account of colonial revivalism began with what he called "the sad decay of vital religion." He quoted such Puritan divines as Samuel Danforth, Increase Mather, Samuel Torrey, and Cotton Mather to make his case for religious declension. In his sermon before the Massachusetts general court on May 11, 1670, Danforth asked "Whether we have not in a great measure forgot our errand into the wilderness." In a 1683 sermon, Torrey left no doubt about his answer to Danforth's question. He wrote "that there hath been a vital decay, a decay upon the very vitals of religion, by a deep declension in the life and power of it." In his 1706 jeremiad *The Good Old Way*, Cotton Mather lamented that "the modern Christianity is, too generally, but a very shadow of the ancient!"[65]

Gillies noted, however, that out of the depths of New England declension came revival. The earliest form was that of covenant renewal. Meeting in 1679, a synod of all the churches convened to consider why God allowed the colonies to suffer at the hands of the Indian sachem Metacom. The conclusion was that King Philip's War had been a divine visitation upon disobedient Christians. Only "a solemn renewing of covenant with God, and one another" could restore God's favor. When "many complied, ... there was a considerable revival of religion among them."[66]

In Gillies's depiction of American awakenings, Northampton enjoyed a special place as a "remarkable revival," the last and greatest of a succession of local awakenings before the Great Awakening beginning in 1739. Northampton was noteworthy as a genuine "work of God," but it was also an inspiration for budding revivalists, who saw it as a beginning of a larger dispensation. Edwards's *Narrative* inspired the Oxford Methodists who would play major roles in promoting transatlantic revivalism. The group's leader John Wesley recorded in his diary: "I read the truly surprising narrative of the conversions lately wrought in and about the town of Northampton, in New England. Surely this is the Lord's doing, and it is marvellous in our eyes." And Gillies noted that when Whitefield arrived in New England, he desired especially to visit Northampton, "having read in England, an account of a remarkable work of conversion there, published by their Pastor the Rev. Mr. Jonathan Edwards."[67] Thus Northampton was more than a local revival; its telling and retelling became an inspiration and model for what Gillies called "the extensive revival in the British Colonies in America, which began chiefly in the end of 1739."[68]

The Great Awakening—the colonial American phase of the revival—was a major chapter in John Gillies's history of "Remarkable Periods of the Success of the Gospel." Published in 1754 in two volumes, *Historical Collections* describes revivals from the first Pentecost to the mid–eighteenth century.[69] The first volume covers great outpourings of God's spirit through the seventeenth century, with the Protestant Reformation receiving most attention. Volume 2 contains about the same number of pages as the first volume but extends only over the first half of the eighteenth century. The colonial American revivals constitute half of that. Thus Gillies devotes about one-fourth of his history to the great awakening. In his account, the American revival, while part of an international awakening, was the feature attraction.

Gillies relied on revival magazines for most of the material in volume

2. Except for a few letters and Whitefield's *Journals*, Prince's *Christian History* is the basis for his description of the American revival. He noted that he extracted material "mostly verbatim." Only on occasion did he choose "the way of Paraphrase, . . . [or] the way of Abridgement."[70] While largely derivative, Gillies's history makes a significant contribution to revivalists' interpretation of the great awakening, giving prominence to the great awakening by presenting it as the extension and culmination of the Reformation. Situating it as one of a very small number of preeminent events in salvation history, Gillies ensured the Great Awakening's eminence among evangelicals. He characterized it as "that extraordinary Revival in the British Colonies in America, which began chiefly in the Year 1740, and continued in 1741, 1742,—spreading through a great many Places."[71]

Gillies viewed the eighteenth-century revival as deliverance. He agreed with other revivalists that the awakening came in a dark chapter of Christianity when opposition from without and sinfulness within the church brought discouragement to the faithful. But, Gillies argued, that has always been the case. He wrote of the church that the "most threatening dangers and lowest times have frequently been soon followed with the most signal appearances in its behalf." God intervenes when his people are under greatest attack, as was the case during "the times preceding the deliverances from Egypt and Babylon, the first promulgation of the gospel, and the Protestant reformation." Scriptural promises and church history teach that when the church "seems in imminent danger of becoming consumed; the power and good-will of him who dwelt in the bush seasonably interposes; and the time of need proves the time for the Lord to work."[72] The eighteenth-century evangelical revival takes its place as one of the church's great deliverances.

Gillies's history fits Jon Butler's paradigm of the Great Awakening as "interpretive fiction"; however, it is a fiction that predates Joseph Tracy's version by more than a century. Indeed, Tracy relied heavily upon *Historical Collections* for his construction of the Great Awakening, adding little original interpretation other than the title. Gillies and other revival inventors operated out of a strong conviction that they were describing and promoting nothing less than a second reformation, an extraordinary dispensation of grace. To the transatlantic community of evangelicals it inspired, that interpretation became an article of faith. But to many outside the revivalist circle, the notion was the result of enthusiasm, overheated imaginations that saw God's hands in human events. Some critics published their own "discoveries" of the revival as artful design, works that revivalists, in turn, charged were "inventions" in the sense of being fabrications. Historians, then, who seek to explain the state of religion in mid-eighteenth-century colonial America confront an array of fictions, inventions and counterinventions, from which they construct their own "interpretive fictions."

Part Three

CONTESTED INVENTIONS,

1742–1745

FROM the outset, opponents challenged the revivalists' invention of the Great Awakening with alternative explanations—counterinventions— that emphasized human machination instead of the work of God. Viewing the "awakening" as a series of events that added up to only a "small thing" antirevivalists in New England and the Middle Colonies attacked the revival with stinging polemics. The debate between those promoting a "remarkable Revival of Religion" and those denouncing "Errors and Disorders" reached its most contentious level in 1743. The two sides disagreed on basic issues, including whether or not there had been a revival, and, if so, what "facts" constituted evidence.

One opponent, Benjamin Prescott of Salem, Massachusetts, charged revival promoters with submitting their own judgments or interpretations as "facts" on the basis of which all Christians should attest to the "great awakening." Prescott claimed that critics subscribed to a higher standard of evidence, that their assessment of the work as "Errors and Disorders" was based on the "facts" of direct observation. In his view, it was "an unreasonable Thing for them [i.e., revivalists] to expect that with a full Reliance on their Judgment, others should join them in giving a positive Attestation thereto." While conceding that genuine revival occurred periodically in local congregations, Prescott objected to revivalists' claims of an extensive awakening throughout the land. He singled out for special criticism awakeners' attempts to convince readers far removed from revival events that they should accept as objective truth the accounts set forth in revival narratives. Prescott thought it a further attempt at artful invention to expect "Persons . . . at a *great Distance* from [an alleged awakening], and having no Acquaintance with the State of Religion" in the congregation claiming a "Work of God" to join in "a positive Attestation to such a remarkable Revival of Religion there."[1] His point was that only participants and eyewitnesses were in a position to opine whether a revival had occurred. To him, the chorus of revival claims orchestrated by enthusiasts in Britain and America rested on assertion backed by hearsay. Part Three explores the polemics each side hurled at the other, and the apologies each offered in its own defense.

CHAPTER 6

The "grand delusion" or "great Mistakes of the present Day"

IN 1781, a group of Connecticut Congregationalists boldly proclaimed the mid-eighteenth-century revivals to be the "GREAT REFORMATION." They recognized, however, that not everyone viewed the revivals as "great" or even as revivals. They noted that from the earliest stirrings at Northampton in the mid-1730s, antirevivalists had been "proportionably Zealous, in their Opposition, to the Zeal with which its Friends [i.e., revivalists] endeavoured to promote and carry it on." Moreover, the revivalist authors accused antirevivalists of artful construction: "The Controversy was managed by all Orders of Men; every Public Board, both Civil and Ecclesiastical, were racking their Invention to find out Ways and Means to embarrass and hinder the Work's going on; at least to check the Disorder, as they call it."[1] In calling the opposition's interpretation "invention," the writers echoed a view Gilbert Tennent had expressed forty years earlier. Tennent explained that his motivation for publishing a revival apology was the circulation of "false reports [that] have been invented and spread industriously."[2]

To the authors of *An Historical Narrative*, the matter was simple: revivalists had merely declared and memorialized what was self-evident, the "GREAT REFORMATION." Their opponents, though, had refused to acknowledge the "great ado" as a revival and had resorted to artful invention to denigrate it. In their usage, invention clearly meant fabrication of something untrue.

From the moment revivalists publicly declared the existence of an extraordinary awakening, antirevivalists challenged their claims. Indeed, Benjamin Colman convinced Jonathan Edwards to publish an account of the 1735–1736 Northampton revival because of the "misinterpretations" and "falsehoods" being spread about religious events in the Connecticut Valley. In England, when George Whitefield established himself as a popular evangelist, one of the established church's severest critics, the bishop of London exposed the revivalist as an enthusiast whose self-serving writings violated standards of Scripture and reason.

Until 1741, opponents preached and published against the revivals as individuals with little coordination. But by 1742–1743, oppositionists began to operate through an informal transatlantic antirevivalist network. In their attacks, antirevivalists vigorously challenged awakeners' assertions of decline and revival. They rejected the revivalists' gloomy portrayal of the prerevival state of religion. And they countered the postrevival declarations that a great awakening had occurred.

Antirevivalists met each revivalist invention with a counterinvention of their own. Charles Chauncy dismissed the awakeners' claim that the revival was authentic because of its uniformity "in different parts of the land." To him the answer lay in human nature: "humane Nature is humane Nature—Persons in different Provinces have the same Passions. If certain Means affect some Persons in one Place, it is nothing Wonderful if the same Means affect some in another."[3] In other words, rather than giving evidence of a uniform work of God, widespread similarities attested to a uniform invention of revival promoters.

From pulpit and press, New Lights (revivalists) and Old Lights (antirevivalists) attacked each other. One of the most dramatic exchanges occurred at Boston's First Church between pastor Thomas Foxcroft, an ardent revivalist, and associate pastor Charles Chauncy, the awakening's most outspoken opponent. Their printed sermons during the revival indicate that the two treated their congregation to a lively debate that clearly differentiated the opposing sides. In a Thursday evening lecture in 1740, Foxcroft provided the audience with "Some Seasonable Thoughts on Evangelic Preaching." He argued against sermons delivered in "a philosophical and unevangelic Strain," adding that the preacher who took such a tack "might as well have taken his Text out of *Seneca's* Morals." Given Chauncy's rationalist proclivities, no doubt the listeners applied Foxcroft's words to his colleague. In another thinly veiled swipe at his associate's views, Foxcroft said that if a preacher's notions of Christianity forbid his preaching awakening sermons, " 'tis justly to be fear'd [he is] in a *different* Scheme, or else a *different* Spirit, from that of the Apostles."[4] The phrase "different Scheme" came close to suggesting that antirevivalists were beyond the Christian pale, and certainly represented their teachings as being antithetical to New Testament truths.

In a rejoinder, also delivered at the Thursday lecture, Chauncy offered "Some Seasonable Advice to those who are New-Creatures." By repeating the adjective "seasonable" found in Foxcroft's lecture title, Chauncy provided a clear signal to the audience that they were about to hear another view on the same question. It also underscored the fact that the discourse would address the current religious stir that had turned New England religion on its head. Chauncy warned against the ill effects of an undue emphasis on the New Birth as advocated by New Lights such as his colleague. In particular, he cautioned those who saw conversion as granting instant and complete grace. He admonished his parishioners to "think not the measure of your *first endowments*, to be greater than it is." Converts must expect to grow and increase in faith, and, Chauncy added, that takes time and diligence. Obviously referring to revivalist enthusiasm that was often given to extravagant claims, he urged prudence: "Take care to keep your *zeal* under the government of *sound judgments.*"[5] He concluded with a reminder that God was a god of order that was manifest among angels, nature, and humankind.

The most publicized debate was that between Chauncy and Jonathan Edwards. On September 10, 1741, Edwards delivered a commencement address at Yale based on 1 John 4:1, which called on Christians to "try the spirits" of preachers because "many false prophets are gone out into the world." In testing the spirits of recent revivals, he identified several "Distinguishing Marks" proving that the "Uncommon Operation That Has Lately Appeared on the Minds of Many of the People of This Land" was in fact a "Work of the Spirit of God." Although intended as an "irenicon" that would foster reconciliation, Edwards's sermon triggered a series of responses that further polarized attitudes toward the revival. Within a month, "'testing the spirits' quickly became a popular pulpit exercise." One example will suffice to illustrate how antirevivalists interpreted the text that Edwards had selected at Yale. John Caldwell, the Presbyterian pastor at Blandford, Massachusetts, declared that most of the so-called conversions reported by awakeners sounded like "an epidemical distemper ... especially [among] the younger women and children."[6] Many other Old Light sermons rang changes on that theme.

In 1743, Edwards and Chauncy waged a press war, wielding diametrically opposed interpretations of the "great ado." On March 24 and again on March 31, the *Boston News-Letter* advertised Edwards's *Some Thoughts Concerning the Revival*. The same pages announced Chauncy's forthcoming *Seasonable Thoughts on the State of Religion*. As one historian has observed, the juxtaposition was "hardly coincidental."[7] Moreover, Chauncy's title page contained a table of contents which mirrored that of Edwards's book. Chauncy accepted that some good had been done, but argued that it had resulted from God's dispensing his grace in his usual, predictable, orderly way. He refuted the revivalist hype about a

4. Charles Chauncy: leading revival critic

"great awakening." In a published response to Edwards's Yale address, he challenged the Northampton pastor's claims that "much hath been done" in this so-called work of God. He warned readers against being taken in by all the immoderate claims that characterized revivalists' publicity. Stripped of hyperbole, the awakening would be far from "great"; indeed, it would be reduced to a "small Thing."[8] Chauncy's implications of invention echoed similar charges by revivalists. This chapter explores the antirevivalists' counterinventions.

5. Jonathan Edwards: revival promoter and theologian

THE REVIVAL AS ARTIFICE

No one was more eloquent in interpreting the Work as revival than Jonathan Edwards. Fending off attacks aimed at some revivalists' bizarre behavior, Edwards attempted to shift the debate from a discussion of means to a consideration of consequences. He argued that the awakening should not be judged "a priori; from the Way that it began, the Instruments that have been employed, the Means that have been made use of, and the Methods that have been taken and succeeded in carrying it on." Edwards himself had questions about some practices, such as lay exhorting. But when the affair was judged "*a posteriori*," he assured his readers, "we are to observe the Effect wrought."[9] He concluded that, excesses notwithstanding, the revival was indeed a work of God that conformed to biblical teachings regarding special acts of divine dispensation.

Charles Chauncy disagreed. While he saw much evidence of "*enthusiastick Heat*" and a "*Commotion in the Passions*," he failed to see "that Men have been made better." He added, " 'Tis not evident to me, that Persons, generally, have a better Understanding of Religion, a better Government of their Passions, a more Christian Love to their Neighbour, or that they are more decent and regular in their Devotions towards God." Instead, Chauncy continued, he observed the "same Pride and Vanity, the same Luxury and Intemperance, the same lying and tricking and cheating, as before. . . . There was certainly no *remarkable* Difference as to these things."[10] In his a posteriori judgment, the awakening was found wanting.

A group of seventy New England antirevivalists formed a rump conference after the annual pastors' convention in May 1743 to reflect on recent religious events, examine evidence revivalists claimed for calling those events a Work of God, and publish their findings. At the conclusion of the deliberations—moderated by the distinguished pastor at Scituate, Massachusetts, Nathaniel Eells—the ministers published their findings in a stinging denunciation of any interpretation recognizing recent activities as emanating from God. They viewed as flimsy the materials from which revivalists invented revival, and charged revivalists with being too credulous: uncritically accepting individuals' conversion accounts based on "secret Impulses" rather than on "the *written Word* [and] the *Rule* of their Conduct." In other words, the awakeners' emphasis on religion of the heart, the "new birth," placed undue weight on unverifiable private experience rather than observable public conduct. The antirevivalists viewed the scheme of salvation as extremely subjective: "none are *converted* but such as know they are converted and the *Time when*." To the critics, the revivalists had slipped into the same error as the antinomians: personal experience transcended "*Scripture and Reason*."[11]

To Chauncy, the events some considered to be of divine origin were human contrivances. Moreover, he believed that Whitefield had instigated the "great ado," and that the so-called revival was coextensive with the Grand Itinerant's antics. The "most glorious Work of Grace going on in *America*," he observed sarcastically in 1742, was in fact "begun by Mr. Whitefield, and helpt forward by those in his way of preaching and acting." Chauncy viewed the whole thing as a product of slick publicity and promotion. Well before the Grand Itinerant arrived in Boston, "The Minds of People in this part of the World, had been greatly prepossest in Favour of Mr. Whitefield from the Accounts transmitted of him, from time to time, as *a Wonder of Piety, a Man of God*, so as *no one was like him*." Dissenting ministers completed the fabrication, mentioning Whitefield by name in their prayers and sermons, presenting him as "the Instrument of *such Extraordinary Good* to so many Souls." Just as the awakening was a product of human invention, so were revival narratives. He warned Scottish readers not to be taken in by the "marvellous Accounts [that] have been sent Abroad of a most glorious Work of Grace going on in America." Expressing his wish that the reports were true, he felt compelled to expose portions that were "known Falsehoods" and others "strangely enlarged upon." He concluded that the printed "Representations" were misleading and unreliable, exhibiting a "wrong Idea of the religious State of Affairs among us." Having damned revivalist accounts as fanciful constructions, Chauncy assured his readers that his own version was no "romantick Representation of Things; but it is the real Truth of the Case without a Figure."[12]

Another antirevivalist described how revival promoters wove fictional tales into their printed accounts of an intercolonial awakening. Writing as an anonymous observer, one writer noticed that in their publicity revivalists frequently changed "the *particular* Phrase, . . . *This glorious Work*, or the glorious Work of God which *is now carrying on in the Land*, into a general Form of Speech, as, 'The Works of Christ,' [or] . . . 'The most glorious Works of Christ.'"[13] In other words, the pamphleteer objected to publicists' making the revival more than it was, bearing witness to what amounted to "*The* Great Awakening" rather than referring to this or that "great awakening" in a particular community. According to this critic, the revival was more rhetoric than reality.

Opponents rejected claims that the so-called revival was self-evident, and exposed the process by which revivalists invented it. When John Caldwell referred to the "fashionable Principles in Religion," he presumed that those revivalist principles had been fabricated.[14] He listed the "chief Promoters of this Work" as not only Whitefield and Tennent but also such local and regional figures as "Pomroy, Buel, Davenport, Morehead, Croswell, Blair, [and] Rowland." Caldwell described how the revivalists constructed their religious program. First, they created the idea of a deplorable state of religion. "They exercise a Zeal against what they call Error and Deadness [in religion]," Caldwell wrote, "tho' by Religion they mean only their own Fancies, and unscriptural Opinions."[15] In other words, the so-called state of declining religion against which the awakeners railed, like other revivalist assertions, was a figment of overzealous imaginations.

A second step in the awakeners' fashioning of revivalism was their definition of which colonial ministers were true to experimental Christianity and which were not. Caldwell quoted from revivalist writings to describe the boundaries revivalists constructed to differentiate themselves from clergymen who did not believe as they did. Jonathan Edwards called "such as will not admit those of this Scheme into their Pulpits, Samaritans." Whitefield gave "an Account of only a very few of the Clergy in these Provinces who are converted, and these such as are in his way." Tennent represented "the Body of the Clergy of this Generation, as Varlets, the Seed of the Old Serpent, Men whom the Devil drives into the Ministry, blind, and dead Men . . . dead Drones, Dupes, Dunces." And Samuel Finley compared "such as are but in doubt, to Followers of Baal."[16]

A third way in which revivalists created a new religious "scheme" was to redefine the relation between humans and the world. According to Caldwell, awakeners denounced the world, especially the unwholesome entertainment and products flowing from a marketplace more and more attuned to satisfying hedonistic appetites. They warned their followers of the consequences of embracing the world; simultaneously they offered comfort in a future spiritual realm. Caldwell framed revivalism's core message as, "Scare 'em a little, and then perswade 'em all is well, and they are sure of Heaven." He questioned the motives of the evangelists, wondering if their efforts were not intended more to raise a following and fill their coffers than to save souls. "Were a Man to establish a Scheme of Religion for his worldly Interest," he mused, "would not this be it, to put on a Shew of Godliness, and pretend to despise the World?"[17] He wondered whether evangelistic cries for piety did not mask their quest for profits.

A final strategy employed in the construction of revivalism was self-promotion. Caldwell suggested that the awakeners knew that publicity was as important in the fashioning process as the religious scheme itself. He noted that revivalists were "perpetually telling us of their Success, of the Numbers that follow them, and the Satisfaction People have in their Performances." He cautioned his readers against accepting this self-defined success. "Look a little farther than the Surface of Things," he admonished, "be not taken with Shew and Appearance for Reality."[18] He wanted them to recognize revivalist literature for what it was: propaganda. Their guide should be their reason and Scripture, not broadsides and headlines.

In 1743, Nathaniel Eells called for discrimination in judging the work going on in American religion. He conceded that "There is, (doubtless) a good Work of God going on in the Country, his Spirit is evidently poured out upon many in one Place and another." But he added, "there is, (doubtless) an evil Work of Satan going on in the Country." He pointed to "all the Noise & Stir, the strange Agitations and Motions, Screaming and Fainting, and Disorders," and expressed his dismay that many attributed those things to "the pouring out of God's Spirit upon his People, and will not allow of any Delusion in such Things." Eells called on reasonable people to distinguish "the genuine and proper Work of God's Spirit from the counterfeit and delusive Work of Satan."[19]

Others joined Eels in protesting the awakeners' claim that a true revival was afoot. One opponent found offensive the extravagant labels revivalists used to describe their work: "by Way of Eminence, [they called it] *The Work, This good Work, and This glorious Work*." He found particularly offensive such claims as Gilbert Tennent's remark that "there is the same Demonstration of the Spirit and power manifested in *This Work*, that attended the preaching of Christ and his Apostles." He concluded that no one had determined exactly what "this Work" was because many revivalists claim "everything," including "Disorders" evidenced by such behavior as "Trances and Screaming." Chauncy believed that some revivalists were too quick to accept as fact private testimony of God's work within individuals, however strange the account might be. Of Thomas Prince, Chauncy wrote that "I do not know any one that had more learning among us, excepting Doct. Cotton Mather." However, when it came to Prince's support of the revival, Chauncy added that "he would have been much greater, had he not been apt to give too much credit, especially to surprising stories. He could easily be imposed on this way."[20] Antirevivalists warned readers that just because someone called recent events a revival did not make them so.

While insisting that revivalists should be precise in defining "The Work" and should provide concrete evidence to substantiate their assertion that it was a Work of God, antirevivalists sometimes made their own unsubstantiated claims. In 1743, Thomas Fleet published *A Letter From a Gentleman in Scotland, To His Friend in New England*, a scathing attack on revivalist publications. The anonymous author of the pamphlet explained his reason for writing the letter in a lengthy subtitle: "wherein many mistakes, relating to these things, [i.e., the Work at Cambuslang] that have been formerly and lately transmitted to this country, are rectified, and the whole affair set in a true and impartial light." In other words, this would be the definitive, unbiased account based on a fair reading of all the evidence. In recommending the pamphlet to readers, the publisher claimed that it was written "in so masterly a way, with elegance of thought . . . that it will sufficiently recommend itself to every candid and ingenuous reader." Then, in a statement that he himself would have lampooned mercilessly had it been written by a revivalist, the publisher added, "there is no need to acquaint the world, either by whom, or to whom, it was written."[21] That is, he asked the reader simply to take the unattributed argument at face value, precisely what antirevivalists accused revivalists of doing. As in other wars, the participants insisted on fair fighting only on the part of their opponents.

Charles Woodmason found in the South Carolina backcountry what Caldwell discovered in New England: revivalists as inventors. While performing his work as an Anglican missionary in that region, Woodmason penned one of the most colorful and scathing denunciations of itinerants. He called them "roving Teachers that stir up the Minds of the People against the Establish'd Church, and her Ministers—and make the Situation of any Gentleman extremely uneasy, vexatious, and disagreeable." Woodmason's impressions came from firsthand experience. "Some few of these Itinerants have encountered me," he wrote; "I find them a Sett of Rhapsodists—Enthusiasts—Bigots—Pedantic, illiterate, impudent Hypocrites—Straining at Gnats, and swallowing Camels, and making Religion a Cloak for Covetousness Detraction, Guile, Impostures and their particular Fabric of Things."[22] The revivalists had "made" religion into something that violated Woodmason's sense of order and propriety. In short, their "invention" was offensive to his Anglican sensibilities.

Some antirevivalists also claimed that zealous promoters were more destroyers than restorers of true religion. In particular, they denounced the awakeners' "Disorders in Practice." They saw in itinerancy both arrogance and censoriousness. Roving evangelists, "without the Knowledge, or contrary to the Leave of the *stated* Pastors in such Places, assemble their People to hear *themselves* preach, arising, we fear, from too great an Opinion of *themselves*, and an uncharitable Opinion of *those Pastors*." Moreover, they violated the sanctity of the ministerial office through encouraging lay exhorters who, with "*no education* and but *low Attainments* in Knowledge, in the great Doctrines of the Gospel, without any *regular Call*, . . . take upon themselves to be *Preachers* of the Word of GOD."[23] The result was spiritual anarchy, as anyone claiming the new birth could speak authoritatively of spiritual matters.

In addition to criticizing itinerants and exhorters, the antirevivalists disapproved of the so-called awakening's tendency to promote division between clergy and laity. "The Spirit and Practice of *Separation* from the *particular Flocks* to which Persons belong," they warned, "is very subversive to the Churches of CHRIST, opposite to the Rule of the Gospel." They also condemned the arrogance bred in the laity who claimed the new birth. Too often they assumed "to themselves the Prerogative of GOD, to look into and *judge* the *Hearts* of their Neighbors, *censure* and *condemn* their *Brethren*." And the critics denounced what they considered to be undue emotionalism that sometimes manifested itself in public worship as crying, moaning, and shouting. They wrote, "the many Confusions that have appeared in some Places, from the Vanity of Mind, and ungoverned Passions of People, either in the Excess of *Sorrow* or *Joy*, with *the disorderly Tumults* and *indecent Behaviours* of Persons, we judge to be so far from an Indication of the *special Presence of* GOD with those Preachers that have industriously excited and countenanced them . . . that they are a plain Evidence of the Weakness of human Nature."[24] To many critics, enthusiastic preachers fabricated the so-called revival by manipulating emotions. Evangelists and exhorters reduced salvation to an inner, private new birth. And the proponents of the awakening labeled those who disagreed as being either misguided or unconverted.

According to antirevivalists, awakeners employed an artful publicity campaign to put critics on the defensive. Charles Chauncy knew firsthand the difficulty of criticizing the popular Whitefield when the Grand Itinerant first arrived in Boston: "to such a height did this Spirit of [popularity] rise, that all who did not express a very high Thought of Mr. *Whitefield*, were lookt upon with an evil Eye; and as to those who declared their Dislike of what they judged amiss of the Times, they were stigmatised as *Enemies of God and true Religion*, yea, they were openly represented, both from the *Pulpit* and the *Press*, as in danger of committing *the Sin against* the *Holy Ghost*, if not actually guilty even of this *unpardonable* Sin."[25] In criticizing the revivalists' propaganda, Chauncy also acknowledged its effectiveness.

Reverend Stephen Williams agreed that Whitefield's advance publicity was seductive. The pastor at Longmeadow in Hampshire County in western Massachusetts was familiar with revivals, having observed the awakenings in nearby Northampton, first under the preaching of Solomon Stoddard and then under that of Jonathan Edwards. Early in 1740 Eleazar Wheelock informed Williams of a more general awakening led by George Whitefield. Later that year Williams read Whitefield's *Journals* with ambivalence. Generally, he approved, noting that the itinerant "Seems to have much of ye presence of God—& he has been instrumental of doing Great things." Again the novelty of Whitefield's message was not the familiar theme of the new birth, but rather his unusual success in preaching the gospel throughout the British Atlantic world. As Williams commented, such success must signify God's power working through the evangelist. But reading Whitefield's self-aggrandizing account of the revival also raised fear in Williams. He expressed his hope that Whitefield could be preserved from "running into any Extreames yt may disserve ye interest of [Christ]." His reservations notwithstanding, Williams invited Whitefield to preach in his pulpit. The performance "confirmed . . . his estimation of Whitefield's inimitable faculty of touching ye affections and passions."[26]

Thus, initially, Williams applauded the revival's influence on people of western Massachusetts. He approved of the numerous religious societies that formed for the purpose of prayer and devotion. He observed an increase in numbers attending lectures and seeking spiritual counsel. He believed that the accelerated activity signified authentic religious experiences. Yet Williams increasingly became concerned about what he considered excesses. He denounced the disruptive itinerancy of his brother-in-law, James Davenport, whose preaching bordered on demagoguery. But his greatest criticism centered on the newly expressed power of awakened lay men and women who "challenged the traditional position of the office he held." The revival had become "a movement of tremendous popular force, a movement in the pews as well as in the pulpits."[27] Religion seemed to be marching to the loud, volatile drumbeat of popular applause rather than to the quiet, steady rhythm of biblical truth.

Williams objected to the fact that itinerants bypassed duly constituted ecclesiastical structures and preached directly to masses. According to one historian of Hampshire County, settled pastors were relegated to the sidelines. "To a great degree, ministers became as much observers as participants. Those who tried consciously and earnestly to excite the spiritual passions of their people often watched in wonder as their congregations went almost wild with both joy and agony." In other words, the settled clergy had lost control, as "everywhere people seemed to have pushed the normal relations between pastor and flock beyond their traditional bounds, and the desire for salvation that gripped many led them to want more and demand more from their ministers."[28] Roving imposters had driven wedges between parishioners and pastors.

Some antirevivalists found ridicule to be effective in attacking the awakeners' use of unorthodox means to propagate their message. One London opponent denounced the Methodists who "preached in the Streets, and even at the Exchange," in order to make a show and attract a crowd. Conceding that revivalists had "not yet come to that extravagancy, as to run about naked," they noted that "their other Methods to raise Mobs on such occasions are notoriously known."[29]

Others were more explicit and systematic in identifying offensive revivalist practices. One correspondent to the *Boston Evening-Post* addressed a question posed by another letter-writer: "What are the great Means and Instruments of keeping up the Spirit of Enthusiasm in the Land?" The writer listed five methods in descending order of their offensiveness to an antirevivalist, and, correspondingly, their effectiveness to promoters of the awakening. First, he cited itinerant preaching as "the great Instrument of *Religious Mischief*; the grand Engine which begun the Work." Second, he claimed that the *Christian History* represented the "most diffusive Evil," reaching an audience on both sides of the Atlantic. Third, the author argued that revivalists had won the public relations war in which "*able and learned Preachers*" were disparaged and "those of a *very different Character*" are promoted." Fourth, he blamed the "Unsteady Conduct" of the settled ministry whose preaching "has sometimes been against and other times been for the work." Fifth, he blasted other pastors who openly encouraged the revival by conducting "itinerations of their own."[30]

For many antirevivalists, itinerancy, advertising, and lay exhorting represented the most offensive practices of the awakeners. In attacking itinerant evangelists, opponents portrayed them in the same unflattering terms as were often employed against peddlers of petty goods. One depiction of early American chapmen will suffice. "The whole race of Yankee peddlers," wrote one harsh critic, "are proverbial for dishonesty. They go forth annually in the thousands to lie, cog, cheat, swindle, in short, to get possession of their neighbour's property in any manner it can be done with impunity. Their ingenuity in deception is confessedly very great. They warrant broken watches to be the best time-keepers in the world; sell pinchbeck trinkets for gold. . . ."[31] Old Lights and Anglicans were equally unflattering of strolling preachers.

Itinerants violated what many pastors considered a sacred trust: their exclusive jurisdiction over spiritual affairs within their own parishes. Itinerants routinely defied that convention. In the 1740s, the revivalist Samuel Davies left his New Jersey home for Virginia to preach his evangelical message where it had not been previously heard. To Anglican clergymen, however, he was an unwanted competitor who disrupted parish churches. According to one minister, if Davies had come into a country where the Church of England was "in the same state of corruption as the Romish Church was at the time of the Reformation," then the clergy would have supported his missionary activities. But "he came 300 Miles from home, not to serve people who had scruples, but to a Country where the Church of England had been Established from its first plantation." Rather than extending the gospel, Davies was merely proselytizing, swaying the affections of church members. The bishop of London, who had oversight of Virginia's ecclesiastical affairs, agreed, maintaining that the Act of Toleration did not protect an itinerant preacher who traveled "over many Counties to make Converts in a Country . . . where till very lately there was not a Dissenter from the Church of England."[32]

Parish ministers also resented the intrusion of uninvited, unlicensed preachers who periodically appeared, attracted large crowds, propagated enthusiastic notions, and left with a promise to return. Itinerants in the 1740s and 1750s seemed to be everywhere. An Anglican clergyman in Virginia, James Maury, warned a colleague of the evils of traveling preachers. "It seems not improper to inform You," Maury wrote, "that the revd Messrs [Samuel] Davies & [John] Todd have lately been guilty of what I think Intrusions upon me, in having preached each of them a Sermon at a Tavern in my Parish." Moreover, he noted that neither had "obtained any properly authenticated License to exercise their Function," an ecclesiastical requirement that soon would become a statutory obligation in Virginia to regulate orderly worship. Maury warned that Davies and Todd had left his parish promising "to range upon our Frontiers" where the Anglican Church's hold was tenuous indeed.[33]

Maury feared the competition of itinerants. They introduced ideas that swayed his parishioners toward heretical notions, sometimes turning the people's affections from their pastors. He noted that "Disaffection in the People to regular Pastors of unblemished Morals & unquestionable Abilities, together with many other unhappy Effects, have usually attended the Ministry of Itinerants & Enthusiasts in this Colony." The pastor at Hanover, Patrick Henry, Sr., described how itinerants' periodic visits kept a parish in disarray: "these Itinerants . . . screw up the People to the greatest heights of religious Phrenzy, and then leave them in that wild state, for perhaps ten or twelve months, till another Enthusiast comes among them, to repeat the same thing over again."[34] Henry led the fight for statutory regulation of what was rapidly becoming a free market of ideas, a prospect that, in his judgment, meant chaos.

The itinerants' advertising practices disturbed Henry because they were effective in alerting large numbers of people to upcoming preaching services. In a letter to a fellow clergyman, Henry warned about Davies's plans for June 1747: "Mr. Davies is to preach at Goochland Court-house next Thursday, from whence he is to travel as far as Roanoke, preaching at certain appointed places in his way." Henry described the advance publicity Davies employed to raise crowds: "circular Letters and Advertisements are dispersed all over the upper parts of this Colony, that the People may have notice of the times & places of meeting. My Informer has one of the circular Letters, and the Advertisement at Goochland Court-house has, I believe, been seen by hundreds."[35] Through advertising, itinerants bypassed parish ministers and invited parishioners to consider an alternative worship experience. Henry knew that such tactics forever changed the relationship he enjoyed with his people, undermining his ability to direct the spiritual instruction of the laity with minimal interference. He now faced competition within his own parish.

Itinerants competed with the settled clergy along a range of issues, including the most sensitive topic of the day: slavery. No dimension of clerical control in eighteenth-century Virginia was as jealously guarded as the religious instruction of slaves. Parish ministers, under the ever watchful and sometimes suspicious eye of slaveholders who dominated local vestries, had long taught African bondsmen and bondswomen the basic tenets of Christianity, always stressing the divine injunction for servants to obey their masters. In the 1750s, Samuel Davies distributed among whites and blacks, many of whom he had taught to read, his assessment of the state of religion among Virginia slaves. The widely circulated pamphlet echoed many of the themes developed by Anglicans, including the central obligation of slave acquiescence in a divinely ordained social structure. Yet the pamphlet contained social dynamite. Davies stated the obvious, observing that the rapid growth of the slave population threatened the security of whites. By distributing his pamphlet among blacks as well as whites, Davies illustrated why the free competition of religious ideas could not be tolerated in Virginia. One letter-writer expressed what must have been a common view of Davies's actions: "Mr. Davies hath sent among our Negroes a Small Pamphlet, I Expect one will be Sent to your Honr wherein you may Perceive Mr. Davies hath much Reproached Virginia. And informs the Negroes they are Stronger than the Whites, being Equal in Number then, & having an Annual addition of thousands. I Can't See any Advantage to the Country, to give this account to the Negroes. . . ."[36] In fact, Davies had already given the pamphlet to slaves. To his enemies, Davies flaunted his disregard of the established church's control. His itinerancy had invaded parish boundaries. His advertising had announced to parishioners an alternative worship experience. And now his pamphlet threatened the very linchpin of Virginia society.

Clerical opposition to itinerant preachers paralleled storekeepers' protest of peddlers' invading their markets. Outsiders created competition by giving consumers choices, thus draining sales from established retailers or forcing them to reduce prices, which led to lower margins. Colonists debated the activities of Whitefield and other "pedlars in divinity," divided over whether their presence represented choice and convenience or competition and confusion.

Opponents compared itinerant revivalists to peddlers of quack medicines. One contributor to the London *Weekly Miscellany* drew a parallel between Whitefield and "an itinerant pretender to the science of physick [who] was cheating the deluded multitude of their money and health." Quack medicine men relied on artifice to sell their potions: "self-commendations, an enumeration of his many and wonderful cures at home and abroad, the honours and rewards he has received from persons of the greatest distinction, his superior skill in his profession, [and] the extraordinary virtues of his packets." Operating in a similar way, revivalists appealed to the ignorant, who take the "man's own testimony for his abilities and integrity."[37] Objecting to itinerant preachers' "disorders, irregularities, and artifices," another critic claimed that the roving evangelists "have no warrant, but their pretended call from Heaven, to preach in any church in the diocese."[38]

To combat the evangelical challenge, antirevivalists sought to restore and strengthen the closed system so thoroughly violated by "enthusiasts" who claimed no other allegiance than to their own sense of divine calling. Charles Chauncy objected to the intrusiveness of the new religious economy. In 1743 he published a strategy to guard against "Errors in Doctrine, and Disorders in Practice." He condemned preachers "who keep not within their own Bounds, but go over into other Men's Labours: They herein intermeddle in what does not belong to them, and are properly Busie-bodies." Chauncy charged Whitefield with "taking so little Care of his own Flock" in Savannah while he intruded frequently in others' parishes. He also proposed that all clerical candidates undergo a "due Trial of their Qualifications" as a safeguard against the ministrations of "raw unqualified Persons." And as a preservative against the "wrong Use of the Passions," he recommended that all Christians should insist on "a due Care to prove All Things" by biblical standards and right reason rather than submitting "blindfold to the Dictates of others." In short, Chauncy adapted the revivalists' message, calling for a new revival to combat confusion and disorder and promote true religion; his would be a "Revival of Discipline."[39]

In 1743, one antirevivalist urged all critics of itinerants to attack the "vagrant Preachers" and to attack hard. The anonymous pamphleteer said that for too long "they have been deafen'd with Applause" by their admirers and "treated . . . with too much Caution" by their opponents. Those who had attacked itinerants had "handled 'em as if they were afraid of hurting 'em." Calling on his colleagues to join him in taking off the polemical gloves, he pleaded that "our Business *now* should be . . . to expose their *Ignorance* and *Impertinence* to the World."[40]

A close second to itinerants as a target of antirevivalist scorn was revivalist printed propaganda, especially the *Christian History*. On March 1, 1743, Thomas Prince placed an advertisement in the *Boston Gazette* announcing a weekly paper devoted to "authentick Accounts" on the progress of the "Revival of Religion." He promised accounts from New England, other American plantations, and all "Parts of Great Britain." Two weeks later Thomas Fleet published the first of a series of attacks against Prince and the *Christian History* that would continue and intensify over the magazine's two-year life. The first assault appeared in the form of a letter taking note of the new weekly and proposing yet another. The letter-writer characterized it as a "Party Affair" written primarily for "Separatists . . . [who] must be glad of a Work of this Nature, wherein they will doubtless find many Miracles recorded." Ridiculing the new periodical, the author expressed his intention to publish a parallel work that would expand on the central theme in Prince's paper: "to publish the *Progress of Enthusiasm* in all *Ages* and *Nations*, with the Confusions consequent upon it." Warming to the task, he continued, "Particularly I shall enlarge upon the *Pagan Enthusiasm*, and explain the *Peruvian*

Priests blowing Courage into the Natives, with other Mechanical *Operations* upon their Minds.''[41] Thus, in the initial thrust against the revivalist magazine, Fleet was able to introduce the major themes of the antirevivalist argument: the revival was rooted in enthusiasm, not Scripture or reason; at its center were self-styled miracles; its history reached into the dark past of pagan superstition; its leaders produced results through means designed to manipulate weak-minded people; and its publications were highly partisan.

Throughout 1743 and until summer 1744, when war news began to dominate, Fleet filled his newspaper with attacks on articles that appeared in the *Christian History* and on the periodical itself. The October 24, 1743, edition of the *Boston Evening-Post* expressed a savagery intimating that the revival magazine was scoring heavily in the print war. In recognition of the weekly's widespread circulation and influence, the article began by suggesting that its "Design and Tendency is to keep up the Spirit of Contention, Division and Separation thro' all the *American* Provinces, and even beyond the *Atlantic*. A most diffusive Evil this!" The paper's real purposes were to "serve a *religious Party*, . . . *to get Money*, [and] to *suppress the Truth*." The writer claimed that Prince published "weekly the Sentiments of weak enthusiastical Men" and circulated this material among new converts and especially separatists. Having savaged the content, the writer conceded that readers "esteem'd [it] . . . almost of equal Authority with the *inspired Writings*," and noted that "it is publickly read on the Lord's Day in several Churches."[42]

Fleet scoffed at Prince's claims that revival narratives appearing in the *Christian History* were "Authentick Accounts." He drew attention first to the fact that in the May 31, 1743, edition of the *Boston Gazette*, Prince had solicited ministers sympathetic to the revival to submit reports on evidence of awakening in their congregations. Second, Fleet questioned whether the scripted revival narratives were sufficient evidence for the claim that a revival was under way. To him the proof was too thin; he pointed out that each rested solely on the "*single Test* of a *participating Minister*," hardly "*authentick Proof*" of anything other than that pastor's hopes and wishes, or, perhaps, delusions.[43] In another attack on what he regarded as unsupported revival claims, Fleet accused Prince of engaging in the "utmost artifice."[44]

At times, Fleet's attacks on the *Christian History* became malicious ad hominem assaults on the revival magazine's editor, Thomas Prince, Jr. In one particularly personal and tasteless denunciation published as an open letter in the *Boston Evening-Post*, Fleet addressed the "undertaker of the *Christian History*" as "Master Tommy." Later he dismissed the materials "the little Master" printed as "flighty." He even accused Prince of dishonesty for reprinting large sections of revivalist books and pamphlets, suggesting that he should instead have directed his subscribers to purchase copies of the reprinted works and pay full price.[45] In that charge, Fleet was demanding that Prince adhere to an editorial standard that he himself did not follow in his own newspaper, which reprinted large excerpts from antirevivalist works.

One antirevivalist strategy was to turn revivalist propaganda back against the promoters who published it. In particular, opposers questioned or reinterpreted the numbers revivalists publicized as evidence of an extensive movement. When Thomas Prince boasted in July 1743 that 111 New England ministers had signed a testimony to the great Work of God, an Old Light responded with a newspaper article putting that figure in context. Rather than showing widespread support within what revivalists boasted to be a revival center, the figure, according to his analysis, exposed the limits of acceptance. He focused on the number of attesters as a percentage of the total number of pastors from each New England colony. The results showed a surprisingly low rate of endorsement, especially given "all the Art and Pains used" to solicit support, a reference to Prince's newspaper campaign inviting ministers who thought the work was of God to either attend a meeting in Boston or submit a written attestation. Only 1 out of 6 Rhode Island ministers signed the testament affirming the revival as a Work of God. Figures from other provinces were also far lower than raw numbers would suggest: 8 of 30 in New Hampshire, 12 of 120 in Connecticut, and 90 of 250 in Massachusetts.[46]

Additional analysis of the ministerial attestation exposed more weakness. The critic noted that the 111 signatures came at a *second* meeting of revivalist ministers, conducted two months after the first meeting. At the initial session, only 68 Massachusetts pastors had subscribed to a statement affirming the revival, and of those, only 39 "subscribed *plumply to the whole of the Testimony and Advice, as it is printed.*" In other words, one-half qualified their support by stating that they agreed only to the "Substance, Scope and End" of the awakening while expressing concerns about some of the "Embellishments, Additions, or doubtful Assertions" some zealous revivalists were making. The critic concluded that it was clear that the ministers who supported the revival were "very much *divided in their Opinions* about the real Extent of the Work, the true Means of it, and the Nature and Degree of the Blemishes and

Hindrances.''[47] Thus what had been presented as concrete evidence of widespread support—111 ministers attesting to a genuine revival—became in the hands of an analytical opposer something far less, qualitatively as well as quantitatively.

No practice brought more scorn from antirevivalists than that of lay exhorting. Some revivalists justified gospel preaching by untrained men precisely because they were uneducated. Like the apostles of the early church, exhorters claimed that the new birth alone qualified them to preach and prevail "against all the Powers of the Earth." Virginia Anglicans opposed "Lay Enthusiasts" who convened meetings and read "sundry fanatical Books" to the audience. They also objected to unordained, uneducated "strolling pretended Ministers" who invaded Anglican parishes without invitation.[48] The result was disorderliness and confusion. If authority were deemed to rest on individual assertions of divine power, the result would be anarchy. To Anglicans, the clerical call was a holy and solemn commission that merited the most assiduous study. Education was necessary to enable men to deliver the gospel in a rational manner. Otherwise, any mechanic or plowman could announce himself a preacher and proclaim the word of God.

When revivalists insisted that they were merely offering men and women a religious choice, Old Lights countered that enthusiasts' notion of lay choice often resulted in confusion and disorder. In a sermon entitled *A Looking-glass for Changelings*, Isaac Stiles admitted that it was honorable for Christians "to Embrace Truth when ever it offers it self to our Choice, . . . to exchange falsehood for truth, darkness for light, and bitter things for sweet." But he argued that the awakening had inspired a different kind of change: "a changing from good to bad, . . . a changing true Maxims and Opinions for false ones: turning away from the truth and turning unto fables." What he decried most could be characterized as an unregulated religious market created by itinerants who offered their followers choice, regardless of how their "product" squared with teachings of the settled ministers. Stiles could not accept the idea that uninformed, lay people should make choices in something as serious as religion. He observed that lay men and women were "given to change in matters of Religion. They seem always as tho' they had their Religion to chuse, in regard they are never fix'd in any thing; but are for ever wavering like a wave of the Sea, driven to and fro and carried about with diverse & strange Doctrines."[49] To Stiles, the solution to the problems created by changelings was to place lay men and women under the leadership of steadfast ministers: "we ought in this case to make

Choice of men that are of fix'd & steady Principles and uniform in their Practice."[50]

Old Side Presbyterians opposed the revivals for their lack of discipline, especially in allowing unlicensed persons to preach. Meeting in Philadelphia, the Pennsylvania Presbytery published in 1741 their reasons for opposing the revivalists. At the center of their concern was a perceived loosening of clerical control over the supply of ministers. Revivalists like the Tennents refused to submit to the synod's examination of ministerial candidates, insisting that anyone who had experienced the new birth and been called by God to preach should be licensed and ordained. Moreover, they proceeded to send forth newly minted preachers from their "Log College," the evangelical seminary established near Neshaminy, in Bucks County, Pennsylvania, to supply experiential pastors. In addition to opposing any ordination other than that sanctioned by the synod, Presbyterian leaders denounced itinerancy. Not only did itinerants make "irregular Irruptions upon the Congregations," they did so without "immediate Relation, without Order, Concurrence or Allowance of the Presbyteries."[51] In other words, they insinuated themselves between the church's governing body and parishioners. They disrupted the controlled, regulated religious market that had operated for decades in the Middle Colonies.

The Presbyterian revivalist Samuel Blair viewed attacks upon Whitefield as evidence of the evangelist's success in attracting church members to his services. To Blair, Whitefield was taking market share from the settled ministry by offering a product superior to their "sapless" message. In 1741, Blair wrote, "If you want to know the Bottom of all [their opposition]; you know that the Work of God, the Power of his Gospel, deep Soul-Exercise about eternal Things, . . . is likely to make a mighty Inroad upon us." From antirevivalists' perspective, "this by all Means must be hindered . . . from prevailing; and a Reduction of Things to their former peaceful, quiet and secure Situation attempted." Opposing clergymen, as Blair saw it, feared that once "People are enlightened and awaken'd by the Word and Spirit of God, they can't be satisfied any longer with sapless, careless Ministers."[52]

Antirevivalists had admired Whitefield from afar, praising his work in England from 1737 through summer 1739. But when he arrived, their attitude changed. Blair noted the alteration: "While Mr. Whitefield kept within due limits without disturbing our Borders, and stay'd beyond the Water, he was a brave Man, and doing much Good; but he is not long here among us but he is quite unsufferable." Likening the present to apostolic times, Blair wrote, "Thus the Pharisees in our Saviour's Time, spoke well of the Prophets that lived in the Days of their Fathers, at a competent Distance from themselves, while in the mean Time they persecuted the Prophets of God which they had among them."[53] When Whitefield began to stir their parishioners' affections against them, anti-revivalist ministers saw the itinerant as an unwelcome competitor.

ANTIREVIVALIST MESSAGE

In the contest of inventions, antirevivalists often found themselves on the defensive, responding to highly publicized charges that they neglected to preach the great Reformation doctrines. Old Lights and Anglicans felt the sting of the awakeners' anticlericalism. In particular, revivalists castigated missionaries sent to America by the Society for Propagating the Gospel in Foreign Parts. Whitefield claimed that most were worse than no minister at all. Always he contrasted his efforts to advance the Kingdom of God with the church's designs to retard it. After his first visit to New York, he wrote, "The heads of the Church of England seemed resolved to shut out the Kingdom of God from amongst them." By contrast, he boasted that since his visit, "as much, if not more good has been done there, than in any other place, in so short a time."[54]

The Anglican clergy insisted that they were as concerned about piety as were their Congregational brethren. In mid-1725, the Massachusetts General Court approved a ministerial petition calling for a synod to "revive decaying Piety, in conformity with the Faith & order of the Gospel." However, the petitioners, pastors led by Cotton Mather, did not include Church of England priests. Timothy Cutler and Samuel Myles, ministers of the two Boston Anglican churches, petitioned Governor William Dummer and the court to include them in the synod. They wrote, "As the episcopal Ministers in this Province are equally concerned with the Petitioners for the Purity of Faith & manner in the Land it is disrespectful to them not to be consulted in this important affair."[55] The court rejected their plea. While royal authorities blocked the Synod of 1725, the ministerial jockeying in anticipation of it revealed deep-seated animosity toward Anglicans.

Excluded by the Congregational clergy and the General Court, the Church of England ministers sought an independent avenue for promoting their faith. Led by Cutler and James Honeyman, the clergy organized themselves into an association for fulfilling their mission "by preaching and practising a profound devotion towards God, all possible Loyalty to his most Sacred Majesty, King George, and a full complacency in the succession established in his most illustrious House." The pastors noted "with great satisfaction that we behold our several congregations in a thriving condition and find in multitudes of our neighbors very easy and open minds to the reception of Truth."[56] But therein lay the problem. Congregationalists had a very different version of the truth and tried to thwart the church's rendition. What ensued and heightened during the evangelical revival was increased competition between advocates of very different conceptions of the gospel and how it should be taught and practiced.

With the establishment of their own ministerial association, and convinced that cooperation with Congregational ministers was impossible, the Anglican clergy embarked upon an aggressive program to expand membership, including proselytizing. Cutler began preaching in neighboring towns such as Braintree, Dedham, and Scituate. And at his own Christ Church, he reported increased membership and attendance, noting that audiences were "seldom without dissenters." He observed on another occasion that "it is not uncommon for Dissenters to visit my congregation, who, many of them, do depart with satisfaction, which many that are inveterately set against the Church labor to overballence by a spirit of zeal and acrimony against me."[57] In 1727 he estimated that attendance "is now encreased to about 700 or 800," up from around 400 two years earlier. By the end of the Great Awakening, Boston had three Anglican churches; Christ Church was the smallest, with about 600 members. Such remarkable growth, four- or fivefold over twenty years, indicates that the church had experienced its own "revival." The number of Cutler's communicants also doubled, from between 40 and 50 in 1724 to 94 in 1726. Before one was admitted to communion, he or she had not only to demonstrate an understanding of the faith but to exhibit sober and upright behavior as the manifestation of faith. Unlike the subjects of "conversions" dissenters often described, Cutler's communicants seldom underwent a sudden transformation from "a remarkable dissoluteness to a virtuous life." Yet Cutler argued that "there are many serious persons belonging to us both young and old, devout in the Church & consciencious in their conversations & maintaining as unblemished characters for all moral virtues as any of the Dissenters with us."[58]

In 1744, the bishop of Landaff quantified Anglican missionary successes in America. He reported that under the auspices of the Society for the Propagation of the Gospel in Foreign Parts, "more than One Hundred Thousand of our own People [i.e., English men and women], and many Thousands of *Indians* and *Negroes*, have been instructed and baptized into the true Faith of our Lord Jesus Christ." It is noteworthy that the bishop, like revivalists in their claims regarding experimental Christianity, referred to the SPG brand of religion as "the true Faith." He indicated that these impressive results came about in no small part through the dissemination of the printed word: "more than One Hundred and Twenty Thousand Volumes of Bibles and Common-Prayer Books, with other Books of Devotion and Instruction, together with an innumerable Quantity of pious small Tracts." Moreover, even in the hotbed of revival fervor, Anglicans were making gains. The bishop noted that the number of church members in New England increased during the awakening, and that "the visionary Feuds concerning Methodism and the New Light [were] being kept within the Bounds of those who began them."[59]

Old Light Congregationalists agreed with Anglican critics. They too believed that the "revival" was more enthusiastic hype than demonstrable reality. They made clear, however, that they supported any genuine Work of God, including whatever portion of the current stir that was an ordinary, reasonable, scriptural manifestation of divine inspiration. Jonathan Ashley, pastor at Deerfield, Massachusetts, objected to a newspaper attack by William Cooper accusing him of not only resisting the Work of God but not understanding what it was. Ashley replied in a letter printed in the *Boston Evening-Post* and also published as a pamphlet. He wrote that "Love to God and our Neighbour, the Lord Jesus Christ has made the Sum of the Work of God, if by it is meant (what ought to be) a Work of God wrought in Men by the Holy Spirit." Like the revivalists, Ashley insisted that the indwelling spirit of God brings about change in persons, not good works of their own. But, differentiating his understanding from that of some zealous promoters, Ashley emphasized that the result of the indwelling spirit is active love, not a censorious attitude that breeds division. Ashley closed his remarks by proclaiming the necessity of "this Work of God" in the lives of all men and women.[60]

Old Lights considered themselves faithful to their Puritan heritage and accused New Lights of fashioning a novel message based more on enthusiasm than on Scripture. In the early 1740s, Charles Chauncy no doubt recalled that just a few years earlier his sermons had been acceptable to those now questioning his views of redemption and other evangelical ideas. No less a revivalist leader than Thomas Prince had invited Chauncy to fill his pulpit on occasion, confident in the younger minister's theological soundness.[61] In Chauncy's reckoning, his theology had not changed; the revivalists were the ones who had introduced new and strange notions.

The evangelical revival underscored the very different conceptions of the gospel held by Anglicans and the awakeners. The revivalists reduced the gospel message to the "one thing needful," a new birth—that is, conversion. Moreover, they emphasized "religion of the heart," seeing the "affections" as the seat of salvation. And they elevated inner experience over doctrinal understanding. They censured those who did not subscribe to their notions, especially the Anglican clergy, often labeling them "unconverted." Ministers of the Church of England saw the gospel in another light. They believed that individuals grew into an understanding of God's love and grace. The standards for correct understanding of gospel truth were Scripture and reason. God was a god of order and harmony and communicated his truths in like manner. The church provided the best means by which people came to know God's grace, and through which they practiced their faith. Ministers understood their primary goal as that of propagating and maintaining Christian practice through teaching and preaching and performing the church's ceremonies.[62] To deny that revivalists believed in reasonable as well as affectionate Christianity, and to claim that Anglicans made no allowance for dramatic conversions, is to oversimplify the matter. But fundamental differences separated the two groups.

No issue more separated pro- and antirevivalists than the relation between individuals and the church. In an evangelistic strategy that bypassed the clergy, awakeners appealed to individuals to work out their own salvation. Evangelicals preached that conversion was a matter solely between a man or woman and God, and that the issue could be settled with certitude: that "all true Converts are as certain of their gracious State as [a] Person can be of what he knows by his outward Sense." Moreover, men and women should assume control of their spiritual lives even if it meant leaving their parish church. Though they denied advocating ecclesiastical separatism, evangelicals did preach that "People [were] under no sacred Tye . . . to their own Pastors . . ., but may leave them when they please, and ought to go where they think they get most Good."[63] In other words, people had a choice, and if their current pastor did not provide sufficient spiritual nurture, they should seek it elsewhere. Because the new birth was experiential—a matter of the heart as well as the head—revivalists believed that everyone, regardless of education, could respond to God's grace.

Antirevivalists viewed the evangelicals' actions differently. They held that many in Whitefield's or Tennent's audiences possessed weak, not independent, minds. They accused the itinerants of "preaching the Terrors of the Law . . . and so industriously working on the Passions and Affections of weak Minds." Such terrifying preaching was aimed at frightening, not enlightening, men and women. Furthermore, according to antirevivalist Presbyterians in Philadelphia, revivalists sought not to expand people's religious choices but to narrow them by controlling who preached in revival services. According to one synod leader, "by Virtue of Mr. Whitefield's Order," only those approved by the Grand Itinerant could preach to the huge audiences gathered on Society Hill.[64]

Competing inventions also involved a contest of canons. In opposing Jonathan Edwards's Calvinism, Charles Chauncy fashioned a scriptural defense that might be called a canon of universal grace. In a sermon published well after the Great Awakening but reflecting ideas he expressed during the revival, Chauncy argued in *Salvation for All Men* the doctrine of universal salvation. His reasoning and the biblical authority he invoked echoed those which John Wesley had employed in 1740 in his sermon on free will, the occasion for the Wesley-Whitefield split. Much of Chauncy's work consisted of lengthy quotations from his own canon of right-thinking theologians, including Jeremiah White, chaplain to Oliver Cromwell and "an eminently pious, good man"; Dr. David Hartley, "a man of known serious piety, a disciple of Mr. John Wesley"; and one, Joseph Nicol Scott, who claimed to have "with repeated care, examined all the passages of scripture that relate to the future punishment."[65] Through his "pious and learned" authorities, Chauncy examined the Bible for texts proving not only that universal salvation was God's design but that grace was a reality for all humans.

Chauncy argued his case by piling text upon text that alluded to the universality of salvation. He held that the New Testament makes clear that Christ became a ransom for all: "See Titus ii.11. *The grace of God, which bringeth salvation to all men, hath appeared, &c.* i Tim. iv.10. Rom. v.18. 1 John ii.2. *If any man sin we have an advocate with the father, Jesus Christ the righteous, who is the propitiation for our sins, and not for ours only, but for the sins of the* WHOLE WORLD."[66] As carefully as he searched the Scriptures for references that fit his case, Chauncy ignored those that discuss divine election. In the contentious religious economy of the eighteenth century, he knew that he must present his own case as authoritatively and persuasively as possible, fully aware that competitors would do the same with their claims.

Old Lights and New Lights also differed over the relative importance of reason and emotion in salvation. Old Lights equated emotionalism and enthusiasm. Chauncy applied the term "enthusiasm" to awakeners in the word's "bad sense, as intending an *imaginary*, not a real inspiration" from God. Enthusiasts deluded themselves and others by mistaking "the workings of [their] own passions for divine communications, and fanc[y] [themselves] immediately inspired by the Spirit of God, when all the while, [they are] under no other influence than that of an overheated imagination."[67]

Critics of the revival believed that awakeners deluded their followers by encouraging them to give priority to emotion over reason. The Harvard faculty warned that feelings too easily succumbed to "Suggestions of the evil Spirit." They maintained that one must always judge religious experience by the standards of reason and Scripture. People must be aware that if religious impulses or impressions "be not agreeable to our Reason, or to the Revelation of the Mind of God to us, in his Word, nothing can be more dangerous than conducting ourselves according to them."[68]

To many revival critics, awakeners, while representing themselves as possessing a catholic spirit, were dissenters in disguise. SPG missionaries were convinced that Whitefield had targeted church members as potential converts to his brand of evangelicalism. Archibald Cummings, the commissary in Philadelphia, agreed, remarking that Whitefield's "character as a clergyman enables him to do the greatest mischief." By heralding his ordination as an Anglican priest, the itinerant, according to Cummings, "thereby fights against the church under her colours, & Judas like betrays her under pretence of friendship, for which reason the Dissenters are exceeding fond of him, cry him up for an oracle & pray publicly for his success, that he may go on conquering & to conquer & in return he warmly exhorts his proselytes from the church to follow them as the only preachers of true sound doctrine." In other words, the commissary believed that the revivalists were really on a mission of proselytizing church members rather than converting the unchurched. Missionary Richard Backhouse of Chester, Pennsylvania, described how "these new Apostles convert the secure [i.e., Anglican] world." They first convince parishioners that they have based their faith on a false foundation: "They tell them they are in a damn'd state, and sentence them immediately to hell." Having raised doubts about their salvation, the evangelists and exhorters, by "incessantly gadding thro' the Country," frighten men and women, who "with throws and pangs are born again."[69] Despite Cummings's public opposition to Whitefield, the commissary lamented that "great numbers" believed everything the evangelist said as if his utterances proceeded from "immediate inspiration."[71] everything the evangelist said as if his utterances proceeded from "immediate inspiration."[70]

ANTIREVIVALIST PUBLICATIONS

As vigorously as revivalists challenged preawakening religious norms and practices, antirevivalists defended them. Though revivalists claimed to uphold the best in American religious tradition—that is, the values and beliefs of the original Puritan immigrants—opponents contested that assertion. Thus two spiritual armies engaged in a struggle to define colonial religious culture: awakeners who accused established ministers of accommodating Protestantism to the world versus antirevivalists who defended their churches against such enthusiastic assaults. It was a cultural contest pitting "outsiders" (revivalists) against "insiders" (antirevivalists). According to one historian, "religious struggles engage people in elaborate strategies that on each side entail affirmation and denial, advancement and repression, of a set of cultural options. Some groups champion themselves as upholders of norms, others as challengers of those norms."[71]

To combat the so-called revivals, some leading critics in Britain and America formed a loose-knit transatlantic communication network. At the center were Church of England clergymen, especially the bishop of London, the church's colonial commissaries, and SPG missionaries. As Whitefield sailed for America in 1739, Bishop Edmund Gibson published a pastoral letter criticizing enthusiasm. Within months, Andrew and William Bradford reprinted the epistle in Philadelphia. By the end of 1740, however, American clergymen needed new ammunition to combat the enthusiasts. "Your Lordship's Letter hath had an hearty Welcome, and been very beneficial where it has reached," wrote Timothy Cutler to Bishop Gibson, "but the Copies of it are very rare." Several months later, Cutler expressed his appreciation to the SPG secretary for "the good books" the society had sent "occasioned by the disorders and confusions Mr. Whitefield and his Disciples have wrought among us." He requested additional copies of a particular antirevivalist work, "The Trial of Mr. Whitefield's Spirit." Cutler was confident that the volume "would highly serve us were it spread abroad."[72]

Correspondence from SPG missionaries informed the bishop of London and the society itself of revival activity in America. In almost 75 percent of Massachusetts missionaries' letters to the SPG secretary between 1739 and 1745, news about the awakening predominated. The incidence of revival reportage was also strong in Pennsylvania, where two-thirds of the letters centered on the "enthusiasts'" activities.[73]

Central to the contest for defining religious culture in the 1740s were competing fictions. Revivalists, for instance, cast themselves as outsiders who challenged clerical insiders. They expressed their antagonism to established institutions through a "language of dissent" that placed leaders of vested interests on the defensive.[74] During Whitefield's 1739–1740 tour, revivalists stayed on the offensive, exploiting popular dissatisfaction with settled ministers and their churches. After his departure, and as more radical itinerants such as James Davenport challenged colonial culture through bizarre behavior, the contest shifted in favor of the insiders, who hammered away at the confusion and disorder revivalists promoted.

From 1740 through 1742, the revivalists continued their mastery of the popular press. In 1740, they published 42 works—mainly short pieces intended for distribution among lay men and women—while the opposition printed 8 (see table 6.1). Antirevivalist literature originated primarily in the Middle Colonies and South Carolina. The Anglican commissaries of Philadelphia and Charleston defended the clergy against Whitefield's charges that they failed to preach Reformation doctrines, and that they themselves had embraced worldly pleasures. Also, a group of Old Light Presbyterians in Philadelphia and New York attempted to expose Whitefield and Tennent as unorthodox itinerants who violated the Westminster Confession. In 1741, evangelicals published 48 works supporting the awakening, while the opposition printed just 9. Again, opponents in the Middle Colonies and South Carolina led the attack, repeating and elaborating on previous charges. The following year, with Whitefield back in England, revivalist titles fell to 29 while those from the opposition rose to 20. For the first time, the center of antirevivalism shifted to New England. As Gilbert Tennent and James Davenport followed Whitefield in extensive itinerancies through that region, and as their attacks

TABLE 6.1

Revivalism and the Colonial Press, 1739–1745

	1739	1740	1741	1742	1743	1744	1745
Total no. of titles pub'd.	133	184	206	231	207	200	197
No. pubs. related to revival	17	50	57	49	51	31	53
% of revival pubs. to total	13	27	27	21	24	15	27
No. prorevival pubs.	17	42	48	29	24	25	26
No. antirevival pubs.	0	8	9	20	26	6	26
Ratio pro- to anti- pubs.	$\frac{17}{0}$	$\frac{5}{1}$	$\frac{5}{1}$	$\frac{1.45}{1}$	$\frac{0.92}{1}$	$\frac{4}{1}$	$\frac{1}{1}$

Source: Charles Evans, comp., *American Bibliography: A Chronological Dictionary of All Books, Pamphlets, and Periodicals Printed in the United States of America from the Genesis in 1639 down to and including the year 1820* (Chicago, 1904), 2:122–198.

against the settled ministry intensified, opposers began to respond in kind.

The year 1743 was the watershed in the revival's print war. Revivalists published 24 works that year, and antirevivalists 26, with New Englanders again at the forefront of opposition. With Whitefield still in England, Thomas Prince of Boston assumed leadership for the revivalists, promoting the transatlantic awakening through the *Christian History*. After regaining the initiative briefly in 1744 by publishing 25 pamphlets to the opponents' 6, revivalists in 1745 witnessed as many titles coming from the opposition press as from their own, as antirevivalists and revivalists each released 26 works. What gave the numerical equalization added significance was that it occurred during Whitefield's return to America on his second preaching tour. The Old Lights had mobilized their forces and greeted the evangelist's return with an orchestrated attack. As he entered Boston, he no doubt saw all over the city a satirical broadside ridiculing his ministry. More damaging for his itinerancy was a series of testimonials published by ministerial associations stating their objections to his preaching in their pulpits. One after the other, dissenting pastors from Salisbury, Andover, Weymouth, Marlborough, Hartford, and New Haven expressed their opposition in the public prints, drowning out the voices of defenders from Fairfield, Taunton, and Windham. Moreover, the presidents and tutors at Yale joined their counterparts at Harvard in representing Whitefield as dangerous to the good order of religion. The tide of publicity had turned decidedly against the revivals, proclaiming in print the end of the great awakening.

In the Middle Colonies, much of the antirevivalist polemics came from the pens of Presbyterians who objected to the Log College preachers' attempts to disregard the Westminster Confession, especially in the ordination of ministers. In a stinging pamphlet, Robert Cross, a pastor who supported the revival while opposing the revivalists, listed the reasons why the Philadelphia Synod could no longer enjoy the fellowship of the revival leaders. First, he condemned their "heterodox and anarchical Principles" that departed from both Scripture and confession. Second, Cross denounced "their . . . proceeding to license and ordain Men to the Ministry of the Gospel, in Opposition to, and in Contempt of . . . [the] Synod." Third, he decried their "making irregular Irruptions upon the Congregations, to which they have no immediate Relation." Fourth, he deplored their "Principles and Practices of rash Judging and Condemning all who do not fall in with their Measures, both Ministers and People, as Carnal, Graceless, and Enemies to the Work of God." Fifth, he condemned "their industriously persuading People to believe, that the Call of God whereby he calls Men to the Ministry, does not consist in their being regularly ordained . . . but in some invisible Motions and Workings of the Spirit, which none can be sensible of but the Person himself. . . ." Sixth, Cross criticized their "preaching the Terrors of the Law in such Manner and Dialect as has no Precedent in the Word of God." Such preaching, he charged, worked on "the Passions and Affections of weak Minds, as to cause them to cry out in a hideous Manner, and fall down in Convulsion-like Fits." And finally, he censured their "preaching and maintaining, that all Converts are as certain of their gracious State, as [a] Person can be of what he knows by his outward Senses; and are able to give a Narrative of the Time and Manner of their Conversion."[75]

Two years later, New England polemicists published a catalog of charges against the revivalists that were similar to those cited by Middle Colony Presbyterians. In a 1743 convention, a group of pastors testified against "Errors in Doctrine" and "Disorders in Practice" committed by revival promoters. Under the former heading, the antirevivalists repeated two of Cross's objections: "that some in our Land look upon what are called *secret Impulses* upon their Minds, without due Regard to the *written Word*, the *Rule* of their Conduct," and "that none are *converted* but such as *know* they are converted, and the *Time when*." The New Englanders also listed practices that Cross had denounced: itinerants' invading settled ministers' parishes without invitation; revivalists' ordaining ministers without "any *special Relation* to a *particular Charge*"; preachers' censuring and condemning their brethren as unconverted and unworthy of proclaiming the gospel; and evangelists' employing a sermonic style designed to arouse "ungoverned Passions of People, either in the Excess of *Sorrow* or *Joy*, with the *disorderly Tumults* and *indecent Behaviours*" of many persons.[76]

The effectiveness of antirevivalism in the public prints is illustrated by its influence on a staunch revivalist, Nicholas Loring, pastor of North Falmouth, Massachusetts. Loring testified that he had "entertain'd a very high Esteem of Mr. Whitefield from the Time of his first coming into New England to this Day." However, when he saw the advertisements of antirevivalist testimonials, his confidence began to erode. "At the opening of his late Visit to New-England," Loring wrote in 1745, "seeing the Testimonies of so many Reverend Gentlemen (advertiz'd in the publick Print) against him, refusing him their Pulpits, and warning the World of him as a dangerous Man, I felt my Regards for him and his Conduct, sensibly to abate." Loring's account attests to the power of advertising. He had not yet read the advertised publications, but the stature of their authors shook his faith. Also, their appearance in the "publick Print" gave the notices added credibility: after careful deliberation, prominent ministers were making known their views of Whitefield in print for all to see. Eventually, Loring acquired copies of the publications and testified that "upon the reading of them, all my hate Prejudice against him [Whitefield], vanish'd like Smoke."[77] Clearly for him, seeing the advertisements and reading the texts had been two distinct experiences. One can only speculate about the impact of the advertisements on those who did not go on to read the texts.

The amount and nature of newspaper coverage reflected publishers' attitudes toward the revival. In some instances editorial decisions had been reached before Whitefield's arrival. How Boston's five newspapers covered the evangelist's first week in Massachusetts signaled what each planned for the rest of his itinerancy. The strongest revivalist printers were Samuel Kneeland, Timothy Green, and John Draper. Since before the Northampton awakening, Kneeland and Green's publication list had contained many evangelical titles, including works by Edwards and Colman. It is not surprising, then, that both of their newspapers, the *New England Weekly Journal* and the *Boston Gazette*, gave Whitefield extensive coverage. The *Journal* devoted three paragraphs, or a total of 31 lines, to the itinerant's arrival, noting the "vast Crowds" following him and the "great Impressions" his sermons made on hearers. It also contained a testimonial from Charleston, South Carolina, characterizing Whitefield's Georgia orphanage as a "little Heaven on Earth."[78] The *Gazette's* coverage was even greater: four paragraphs and 40 lines, including the same testimonial.[79] Similarly, the revivalist John Draper devoted two paragraphs of 55 lines in his *Boston Weekly News-Letter* to Whitefield's first week.[80]

Boston's two other newspaper publishers, E. Huske of the *Boston Weekly Post-Boy* and Thomas Fleet of the *Boston Evening-Post*, were much more restrained in their coverage. Huske included a single paragraph of 14 lines on Whitefield's first week. Fleet also devoted just one paragraph but limited it to 4 lines, acknowledging that Whitefield preached to "very large Assemblies, and with great Applause."[81] Over the following weeks, Huske and Fleet would become far less charitable to the revivalists.

In the September 29 edition of the *Evening-Post*, Fleet expressed his relief upon Whitefield's leaving Boston. He wrote, "this Morning the Reverend Mr. Whitefield set out on his Progress to the Eastward, so that the Town is in a hopeful Way of being restor'd to its former State of Order, Peace and Industry." To that John Draper replied in the *Boston Weekly News-Letter*, "the Generality of sober and serious Persons of all Denominations among us (who perhaps are as much for maintaining Order, Peace and Industry, as Mr. *Evening-Post* and Company) have been greatly Affected with Mr. Whitefield's Plain, Powerful and Awakening Preaching." He charged Fleet with the "Spirit of the Jews" who opposed the apostle Paul's preaching at Antioch, and the "Spirit of the Gadereens" whom Jesus rebuked.[82]

Fleet retorted that Draper had taken his statement out of context. The key to understanding the original article was the juxtaposition of an account of unruly soldiers leaving Boston at the same time Whitefield departed. Fleet claimed that his comment concerning the restoration of peace and order referred, not to Whitefield's going, but to the soldiers'. He accused Draper of overlooking the conjunction "and" that made Fleet's intentions clear. Moreover, Fleet contended that he "never made the least Opposition to the Rev. Gentleman" and encouraged Whitefield's continued preaching "till we are become more sober and industrious." He admitted that in his newspaper coverage he had "not followed him so far as some others." In Fleet's view, people had a choice among religious styles and expressions. Revivalism was one alternative, offering services at times and places other than those fixed by most parish ministers. But if people chose to follow "their secular employments on appointed times and worship under the ministry of their own pious Pastors, they should not be stigmatiz'd as Atheists, Profligates, or very irreligious Persons."[83] Similarly, newspaper publishers were free to give as much or as little attention to a particular religious practice as they desired.

Whitefield's censorious remarks about revered clerical leaders and educational institutions rallied antirevivalists. On April 7 the publication of his so-called New England Journal became the basis of a heated discussion in Boston newspapers.[84] Two passages in particular offended New Englanders, including some who supported the revival. Of Harvard, Whitefield had recorded in his *Journals* during his visit in 1740, "Discipline is at a low ebb. Bad books are become fashionable among the tutors and students. Tillotson and Clark are read, instead of Shepard, Stoddard, and such-like evangelical writers." And of New England clergymen, he generalized, "Many, nay most that preach, I fear, do not experimentally know Christ."[85] Upon reflection a more mature Whitefield rued the intemperate passages. "In my former Journal, taking things by hearsay too much," he confessed in the 1756 revision, "I spoke and wrote too rashly of the colleges and ministers of New England." Belatedly, he asked "public pardon from the press," acknowledging that his words were "rash and uncharitable and though well-meant, . . . did hurt."[86]

William Brattle, while pledging his continued support of the revival, attacked what he characterized as Whitefield's intemperate, ill-informed 1740 assaults on Harvard and New England clergymen. Confessing his belief that Whitefield "has been instrumental in awakening and stirring up People to a serious Concern for the Salvation of their precious Souls," Brattle asserted that the evangelist was not infallible. He took exception to Whitefield's censure in a series of newspaper articles that became the front-page story in five issues of the *Boston Gazette.* He charged Whitefield with being "partial" in his assessment of Harvard and "uncharitable" in his evaluation of ministers. Brattle hoped that Whitefield's writings would not do "as much Hurt to Religion as his Preaching did Good."[87]

Long after Whitefield's departure for England in early 1741, the revival continued to raise the scorn of its opponents. In Boston, Timothy Cutler identified the press as a continuing fount of awakening notions that kept people astir. Almost two years after Whitefield left the colonies, Cutler wrote, "Books of this unhappy tendency, Books Calvinistic, Enthusiastical, and Antinomian do abound; the Press here never had so full employ before, nor were people ever so busy in reading."[88] And in Virginia, six years after the northern revival had subsided, Anglicans confronted revivalism at every turn. One antirevivalist appealed to the House of Burgesses for help in stemming the tide of enthusiasm sweeping the western counties of Hanover, Henrico, and Goochland. The writer reported "numerous assemblies, especially of the common people" who met on a "pretended religious account, convened sometimes by merely lay enthusiasts." Moreover, groups of men and women met without a trained clergyman presiding and "read sundry fanatical books and used long extempore prayers and discourses." On other occasions, "strolling pretended ministers" such as Whitefield disciple John Cennick led services.[89] From Boston to Williamsburg, revivalists seemed to be on the attack with an army of lay exhorters as well as evangelists, firing endless rounds from pulpit and press.

As revivalists promoted a transatlantic awakening through an informal letter-writing and publishing network, antirevivalists countered with a similar strategy. When Scottish and New England awakeners exchanged accounts of success to promote revival on both sides of the Atlantic, Old Lights countered with what Charles Chauncy called an "antidote" of their own. In a published letter to George Wishart, an Edinburgh minister, Chauncy refuted claims made in a revivalist pamphlet of a "glorious Work of Grace going on in America." Chauncy retorted that the propaganda was a fabrication: "Some of the Things related are known Falsehoods, others strangely enlarged upon; and the Representations, in general, such, as exhibit a wrong Idea of the religious State of Affairs among us."[90] He then proceeded to give his interpretation of events. First came advance publicity that "greatly prepossest" people in favor of the revivalists; then ensued a highly promoted, staged series of extravagances aimed at attracting the "Vulgar"; and finally came "marvellous Accounts" disseminated abroad about a great revival of religion. The tone was one of warning lest Scots be similarly deceived.[91]

Antirevivalists discovered that the same market which revivalists exploited enabled them to reach a broad audience with a variety of cultural productions. Whitefield and other revivalists had blasted the thriving theater in mid-eighteenth-century London as a worldly lure of the devil. As the popular evangelist escalated his public assault on plays and playhouses, leading actors and playwrights countered with attacks against the self-promoting preacher. In such productions as *Will and No Will* and *The Mock Preacher*, playgoers saw the Methodists ridiculed as enthusiastic purveyors of superstitions. But the most scathing attack came in Samuel

Foote's *The Minor,* first performed at David Garrick's Drury Lane Theatre in 1760. Foote focused his ridicule on a cross-eyed character, Dr. Squintum, an obvious caricature of Whitefield. A madam of a brothel, Mrs. Cole, attended one of Squintum's sermons, where the preacher "stept in with his saving grace, got me regenerate, and another creature." Though converted, Cole "continued to ply her illicit trade, prompting another character to observe 'with what ease she reconciles her new birth to her old calling!'" Then Mrs. Cole introduced one of her young girls to a "life of methodism and prostitution with the words: 'Don't you remember what Mr. Squintum said? A woman's not worth saving that won't be guilty of a swinging sin; for they have matter to repent upon.'"[92] *The Minor's* box-office success encouraged Garrick and Foote to follow up with other satires, most notably *The Register Office* and *The Methodist.*

In addition to playwrights and actors, painters and cartoonists lampooned revivalists. William Hogarth, who was equally critical of the Anglican Church's lifelessness, ridiculed the awakeners' "enthusiasm." His *Enthusiasm Delineated* depicts a congregation displaying all sorts of emotionalism. Obviously contrasting this service with that of *The Sleeping Congregation,* Hogarth replaced the hourglass of the earlier painting with a thermometer that registered the congregation's reaction to the service—from zero to higher degrees labeled "Luke Warm," "Love Heat," "Lust Hot," "EXTACY," "Convulsion Fits," Madness," and "Revelation." The Bible is opened to the words "I speak as a Fool." The sounding board above Whitefield's head is cracked with "the noise of his enthusiasm."[93]

Revivalists also were targets of men of letters. In *The History of the Adventures of Joseph Andrews,* Henry Fielding introduced Parson Adams, who wishes to realize worldly gain from his profession. Beset by "the hardships suffered by the inferior clergy," Adams desires to enter the marketplace of printed sermons, hoping to profit as Whitefield and Wesley had. He is confident that his solid orthodoxy would outsell the revivalists' "nonsense and enthusiasm." But from a bookseller, Adams learns that sales appeal, not theology, gets the attention of printers. The bookseller tells him that "for my part, the copy that sells best, will be the best copy in my opinion; I am no enemy to sermons but because they don't sell: for I would as soon print one of Whitefield's, as any farce whatever."[94] Adams's only hope would be to "puff" his sermon. The bookseller suggests that "we could say on the title page, published at the earnest request of the Congregation, or the Inhabitants," or they could make some other bold claim.[95] Fielding's message is clear: Whitefield's sermons sold, not because of correct theology, but because he was a slick self-promoter.

By 1743, antirevivalists on both sides of the Atlantic had succeeded in engaging revivalists in a battle of inventions. They managed to shift much of the reading public's attention away from the revival itself to the debate over whose *account* was more accurate. That summer in Boston, rival groups of ministers met in separate conventions, claimed to weigh the evidence in an impartial way, and reached solemn conclusions regarding the recent Work. Was it a genuine revival, or was it enthusiastic bombast? Revivalists polled their 111 convening pastors, and a majority attested that "there has of late been a happy Revival of Religion." Antirevivalists polled their 68 convening pastors, and a majority lamented the prevalence of "errors and disorders" that had been paraded as revival. The story then became one of whose view was correct, whose "poll" more convincing. One participant in the debate acknowledged that the battle of polls and testimonies would not be decided by the ministers. Rather, "serious Christians [i.e., laypersons] will judge" the matter.[96] Exactly who those "serious Christians" were was itself a matter of much debate.

CHAPTER 7

"This is the Lord's Doing"

As BOSTON'S temperatures climbed in July 1743, the rhetorical battle between New England's pro- and antirevival factions also got a lot hotter. Seething ever since the awakening's opponents had met in convention in May to denounce the revival as the handiwork of enthusiasts rather than the Work of God, Boston's revivalist ministers convened on July 7 to respond. As they began their deliberations, however, the awakeners assumed a neutral, impartial voice suitable for persons seeking a fair evaluation of all pertinent evidence. They observed that the intercolonial revival had become a major news story, "an Affair which has in some Degree drawn every One's Attention, and been the Subject of much Debate both in Conversation and Writing." While asserting that they were discussing a well-known phenomenon, the writers turned to the question of meaning: "the grand Question is," they wrote, "Whether it be a Work of God, and how far it is so?"[1]

At the same time, a group of revivalist ministers from the Middle Colonies dealt with the same issue and sought to establish that the recent religious stirrings were indeed a genuine Work of God. They believed that it was important to make a strong case supported by strong evidence from believable sources in different parts of British North America and beyond. Claims that the event was not a revival of religion made it imperative that a convincing argument be advanced. "Here we must observe," the New Lights from Pennsylvania and New Jersey wrote, "that divers false Reports have been invented and spread industriously both by Word and Writing, in order to blacken the Characeters of several Ministers, who God has been pleas'd of his pure Goodness to honour with Success."[2]

Both sets of ministers declared their strong convictions that the work was indeed a genuine revival of religion. The Bostonians noted that "the most serious and judicious, both Ministers and Christians, have look'd upon it to be, in the main, a genuine Work of God, and the Effect of that Effusion of the Spirit of Grace, which the faithful have been praying, hoping, longing and waiting for." But, while affirming it to be an extraordinary outpouring of God's grace, the same people acknowledged "some

Circumstances attending it, to be from natural Temper, human Weakness, or the Subtilty and Malice of Satan permitted to counter-act this Divine Operation."[3]

Similarly, the Middle Colony revivalists gave "publick Testimony to the Reality and Truth of the late Revival of Religion in this Land; or to what is call'd generally and justly the Work of God." They defined it as a "Work of Conviction and Conversion spread not long since in many Places in these Provinces, with such Power and Progress, as even silenc'd for a Time the most malignant Opposers." It was accompanied by "astonishing Displays of the Divine Almightiness, in alarming multitudes of secure Sinners out of their fatal Stupor, and exciting in them the utmost Solicitude about the everlasting Concerns of their Souls, many of which gave us a Rational and Scriptural Account of their Distress and afterwards of their Deliverance from it, agreeable to the Method of the Gospel of Christ." Answering those who charged that misconduct on the part of some sullied the whole, the attesters asked, "What if there were some Things exceptionable in the Conduct of some of the Instruments and Subjects of this Work, is this so strange an incident in a State of Imperfection, as to give us ground of Surprise and Prejudice against the whole Work?"[4]

When they surveyed the religious landscape in the early 1740s, revivalists were certain that they were witnessing a great revival. According to Jonathan Dickinson, Christians had seen a "Display of God's Special Grace" in what he called "The Work of God, in the Conviction of Sinners, so remarkably of late began and going on in these American Parts." In their preface to Dickinson's account of the revival, Benjamin Colman and other Boston ministers bore testimony to "what is call'd the present Work of God in the Lord." They believed it possible and necessary to separate what was "a glorious Display of the divine Power and Grace" and "those Disorders, Errors, and Delusions, which are only the unhappy Accidents."[5]

APOLOGIES: DEFENDING THE REVIVAL AS THE WORK OF GOD

Before they themselves faced charges of inventing the great awakening, revivalists had accused others of tainting true religion with human invention. In 1738, Jonathan Dickinson had engaged in a pamphlet skirmish with an SPG missionary over what constituted true worship. For the Elizabeth-Town pastor the matter hinged on authorship: if church faith and practice came from God as set forth in Scripture, they were authentic; if, however, they arose from human reason based on the notion that people can save themselves, then that worship was false. In remarks addressed to the Anglican minister John Beach, Dickinson asserted, "all human Inventions and Impositions in the worship of God are *vain Worship*." He hastened to say of the Anglicans that "they have such [i.e., some] Worship among them, as is not of *human Invention*."[6] The clear implication was that the church contained other elements that were fabricated. Dickinson made the charge explicit by citing the influence of Arminians who in matters of faith and practice shifted the focus from sovereign Creator to independent creatures.

Their strong Calvinism convinced awakeners that revival could come only from God, that there could be no place for human invention. Therefore, the most hurtful and serious charge revivalists had to answer was that the work they had encouraged and promoted was not the work of God. Throughout 1742 and 1743, antirevivalists in the Middle Colonies and New England had published polemical pamphlets whose main purpose was to expose the awakening as a human work. They called into question the centerpiece of the revival: the New Birth itself. Anyone, they argued, could claim to have experienced conversion, because it was an internal process known for sure only by the individual and God. Scripture, reason, church tradition—more objective standards for judging the authenticity of one's religious experience—had been ignored, and personal experience reigned supreme. Observable behavior, the polemicists contended, suggested anything but a work of God. Crying out in worship services and falling on the floor during sermons seemed to disrupt, not promote, God's Word. And, they claimed, the public conduct of converts did not improve after the New Birth. If anything, conversion produced arrogance, division, and censoriousness.

Refusing to acknowledge the revival as the work of God, opponents hammered away relentlessly at its human architects and their weaknesses. They cited the most extreme measures of radicals such as James Davenport to tar all evangelicals. And they focused on the innovative measures evangelists employed as clear evidence that human engines drove the awakening. For instance, they argued that preaching the "terrors" of the Gospel in highly emotional tones was bound to produce emotional outbursts among the less educated. And if preachers conducted services daily and filled people's minds with nothing but religion, the result would certainly be a stir about things divine; but, said the polemicists, to see the hand of God was a stretch. Finally, opponents explained the spread of the revival by pointing to the power of example. Through all the publicity, people in one region would have read about how persons in other areas had behaved and would emulate them when revival services began in their community.

Apologists refuted the attacks one by one. They countered that the revival was in reality the work of God; that its measures and manifestations were scriptural and doctrinal; that the work was consistent with great effusions of the past; that the inward work of God had clearly discernible outward manifestations that were marks of divine operation; that extremes and errors were to be expected in a mass movement but did not discredit it; that the work's spread among a large number of people in distant and diverse communities argued for a single divine origin; and that the human means employed to prepare persons to receive God's grace were instruments that God used for his ends, and not the engines of the work.

In making their case, apologists sought to back their contention with evidence they deemed incontrovertible. American revivalists publicized widely the apologies written by Scottish evangelicals. One oft-quoted Scot was William McCullough, pastor at Cambuslang, the Scottish revival's epicenter, who argued that the awakening "is supported by all that Kind of Evidence that Things of this Nature are capable of." In other words, if one acknowledges the existence of extraordinary effusions of God's grace at all, he or she will concede that the present work is genuine. Recognizing the skepticism among doubters and the enthusiasm of some supporters, another Scot, James Robe, sought to lay out a case based on a solid factual foundation. "I am to confine myself to a simple Narration of Facts," he began, "as the Evidences on which the Opinion of many concerning the present happy Change that is wrought on that People, is founded." He pledged to restrict his comments to the evidence, "leaving it to [readers] to draw proper Conclusions from the Facts, after comparing them with Scripture Rules and Instances."[7]

Like his American counterparts, Robe relied upon numbers to support his contention that the revival was truly an extraordinary work of God. Large numbers of converts set this occasion apart from the ordinary working of God's grace. He conceded, however, that the large crowds also included some persons who were impostors. He argued that it was "natural to expect, when on a singular Occasion of this Sort, great Numbers of People from adjacent Towns and Country, came flocking to a Place that became so remarkable . . . that in such a promiscuous Multitude some Counterfeits would readily happen." But, he added, conscientious ministers conducted a "strict Examination" of individuals professing a conversion experience to ensure that the "Work was solid."[8]

To lend weight to his narrative, Robe cited specific statistics in tracing the origins of the revival. The Cambuslang awakening began in January 1742, when "90 Heads of Families" petitioned their minister to conduct a weekly lecture stressing the necessity of regeneration. Then, in February, a large number of men and women gathered for a general prayer meeting, and as word of that meeting spread, subsequent meetings attracted even larger crowds. After Pastor William McCullough gave a sermon in February, "about fifty, came to the Minister's House, under Convictions and alarming Apprehensions about the State of their Souls." Again, news of this event spread, and soon "Numbers daily" came to hear the Word, and McCullough responded with daily sermons. The results were extraordinary: "the Number of Persons awaken'd to a deep Concern about their Salvation . . . has amounted to above 300."[9] Ninety heads of family, fifty under conviction, three hundred awakened: for Robe these figures represented concrete facts that were beyond dispute. Nothing vague or ambiguous about this account.

Aware that detractors expressed skepticism over the so-called conversions, Robe cited evidence that good works followed professions of faith. He reported a "visible Reformation of the Lives of Persons who were formerly notorious Sinners; particularly, the laying aside of Cursing, Swearing and Drinking to excess, among those who were addicted to that Practice." Persons who had mistreated their neighbors not only expressed "Remorse for Acts of Injustice" but made public "Restitution." To Robe, the evidence pointed to an obvious conclusion. "The Sum of the Facts I have presented," he concluded, "is That this Work was begun and carried on under the Influence of the great and substantial Doctrines of Christianity." Convinced that any reasonable reader would agree with his conclusion, he added, "Now I have given you a plain and simple Account of the most material Facts relating to this extraordinary Work at Cambuslang," and "I leave it now to you to judge how far such Facts make it evident, that this Work is from God."[10]

American apologists also supported their claims with facts of their own. Critics had charged that God might indeed have performed a great work within individuals and congregations, but such inward, secret work, they argued, could be known only by the persons or churches experiencing it. Those "facts," they maintained, were not real to anyone who had not experienced them, and therefore the publication of such facts would serve no useful purpose. Revival promoters countered that conversions and revivals were facts that were real and could and should be reported abroad as reliable evidence. Ministers were capable of authenticating true works of God by examining converts against rational and scriptural standards. In their testimony, supporters wrote:

> With respect to numbers of those who have been under the impressions of the present day, we must declare there is good ground to conclude they are become real Christians; the account they give of their conviction and consolation agreeing with the standard of the Holy Scriptures, corresponding with the experiences of the saints, and evidenced by the external fruits of holiness of their lives; so that they appear to those who have the nearest access to them, as so many epistles of Christ, written, not with ink, but by the Spirit of the living God, attesting to the genuineness of the present operation, and representing the excellency of it.[11]

In other words, the attesters argued that in examining those who claimed to have experienced the New Birth, they had followed precisely what their opponents prescribed for assessing authenticity: first, try the converts' "impressions" by scriptural standards; and second, critique behavior as well as testimony in measuring change.

Revivalists also defended their definition of "this Work," the term often used for the awakening. In pressing supporters for clarification, antirevivalists suggested that "this Work" included dangerous innovations absent from both Scripture and the history of the early New England Puritans. Theophilus Pickering of the Second Church in Ipswich tried to get Daniel Rogers of the First Church to admit that "by 'This Work' [revivalists] meant more than they were willing to confess, and that it included 'some effects attendant, as visible signs or open discoveries' of the Spirit's operations." Rogers retorted that he and other promoters were making no special claims for the disruptive behavior manifested by some; they were, indeed, attributing no novelty to the present revival. He explained that by " 'This Work—This Work of God,' we mean God's work of convicting and converting sinners; and we do not mean to distinguish it from the convincing and converting work of God, carried on in New England in the days of our fathers, or anywhere else in any age of the Christian church; for we suppose God's work in convincing and converting sinners to be ever the same, as to the substantial parts of it."[12] Rogers refused to allow Pickering to put words in his mouth.

In spring 1742, the revival came under its heaviest attack in both the Middle Colonies and New England. At the core of the assault was the assertion that the work throughout the land was not of God. Rather, according to the polemicists, it was a display of hubris and excess by overwrought enthusiasts who found easy prey among the poorer, less learned members of society. In both regions, recent behavior of some revivalists fueled such charges. In New Jersey, Robert Cross, who had been an early supporter, became one of the revival's severest critics. And in New England, James Davenport's extravagant claims of divine inspiration tarred him and all other itinerants with the brush of enthusiasm. Revivalists defended their movement through convening ministerial associations and presbyteries and issuing defenses of the divine authorship of the awakening. The New York Presbytery, led by Jonathan Dickinson of Elizabeth-Town, New Jersey, and Ebenezer Pemberton of New York City, explained why they deemed it necessary to publish apologies. "We protest," they wrote after meeting in May 1742, "against *all those Passages* in any of the Pamphlets which have been published in these Parts, which seem to reflect upon the Work of *divine Power and Grace* which has been carrying on in so wonderful a Manner in *many of our Congregations*." They then declared to "all the World, that we look upon it to be the indispensable Duty of all our Ministers to encourage *that Glorious Work* with their most faithful and diligent Endeavours."[13]

Apologists on both sides of the Atlantic spoke out from the pulpit and the press in defense of the revival. Gilbert Tennent led the New Brunswick Presbytery in thanking God for raising up "*Witnesses* in diverse Parts of the World to appear for his Cause by *publick Attestations* and *Defences*." They mentioned several by name that they found especially effective in countering "misrepresentations": Jonathan Edwards's *Distinguishing Marks* and *Some Thoughts Concerning the Present Revival*, James Robe's *Narrative of the Extraordinary Work at Cambuslang*, Alexander Webster's *Divine Influence: The True Spring of the Extraordinary Work at Cambuslang*, and Jonathan Dickinson's *Display of God's Special Grace*, all of which came from colonial presses in 1742–1743. The fact that Scottish revivalists were writing defenses similar to those penned by Americans lent weight to the argument that the work on both sides of the Atlantic emanated from the same divine source.[14]

Stung by charges of fellow Presbyterians that revivalists had violated every tenet of church government, many New Jersey revivalists separated from the Philadelphia Presbytery and formed the New Brunswick Presbytery. Reading published attacks from former colleagues such as Robert Cross and John Thomson, members of the new organization under Gilbert Tennent's leadership responded. They claimed that "divers *false Reports* have been invented and spread industriously both by Word and

Writing, in order to blacken the Characeters of several Ministers whom God has been pleas'd of his pure Goodness to honour with Success." To the revivalists, the attacks were wholly groundless because of overwhelming evidence pointing to God's authorship of the work. The apologists laid out what to them was clear proof that the work was of divine origin: "astonishing Displays of the divine Almightiness, in alarming Multitudes of secure Sinners out of their fatal Stupor"; "poor Souls flock'd to the dear Immanuel"; "*Multitudes* in our religious Assemblies, trembled like the *Jailor* (as described in the *Acts of the Apostles*)"; and "these Sensations [in converts] have been followed by a *Gospel Conversation*" and altered behavior. The conclusion was clear: "In short, we are fully perswaded that we have had all that *Evidence* of the Reality of a *Work of God* among us, which can be reasonably expected in the present State of Things, since Miracles have ceased."[15] Given the indisputable signs of revival, the revivalists concluded that "it is shocking to think that any should dare to oppose a Work attended with such commanding Evidence as has been among us!"[16]

The disagreement among New England ministers over the meaning of religious events in the early 1740s was a matter of emphasis. When they met at their annual convention in Boston on May 25, 1743, revival critics outmaneuvered revivalists and produced a printed testimony that focused on "errors in doctrine" and "disorders in practice." Only after listing six specific criticisms in each category did the authors, who won approval of the draft by a narrow vote, even mention the possibility of revival. In the last paragraph, the attesters wrote, "where there is any special revival of pure religion in any parts of the land at this time, we would give unto God all the glory."[17] Clearly the majority was saying that what dominated the religious scene was a great noise generated by self-promoting enthusiasts with only scattered evidence of real revival. Revival promoters believed that the antirevivalists had distorted the sentiments of most ministers present by emphasizing in great detail reported instances of errors and disorders while barely acknowledging the work of God.

Revival promoters protested the published testimony and the process that produced it. Joshua Gee, a strong supporter of the awakening, charged that antirevivalists had pushed their version of the testimony through the convention with much bad faith. First, he claimed, revivalists had understood that the testimony would first attest to "a revival of religion in many parts of the land" and then testify against "errors and disorders." When that did not happen and revivalists voiced their objections, Gee said that "they were interrupted in a rude manner, and treated with open contempt."[18] Moreover, Gee argued that the final document had received only thirty-eight votes, a bare majority, and that number resulted from the presence of many antirevivalists who did not belong to the Boston convention. The implication was that they were invited for the express purpose of ensuring a testimony denouncing the revival.

To set the record straight, revivalists, led by Thomas Prince, called a special meeting of "friends of the revival." The active recruitment campaign resulted in a gathering of supporters, an overwhelming majority of whom subscribed to a testimony expressing unqualified conviction that what had occurred in the land was the "happy Revival of Religion." The tone was entirely different from that of the earlier declaration. Here the emphasis was on the fact of a great and general awakening that was the work of God. Only after that point was established did the subscribers acknowledge that regrettable errors and disorders had attended the work in some instances.

One of the greatest challenges confronting apologists was the antirevivalist charge that "vast iniquities, error, discord, and enthusiasm" suffused the revival. The problem was that there were indeed within the awakening many expressions of those ills. But to call them pervasive was, according to Jonathan Parsons of Lyme, Connecticut, "generally groundless." He expressed his opinion that "things have been misrepresented." While conceding the presence of enthusiasm and fanaticism, he noted that "generally speaking, there has been a great reformation of that evil: our new converts as far as I can observe, are very prudent on that account: they suspend giving any judgment at all, on either side." Parsons described the measures he took to authenticate genuine conversion experiences; he carefully examined converts within his own congregation and visited neighboring communities where revival visited and talked to converts. He reported that this firsthand examination did not confirm the sweeping denunciations opponents made. Moreover, he suggested that revival opponents were guilty of just such rash judgments as they accused revivalists of making.[19]

The zeal of some revivalists and the virulence of most antirevivalists prompted awakeners to develop a systematic apology in support of their beliefs. Beset by excesses from within the movement and besieged by relentless attacks from without, defenders of the great awakening sought to define a "Work of God" with greater clarity. In 1741, Jonathan Edwards, taking on the daunting task of explaining the unusual, published

The Distinguishing Marks Of a Work of the Spirit of God. Specifically, he focused on "that uncommon Operation that has lately appeared on the Minds of many of the People of this Land," and on the "extraordinary Circumstances with which this Work is attended."[20] Opponents singled out the "uncommon" and "extraordinary" to prove that the work was not of God but flowed from overheated imaginations that invented strange notions. Some supporters, on the other hand, exhibited "strange" behavior and held it up as evidence of God's Spirit at work within them. Edwards sought to set rational and scriptural boundaries for understanding how the Spirit of God operated.

At the outset, Edwards defended the revival against charges that it should be dismissed as emanating from God because it was "carried on in a way very unusual and extraordinary." He argued that the rule one must apply in judging a work of God's Spirit is the Bible, not "what we have been used to, or what the church of God has been used to." He explained that "God has heretofore wrought in an extraordinary manner; he has brought those things to pass that have been new things, strange works; and has wrought in such a manner as to surprise both men and angels; and as God has done thus in times past, so we have no reason to think but that he will do so still."[21] One need only read the Scriptures to be reminded that God on occasion brought about "sudden changes," as at Pentecost. And God made promises of future deliverances of his people—promises whose swift fulfillment will confound those who confine his actions to ordinary operations: "Who has heard such a thing? Who has seen such things? Shall a land be born in one day? Shall a nation be brought forth in one moment? For as soon as Zion was in labor she brought forth her sons [Isa. 66:8]." Revivalists believed that they were witnessing just such a deliverance in the eighteenth century.

While stating his opposition to excesses of some revivalists, like James Davenport, Edwards argued that even those "imprudences and irregularities" were signs that the awakening was a work of God. He maintained that God pours out his grace to "make men holy," not to "make them politicians." Appealing to reason, he continued, "'Tis no wonder at all, that in a mixed multitude of all sorts, wise and unwise, young and old, or weak and strong natural abilities, that are under strong impressions of mind, there are many that behave themselves imprudently." Such behavior can be accounted for "from the weakness of human nature, together with the remaining darkness and corruption of those that are yet the subjects of the saving influences of God's Spirit." Moreover, the Bible attests to "manifold imprudences" attending the work of God.

Edwards cited the church at Corinth, a congregation celebrated for "being blessed with large measures of the Spirit of God" yet also a people given to "great and sinful irregularities," including speaking in tongues wherein they claimed "immediate inspiration of the Spirit of God."[22] Far from discrediting the revivals, excesses and imprudences provided evidence of an extraordinary work of God.

Edwards warned that all revivals witness backsliding: some persons initially express great zeal only to slip into heresy and even opposition. Having conceded that some "fall away into gross errors or scandalous practices," he denied that such apostasy was an "argument that the work in general is not the work of the Spirit of God." He contended, "that there are some counterfeits, is no argument that nothing is true: such things are always expected in a time of reformation." To illustrate, he cited the example of Nicolas, a deacon elected by the Jerusalem Christians at Pentecost. In that first great "extraordinary pouring out of the Spirit, [he was] a man full of the Holy Ghost, and was chosen out of the multitude of Christians to that office." Yet the Acts of the Apostles also records Nicolas's backsliding, noting that after Pentecost he "fell away, and became the head of a set of vile heretics, of gross practices."[23] Edwards was well aware that backsliders abounded in the mid–eighteenth century, and while their actions embarrassed revivalists, they did not compromise the revival itself.

Edwards summed up his case that recent events amounted to a work of God much as a lawyer would argue in court. The verdict must rest on two things: "facts and rules." To him the facts were indisputable: thousands had come under conviction and experienced conversion in "all parts of the land, and in most of the principal, and most populous, and public places." And the revival had extended over a long period of time, providing people with a "great deal of opportunity to observe the manner of the work." A much more certain determination could be made in such a case as this, when the work of God "is observed in a great multitude of people of all sorts, and in various different places, than when it is only seen in a few." The overwhelming evidence in this instance, Edwards claimed, supported his position. Having established the facts of an extraordinary work of God, he turned to the rule by which those facts must be interpreted. In spiritual matters, for Christians, that can mean only the Bible, particularly the New Testament. When he applied the "rules of the Apostle" in Acts to the facts of the eighteenth-century awakening, Edwards concluded that they "clearly and certainly shew it to be the work of God."[24]

In discussing signs, Edwards took a position opposite that of his rival, Charles Chauncy. While Chauncy focused on the human instruments that produced the "great ado," Edwards emphasized results that he claimed could emanate only from God. To Chauncy, the so-called revival was a "repudiation of signs." For instance, in discussing the evils of itinerancy, he asked, "what is the Language of this going into *other Men's* Parishes?" To him the answer was clear: itinerancy was a "violation of a traditional language of deference" that called into question "the right relation between pastor and people." Edwards argued that the revival transcended human understanding of cause and effect. He believed that one can see God's effusive grace only through "'the effect wrought,' and not from 'the way it began, the instruments . . . employed, the means that have been made use of, [or] the methods that have been taken . . . in carrying it on.'" He pointed to the biblical analogy of the wind: "we hear the sound, we perceive the effect."[25] In his view, Chauncy and other opponents had it all wrong: they argued from cause to effect and concluded that novel, noisy causes surely betokened a work of human rather than divine origin. Edwards and his fellow revivalists concluded that the wondrous effects being wrought could originate only in the Almighty.

Apologists in the Middle Colonies faced two challenges in defending the revival as a genuine Work of God. First, they had to answer charges that the present ado was novel in the annals of Christian history. Old Lights posed the question this way: "How comes it to pass, that we hear so much of these Things of *late*, which former Times and Ages knew so little about?" To skeptics and critics, innovation raised the suspicion of human invention. Without precedent in Scripture and tradition, new measures could be explained only as coming from the fancy of promoters.

Second, apologists had to explain why one should believe that the large crowds and unusual audience reactions were God's work as opposed to the natural effects of publicity and performance. Opponents attributed the huge gatherings to endless promotion and to the circuslike atmosphere that prevailed. Critics claimed that New Light evangelists were masters at playing on their listeners' emotions, manipulating them at will to produce gales of laughter or cataracts of tears.

Like Edwards, Jonathan Dickinson published a systematic defense of the revival. The Elizabeth-Town, New Jersey, pastor chose a dialogic format to make his case that what was occurring was indeed a Work of God. Presenting his ideas as answers to questions raised by a skeptical church member, Dickinson pointedly responded to objections raised across the northern colonies. He addressed the issue of novelty and innovation in discussing the question "How comes it to pass, that we hear so much of these Things of *late*, which former Times and Ages knew so little about?" He defended revivalists' emphasis on the new birth and their preaching styles by considering them within the context of biblical and church history. To his inquisitor, he answered, "I must inform you, that the Fact is quite contrary to your Supposed. Read all the most famous Authors upon practical Godliness, from the Beginning of the Reformation; and you'd find that they teach the same Doctrines I have now insisted on. Read the Narratives of particular Conversions, and you'll find that the Work has always been carried on in Men's Hearts, in a Method substantially the same with what I have described."[26]

Dickinson considered the extensive geographic spread of the revival to be convincing evidence of its divine origin. He asked his doubting parishioner, "Whence is it that we hear of so much of these Things now, but from the more plentiful Effusion of the blessed Spirit? Whence is it that this blessed *Work has spread so extensively, far and near . . .?*" Answering his own question, Dickinson declared, "Certainly *this is the Lord's Doing; and it is marvellous in our Eyes.*" Moreover, in response to charges that the awakenings were human inventions, he concluded, "there could be no Conspiracy, Collusion, or Endeavours of Imitation, in Persons so far removed from, and so unacquainted with one another."[27]

By 1743, American apologists found that many persons who opposed Whitefield tried to equate the revival with the Grand Itinerant and tar the awakening with the same brush used to discredit the controversial evangelist. Whitefield had been fiercely attacked even by some revival supporters because of his published criticisms of the New England ministry and of Harvard College. After his departure in 1741, Americans read in his last *Journal* that he questioned whether most clergymen had themselves experienced the New Birth, and he accused Harvard's faculty of ignoring the sound books of their Puritan forebears and embracing the works of rationalists and deists. Again, defenders of the American awakening enlisted the aid of Scottish revivalists. In 1743, Kneeland and Green reprinted another apology for the Cambuslang revival, this one written by an Edinburgh pastor, Alexander Webster. In his *Divine Influence: The True Spring of the Extraordinary Work at Cambuslang*, Webster took on those who "artfully connect this Affair with the Reverend Mr. Whitefield, hoping that those who don't judge Favourably of him, will, for *this Reason*, entertain sorry Notions of what has pass'd." He also refuted the argument of others that the large crowds and emotional outbursts associated with the awakening resulted primarily from Whitefield's *"fervent Address,"* that it was all the *"Effect of Mechanism."* Webster stated his opinion that "Mr. Whitefield is *entirely* out of the Question." He pointed out that when Whitefield was first in Scotland, he did not preach at Cambuslang, that the revival there started four months after Whitefield's departure, and that long before the evangelist returned, the awakening had spread far beyond Cambuslang.[28] Without doubt, American revivalists welcomed a clear statement separating the Work of God ongoing on both sides of the ocean from the boisterous, and at times embarrassing, Whitefield revival.

As for antirevivalist criticism of itinerancy itself, revival apologists defended the practice as a positive means of spreading the gospel. They pointed out that the practice began when clergymen excluded certain evangelicals from their pulpits and branded them deluded enthusiasts. Undaunted, and determined to fulfill the Great Commission, itinerants delivered their message of the new birth throughout the British Atlantic world. They did not, however, operate in a free competitive religious marketplace. While the colonial religious economy was "virtually unregulated" in comparison to that in England, itinerants were unwelcome competitors for clergymen who had enjoyed the privileges and profits guaranteed by law and custom.[29] Perhaps revivalists' greatest challenge to the old order was their disregard for the parish structure. The New Jersey evangelical Gilbert Tennent proclaimed that seekers after the true gospel should not allow ecclesiastical structures to restrict their spiritual options. Specifically, he encouraged his followers to ignore parish boundaries in the "Getting of Grace and Growing in it." While pointing out the scriptural admonition to hear the Word preached, Tennent questioned "why we should be under a fatal Necessity of hearing . . . our Parish-Minister." He added that he had "known Persons to get saving Good to their Souls, by Hearing over their Parish-line." He urged evangelicals to choose from among the growing variety of printed and preached sermons, "seeing at one time we cannot hear all, neither doth the Explication and Application of all, equally suit such a Person, in such a Time, or Condition, or equally quicken, and subserve the Encrease of Knowledge."[30]

Tennent's views suggest that revivalists' definition of their market differed greatly from that of the settled ministry. Whitefield declared "the whole World [his] Parish." Moreover, he announced that he was subject to no specific local jurisdiction; rather, he was a "Presbyter at large.''[31] In other words, he and other itinerants had an expansive view of their audience, one that extended throughout the British Atlantic world, ignoring social, ecclesiastical, and even national boundaries. He refused to operate within denominational structures, pleading with "ministers and teachers of different communions [to] join with one heart and one mind to carry on the Kingdom of Jesus Christ.''[32] Further, he counted church members as well as nonmembers among those needing to hear the gospel—that is, his particular brand of the gospel. To him, denominational affiliation meant little. Persons subscribing to the loftiest creeds could still be unconverted, "dead in Trespasses and Sins." He warned that instead of "overcoming the World [many were] immersed in it." He urged them to make the attainment of salvation "the one Business of [their] Lives.''[33]

POLEMICS: ATTACKING OPPONENTS OF THE WORK OF GOD

Revivalists not only defended the work as an operation of the Holy Spirit, they attacked antirevivalists on a wide front. One of the surest signs that the revival was a mighty work of God was the intense opposition that rose up against it, especially on the part of professing Christians. Edwards reminded readers that from Christ's coming into the world, religious leaders had opposed him primarily because the manner of his arrival did not conform to their expectations or threatened their authority. And so it was now. Edwards viewed the great awakening as nothing less than "Christ . . . come down from heaven into this land, in a remarkable and wonderful work of his Spirit." Many religious leaders of New England, like those in ancient Judea, opposed the revival, not reckoning it as a great outpouring of grace but looking upon it as "confusion and distraction." When Christ first came, some of the greatest Jewish leaders, scribes and Pharisees, "had a great spite against the work, because they saw it tended to diminish their honor, and to reproach their formality and lukewarmness. Some upon these accounts, maliciously and openly opposed and reproached the work of the Spirit of God, and called it the work of the Devil.''[34] Edwards's message for his day was clear: if you oppose the revival, you are opposing Christ and thereby linking yourself with those whom Christ condemned for opposing him in Judea.

Promoters in the Middle Colonies and New England answered their opponents' sallies blow for blow. One of the Log College men, Samuel Finley, published a blistering polemic against John Thomson, one of the leading revival opposers in the Philadelphia Synod. Ridiculing Thomson's explanation of doctrinal matters, Finley called his equating repentance and conviction "an Imposition on the Ignorant and Credulous, and a manifest Perversion of the Use of Language." Warming to the occasion, he exclaimed, "What! to substitute one Word in place of another, contrary to the known Acceptation of the Word? How awkward, and abusive!" Finley proceeded to lecture Thompson on correct grammar: "'Tis true, Repentance does presuppose Conviction; yet they are no more the same than the Relative and Antecedent are."[35]

Finley then turned against Thomson one of the polemical missiles he and other antirevivalist Presbyterians had hurled. Thomson had accused the awakeners of "rash Judging," especially after Gilbert Tennent published his sermon on unconverted ministers. By that locution, Thomson meant that revivalists dared to render judgments on God's dealing with individuals, making assertions as to who had and who had not undergone the New Birth. Finley answered the charge by claiming that opponents were guilty of rash judging in condemning the "Work of God as the Work of the Devil," especially in light of the overwhelming evidence of God's hand in the affair. "Is it not Rash Judging," he asked, "in Propriety and Strictness of Speech, when they judge not only without Evidence, but contrary to it?" He then added that the term was "too soft; 'tis rather a furious and vicious *Out-facing the Truth*." To Finley, the antirevivalists were disingenuous. On the one hand they conceded that as a result of the Work, "the Lives of many are more holy in Appearances," while on the other judging the "Subjects and Promoters of it [the revival], to be acted upon by the Devil."[36]

According to Finley, the antirevivalists were guilty of more than rash judging; they had prejudged the work and condemned it without awaiting its fruits. He reminded his readers that the opponents "used to bid us wait until the After-fruits would discover it" before calling the work an operation of the Holy Spirit. Yet "they did not wait for such Evidence themselves, to form a Judgment that Satan was at the Helm." Finley said he could understand rendering a negative assessment after witnessing the work "carried on by disorderly Persons, in a disorderly Manner." But, he asked, "how then can they account for their Opposition to the *first* Appearance of it, before they had any Disorder to complain of?" He noted that the work first appeared at Fagg's Manor, under the ministry of Samuel Blair, "an orderly settled Minister in that Place." He explained that "here was no disorderly Person, no breaking into other Men's Congregations, nor irregular Candidates." Despite the absence of practices that even some revivalists later denounced, "some of our Opposing Ministers condemned the Work as Enthusiasm and Delusion, before they had seen or conversed with these Persons, who were the Subjects of it."[37]

Finley accused revival opponents of escalating their negative campaign in a desperate reaction to the awakening's success. When the work spread into the opposers' own communities and congregations, "their Anger kindled into Rage." Unable to turn the revival's tide because it was propelled by God's Spirit, the antirevivalists, according to Finley, resorted to childish name-calling and labeling: "they called their [converts'] Conviction and Sorrow, Melancholy; their Devotion and Seriousness, Hypocrisy or Grimace; and their Joys must be Enthusiasm and Delusion." Opposers like Thomson stigmatized promoters with the "Name of *the blazing Professors now-a-days*" and called their ministries "*Novelties, itching Ears, glaring Shews, vain Boasts*, and such like." Finley admitted that the strategy worked among some: "By these . . . Methods, they prejudiced many against the Ministers, and others against the Work of God." Seeing their attack working, the opponents accelerated their negative assault: "Hereupon the Cry arose about Disorders, Irregularity, and all the Train of Confusions, Schemes, Factions and Parties, so strenuously insisted upon ever since."[38]

Speaking from the radical wing of the revivalist movement, Andrew Croswell waged a bare-knuckle attack against the opposition, characterizing their criticism as a series of denials, exaggerations, and fabrications. He accused antirevivalists of dismissing the entire work by attributing "it all to the Devil and Enthusiasm." He contended that opponents counted on many persons' accepting uncritically such labeling without demanding real evidence. Croswell argued that opponents misrepresented the awakening by making "great Stories of little ones, and . . . represent[ing] Things in the worst Colors." They selected the most unusual and outrageous behavior observed at revival services and portrayed it as characteristic of all in attendance. Finally, he argued, opposers simply lied; they "tell Stories which have been chained upon the present Work, the Subjects and Instruments of it, that have no Foundation at all."[39]

While Finley and Croswell focused on the antirevivalists' unscrupulous tactics, Joshua Gee of Massachusetts aimed his polemic at the results of those tactics. Gee taxed New England antirevivalists with not only assaulting revivalists but undermining the Work of God at home and abroad. The primary target of his attack was a testimony published by a group of ministers condemning not only doctrinal errors and disorderly practices but the revival itself. As Gee saw it, the report damaged all chances of propagating the Gospel because it "gave the Enemies of Religion ... great Advantage to obstruct the Revival and Progress of vital Christianity." Addressing Nathaniel Eells, pastor at Scituate, who alone had signed the testimony, Gee accused the pastors of misleading the public. He claimed that the published report suggested widespread if not unanimous support for the views expressed. But, according to Gee, the facts suggested something far different. He noted that only one-third of the ministers of Massachusetts had attended the convention, and that of those present, only a small majority voted against attesting to the revival as an operation of God's grace. While there was much debate, with many believing that it was a Work of God, the testimony "would make the World believe there was a general Agreement in the Votes ... which relate to the Revival of Religion."[40]

An oft-repeated theme in revivalist polemics was the charge that those who opposed the awakening were not Christians or at least had imbibed heretical principles. Revival promoters claimed that antirevivalists were related spiritually to Archbishop John Tillotson, whose rationalist inter-pretation wrote Christ out of the gospel. According to Thomas Foxcroft, one could point to scores of sermons written by antirevivalists that "run to a faulty Excess upon a philosophic strain." To illustrate, he decided to "single out Dr. Tillotson's two Discourses on Matthew 6.33." Foxcroft said that both works lacked "a Regard to the Things which concern the Lord Jesus Christ." And, he warned his American readers, where the necessity of the New Birth in Christ is not preached and "where a great and universal Neglect of preaching Christ hath prevailed in a Christian Nation, it hath given a fatal Occasion to the Growth of Deism and Infidelity."[41]

According to another polemic, Old Lights acted in bad faith, misrepresenting certain aspects of the revival out of their ignorance of how God's grace worked. Thomas Prince thought that was the case regarding antirevivalist ridicule of "Joys or Consolations" sometimes expressed outwardly by those undergoing a conversion experience. To opposers, such emotional outbursts were feigned, part of the sham orchestrated by manipulating evangelists and their weak-minded followers. Defending the emotions, Prince pointed out that they were grounded in New Testament faith, that "the *Consolations* of some were weaker, of others, stronger: In some they rose to *Joys*: in some few to *Joy unspeakable* and *full of Glory*, as the Apostle speaks." He explained that such expressions were "unfeigned" and were the "*natural Effects* of an extraordinary intense *Exercise* of Soul." He claimed that opponents greatly exaggerated the instances of emotional displays. He reported that he "never saw one either in Town or Country, in what some wrongly call a *Vision, Trance or Revelation.*"[42] His message was clear: the problem was not the ocurrence of disruptive behavior but the ignorance and exaggeration of critics.

No revivalist polemic drew more comment from antirevivalists than Gilbert Tennent's widely publicized and circulated sermon against unconverted ministers. Tennent's attack represented what one historian calls an "inverted Jeremiad," a sermon that shifts the blame for spiritual decline from lay men and women to "the ministers and the colleges that trained them."[43] Tennent called opponents of the revivals modern-day Pharisees who were "great Strangers to the feeling Experience" of the New Birth. He declared that laypersons seeking true religion should leave "the Ministry of natural Men" and seek out a pastor who will provide the "most Good for [their] precious Soul[s]." In short, "Pharisee-Teachers, having no Experience of a special Work of the Holy Ghost, upon their own Souls, are [not] . . . fitted for, Discoursing, frequently, clearly, and pathetically, upon such important Subjects."[44]

By branding antirevivalist ministers as "unconverted," Tennent defined the competition for souls as a zero-sum endeavor. While they opposed the regulated religious market defined by parish boundaries, and though they sought to compete in an open religious market, revivalists nevertheless sought a monopoly. They believed that their representation of the gospel was the only true one. Truth was indivisible, and it rested securely on the revivalist side. Those offering a different version were impostors and must be exposed as such.

DIFFERENTIATION: DISTINGUISHING THE WORK OF GOD FROM ENTHUSIASM

For all the attacks from outsiders, perhaps the greater challenge facing revival promoters was the extreme, sometimes bizarre, behavior of some within their own camp. In 1742, several events caused revival promoters great embarrassment and presented opposers with new ammunition with which to attack the movement. The May 3 issue of the *Boston Post-Boy* reported an odd incident that had occurred in March of that year in South Carolina. Hugh Bryan, a wealthy planter and revival convert, for several days entered a trancelike state in which he conversed with an invisible spirit that he interpreted to be the Holy Spirit. According to an anonymous account, the spirit "directed him to go and take him a Rod, of a certain Shape and Dimension, from such a Tree, in such a Place as he told him of and therewith to go and smite the Waters of the River, which should thereby be divided, so as he might go over, on dry Ground." Bryan obeyed the voice, and fell "a smiting, splashing and spluttering the Water . . . till he was quite up to the Chinn." His brother, Jonathan, saved him from drowning. The writer, obviously an opponent of the revival, concluded that the episode was "the Workings of White-fieldianism in its native Tendency."[45]

A year later, Thomas Fleet, the antirevival editor of the *Boston Evening-Post* continued to cite the Bryan incident to demonstrate how the so-called Work of God was more the manifestation of "Enthusiasm." At every opportunity, Fleet reported accounts of "Appearances"—a term that included all instances of revelations, trances, visions, and impulses—and "Bodily Effects," physical expressions of those appearances, such as screaming, crying, rolling, jerking, and fainting. Thus he delighted in reprinting extracts from a letter on the state of religion in South Carolina that spoke of "Trances, Visions and Revelations among Blacks and Whites." The mention of "Blacks" (in other accounts Fleet listed women or children or the mentally deranged) reminded readers that revival promoters preyed upon the weak and unlearned members of society. The report concluded that "ever since the famous Hugh Briant [*sic*], sousing himself in the River *Jordan*, in order to smite and divide its Waters," South Carolinians had attributed such antics to "the Delusion of the Devil."[46]

Revival supporters recognized the damage that Hugh Bryan had done their cause. Ebenezer Turell, pastor at Medford in Massachusetts, referred to the water-parting incident in a 1742 pamphlet, "Methinks the Carolina Story lately printed (which you have read) is enough to deter one from such Things," that is, appearances. He feared, however, that the strange episode was not an isolated occurrence. He expressed his opinion that the appearances and bodily distresses had "been promoted and augmented of late in some by an unskillful handling of the Word."[47] In other words, they were part of an invention fabricated by overzealous and often uneducated revival supporters.

A second event titillated readers throughout colonial America in a much-publicized episode that chagrined revival promoters, prompting them to differentiate between what was clearly the Work of God and what was attributable to human weakness or even diabolic intervention. James Davenport, an itinerant preacher from Southold on Long Island, toured New England in 1742, much as George Whitefield and Gilbert Tennent had done the two previous years. But, unlike his predecessors, Davenport managed to run afoul of the magistrates, who viewed many of his practices as disturbing the peace, such as leading throngs of singing, dancing followers on unauthorized parades through the streets of Boston. Pastors on both sides of the revival question grew alarmed at Davenport's insistence that people should leave their churches because all of them were corrupt owing to the ministers' unconverted state. When Connecticut pastors accused Davenport of subverting good ecclesiastical order, the magistrates agreed, called his public behavior outrageous, and expelled him from the colony. More important for the revival movement, Davenport also alienated most of the revivalist pastors in the region with behavior they deemed extreme and irrational. They recognized that Davenport's antics provided revival critics with a new arsenal for attacking the Work of God.

In 1742, Boston's leading promoters of the awakening, including Benjamin Colman and Thomas Prince, published a stinging testimony against Davenport. What made their task particularly unpleasant, they wrote, was that Davenport's recent behavior had dashed the high hopes they had formed when they first learned of his plans to preach in New England. On the basis of those early reports, the ministers said that "he appear'd to us to be *truly pious.*" They had hoped that God would use him as an "*Instrument of Good to many Souls.*" But, alas, they found themselves in July 1742 bearing testimony against him. Among the practices they found most objectionable and, therefore, harmful to the revival was "His *judging* some *Ministers* . . . to be unconverted" and thinking God had called him to "*demand* of his Brethren . . . an Account of their Regeneration." They also denounced his encouraging "*private Brethren,* i.e., not Ministers, to pray and exhort in Assemblies gathered for that purpose."[48]

Davenport paid no heed to his corevivalists' admonitions. By spring 1743, he had become quite delusional, believing not only that the church was corrupt but that the world itself was infested by undesirable things. On March 6, in one of the most public spots in New London, Connecticut, Davenport and some of his followers started a huge bonfire. First, they tossed into it "Numbers of Books, principally on Divinity." Included was one of Charles Chauncy's works, an understandable target of an itinerant's ire. But other works destroyed were Protestant classics such as Bishop Beveridge's *Thoughts* and Russell's *Seven Sermons*. There was even a book by one of the revival's leading publicists, Benjamin Colman. As they burned the books, Davenport and his faithful shouted, "Thus the Souls of the Authors of those Books, those of them that are dead, are roasting in the Flames of Hell." And they warned that writers still living faced a similar fate unless they repented. The book burning was only the beginning. Next, Davenport cried out against idolatry, suggesting that many within his own circle were guilty of "idolizing their Apparel, and should therefore divest themselves of those Things especially which were for Ornament, and let them be burnt." Immediately his most unquestioning disciples began to strip off their clothes and toss them on the fire. They then turned on anyone in the crowd wearing something they deemed ostentatious, and demanded that the wearer tender it as a burnt offering.[49]

More than books and clothing went up in flames that night. Davenport's ministry disintegrated as well. Despite his published recantation a year later in which he claimed that he had been under the influence of the "*false Spirit*," he never again enjoyed the confidence of evangelicals, who blamed him for doing great disservice to the revival.[50] And the bonfire spread into a firestorm of criticism aimed at all itinerants. Shortly after Davenport's confession appeared in print, George Whitefield returned to Boston and faced withering censure. As the best-known of the grand itinerants, he had to answer for the sins of them all, and Davenport's proved to be damning indeed.

While New England revivalists tried to put distance between themselves and Davenport, Gilbert Tennent was attempting to separate his brand of revivalism from that of the Moravians, whose teachings were too antinomian for him. Antinomianism was a heresy teaching that Christians were freed by the gospel's grace from the necessity of observing the moral law. Tennent published a treatise in 1743 exposing fundamental differences between Moravian Pietists and Presbyterian revivalists in New York, New Jersey, and Pennsylvania. To a sermon entitled *The Necessity of Holding Fast the Truth*, he appended remarks "relating to errors lately vented by some Moravians." Referring to the Middle Colonies, Tennent deplored "the mischievous effects of the Moravian Conversation in some Places in this part of *America*, in corrupting religious Persons with false Notions of divine Things, and in making unhappy Divisions among them." He accused them of antinomianism, quoting Count Nicholas Zinzendorf in his belief "that it is not needful to preach the Law, but hurtful, under the Gospel Dispensation." Tennent also charged

Moravians with enthusiasm or immediate inspiration. He said that Zinzendorf held the position that elders and ministers "dare speak nothing, but what Christ works in them." Tennent declared that at New Brunswick he saw the effects of such arrogant claims among laypersons. He reported that two Moravian women publicly avowed that they had ceased sinning: "the first said, that she had neither sinned, nor doubted in eighteen Years; and the latter said that she had not sinned in four Years."[51]

After enumerating a long list of doctrinal errors, Tennent summarized his complaints by accusing the Moravians of inventing—that is, fabricating—a false brand of religion. According to his perspective, the sect substituted immediate inspiration for human reason and scriptural revelation. Tennent dismissed their "Doctrine of Simplicity" as "real Folly and implicit Faith, a believing of Nonsense, Contradictions, and mysterious Gibberish." Moreover, he charged the Moravians with being "exceeding artful in ... inculcat[ing] this popish Doctrine," saying that they used "Fox-like Shifts, to evade the Discovery of their heretical and horrible Principles." Tennent wanted evangelicals to know that Moravian "detestable Delusions" were not part of the "remarkable Work of God" under way in America.[52] The purpose of his public exposure was to uncover (or invent, in the positive sense) their true design as a cunning fabrication (or invention, in the negative sense).

What Tennent in the Middle Colonies and his counterparts in New England faced was a revival that had many different dimensions and voices. It was never monolithic. Rather, it had many and diverse followers who crafted competing inventions. Most revivalists, however, fell into one of two categories: moderates and radicals, with the distinction resting on how awakeners in each viewed the workings of God's Spirit. To moderates, the awakening was first a work of God that conformed to recognizable scriptural signs. The Bible set forth how God's Spirit would operate during seasons of extraordinary effusions, and moderates were suspicious of those who claimed to receive direct divine revelation or inward impulses that took precedence over biblical authority. The revival was, second, led by educated and ordained ministers, although there was considerable dispute over what constituted a proper education, and what the appropriate ordination body was. Moderates believed that God was a god of order and would not entrust the propagation of the gospel to uneducated persons who claimed to have received a divine message entrusted only to them. Moderates also found disturbing the importance that some attached to convulsions, fits, and faintings evident in some revival services. That such things could attend a conversion they did not deny; that these experiences should be encouraged and held up as convincing signs of conversion they regretted.

Radicals included revivalists who reached the conclusion that the only way they could practice "pure and undefiled" religion was to withdraw from their existing congregations and form new churches. As withdrawing radicals, known as Separatists, formed new congregations, moderates sought to distance themselves from what they considered to be a dangerous and even heretical stance. Beginning in 1741, some revivalists removed themselves from their churches, and by 1745 forty-two Separate congregations had been raised in New England. The Confession of Faith of one of these new bodies highlights some of their central tenets. The Mansfield, Massachusetts, Separatists vowed, for example, that "all doubting in a believer is sinful, being contrary to the command of God." Moreover, they held that "every brother that is qualified by God for the same, has a right to preach according to the measure of faith, and that the essential qualification for preaching is wrought by the Spirit of god; and that the knowledge of the tongues and liberal sciences are not absolutely necessary."[53]

Radicals were some of the revival's ablest polemicists, but, to moderates, they were at the same time some of its greatest irritants. No one was a more ardent revivalist than Andrew Croswell, pastor at Groton, Connecticut. At Harvard he, like Whitefield at Oxford, had been a servitor because of his lowly social standing. At Groton, Croswell and his congregation experienced an awakening inspired by events in Northampton. During that time, he had a personal awakening and thereafter made the necessity of the New Birth the centerpiece of his preaching. He became one of Whitefield's fiercest defenders when the itinerant came under attack by either Old Lights or Anglicans. By 1741, however, he began championing some persons and practices that made him an embarrassment for more moderate revivalists. First, even after Davenport's performance at New London, Croswell pointed out with pride that he had been the one to introduce Davenport to New England in the first place, and that he had encouraged the eccentric preacher to expand his ministry. Second, he was one of the first and most zealous promoters of lay exhorters, claiming that anyone filled with the Holy Spirit was qualified to preach the gospel regardless of educational attainment. Third, he launched a public attack against one of the moderates' chief spokesmen, Jonathan Dickinson, in a pamphlet war over what was and what was not a display of God's grace. He also accused other revival promoters of being tepid in their support of the awakening because they refused to embrace Separatism. Finally, Croswell became a Separatist leader, arguing that true believers had a duty to separate themselves from ministers and congregations that had not experienced the indwelling spirit.[54]

Moderates were concerned that radical beliefs and practices discredited all revivalists. Therefore, to distinguish between the genuine work of God and the excesses of zealots, moderates published works in the early 1740s clarifying their position. Moderate voices included those of the most prolific writers throughout the Great Awakening: in New England, Jonathan Edwards, Benjamin Colman, William Cooper, and Thomas Prince; in the Middle Colonies, Jonathan Dickinson, Gilbert Tennent, Samuel Blair, and Ebenezer Pemberton. The best-known radicals were James Davenport, Andrew Croswell, and Ebenezer Frothingham, who were considered extremists by moderates most especially for their emphasis on lay exhorting and separatism. Moderates such as the ministers of the Windham [Connecticut] Association thought that such views were not only wrong but hurtful to the revival itself. Their published denunciation of Separatist notions was intended to differentiate between God's work and that of the Devil. As they saw it, Separatists had fallen victim to Satan's wiles, which deluded some by "filling their minds with flashes of joy and false comforts," leading to spiritual arrogance and censoriousness.[55]

In 1742, a moderate revivalist, Ebenezer Turell, published two pamphlets designed to clarify what the revival was, and what some zealots had tried to make it into. The Medford, Massachusetts, pastor constructed his argument in a fictional dialogue between a minister and his neighbor, with the latter asking a series of questions about current religious affairs. He asked first, "What is the Work of God?" The minister replied that it was "the Work of [God's] Grace wrought on the Hearts of Many by his Word and Spirit." The work emanated from God: "the Blessed Spirit has been sent down to convict, convince, and convert Sinners, and to quicken, enliven and comfort the Saints." He concluded by asserting that "a conspicuous Reformation is wro't in some Places." The neighbor followed up by asking if God's Spirit had not been present with Puritans from the first settlement in New England. The minister replied that it had, but added that it has been evident "more especially through the *acceptable Year of the Lord* that has rowl'd over us." He explained that "there has been such a Revival and Increase of it as well deserves to be distinguished and called the *Work of God*, or the *outpouring of the Spirit* as others express it." The minister interpreted the present work as a "partial Accomplishment of some gracious *Prophecies* and *Promises*, on which the faithful People of God in the Land have long *waited* and hoped."[56]

Turell then turned the dialogue toward human excesses that had tainted the revival. The minister expressed his opinion to his neighbor that if the Work of God had been left alone in its unadorned state and not been placed "in uncertain Appearances," there would have been less opposition to it. The neighbor said that he had been told that "the great Degree of Persons' Distress, and the Suddenness of Conversion, as well as the Number, distinguished it from all other Works of this Nature." While conceding that God works in diverse ways, the minister stated his fears that much distress "has been promoted and augmented of late in some by an unskillful handling of the Word." In other words, the minister believed that some extremists had invented a revival style in which outcries were a centerpiece. He deplored the fact that untrained zealous self-appointed preachers encouraged "Negroes and the most ignorant of the Principles of Religion to become Exhorters, even in considerable Assemblies, and Women to become Teachers." Moreover, he lamented, such persons laid great "*Weight* on their *Agonies, Screamings Out, Convulsions*, etc."[57] Finding no biblical support for such emotional demonstrations in a genuine Work of God, Turell concluded that they were inventions of ignorant, misguided people.

Turell explained in another pamphlet why he, a revival promoter, would publish a work against others who represented themselves as revivalists. He explained that he had gone public with his criticism of what he considered to be excesses "to let the World see, that the Friends and Promoters of the good Work, are not wholly ignorant of Satan's Devices & Endeavours to sully its Glory." He told readers that he saw "a plain difference between the Gold, Silver, and precious Stones; and the wood, Hay and Stubble clumsily tost on the Foundation." He hoped that as a result of his denunciation of beliefs and practices advanced by some in the name of a genuine revival, "the Opposers & Enemies of the Work may no longer say, 'That we swallow down every Thing; and attribute all Appearances to the God and Spirit of Order.'" He also expressed his disapproval of many in his own congregation who followed every itinerant and exhorter who came along out of a "vain Curiosity and Affectation of *Novelty*." Turell reiterated his admiration for the work of Whitefield and Tennent but warned that "some who have since ap'd [the great itinerants] are Authors of much Confusion and Division."[58]

Thomas Prince shared Turell's views, but he believed that a joint statement by leading moderates needed to be published affirming their belief that the present work was truly of God, while at the same time expressing concern over excesses. Accordingly, he led the effort to organize a meeting in Boston of all New England ministers who "are persuaded there has of late been a happy Revival of Religion, thro an extraordinary divine Influence, in many Parts of the Land, and are Concerned for the Honour and Progress of the remarkable Work of God." He invited the pastors to come to Boston "to give an open conjunct Testimony to an Event so surprizing and gracious, as well as against those Errors in Doctrine and Disorders in Practice, which . . . have attended it, and in any Measure blemish'd its Glory, and hindred its Advancement."[59]

A month after issuing the invitation, Prince recognized that the conference needed to address clearly the issue of appearances, particularly what distinguished some as the Work of God and others as enthusiasm. He knew that the "Terrors & Joys" often described as attending awakenings had given rise to much "Debate & Contention." Thus he solicited more precise information about the rise, nature, and operation of those "Appearances." He asked ministers to submit "authentick Accounts of the Numbers of Men, Women, Children, Indians and Negroes, and Persons of Infamous Characters, as profane Swearers, Thieves, Cheats, Liars, Slanderers, Drunkards and tavern-Haunters, Adulterers and Fornicators, and the like, that have appear'd to be under the late remarkable Work." He wanted to know "how many of each Sort have been struck or in Terror and, how many have received Joy; [and] what Fruits of Piety have been most conspicuous in 'em." Prince concluded with a plea that all reports be "well-vouched Accounts of such Events."[60]

Prince believed that the best way to silence critics of the great awakening was to pile up evidence pointing to its existence. He agreed with Alexander Webster that the best evidence was that of respected ministers who attested to the revival. In making his case that the Work at Cambuslang was from God, Webster informed his readers that the "*Number* of Witnesses are Many; —Their Characters *fair* and *good.*" And, he said, "They attest only to a *Fact.*" In support of those who testified to the revival as a divine work, Webster wrote, "I think their *Veracity* is beyond all *reasonable Suspicion.*" He then argued that to dismiss the testimony of such impeccable witnesses was to be prejudiced and stiff-necked. "Men must be deeply imbarqued in the Opposition," he concluded, "who can suppose such a *Number* of Ministers, Preachers and others, hitherto of *untainted Fidelity,* living in *distant Corners,* and very *different* as to their Opinions in some Respects, all in League with Hell, and associate together to lye unto the Holy Ghost, that, if *possible, they may deceive the very Elect.*"[61]

When opponents charged American revivalists with fabrication and exaggeration, Prince, then, solicited attestations from reputable ministers that the work was a genuine revival of religion. He filled the pages of his *Christian History* with testimonies from ministers and laymen. In the first volume, primarily covering the year 1743, he printed in the magazine twenty-four "Attestations to the Revival of Religion" from New Englanders, including statements from Massachusetts, Connecticut, New Hampshire, and Rhode Island. He also published eight attestations from Scotland, where the revival's spread could be partly attributed to a strong New England influence. The second volume of the *Christian History* revealed further fruits of Prince's solicitation efforts, especially in colonial regions outside New England. He printed testimonials from ministers and laymen in New York, New Jersey, Pennsylvania, and Delaware.

Samuel Kneeland and Timothy Green joined Prince in defending the revival as the remarkable Work of God by printing endorsements from eminent British dissenters in the *New-England Weekly Journal.* In a letter to William Shurtliff of Portsmouth, New Hampshire, Isaac Watts weighed in on the side of moderation. The London pastor expressed his delight "to see the Grace of God break out afresh in so powerful a manner in so many Places of our Plantations in *America.*" While endorsing the colonial revival and affirming that it did indeed emanate from God, he pointed out that regrettably there was evidence of "humane Weaknesses and Imperfections."[62] Watts's endorsement thus sounded the same themes of celebration and caution developed within American moderate ministerial attestations: the intention to declare and promote the genuine Work of God, while exposing and opposing extreme actions that undermined it.

When one reflects on the apologetic and polemical rhetoric of revivalist literature, two conclusions emerge. First, inventing the Great Awakening was highly perspectival. Moderates and radicals alike sought to tell the revival story from their particular perspectives, giving it color based on the inventor's theological, personal, and regional orientation. The result was that even in the telling the Great Awakening lacked the uniformity that its promoters cited as proof that it emanated from God. Rather, rival claims indicate that human influence gave the revival an all too human texture. In their accounts, moderates affirmed that the awakening was "a blessed Outpouring of the Spirit of God in this Country," but conceded that the work had been attended by a "Mixture of Enthusiasm and false Religion." In their versions, radicals likewise viewed the revival as a divine movement, but they charged that moderates were "tepid" in promoting "pure and undefiled religion." From their vantage point, radicals saw moderates' opposition to Separatism as evidence that they were more concerned about compromise than principle. And radicals saw themselves, in contrast to the weak-kneed moderates, as the true warriors in the raging cultural war. As a result of the internecine battles, when one turns to revivalist literature to understand what occurred in the mid–eighteenth century, one realizes that the challenge is not primarily a matter of determining whether there existed an overarching event called *the* Great Awakening, but one of grasping the presence of multiple inventions of *the* Great Awakening. Read Edwards, and one uniform account presents itself. Read Croswell, and another appears.

The second conclusion is suggested by the revivalists' polemical writings. In reading them, one encounters impenetrable boundaries between revivalists and antirevivalists. One can hardly imagine how a person could move back and forth between rival camps, with one side heralding events as authentic revival and the other calling them human delusion. And yet many people, including some identified as leaders in either camp, did move across the invented lines of demarcation. Nathaniel Eells was the moderator of the Boston convention that published one of the most scathing denunciations of the "errors and disorders" that awakeners had paraded as revival. Yet he also signed the revivalist convention's manifesto affirming the presence of a "happy Revival" in the land. True, he qualified his support by concurring with the substance of the report while expressing his belief that in the final publication, the "great Disorders were not sufficiently testify'd against." One of the revival's foremost leaders, Benjamin Colman, joined Eells in that demurral. Eells's and Colman's signatures attesting to the same judgment indicate that the Great Awakening *as reported* is an invention with very sharply etched divisions that obscure a much richer and more intricately shaded continuum of positions.

"The late Revival of Religion"

WRITING IN 1749, Gilbert Tennent pronounced the revival over. He wrote that "the *Church* is now in its ordinary *State*" By contrast, he explained, "Some Years past, the *Church* in this *American Wilderness* was in an extraordinary Situation, by Reason of a very uncommon *Effusion* of divine *Influence*, in the *Conviction*, and *Conversion* of Sinners, (to all Appearance) in much greater Numbers than what is usual." Tennent no longer saw evidence of revival: no huge crowds gathered to hear itinerant preachers, no large ingathering of souls being converted. Instead, he regretted to report, the ecumenical spirit of the revival had been replaced by "contending *Parties*" bent on making fine doctrinal distinctions the basis for "true" religion. He lamented that differences of "*Sentiment* about *lesser Matters* and warm *Disputes pro* and *con* respecting them" had destroyed the great awakening that had de-emphasized denominational and sectarian distinctions.[1]

In addition to declaring the revival over, promoters ceased to produce publications heralding and promoting a great awakening. In 1746, Thomas Prince wrote and published a work entitled *The Salvation of God*. Given his prominent role as one of the chief publicists of the colonial revivals, one would expect a sermon with that title to be an update on the extraordinary outpouring of God's spirit in America, the theme of Prince's publications for the previous several years. The language in the discourse sounded familiar. He wrote of the "Greatness of that Salvation God has given us" first in Europe and second in North America. However, in 1746, he spoke not of God's deliverance of sinners from their transgressions in a spiritual revival but of God's deliverance of the English from the French during a time of war. The sermon discussed events in Scotland and New England, also the geographic foci of Prince's *Christian History* during the previous two years. Now, though, he exulted in the defeat of the Pretender and the rebellion he had fomented in Scotland. And he gave thanks for New England's stunning victory at Fort Louisbourg.[2]

During 1743–1745 Prince had solicited revival news from every minister who believed that the "present Work" was a "remarkable Work of

God," and he had published every scrap of revival news he could gather. However, late in 1745, he issued the last edition of the *Christian History*. Similarly, newspapers that had devoted their front pages to revival stories barely mentioned revival in 1746: the "great awakening" had ceased to be a major news story worthy of extensive coverage. Only 5 percent of colonial publications in that year were about the revival, as compared to 35 percent the previous year. While war explains part of the shift of focus away from the awakening, it cannot bear the entire burden.

Revivalists offered theological explanations for the awakening's end. In their view of the divine economy, God's was the invisible hand that directed his grace to work within individuals he had elected for salvation. In the waning days of the eighteenth-century awakening, ministers feared that God was withdrawing his hand. When the Northampton revival of the mid-1730s had drawn to a close, Jonathan Edwards implored the Almighty not to "forsake the work of his own Hand."[3] Though they regretted the decline, revivalists knew that, by definition, revivals were "extraordinary" effusions of his mercy limited to finite "seasons of grace." Only God knew their duration.

Evangelicals who believed that the great ado in many parts of America had been a work of God cited evidence of its decline. Throughout the debate over the Great Awakening, New Lights and Old Lights offered different evidence in support of their respective positions. The latter had emphasized the revivalists' new measures—itinerant evangelism, extemporaneous preaching, lay exhorting—as instigating dangerous innovations that produced error and confusion. For their part, New Lights had stressed results of their efforts—crowds, conversions, charitable giving—as compelling evidence of a genuine revival of religion. By 1746, many revival supporters could no longer detect those indicators of revival.

As early as 1746, no semblance of an extensive, uniform, intercolonial revival could any longer be found. Several factors explain why the revival ended both as observable and as reported event. First, three years of intense contestation between revivalists and antirevivalists had resulted in a zero-sum game. Every assertion promoters advanced met with a counterassertion argued with logic as convincing and evidence as compelling. More important, the contestation revealed to many the fictive nature of the revival in its reported form. It was apparent that for many persons, the revival was not "really real" and therefore was unlikely to win adherents beyond the base constituencies that had emerged at its onset.

While antirevivalist attacks had placed awakeners on the defensive, problems within the revival movement contributed to its decline. Revival promoters believed, in any case, that extraordinary effusions of God's grace were discreet events over a definite period, one with a beginning and an ending. By 1745, it was clear to most revivalists that the intercolonial and transatlantic revival was over. When George Whitefield approached New England in December 1744 to begin his second American preaching tour, he expressed his hope for "as glorious a revival" as he had witnessed in 1739–1741. However, he soon learned that while signs of an awakening persisted in some places, "there was a general complaint of a withdrawing of the remarkable outpouring of the Spirit of God."[4] As Whitefield preached around Boston, he began to refer to the "great awakening" as "the late great and glorious work of God in New England."[5] Though he preached the same message as before and continued to pray for God's sending revival, he recognized that the recent outpouring was a thing of the past.

At a Boston conference of leading revival promoters, Whitefield learned why the awakening had subsided. Benjamin Colman, Joseph Sewell, Thomas Foxcroft, and Thomas Prince informed the Grand Itinerant that "for near two Years after [his] departure from New England" the "work of God had went on in a most glorious manner," but "then a chill came over the . . . work." The ministers cited several reasons for the chill. First, they mentioned the "imprudence of some Ministers who had been promoters," a reference to the acts of extremists such as James Davenport and Andrew Croswell. Then they discussed the negative effects of some of Whitefield's own indiscretions, specifically some passages in his *Journals* indicating that he "found the generality of Preachers preached an Unknown Christ, [and] that the Colleges had darkness in them." The Boston pastors told Whitefield that such intemperate comments had caused many of their colleagues to fear that he was "a means of promoting separations," and that many no longer welcomed him to their pulpits.[6]

With the great and general awakening over, then, what does the evidence suggest about this extraordinary event's nature and scope? First, the colonial American revival was both regional and intercolonial. It was regional in that it emanated from and burned brightest in the two revival regions of New England and the Middle Colonies. There, ministers and their congregations inherited a rich revival tradition stretching for decades into the past. They knew how to "pray down" and "preach up" revivals, and they knew how to recognize an awakening as a genuine work of God. Thus the Great Awakening was primarily a religious event rooted in a particular branch of evangelical culture. Outside the revival regions, the awakening was scattered. Nevertheless, it was intercolonial in scope. Because itinerant preachers roamed the length and breadth of the colonies for more than five years, and because of the widespread distribution of printed materials, men and women in every corner of the colonies were aware of the revival and responded to it in some way. Much-publicized crowds at revival preaching services tell only part of the story regarding the awakening's extent. When Maryland doctor and bon vivant Dr. Alexander Hamilton made his tour from Annapolis to York, Maine, in 1744, he heard talk of the revival in the most unlikely places. In taverns from Charlestown, Massachusetts, to North East, Maryland, Hamilton found the revival to be a major topic of conversation, and he noted disapprovingly that everyone, unlettered as well as learned, engaged in spirited discussion of the New Light religion.[7]

However, Hamilton's journey also illustrates the geographic limits of the revival. He traveled through some regions where the so-called great awakening was a nonevent, evoking indifference instead of debate. Hamilton found the people of Albany, New York, for example, to be far more concerned about the Indian trade than about spiritual matters. Of them he observed, "As to religion they have little of it among them and enthusiasm not a grain." Issues central to the awakeners, such as justification and regeneration, were not part of their daily discourse. In contrast to evangelicals in the Raritan Valley, they had no expectation of an extraordinary outpouring of God's grace, and they gave no evidence of witnessing such an event. Similarly, Hamilton described little evidence of revival among Anglicans in the Chesapeake, noting that they came from a tradition foreign to that of evangelical revivalism.[8]

Second, the Great Awakening was a religious invention. More specifically, it was a sequenced invention, alternating in character between that word's two eighteenth-century meanings: fabrication and invention. In the 1730s, men and women in the revival regions of New England and the Middle Colonies looked for a long-awaited awakening. Believing in human means to promote revival, they constructed a program of prayer meetings and special sermons designed to produce revival. Then, as the strategy worked in increasing discussion of religion, crowds at services, and numbers converted, revivalists discovered and announced the existence of a "great awakening." Encouraged by what they witnessed and hoping for a wider awakening, promoters disseminated publicity of the colonial events throughout the Atlantic world, complete with scripts for local revivals. As the manufactured revival accounts helped inspire similar experiences in such remote places as Cambuslang and Kilsyth, Scotland, Anglo-American revivalists viewed the local events as part of the "same work." In other words, in connecting scattered awakenings emanating from a few centers rich in revival tradition, a transatlantic network of revival promoters discovered a single "general awakening" over a global expanse and publicized it as a genuine Work of God similar to that at Pentecost and the Protestant Reformation.

The revivalists' invention was cultural in nature, with its success depending upon persons who shared a set of beliefs about the way God dispensed grace. When awakeners introduced the revival to groups beyond the evangelical culture, they witnessed unintended consequences—that is, those groups often fashioned their own inventions. Revivalists attempted to convey the necessity of the new birth to Native Americans along the frontiers of New England and the Middle Colonies. Sometimes missionaries, like Yale graduates Eleazar Wheelock and David Brainerd of Massachusetts, undertook the task of educating and evangelizing Indians. Laymen, such as one Pennsylvania Indian trader, took translations of revival sermons to tribes in the interior. However, the awakening among Native Americans was spotty and local at best. Without an evangelical revival tradition, the Indians must have found the fantastic claims of the revivalists strange indeed. They knew little of church history, especially the so-called midnight of the church that necessitated revival in the first place, nor did they understand such Reformation principles as justification, redemption, and sanctification, or rival interpretations of those ideas by Calvinists and Arminians. Moreover, at the same time Anglo-Americans were discovering a "great awakening," many Indians were finding or inventing their own version. According to one historian, a cluster of Native Americans in the Susquehanna and Ohio Valleys began in the late 1730s to follow "prophets" who proclaimed the necessity of a new spiritual encounter, but, unlike that of white revivalists, this one was rooted in nativist traditions. Fired by "vision[s] of God," seers admonished their followers against embracing English mores and trade, and urged them to revive the beliefs and "ceremonies of their ancestors."[9] In the midst of a revival of their own making, Indians paid scant attention to outside evangelists representing those who, from the native perception, had contributed to their own spiritual and material decline.

Third, the Great Awakening was a contested event, part of a colonial cultural war. Many Protestant clergymen and laypersons found the revivalist message to be rank enthusiasm spilling out of overheated passions.

In their view it was primarily the result of artful preachers who discovered that their emotional message appealed to the "vulgar" masses. Seeing some of their own parishioners lured away, antirevivalists mounted a counteroffensive designed to discredit the so-called revivals as more hype and bombast than the genuine work of God. Then, in a print war of invention and counterinvention, the opposing sides debated religious events of the day and reached opposite conclusions about their meaning. While revivalists discovered a true awakening, antirevivalists found "errors and disorders" that undermined good order in America's churches. By 1743, the battle of the presses had intensified and took on a life of its own. The focus shifted from events that gave rise to the dispute in the first place to rival published accounts of events. The two sides debated which side's version was more convincing and plausible. Each accused the other of gross fabrications based on thin or even false evidence, partial reading of that evidence, and misrepresentation of the other's position. Persons who found validity in parts of each side's interpretation found it increasingly difficult to be heard over the strident voices of extremists.

Given the highly charged atmosphere in which revival accounts were written and published, some contemporaries worried about the accuracy of those early versions. Writing in 1751, Jonathan Edwards reflected on "that extraordinary awakening ... about sixteen years ago" as both event and reported event. He viewed it as an occurrence of specific duration, ending in 1745. Even after witnessing some "glaring false appearances and counterfeits of religion" during that period, he clung to the conviction that "there was a very glorious work of God wrought . . ., and there were numerous instances of saving conversion." While persisting in his belief that the revival had been the work of God, Edwards expressed concern that he and other promoters had overstated the results. He feared, for example, that "the number of true converts was not so great as was then imagined."[10] And he acknowledged a great gap between the revival as it was and the revival as it was reported, and could understand how some could conclude that "all the famed awakenings and revivals of religion in that place prove to be nothing." In other words, Edwards knew that because of exaggeration and hype, to many the Great Awakening was indeed reduced to a "small Thing."

Thomas Prince also worried about his depiction of the revival; but his concern was the opposite of Edwards's. Prince feared that he had understated the work of God. In the final issue of the *Christian History*, Thomas Prince explained what he had attempted to do in publishing the revival magazine. He wrote in his closing lines: "we have given a Specimen of that wondrous Work of God which has been in the midst of these Years revived in many Parts of Great Britain and America." In that statement, Prince let subscribers know that they had seen but a "specimen," a sample of the revival through the narratives and attestations he had printed. He added that "there are some remarkable Narratives yet unprinted and others daily expected." Prince reminded readers that the great subject matter he had dealt with was nothing less than "that wondrous Work of God." By that designation he meant a single, unitary event emanating from a divine source. He underscored the fact that the work was extensive, overspreading "many Parts of Great Britain and America." This had been no local or regional affair but rather intercolonial and transatlantic.[11] His magazine had borne witness primarily to the American phase of the great awakening. But, like Edwards, Prince fretted over the documents revivalists were leaving future generations.

A hundred years later, evangelical and historian Joseph Tracy read the surviving record of the mid-eighteenth-century revival and supplied the name by which subsequent generations would know the event Prince had described: The Great Awakening. The title was Tracy's contribution to the process of inventing the eighteenth-century colonial revival. But the substance was Prince's and his fellow promoters'. Tracy acknowledged that "the leading authority" for his creation was the *Christian History*. He saw the magazine as carefully constructed: a work containing "accounts which were then esteemed favorable," and, therefore, "published for the sake of promoting the revival." In other words, Prince's periodical was a cultural invention suited to the beliefs and needs of mid-eighteenth-century Calvinist revivalists. From his perspective, Tracy found in it "many things which no one now would commend."[12] For succeeding generations of evangelicals, the colonial invention had to be reinvented in order to fit changing social and cultural circumstances. Thus Tracy and other nineteenth-century Arminian revivalists set about the task of inventing their own Great Awakening.

Notes

Introduction

1. All anecdotes taken from *Christian History, Containing Accounts of the Revival and Propagation of Religion in Great-Britain and America*, 2 vols. (Boston, 1744 and 1745), 2:21, 27, 107, 261, 300. A total of 104 issues were published from March 5, 1743, through February 23, 1745. In addition to appearing as a weekly publication, *The Christian History* also appeared in two bound volumes published in 1744 and 1745, each containing 52 issues.

2. C. C. Goen, ed., *Jonathan Edwards: The Great Awakening*, vol. 4 of *The Works of Jonathan Edwards*, ed. John E. Smith et al. (New Haven, 1972), 219.

3. Ibid., 220–221.

4. See *The Testimony and Advice of an Assembly of Pastors of Churches in New-England, At a Meeting in Boston July 7, 1743. Occasion'd By the late happy Revival of Religion in many Parts of the Land* . . . (Boston, 1743), 5, 10.

5. Charles Chauncy, *The Late Religious Commotions in New-England considered. An Answer To the Reverend Mr. Jonathan Edwards' Sermon, Entitled The Distinguishing Marks of a Work of the Spirit of God, applied to that uncommon Operation that has appeared in the Minds of many of the People of the Lord* (Boston, 1743), 2.

6. Jon Butler, "Enthusiasm Described and Decried: The Great Awakening as Interpretative Fiction," *Journal of American History* 69 (September 1982): 306–309.

7. Joseph A. Conforti, *Jonathan Edwards, Religious Tradition and American Culture* (Chapel Hill, 1995), 4.

8. Clifford Geertz, *The Interpretation of Cultures* (New York, 1973), 112.

9. *Boston Evening-Post*, October 31, 1743.

10. Joseph Trapp, *The Nature, Folly, Sin, and Danger of being Righteous Over-much* (London, 1739), 9.

11. [Jonathan Edwards], *The History of the Work of Redemption*, vol. 2 of *The Works of President Edwards*, 8 vols. (Worcester, Mass., 1808), 317.

12. Definition found in Ephraim Chambers, *Cyclopaedia: Or, An Universal Dictionary of Arts and Science*, 2 vols. (London, 1938). I benefited from Garry Wills's analysis of the eighteenth-century meanings of "invention." See Garry Wills, *Inventing America: Jefferson's Declaration of Independence* (New York, 1978), 364.

13. Thomas Fowler, ed., *Locke's Conduct of the Understanding* (New York, 1971), 30–31.

14. Jonathan Dickinson, *A Display of God's Special Grace* (Boston, 1742), title page, 4, and 29.

15. *Christian History*, 1:106.

16. For fuller discussion of "emplotment," see Hayden White, *Tropics of Discourse: Essays in Cultural Criticism* (Baltimore: 1978), 81 ff.

17. Edmund Morgan sees the revivals as introducing "an unacknowledged popularity contest among ministers" wherein the "ability to affect people" proved more important than erudition. See Edmund S. Morgan, *Inventing the*

People: The Rise of Popular Sovereignty in England and America (New York, 1988), 296–297.

18. *Christian History*, 1:2.

Chapter 1
". . that Religion may revive in this Land"

1. David D. Hall, *The Faithful Shepherd: A History of the New England Ministry in the Seventeenth Century* (Chapel Hill, 1972), 15–16.

2. Ibid., 61.

3. See R. T. Kendall, *Calvin and English Calvinism to 1649* (New York, 1979).

4. Cited in Mark A. Noll, David W. Bebbington, and George A. Rawlyk, eds., *Evangelicalism: Comparative Studies of Popular Protestantism in North America, the British Isles, and Beyond, 1700–1990* (New York, 1994), 6.

5. Hall, *The Faithful Shepherd*, 62.

6. Ibid., 249–251.

7. Cedric Cowing, *The Saving Remnant: Religion and the Settling of New England* (Urbana, Ill., 1995), 10, 297–298.

8. Ibid., 27, 34.

9. Marilyn Westerkamp, *Triumph of the Laity: Scots-Irish Piety and the Great Awakening, 1625–1760* (New York, 1988), 24–25. For a fuller discussion of the Holy Fairs, see Leigh E. Schmidt, *Holy Fairs: Scottish Communions and American Revivals in the Early Modern Period* (Princeton, 1989).

10. Schmidt, *Holy Fairs*, 3.

11. David A. Ramsey and R. Craig Koedel, "The Communion Season—An Eighteenth-Century Model," *Journal of Presbyterian History* 54 (Summer 1976): 203, 206.

12. Ibid., 210–211.

13. For the idea of "Evangelicall History," see the work of a seventeenth-century Puritan minister who led a revival in his congregation at Roxbury, Massachusetts: Samuel Danforth, *A Brief Recognition of New-England's Errand into the Wilderness* (Cambridge, Mass., 1671), 22.

14. Edmund S. Morgan, *Visible Saints: The History of a Puritan Idea* (New York, 1963), 3, 138.

15. On sacramental theology in New England Puritanism, see E. Brooks Holifield, *The Covenant Sealed: The Development of Puritan Sacramental Theology, in Old and New England, 1570–1720* (New Haven, 1974), 139 ff.

16. David Levin, ed., *Bonifacius: An Essay Upon the Good by Cotton Mather* (Cambridge, Mass., 1966), xviii, xxii, 21–27.

17. Cited in James Tanis, *Dutch Calvinistic Pietism in the Middle Colonies: A Study in the Life and Theology of Theodorus Jacobus Frelinghuysen* (The Hague, 1967), 175.

18. William James, *Varieties of Religious Experience: A Study in Human Nature* (1902; reprint, New York, 1982), 157–159. For Alline's religious views, see George Rawlyk, *Ravished by the Spirit: Religious Revivals, Baptists, and Henry Alline* (Montreal, 1984); and George Rawlyk, *Wrapped Up in God: A Study of Several Canadian Revivals and Revivalists* (Burlington, Ontario, 1988).

19. James, *Varieties of Religious Experience*, 80–83.

20. Isaac Watts, *An Humble Attempt Towards the Revival of Practical Christians,* 3d ed. (London, 1742), iii.

21. "Diary of the Rev. Thomas Prince, 1737," *Publications of the Colonial Society of Massachusetts* 19 (April 1917): 335–336.

22. Darrett Rutman, *The Great Awakening: Event and Exegesis* (New York, 1970), 144–148.

23. Danforth, *A Brief Recognition,* 9–13, 18.

24. Patricia U. Bonomi and Peter R. Eisenstadt, "Church Adherence in the Eighteenth-Century British American Colonies," *William and Mary Quarterly* 39 (April 1982): 248; H. Richard Niebuhr, *The Social Sources of Denominationalism* (1929; reprint, Hamden, Conn., 1954), 167.

25. Ibid., 256–261.

26. William G. McLoughlin, ed., *Lectures on Revivals of Religion by Charles Grandison Finney* (Cambridge, Mass., 1960), 9.

27. Bonomi and Eisenstadt, "Church Adherence," 246–247.

28. *George Whitefield's Journals* (London, 1960), 387–388.

29. Goen, *Jonathan Edwards,* 146.

30. Jonathan Edwards, *The Distinguishing Marks of a Work of the Spirit of God* (Boston, 1741), 46.

31. Josiah Smith, *The Character, Preaching, etc. Of the Reverend Mr. George Whitefield, Impartially Represented and Supported, in a Sermon* (Boston, 1740), 19.

32. Kenneth A. Lockridge, *The Diary, and Life, of William Byrd II of Virginia, 1674–1744* (New York, 1987), 138–139.

33. *Whitefield's Journals,* 389.

34. Daniel Boorstin, *The Americans: The Colonial Experience* (New York, 1958), 137.

35. Richard J. Hooker, ed., *The Carolina Backcountry on the Eve of the Revolution: The Journal and Other Writings of Charles Woodmason, Anglican Itinerant* (Chapel Hill, N.C., 1953), 42–47.

36. Gilbert Tennent, *The Necessity of Religious Violence in Order to Obtain Durable Happiness* (New York, 1735), 39–40.

37. Solomon Stoddard, *The Efficacy of the Fear of Hell to Restrain Men from Sin* (Boston, 1713), 5.

38. Ibid., 9–10.

39. For a general discussion of the Enlightenment in the colonies, see Henry May, *The Enlightenment in America* (Cambridge, Mass., 1976).

40. J.C.D. Clark, *English Society, 1688–1832: Ideology, Social Structure and Political Practice during the Ancien Regime* (Cambridge, England, 1985), 279–280.

41. Ibid., 282.

42. Norman Fiering, *Moral Philosophy at Seventeenth-Century Harvard: A Discipline in Transition* (Chapel Hill, N.C., 1981), 244.

43. *General Magazine and Historical Chronicle,* February 1741.

44. See, for example, Louis Wright and Marion Tinling, eds., *The Secret Diary of William Byrd of Westover, 1709–1712* (Richmond, Va., 1941), 16.

45. For discussion of Tillotson's writings in the colonies, see Norman Fiering, *Jonathan Edwards's Moral Thought and Its British Context* (Chapel Hill, N.C., 1981), 227 ff.; quotations from 228, 230.

46. Ibid., 239.

47. Richard B. Davis, *A Colonial Southern Bookshelf: Reading in the Eighteenth Century* (Athens, Ga., 1979), 68–69.

48. Richard Allestree, *The Whole Duty of Man: Laid Down In a plain and familiar Way, for the Use of all, but especially the meanest Reader* (Williamsburg, Va., 1746), vii–vii.

49. Ibid., xvii–xx.

50. See Michael Crawford, *Seasons of Grace: Colonial New England's Revival Tradition in Its British Context* (New York, 1991), 22.

51. Ibid., 23. Biblical quotations from *The Oxford Annotated Bible* (New York, 1962).

52. "Diary of the Rev. Thomas Prince," 349.

53. Stoddard, *Efficacy of the Fear of Hell*, 193–204.

54. Increase Mather, *Discourse Concerning Faith and Fervency in Prayer* (Boston, 1710), 65.

55. Cited in Crawford, *Seasons of Grace*, 43.

56. Cotton Mather, *Religious Societies. Proposals For the revival of Dying Religion, By Well Ordered Societies For that Purpose* (Boston, 1724), 2–3.

57. Jonathan Edwards, *An Humble Attempt to Promote Explicit Agreement and Visible Union of God's People in Extraordinary Prayer for the Revival of Religion and the Advancement of Christ's Kingdom on Earth* (Boston, 1747).

58. Stoddard, *Efficacy of the Fear of Hell*, 185–186.

59. Watts, *An Humble Attempt*, 13, 19, 44, 54, 57, 62.

60. Tennent, *Necessity of Religious Violence*, 39.

61. Gilbert Tennent, *The Danger of Forgetting God, Describ'd and the Duty of Considering Our Ways Explain'd* (New York, 1735), 23–24.

62. Ibid., 10.

63. Gilbert Tennent, *The Danger of an Unconverted Ministry, Considered in a Sermon on Mark VI.34 . . .* (Boston, 1742), 6–8, 11–13.

64. Ibid., 17, 20.

65. Kenneth Silverman, *The Life and Times of Cotton Mather* (New York, 1985), 299–300.

66. Cited in Timothy L. Smith, *Whitefield and Wesley on the New Birth* (Grand Rapids, Mich., 1986), 65.

67. Ibid., 66–67, 110–116.

68. Cited in Crawford, *Seasons of Grace*, 186–187.

69. Jonathan Edwards, *A Faithful Narrative of the Surprising Work of God in the Conversion of Many Hundred Souls in Northampton, and the Neighbouring Towns and Villages of the County of Hampshire, in the Province of the Massachusetts-Bay in New-England* (Boston, 1738). For Hutchinson's conversion, see 56–65; for Bartlet's, see 65–72.

70. For the "consumer revolution," see Neil McKendric, John Brewer, and J. H. Plumb, eds., *The Birth of a Consumer Society: The Commercialization of Eighteenth-Century England* (Bloomington, Ind., 1982); T. H. Breen, "An Empire of Goods: The Anglicization of Colonial America, 1690–1776," *Journal of British Studies* 25 (October 1986): 467–499, and " 'Baubles of Britain': The American and Consumer Revolutions of the Eighteenth Century," *Past and Present* 119 (May 1980):

73–104; Ralph Davis, *A Commercial Revolution: English Overseas Trade in the Seventeenth and Eighteenth Centuries* (London, 1967); John J. McCusker and Russell Menard, *The Economy of British America, 1607–1789* (Chapel Hill, N.C., 1985); Roy Porter, *English Society in the Eighteenth Century* (New York, 1982); and Lorna Weatherill, "A Possession of One's Own: Women and Consumer Behavior in England, 1660–1740," *Journal of British Studies* 25 (April 1986): 131–156.

71. For example, reports on enormous crowds in newspapers appeared as if they were official counts from objective observers when in fact they originated with Whitefield or one of his associates. Later in his ministry, Whitefield admitted that some of the counts were greatly exaggerated. See *Whitefield's Journals*, 31.

72. Stoddard, *Efficacy of the Fear of Hell*, 187–188.

73. Ibid., 190.

74. Ibid., 191.

Chapter 2
"the *first fruits* of this extraordinary and mighty Work of God's Special Grace"

1. Dickinson, *A Display of God's Special Grace*, 32.

2. Goen, *Jonathan Edwards*, 155–156.

3. Tanis, *Dutch Calvinistic Pietism in the Middle Colonies*, 43, 49, and 66.

4. See John Gillies, *Historical Collections Relating to Remarkable Periods of the Success of the Gospel*, 2 vols. (Glasgow, 1754), 2:28–29 and 320. Hereafter referred to as the Glasgow edition.

5. Thomas Pears and Guy Klett, eds., "Documentary History of William Tennent and the Log College," *Journal of the Department of History of the Presbyterian Historical Society* 28 (March 1950): 48.

6. Thomas Pears, ed., "William Tennent's Sacramental Sermon," *Journal of the Department of History of the Presbyterian Church in the U.S.A.* 19 (June 1940): 76–77.

7. Ibid., 83.

8. Ibid., 78.

9. Charles Maxson, *The Great Awakening in the Middle Colonies* (1920; reprint, Philadelphia, 1958), 28–29.

10. Ibid., 27–28.

11. Milton J. Coalter, *Gilbert Tennent, Son of Thunder: A Case Study of Continental Pietism's Impact on the First Great Awakening in the Middle Colonies* (New York, 1986), 23.

12. Ibid., 41–42.

13. Ned Landsman, "Revivalism and Nativism in the Middle Colonies: The Great Awakening and the Scots Community in East New Jersey," *American Quarterly* 34 (Summer 1982): 150–151.

14. Cited in ibid., 158–159.

15. Ibid., 163.

16. Perry Miller, *Jonathan Edwards* (1949; reprint, Amherst, Mass., 1981), 35–40.

17. Jonathan Edwards, *God Glorified in the Work of Redemption, By the Greatness of Man's Dependence Upon Him, in the Whole of It* (Boston, 1731), preface.

18. Edwards, *Faithful Narrative*, 5–6.

19. Ibid.

20. Samuel Wigglesworth, *An Essay for Reviving Religion* (Boston, 1733), 15.

21. Edwards, *Faithful Narrative*, 5.

22. Samuel Wigglesworth, *A Religious Fear of God's Tokens Explained and Urged* (Boston, 1728), 9, 17.

23. Edwards, *Faithful Narrative*, 9.

24. Goen, *Jonathan Edwards*, 83. See also Miller, *Jonathan Edwards*, 133–134.

25. Ibid., 63, 69–70

26. Mark Valeri, "The Economic Thought of Jonathan Edwards," *Church History* 50 (March 1991): 39.

27. Edwards, *Faithful Narrative*, 11–12.

28. Ibid., 7–8.

29. Ibid., 18–20.

30. Ibid., 7–8.

31. Ibid., 25–26.

32. Patricia J. Tracy, *Jonathan Edwards, Pastor: Religion and Society in Eighteenth-Century Northampton* (New York, 1980), 113.

33. Edwards, *Faithful Narrative*, 26.

34. Ibid., 31–32.

35. Goen, *Jonathan Edwards*, 564.

36. Ibid., 205–206.

37. Cited in Tracey, *Jonathan Edwards Pastor*, 29 and 64.

38. Goen, *Jonathan Edwards*, 565.

39. Ibid., 538.

40. *New England Weekly Journal*, May 12, 1735.

41. Ibid.

42. Clarence Faust and Thomas Johnson, eds., *Jonathan Edwards: Representative Selections, with Introduction, Bibliography, and Notes* (1935; reprint, New York, 1962), 73–83.

43. Goen, *Jonathan Edwards*, 159–173.

44. Ibid., 191–201.

45. From Isaac Watts's preface to Jonathan Edwards's *A Faithful Narrative* (London, 1737), cited in Goen, *Jonathan Edwards*, 137.

46. Goen, *Jonathan Edwards*, 130–132.

47. Ibid., 134–135.

48. Isaac Watts, *Logick: Or, the Right Use of Reason in the Enquiry After Truth*, 4th ed. (London, 1731), 46, 273, 307, and 355.

49. Ibid., 136.

50. Ibid., 37.

51. Ibid., 141.

52. Ibid., 40.

53. Ibid., 143.

54. Edwards, *Faithful Narrative*, 4–7.

55. Cited in Goen, *Jonathan Edwards*, 130–137.

56. For glosses cited, see the London edition of the *Faithful Narrative*, 24–28 and 56.

57. William Williams to Benjamin Colman, April 28, 1735. Benjamin Colman Papers, 1641–1763. Massachusetts Historical Society, Boston. For Williams's role in the Connecticut River revivals, see Philip F. Gura, "Sowing for the Harvest: William Williams and the Great Awakening," *Journal of Presbyterian History* 56 (Winter 1978): 326–341.

58. Benjamin Colman, *The Merchandise of a People: Holiness to the Lord* (Boston, 1736), i–ii, 6, 10–11.

59. Goen, *Jonathan Edwards*, 112.

60. *The Declaration of the Association of the County of New-Haven in Connecticut* (Boston, 1745), 4.

61. See *The Christian History*.

62. Goen, *Jonathan Edwards*, 138.

63. Gillies, *Historical Collections*, Glasgow edition, vi.

64. Pearsall probably referred to William Williams, *The Duty and Interest of a People* (Boston, 1736). Colman had attached to that sermon part of a letter from Edwards "Giving an Account of the late wonderful Work of God in those Parts."

65. R. Pearsall to Benjamin Colman. Warminster, April 15, 1739. Colman Papers.

66. Jonathan Edwards to Benjamin Colman. May 19, 1737. Colman Papers.

67. Ibid.

68. If one's diary entries are an indication of what preoccupies one's thinking, the Northampton revival was not noteworthy to Thomas Prince in 1737. Though the minister, who would become a leading revivalist in the 1740s, recorded his thoughts on propagating the gospel in general, he did not mention the awakening in western Massachusetts. And, while he mentioned the falling balcony at the Northampton meetinghouse, he did not attach any providential meaning to the event. See "Diary of the Rev. Thomas Prince," 341.

69. *Whitefield's Journals*, 31.

Chapter 3
"imported Divinity"

1. Cited in Edwards, *Faithful Narrative*, i and v.

2. For Foxcroft's comments, see his preface to Jonathan Dickinson, *The True Scripture-Doctrine Concerning Some Important Points of Christian Faith* (Boston, 1741), i–iv.

3. Cited in Richard L. Bushman, ed., *The Great Awakening: Documents on the Revival of Religion, 1740–1745* (New York, 1970), 6–7.

4. Charles Chauncy, *A Letter from a Gentleman in Boston, to Mr. George Wishart, One of the Ministers of Edinburgh, Concerning the State of Religion in New-England* (Edinburgh, 1742), cited in Bushman, *The Great Awakening*, 116–117.

5. Edwards, *Distinguishing Marks*, 16, 18.

6. *Pennsylvania Gazette*, November 8, 1739.

7. Goen, *Jonathan Edwards*, 219.

8. Cited in Schmidt, *Holy Fairs*, 207.

9. For Whitefield's autobiography, see "A Short Account of God's Dealings

With George Whitefield From His Infancy to His Ordination, 1714–1736," in *Whitefields Journals*, 35–72.

10. The students were also known as Methodists because they lived by an exact method that regulated everything they did: how they spent each hour and each penny. After 1740, Methodists split into two groups: one, headed by John Wesley, embraced the Arminian notion of free will; the other, led by George Whitefield, adhered to the Calvinist idea of predestination, albeit of the evangelistic variety. The modern Methodist denomination originated in the 1780s under John Wesley's inspiration.

11. *Whitefield's Journals*, 53, 58.

12. Frank Baker, *John Wesley and the Church of England* (Nashville, 1970), 212–213.

13. Cited in Baker, *John Wesley and the Church of England*, 63.

14. Charles Grandison Finney, *Lectures on Revivals of Religion* (1835; reprint, Cambridge, Mass., 1960), 181.

15. Ibid., 250–251.

16. James Boswell, *The Life of Samuel Johnson* (London, 1831), 1:45.

17. Finney, *Lectures on Revivals*, 260–261.

18. *Whitefield's Journals*, 216.

19. J. A. Leo Lemay and P. M. Zall, *The Autobiography of Benjamin Franklin: A Genetic Text* (Knoxville, Tenn., 1981), 107.

20. Harry S. Stout, "Religion, Communications, and the Ideological Origins of the American Revolution," *William and Mary Quarterly* 34 (October 1977): 525–527.

21. Cited in Harry S. Stout, *The Divine Dramatist: George Whitefield and the Rise of Modern Evangelicalism* (Grand Rapids, Mich., 1991), 9.

22. Quoted from ibid., 41.

23. Lucien Febvre and Henri-Jean Martin, *The Coming of the Book: The Impact of Printing, 1450–1800*, trans. David Gerard (London, 1976), 288.

24. Gillies, *Historical Collections*, 34.

25. Luke Tyerman, *The Life and Times of the Rev. John Wesley, M.A.: Founder of the Methodists*, 3 vols. (New York, 1872–1875), 2:65–66.

26. *Connoisseur*, November 13, 1755, 160.

27. Figures cited in issues of *Daily Advertiser* and in *Whitefield's Journals*.

28. Alan Jenkins, *The Stock Exchange Story* (London, 1973), 20.

29. George Whitefield, *A Faithful Narrative of the Life and Character of the Reverend Mr. Whitefield, . . . Containing an Account of his Doctrines and Morals; his Motives for Going to Georgia; and his travels through several Parts of England* (London, 1739).

30. *A Faithful Narrative of the Life and Character of the Reverend Mr. Whitefield, B.D. From His Birth to the Present Time* (London, 1739), 5, 9, and 15.

31. Tristram Land, *A Letter to the Rev. Mr. Whitefield. Designed to Correct his Mistaken Account of Regeneration or the New Birth* (London, 1739), 2.

32. See Edmund Gibson, *Observations upon the Conduct and Behaviour of a Certain Sect Usually Distinguished by the name of Methodists* (n.p., 1740), 1–3.

33. *The Progress of Methodism in Bristol: or, the Methodist Unmask'd* (Bristol, 1743), 20, 38.

34. For an excellent discussion of the letter-writing network, see Susan Durden

[O'Brien], "A Transatlantic Community of Saints: The Great Awakening and the First Evangelical Network, 1735–1755," *American Historical Review* 91 (December 1986): 811–832; quotation from 815.

35. Letter from R. Pearsall to Benjamin Colman. Colman Papers.

36. Ibid.

37. Ibid.

38. See Harold P. Simonson, ed., *Selected Writings of Jonathan Edwards* (New York, 1970), 35.

39. See Elisabeth Dodds, *Marriage to a Difficult Man: the "Uncommon Union" of Jonathan and Sarah Edwards* (Philadelphia, 1971), 69.

40. On eighteenth-century Americans as a calculating people, see Patricia Cohen, *A Calculating People: The Spread of Numeracy in Early America* (Chicago, 1982).

41. See, for example, *Pennsylvania Gazette*, May 31 and June 28, 1739.

42. *Gentleman's Magazine*, August 1739.

43. *New England Weekly Journal*, November 13, 1739. In a similar experiment conducted and reported in Philadelphia by Benjamin Franklin, the space allotted per person was two square feet, half that cited in the London exercise. Franklin, however, determined that 30,000 people assembled in a semicircle in front of Whitefield could easily hear the evangelist.

44. Ibid.

45. Ibid., September 1739.

46. Goen, *Jonathan Edwards*, 262.

47. *Christian History*, 2:379.

48. *New England Weekly Journal*, November 27, 1739.

49. Francis G. Walett, "The Diary of Ebenezer Parkman, 1739–1744," *Proceedings of the American Antiquarian Society* 12 (April 1962): 109.

50. *New England Weekly Journal*, June 3, 1740.

51. See *Three Letters to the Reverend Mr. George Whitefield* (Philadelphia, 1739), 12.

52. Ibid., 3–5.

53. Ibid., 11.

54. From *Common Sense*, May 19, 1939, as reprinted in *London Magazine or Gentleman's Monthly*, May 1739, 238.

55. See *Whitefield's Journals*, 155.

56. For discussion of Whitefield's use of commercial tropes, see Frank Lambert, *"Pedlar in Divinity": George Whitefield and the Transatlantic Revivals, 1737–1770* (Princeton, 1994), 46–51.

57. For detailed discussion of how Whitefield constructed an exportable revival campaign, see Lambert, *"Pedlar in Divinity"*, and Stout, *Divine Dramatist*.

58. See, for example, *Virginia Gazette*, March 24, 1738.

59. John Gillies, *Memoirs of Reverend Mr. George Whitefield*, (New York, 1774), 13.

60. Population figures taken from Series Z 1–19, *The Statistical History of the United States from Colonial Times to the Present*, 2 vols. (Stamford, Conn., 1965), 2:1168.

61. Isaiah Thomas, *The History of Printing in America*, 2 vols. (Worcester, Mass., 1810), 1:210.

62. Ibid., 2:192.

63. Ibid., 205.

64. *Whitefield's Journals*, 416–417.

65. J. M. Bumsted, "Revivalism and Separatism in New England: The First Society of Norwich, Connecticut, as a Case Study," *William and Mary Quarterly* 24 (October 1967): 596.

66. James Walsh, "The Great Awakening in the First Congregation of Woodbury, Connecticut," *William and Mary Quarterly* 28 (October 1971): 544.

67. For description of an army encampment, see Fred Anderson, *A People's Army: Massachusetts Soldiers and Society in the Seven Years' War* (New York, 1984), 74.

68. Charles Chauncy, *Enthusiasm described and caution'd against. A Sermon Preach'd . . . the Lord's Day after the Commencement . . .* (Boston, 1742), 13. On the meanings of enthusiasm, see David S. Lovejoy, *Religious Enthusiasm in the New World: Heresy to Revolution* (Cambridge, Mass., 1985).

69. Samuel Blair, *A Short and Faithful Narrative of the late Remarkable Revival of Religion in the Congregation of New-Londonderry and other Parts of Pennsylvania* (Philadelphia, 1744), 13, 15.

70. See *Whitefield's Journals*, 461.

71. Ibid., 31–32.

72. For Whitefield's crowd estimates, see ibid., 323–507.

73. Ibid.

74. Thomas, *History of Printing in America*, 2:156–157.

75. Thomas Prince, *A Chronological History of New England* (Boston, 1736), iv.

76. Cited in *Dictionary of American Biography*, 22 vols. (New York, 1958–1964), 8:232.

77. Frank Lambert, "Subscribing for Profits and Piety: The Friendship of Benjamin Franklin and George Whitefield," *William and Mary Quarterly* 50 (July 1993): 529–554.

78. Cited in Lambert, *"Pedlar in Divinity"*, 478, 488.

79. Benjamin Colman to Drs. Guyse and Watts, October 3, 1740. Colman Papers.

80. See, for example, George Whitefield to Benjamin Colman, January 24, 1739/40. Colman Papers.

81. Benjamin Colman to George Whitefield, December 3, 1739, in *Three Letters to the Reverend Mr. George Whitefield* (Philadelphia, 1739), 3–4.

82. Ibid., 3, 5.

83. Benjamin Colman, *Souls Flying to Jesus Christ* (Boston, 1741), 6.

84. Henry Abelove, "Jonathan Edwards' Letter of Invitation to George Whitefield," *William and Mary Quarterly* 29 (July 1972): 488–489.

85. *Whitefield's Journals*, 475–477.

Chapter 4
The "Revival at . . ."

1. *Christian History*, 1:254–258.

2. Ibid., 236–252.

3. See Ebenezer Pemberton, *Discourses on Various Texts* (Boston, 1741).

4. *Christian History*, 1:259–269.

5. Many revival accounts published during and after the Great Awakening bear in their titles their affinity with the Northampton original. See Samuel Buell, *A Faithful Narrative of the Remarkable Revival of Religion, in the Congregation of East-Hampton, on Long Island* (New York, 1766); Eden Burroughs, *A Faithful Narrative of the Wonderful Dealings of God* (Concord, N.H., 1792); James Robe, *A Faithful Narrative of the Extraordinary Work of the Spirit of God, at Kilsyth* (London, 1743); Eleazar Wheelock, *A Plain and Faithful Narrative of the Original Design, Rise, Progress and State of the Indian Charity-School at Lebanon, in Connecticutt* (Boston, 1743).

6. Kneeland and Green published Thomas Prince's circular letter on a single sheet, 19.5 × 14 cm. It bore as a title the first part of the text, *It being earnestly desired by many pious and judicious people, that particular Accounts of the Revival of Religion in every Town* . . . (Boston, 1743).

7. Coalter, *Gilbert Tennent, Son of Thunder*, xii and xvii.

8. John B. Frantz, "The Awakening of Religion among the German Settlers in the Middle Colonies," *William and Mary Quarterly* 33 (April 1976): 288.

9. W. R. Ward, *The Protestant Evangelical Awakening* (Cambridge, England, 1992), 134–138.

10. Ibid., 100–101.

11. See Theodore Tappert and John Doberstein, trans., *The Journals of Henry Melchior Muhlenberg*, 3 vols. (Philadelphia, 1942), 1:73–74.

12. Ibid. For the exchange between Zinzendorf and Muhlenberg, see 76–80.

13. Ibid., 92–93.

14. Ibid., 134–138. See also Donald D. Housley, "The Response of Conservative Presbyterians to the Great Awakening in the Middle Colonies," *Susquehanna University Studies* 8 (June 1970): 301–314.

15. On the controversy between Old Side and New Side Presbyterians, see Leonard J. Trinterud, *The Forming of an American Tradition: A Re-examination of Colonial Presbyterianism* (Philadelphia, 1949), 191–195.

16. For an insightful study on the empowerment of the laity, see Westerkamp, *Triumph of the Laity*.

17. John Webb, *Some Plain and Necessary Directions To Obtain Eternal Salvation*, 2d ed. (Boston, 1741). See unpaginated preface.

18. *Christian History*, 2:393.

19. Joseph Sewall, *The Holy Spirit Convincing the World of Sin, of Righteousness, and of Judgment* (Boston, 1741), 1.

20. Cited in Gerald McDermott, *One Holy and Happy Society: The Public Theology of Jonathan Edwards* (State College, Pa., 1992), 83–86.

21. *Boston Post-Boy*, December 8, 1740.

22. Ibid.

23. Ibid., 192–195.

24. Rosalind Remer, "Old Lights and New Money: A Note on Religion, Economics, and the Social Order in 1740 Boston," *William and Mary Quarterly* 47 (October 1990): 566–567.

25. John L. Brooke, *The Heart of the Commonwealth: Society and Political Culture in Worcester County, Massachusetts, 1713–1861* (Cambridge, England, 1989), 69–70.

26. Bumsted, "Revivalism and Separatism in New England," 596–598.

27. Ibid., 600.

28. Walsh, "The Great Awakening in the First Congregation of Woodbury, Connecticut," 551–555.

29. Philip J. Greven, Jr., *Four Generations: Population, Land, and Family in Colonial Andover, Massachusetts* (Ithaca, N.Y., 1970), 279.

30. Rodger M. Payne, "New Light in Hanover County: Evangelical Dissent in Piedmont Virginia, 1740–1755," *Journal of Southern History* 61 (November 1995): 682–685.

31. See Robert Leland Bidwell, "The Morris Reading-Houses: A Study in Dissent," MS 7:3, Virginia Historical Society, 7–9, 23–24, 29.

32. Ibid., 34.

33. Payne, "New Light in Hanover County," 665, 672–673.

34. George Pilcher, *Samuel Davies: Apostle of Dissent in Colonial Virginia* (Knoxville, Tenn., 1971), 29.

35. Ibid., 29–30.

36. Gillies, *Historical Collections*, Glasgow edition, 2:332–333.

37. Payne, "New Light in Hanover County," 688.

38. *Virginia Gazette*, October 24, 1745.

39. Gillies, *Historical Collections*, Glasgow edition, 2:330.

40. Marcus Rediker, "'The Outcasts of the Nations of the Earth': The New York Conspiracy of 1741 in Atlantic Perspective" (Paper presented to the Cultural History Workshop, Department of History, Purdue University, April 20, 1995), 19–20. For a broader examination of the awakening and slaves, see Albert Raboteau, *Slave Religion: The "Invisible Institution" in the Antebellum South* (Oxford, 1978). See also Stephen Stein, "George Whitefield on Slavery: Some New Evidence," *Church History* 42 (June 1973): 243–256.

41. Cited in Rediker, "'The Outcasts of the Nations,'" 19–20.

42. Jon Butler, *Awash in a Sea of Faith: Christianizing the American People* (Cambridge, Mass., 1990), 166.

43. Cited in Rhys Isaac, *The Transformation of Virginia, 1740–1790* (Chapel Hill, N.C., 1982), 166.

44. Ibid.

45. See Colman's remarks in his preface to Smith's ordination sermon, *A Discourse Delivered at Boston, on July 11, 1726. Then Occasion'd by the Author's Ordination* (Boston, 1726), iii.

46. See Isaac Chanler, *New Converts Exhorted to Cleave to the Lord* (Boston, 1740).

47. Benedict Anderson coined the phrase "imagined community" to describe how popular print such as newspapers "creates . . . [an] extraordinary mass ceremony: the almost precisely simultaneous consumption" of the same material such that thousands of readers, though separated by many miles, are aware that others are engaged in the same enterprise. See Benedict Anderson, *The Imagined Community: Reflections on the Origins and Spread of Nationalism* (London, 1983), 28, 38–39.

48. William Seward, *Journal of a Voyage From Savannah to Philadelphia and From Philadelphia to England* (London, 1740), 55–56.

49. On Kneeland and Green's circular letter, see n. 6, above, this chapter.

50. Circular letter.

51. Ibid.

52. This discussion involves only North American revival narratives, not those from England or Scotland. For Crawford's analysis, see Crawford, *Seasons of Grace*, 185.

53. *Whitefield's Journals*, 352 and 486.

54. *Christian History*, 1:255.

55. Ibid., 2:126–127.

56. Ibid., 414–415.

57. Ibid., 1:261.

58. Ibid., 268.

59. Ibid., 2:322–323.

60. Ibid., 323.

Chapter 5
"... similar facts ... are now united"

1. See table 4.1.

2. *Whitefield's Journals*, 529.

3. See William Cooper's preface to Jonathan Edwards, *The Distinguishing Marks of a Work of the Spirit of God* (Boston, 1741), xvii.

4. Ibid., 224–225.

5. Gillies, *Historical Collections*, 337.

6. *Whitefield's Journals*, 31.

7. Durden [O'Brien], "A Transatlantic Community of Saints," 811.

8. Ibid., 824.

9. Cited in Lambert, *"Pedlar in Divinity"*, 159.

10. Ibid., 132.

11. Ian Steele, *The English Atlantic, 1675–1740: An Exploration of Communication and Community* (New York, 1986), 135–136.

12. *Tercentenary Handlist of English and Welsh Newspapers, Magazines and Reviews* (London, 1920).

13. Susan Durden [O'Brien], "Eighteenth-Century Publishing Networks in the First Years of Transatlantic Evangelicalism," in *Evangelicalism: Comparative Studies of Popular Protestantism in North America, the British Isles, and Beyond, 1700–1990*, ed. Mark A. Noll, David W. Bebbington, and George A. Rawlyk (Oxford, 1994), 45–46.

14. Cited in ibid., 46.

15. Ibid., 47.

16. *Boston News-Letter*, May 26, 1743.

17. Durden [O'Brien], "Eighteenth-Century Publishing Networks," 38–39. See also S. J. Royal, "Religious Periodicals in England during the Restoration and Eighteenth Century," *Journal of Rutgers University* (1971): 27–33.

18. Durden [O'Brien], "Eighteenth-Century Publishing Networks," 39.

19. Cited in ibid., 43–44.

20. For Franklin's sale of Whitefield's works, see manuscript copy of Benjamin Franklin's Ledger "D" located at the American Philosophical Society (Philadelphia). See also George S. Eddy, ed., *Account Books Kept by Benjamin Franklin*, 2

vols. (New York, 1929); and C. William Miller, *Benjamin Franklin's Philadelphia Printing, 1728–1766: A Descriptive Bibliography* (Philadelphia, 1974).

21. Durden [O'Brien], "Eighteenth-Century Publishing Networks," 43.

22. See preface to Dickinson, *Display of God's Special Grace*, ix–x.

23. See Leigh Eric Schmidt, "Sacramental Occasions and the Scottish Context of Presbyterian Revivalism in America," in *Scotland and America in the Age of the Enlightenment*, ed. Richard B. Sher and Jeffrey R. Smitten (Princeton, 1990), 60–67.

24. David Campbell, *Sacramental Meditations On the Sufferings and Death of Christ*, 2d ed. (Boston, 1740), iv.

25. Ibid.

26. Goen, *Jonathan Edwards*, 538. For a fuller discussion of the awakenings in Scotland and their links with the American revivals, see Arthur Fawcett, *The Cambuslang Revival: The Scottish Evangelical Revival of the Eighteenth Century* (London, 1971). Scottish converts frequently mentioned the effects of news from the American revivals on their own new births; see T. C. Smout, "Born Again at Cambuslang: New Evidence on Popular Religion and Literacy in Eighteenth-Century Scotland," *Past and Present* 97 (November 1982): 114–127.

27. John Erskine, *The Signs of the Times Considered: or, The High Probability, that the present* APPEARANCES *in New England, and the West of* Scotland, *are a* PRELUDE of the Glorious Things promised to the CHURCH in the latter Ages (Edinburgh, 1742), 10, 17–18.

28. Gillies, *Historical Collections*, Glasgow edition, 2:399.

29. Ibid., 401–402.

30. Ibid.

31. Seward, *Journal of a Voyage*, 30–31.

32. See preface to Colman, *Souls Flying to Jesus Christ*.

33. Susan Durden [O'Brien], "A Study of the First Evangelical Magazines, 1740–1748," *Journal of Ecclesiastical History* 27 (July 1976): 258.

34. "The Christian's Amusement," *Proceedings of the Wesley Historical Society* 11 (1917–1918): 183.

35. Durden [O'Brien], "First Evangelical Magazines," 258.

36. "The Christian's Amusement,' 184–185.

37. John Lewis to Mrs. James, January 31, 1740/41. Trevecca Letters. National Library of Wales, Aberystwyth, Wales.

38. Cited in Durden [O'Brien], "First Evangelical Magazines," 259–260.

39. Lewis to Mrs. James, January 31, 1740/41. Trevecca Letters.

40. Durden [O'Brien], "First Evangelical Magazines," 261.

41. Cited in ibid.

42. *Weekly History*, June 12, 1742.

43. Ibid., June 26, 1742.

44. Ibid., June 13, 1741.

45. Ibid., July 18, 1741.

46. Ibid., July 4, 1741.

47. Ibid., June 27, 1741.

48. Durden [O'Brien], "First Evangelical Magazines," 266–267.

49. Cited in ibid., 270.

50. Goen, *Jonathan Edwards*, 59, 538.

51. Ibid.

52. *Boston Evening-Post*, October 24, 1743.

53. Webb, *Some Plain and Necessary Directions To Obtain Eternal Salvation*, unpaginated prefacc.

54. John Flavel, *The Great Design and Scope of the Gospel Opened. An Extract from the Rev. Mr. Flavel's England's Duty* (Boston, 1741). See Byles's prefatory remarks in unpaginated preface.

55. *Christian History*, 1:258.

56. The complete title of Gillies's work is *Historical Collections Relating to Remarkable Periods of the Success of the Gospel.*

57. Ibid., vi.

58. Ibid.

59. Ibid., v.

60. Ibid., vi–viii.

61. Ibid.

62. Ibid., 9.

63. Ibid., 239.

64. Ibid., 272–292.

65. Ibid., 279–281.

66. Ibid., 281.

67. Gillies, *Memoirs of the Rev. George Whitefield*, 73.

68. Gillies, *Historical Collections*, 272.

69. This is the two-volume 1754 Glasgow edition of Gillies, *Historical Collections*.

70. Ibid., 1:preface.

71. Ibid. This heading is in vol. 2.

72. Ibid., 1:ix–x.

Part Three
Introductory Section

1. Benjamin Prescott, *A Letter to the Reverend Mr. Joshua Gee, In Answer to His of June 3, 1743. Address'd to Mr. Nathaniel Eells, Moderator of the late Convention of Pastors in Boston* (Boston, 1743), 22–23.

Chapter 6
The "grand delusion" or "great Mistakes of the present Day"

1. *An Historical Narrative And Declaration Shewing the Cause and Rise of the Strict Congregational Churches in the State of Connecticut* (Providence, 1781), 5.

2. Gillies, *Historical Collections*, 423.

3. Charles Chauncy, *An Answer to the Reverend Mr. Edwards' Sermon on the Distinguishing Marks of a Work of the Spirit of God* (Boston, 1743), 8.

4. Thomas Foxcroft, *Some Seasonable Thoughts on Evangelic Preaching: Its Nature, Usefulness, and Obligation* (Boston, 1740), 30–31.

5. Charles Chauncy, *The New Creature Describ'd* (Boston, 1741), 35, 39, 42.

6. Cited in Goen, *Jonathan Edwards*, 52–53, 56–58.

7. Ibid., 81.

8. Charles Chauncy, *The Late Religious Commotions in New-England considered. An Answer To the Reverend Mr. Jonathan Edwards' Sermon, Entitled The Distinguishing Marks of a Work of the Spirit of God, applied to that uncommon Operation that has lately appeared in the Minds of many of the People of the Lord* (Boston, 1743), 2.

9. Jonathan Edwards, *Some Thoughts Concerning the Present Revival of Religion in New-England* (Boston, 1742), 2.

10. Chauncy's remarks concerning the revival's effects on behavior cited in Bushman, *The Great Awakening*, 120.

11. *The Testimony of the Pastors of the Churches in the Province of the Massachusetts-Bay in New-England, at their Annual Convention in Boston, May 25, 1743. Against several Errors in Doctrine, and Disorders in Practice . . .* (Boston, 1743), 6.

12. Chauncy, *Letter from a Gentleman in Boston*, 17–24.

13. *Mr. Parsons Corrected. . . . In a Letter to a Friend* (Boston, 1743), 11.

14. John Caldwell, *An Impartial Trial of the Spirit Operating in this Part of the World, By Comparing the Nature, Effects and Evidences, of the Present Supposed Conversion with the Word of God* (Boston, 1742), i.

15. John Caldwell, *The Scripture Characters or Marks of False Prophets or Teachers* (Boston, 1742), 30–31.

16. John Caldwell, *The Nature, Folly, and Evil of Rash and Uncharitable Judging* (Boston, 1742). See page 5 of the appendix.

17. Caldwell, *Scripture Characters*, 31.

18. Ibid., 14, 30.

19. Nathaniel Eells, *Religion is the Life of God's People* (Boston, 1743), 30.

20. Cited in *Collections of the Massachusetts Historical Society*, 1st ser., 10 (1809): 164.

21. See title page of *A Letter From a Gentleman in Scotland, To His Friend in New England* (Boston, 1743).

22. The Journal of the Reverend Charles Woodmason: "Journal of C. W. Clerk. Itinerant Minister in South Carolina 1766, 1767, 1768," in Hooker, *Carolina Backcountry on the Eve of the Revolution*, 42–47.

23. *Testimony of the Pastors*, 6–7.

24. Ibid.

25. See Bushman, *Great Awakening*, 117.

26. Cited in Gregory H. Nobles, *Divisions throughout the Whole: Politics and Society in Hampshire County, Massachusetts, 1740–1775* (Cambridge, England, 1983), 44–45.

27. Ibid., 45–46.

28. Ibid.

29. *Weekly Miscellany*, January 31, 1741.

30. *Boston Evening-Post*, October 24, 1743.

31. Cited in Richardson Wright, *Hawkers and Walkers in Early America: Strolling Peddlers, Preachers, Lawyers, Doctors, Players, and Others, from the Beginning to the Civil War* (Philadelphia, 1927), 28.

32. William S. Perry, ed., *Historical Collections Relating to the American Colonial Church*, 5 vols. (1870; reprint, New York, 1969), 1:372. For a discussion of itinerancy and how it challenged social and ecclesiastical organizations, see Timothy D. Hall, *Contested Boundaries: Itinerancy and the Reshaping of the Colonial American Religious World* (Durham, N.C., 1994).

33. Cited in Karen O. Kupperman, ed., *Major Problems in American Colonial History* (Lexington, Mass., 1993), 374–375.

34. Ibid., 373–375.

35. Ibid., 373.

36. Ibid., 376.

37. *Weekly Miscellany*, May 5, 1739. This was an Anglican newspaper hostile to the Methodists, particularly Whitefield.

38. Ibid., February 10, 1738.

39. Charles Chauncy, *Seasonable Thoughts on the State of Religion in New-England* (Boston, 1743), 47, 415, 419, 423–424.

40. *Mr. Parsons Corrected*, 11.

41. *Boston Evening-Post*, March 14, 1743.

42. Ibid., October 24, 1743.

43. Ibid., July 4, 1743.

44. Ibid., May 30, 1743.

45. Ibid.

46. Ibid., August 15, 1743.

47. Ibid.

48. See Perry, *Historical Collections*, 1:381.

49. Isaac Stiles, *A Looking-glass for Changelings. A Seasonable Caveat against Meddling with them that are given to Change . . .* (New London, Conn., 1743).

50. Ibid.

51. *A Protestation Presented to the Synod of Philadelphia* (Philadelphia, 1741), 2, 10.

52. Samuel Blair, *A Particular Consideration of a Piece, Entitled, The Querists* (Philadelphia, 1741), 7.

53. Ibid., 9.

54. *Whitefield's Journals*, 388–389.

55. Perry, *Historical Collections*, 3:170–173.

56. Ibid., 177–178.

57. Ibid., 185, 298.

58. Ibid., 163.

59. John Lord, bishop of Landaff, *A Sermon Preached Before the Incorporated Society for the Propagation of the Gospel in Foreign Parts* (London, 1744), 31.

60. *Boston Evening-Post*, February 7, 1743.

61. "Diary of the Rev. Thomas Prince," 337.

62. For the Anglican conception of ministry, see Butler, *Awash in a Sea of Faith*, 164 ff.

63. *Protestation Presented to the Synod of Philadelphia*, 11.

64. Ibid., 3, 11.

65. Charles Chauncy, *Salvation for All Men, Illustrated and Vindicated as a Scripture Doctrine in Numerous Abstracts from a Variety of Pious and Learned Men* (1782; reprint, New York, 1975), i–ii, 19.

66. Ibid., 7.

67. Ibid., 4–5.

68. *Testimony of the President, Professors, Tutors, and Hebrew Instructor of Harvard College, against George Whitefield* (Boston, 1744), 4. See also Ross W. Beales, Jr., "Harvard and Yale in the Great Awakening," *Historical Journal of Massachusetts* 14 (January 1986): 1–10.

69. Perry, *Historical Collections*, 3:203, 217.

70. Ibid., 210–211.

71. R. Laurence Moore, *Religious Outsiders and the Making of Americans* (New York, 1986), xiii.

72. Perry, *Historical Collections*, 3:348, 357–357.

73. Letters surveyed are found in ibid., vols. 2 and 3.

74. Moore, *Religious Outsiders*, xi, xiv.

75. Robert Cross, *A Protestation Presented to the Synod of Philadelphia* (Philadelphia, 1741), 9.

76. *Testimony of the Pastors*, 5–13.

77. *A Letter From the Reverend Mr. Nicholas Loring of North Falmouth In the County of York, To the Reverend Mr. Thomas Smith* (Boston 1745), 3.

78. *New England Weekly Journal*, September 20, 1740.

79. *Boston Gazette*, September 22–29, 1740.

80. *Boston Weekly News-Letter*, September 18–25, 1740.

81. *Boston Weekly Post-Boy*, September 22, 1740; *Boston Evening-Post*, September 22, 1740.

82. *Boston Evening-Post*, September 29, 1740; *Boston Weekly News-Letter*, September 25–October 2, 1740.

83. *Boston Evening-Post*, October 6, 1740.

84. George Whitefield, *A Continuation of the Reverend Mr. Whitefield's Journal to Savannah, June 25, 1740 to his Arrival at Rhode-Island, his Travels to the other Governments of New-England, to his Departure from Stamford in Connecticut for New York* (Boston, 1741).

85. *Whitefield's Journals*, 462, 482.

86. Ibid., 462.

87. *Boston Gazette*, April 13–20, 1741.

88. Perry, *Historical Collections*, 3:367.

89. Ibid., 1:381.

90. Chauncy, *Letter from a Gentleman in Boston*, 5.

91. Ibid., 5–15.

92. Cited in Stout, *Divine Dramatist*, 244–245.

93. Ronald Paulson, comp., *Hogarth's Graphic Works*, 2 vols. (New Haven, 1970). For a plate of *Enthusiasm Delineated*, see 2:231; for text describing it, see 1:244–247. For a plate of *The Sleeping Congregation*, see 2:151; for text describing it, see 1:170–171.

94. Henry Fielding, *The History of the Adventures of Joseph Andrews, and of his Friend Mr. Abraham Adams*, 2 vols. (London, 1742), 1:117–120.

95. Ibid., 17.

96. Joshua Gee, *A Letter to the Reverend Mr. Nathaniel Eells, Moderator of the Late Convention of Pastors in Boston* (Boston, 1743), 13.

Chapter 7
"This is the Lord's Doing"

1. See preface to Dickinson, *Display of God's Special Grace.*

2. Ibid., v.

3. Ibid., i–ii.

4. Ibid., v–vi.

5. Ibid., title page, v.

6. Dickinson, *The Reasonableness of Nonconformity to the Church of England* (Boston, 1738), 126.

7. James Robe, *A Short Narrative of the Extraordinary Work at Cambuslang in Scotland, In a Letter to a Friend With proper Attestations by Ministers and Others* (Philadelphia, 1742), 3.

8. Ibid., 3–4.

9. Ibid., 4–5.

10. Ibid., 8–9.

11. *The Testimony and Advice of an Assembly of Pastors of Churches in New England, at a meeting in Boston, July 7, 1743, Occasion'd by the late happy Revival of Religion in many parts of the Land* (Boston, 1743).

12. Cited in Joseph Tracy, *The Great Awakening: A History of the Revival of Religion in the Time of Edwards and Whitefield* (Boston, 1841), 330–331.

13. Dickinson, *Display of God's Special Grace*, v.

14. *Christian History*, 2:291.

15. Ibid., 286.

16. Ibid., 287.

17. See *The Testimony of the Pastors of the Churches in the Province of the Massachusetts-Bay, in New-England, at their Annual Convention in Boston, May 25, 1743. Against several Errors in Doctrine, and Disorders in Practice, Which have of late obtained in various Parts of the Land* (Boston, 1743).

18. Gee, *Letter to the Reverend Mr. Nathaniel Eells*, 13.

19. Gillies, *Historical Collections*, Glasgow edition, 2:250.

20. See title page, Edwards, *Distinguishing Marks.*

21. Goen, *Jonathan Edwards*, 228.

22. Ibid., 241.

23. Ibid., 245.

24. Ibid., 260–264.

25. Cited in Amy Schrager Lang, "'A Flood of Errors': Chauncy and Edwards in the Great Awakening," in *Jonathan Edwards and the American Experience*, ed. Nathan O. Hatch and Harry S. Stout (New York, 1988), 165–166.

26. Dickinson, *Display of God's Special Grace*, 28.

27. Ibid., 28–29.

28. Alexander Webster, *Divine Influence: The True Spring of the Extraordinary Work at Cambuslang and Other Places in the West of Scotland* (Boston, 1743), 12.

29. Roger Finke and Rodney Stark, *The Churching of America, 1776–1990: Winners and Losers in Our Religious Economy* (New Brunswick, N.J., 1992), 18.

30. See Tennent, *Danger of an Unconverted Ministry*, 14.

31. I have elaborated elsewhere on Whitefield's conception of his mission. See *"Pedlar in Divinity"*, 14.

32. *Whitefield's Journals*, 230.

33. George Whitefield, *Sermons on Various Subjects*, 2 vols. (Philadelphia, 1740), 2:29.

34. Goen, *Jonathan Edwards*, 271.

35. Samuel Finley, *Clear Light Put Out in Obscure Darkness. Being an Examination and Refutation of Mr. Thompson's Sermon, Entituled, The Doctrine of Conviction set in a clear Light* (Philadelphia, 1743), 26.

36. Ibid., 52.

37. Ibid., 52–53.

38. Ibid., 53–54.

39. Andrew Croswell, *A Letter from the Revd Mr. Croswell, To the Revd Mr. Turell, In Answer to his Direction to the People* (Boston, 1742), 15–16.

40. Gee, *Letter to the Reverend Mr. Nathaniel Eells*, 7–10.

41. Foxcroft, *Some Seasonable Thoughts on Evangelic Preaching*, 32–33.

42. *Christian History*, 2:403.

43. Harry Stout, *The New England Soul: Preaching and Religious Culture in Colonial New England* (New York, 1986), 194.

44. See Tennent's sermon in Bushman, *The Great Awakening*, 90–93.

45. *Boston Post-Boy*, May 3, 1742.

46. *Boston Evening-Post*, May 9, 1743.

47. Ebenezer Turell, *Mr. Turell's Dialogue Between a Minister and his Neighbour about the Times* (Boston, 1742), 6–7.

48. Cited in *Christian History*, 2:407.

49. *Boston Weekly Post-Boy*, March 28, 1743.

50. For Davenport's recantation, see James Davenport, *The Reverend Mr. James Davenport's Confession and Retractions* (Boston, 1744).

51. Gilbert Tennent, *The Necessity of Holding Fast the Truth . . . with an Appendix Relating to Errors lately vented by some Moravians in those Parts* (Boston, 1743), 73, 81, 98.

52. Ibid., 99–100, 104, 110.

53. Cited in Tracy, *The Great Awakening*, 317–318.

54. Leigh E. Schmidt, "'A Second and Glorious Reformation': The New Light Extremism of Andrew Croswell," *William and Mary Quarterly* 43 (April 1986): 217–219.

55. *A Letter from the Associated Ministers of the County of Windham, to the People in the Several Societies in Said County* (Boston, 1745).

56. Turell, *Mr. Turell's Dialogue*, 4–5.

57. Ibid., 5–6, 21.

58. Ebenezer Turell, *Mr. Turell's Directions to his People with Relation to the present Times; with the Reasons why it is made publick* (Boston, 1742), ii–iii, 10–11.

59. *Boston Gazette*, May 31, 1743.

60. Ibid., June 28, 1743.

61. Webster, *Divine Influence*, 5.

62. Cited in Crawford, *Seasons of Grace*, 178.

Epilogue
"The late Revival of Religion"

1. Cited in Alan Heimert and Perry Miller, eds., *The Great Awakening: Documents Illustrating the Crisis and Its Consequences* (New York, 1967), 372–373.

2. Thomas Prince, *The Salvation of God in 1746* (Boston, 1746), 18–19.

3. See Jonathan Edwards to Benjamin Colman, May 19, 1734. Colman Papers.

4. *Whitefield's Journals*, 515, 523.

5. Ibid., 526.

6. Ibid., 528–529.

7. Carl Bridenbaugh, ed., *Gentleman's Progress: The Itinerarium of Dr. Alexander Hamilton, 1744* (Chapel Hill, N.C., 1948), 117, 197.

8. Ibid., 27, 74.

9. Gregory E. Dowd, *A Spirited Resistance: The North American Indian Struggle for Identity, 1745–1815* (Baltimore, 1992), 27–29.

10. Goen, *Jonathan Edwards*, 565.

11. *Christian History*, 2:416.

12. Tracy, *The Great Awakening*, iii.

Selected Bibliography

Primary Documents

Printed pamphlets and books for and against the revivals abound in the period, 1735–1745. For individual titles, see Charles Evans, ed. *American Bibliography: A Chronological Dictionary of All Books, Pamphlets, and Periodicals Printed in the United States of America from the Genesis in 1639 down to and including the year 1820*, 14 vols (Chicago, 1904). Newspapers also constitute a rich source for the "great awakening," including those published in Great Britain and in British North America.

Abelove, Henry. "Jonathan Edwards' Letter of Invitation to George Whitefield." *William and Mary Quarterly* 29 (July 1972): 487–489.

An Account of the Most Remarkable Particulars Relating to the Present Progress of the Gospel. Autumn 1742–autumn 1743.

Allestree, Richard. *The Whole Duty of Man: Laid Down In a plain and familiar Way, for the Use of all, but especially the meanest Reader*. Williamsburg, Va., 1746.

Blair, Samuel. *A Short and Faithful Narrative of the late Remarkable Revival of Religion in the Congregation of New-Londonderry and other Parts of Pennsylvania*. Philadelphia, 1744.

Boswell, James. *The Life of Samuel Johnson*. London, 1831.

Bridenbaugh, Carl, ed. *Gentleman's Progress: The Itinerarium of Dr. Alexander Hamilton, 1744*. Chapel Hill, N.C., 1948.

Bushman, Richard L., ed. *The Great Awakening: Documents on the Revival of Religion, 1740–1745*. New York, 1970.

Caldwell, John. *An Impartial Trial of the Spirit Operating in this Part of the World, By Comparing the Nature, Effects and Evidences, of the Present Supposed Conversion with the Word of God*. Boston, 1742.

———. *The Nature, Folly, and Evil of Rash and Uncharitable Judging*. Boston, 1742.

———. *The Scripture Characters or Marks of False Prophets or Teachers*. Boston, 1742.

Chauncy, Charles. *Enthusiasm described and caution'd against. A Sermon Preach'd . . . the Lord's Day after the Commencement. . . .* Boston, 1742.

———. *A Letter from a Gentleman in Boston, to Mr. George Wishart, One of the Ministers of Edinburgh, Concerning the State of Religion in New-England*. Edinburgh, 1742.

———. *The* outpouring *of the* HOLY GHOST. Boston, 1742.

———. *Seasonable Thoughts on the State of Religion in New-England*. Boston, 1743.

The Christian Amusement containing Letters Concerning the Progress of the Gospel both at Home and Abroad etc. Together with an Account of the Waldenses and Albigenses . . . (London). September 1740–March 1741.

The Christian History, Containing Accounts of the Revival and Propagation of Religion in Great-Britain and America (Boston). March 1743–February 1745.

The Christian History or General Account of the Progress of the Gospel in England, Wales, Scotland and America, as far as the Rev. Mr. Whitefield, His Fellow Labourers and Assistants are concerned (London). Autumn 1743–1748.

The Christian Monthly History or an Account of the Revival and Progress of Religion Abroad and at Home (Edinburgh). November, 1743–January 1746.

Colman, Benjamin. *The Merchandise of a People: Holiness to the Lord.* Boston, 1736.

———. *Souls Flying to Jesus Christ.* Boston, 1741.

Croswell, Andrew. *A Letter from the Revd Mr. Croswell, To the Revd Mr. Turell, In Answer to his Directions to the People.* Boston, 1742.

Davenport, James. *The Reverend Mr. James Davenport's Confession and Retractions.* Boston, 1744.

The Diary of Reverend Daniel Rogers, 1740–1751. Original manuscript owned by the New York Historical Society.

Dickinson, Jonathan. *A Display of God's Special Grace. In a familiar Dialogue between a Minister and a Gentleman of his Congregation about The Work of God, in the Conviction of Sinners, so remarkably of late began and going on in these American Parts.* Boston, 1742.

———. *The True Scripture-Doctrine Concerning Some Important Points of Christian Faith.* Boston, 1741.

Edwards, Jonathan. *Discourses on Various Important Subjects, Nearly Concerning the great affair of the Souls Eternal Salvation.* Boston, 1739.

———. *The Distinguishing Marks of a Work of the Spirit of God.* Boston, 1741.

———. *A Faithful Narrative of the Surprizing Work of God.* London, 1737.

———. *Some Thoughts Concerning the Present Revival of Religion in New-England.* Boston, 1742.

———. *A Treatise Concerning Religious Affections.* Boston, 1746.

Eells, Nathaniel. *Religion is the Life of God's People.* Boston, 1743.

Fausts, Clarence, and Thomas Johnson, eds. *Jonathan Edwards: Representative Selections, with Introduction, Bibliography, and Notes.* 1935. Reprint, New York.

Finley, Samuel. *Clear Light Put Out in Obscure Darkness. Being an Examination and Refutation of Mr. Thompson's Sermon, Entituled, The Doctrine of Conviction set in a clear Light.* Philadelphia, 1743.

Finney, Charles Grandison. *Lectures on Revivals of Religion.* 1835. Reprint, Cambridge, Mass., 1960.

Foxcroft, Thomas. *Some Seasonable Thoughts on Evangelic Preaching: Its Nature, Usefulness, and Obligation.* Boston, 1740.

Garden, Alexander. *Regeneration, and the Testimony of the Spirit.* Charleston, S.C., 1740.

Gee, Joshua. *A Letter to the Reverend Mr. Nathaniel Eells, Moderator of the late Convention of Pastors in Boston.* Boston, 1743.

George Whitefield's Journals. 1739–1741. Reprint, London, 1960.

Gibson, Edmund. *Observations Upon the Conduct and Behaviour of a Certain Sect Usually Distinguished by the Name of Methodists.* London, 1741.

Gillies, John. *Historical Collections Relating to Remarkable Periods of the Success of the Gospel.* 1754. Reprint, London, 1981.

———. *Memoirs of Rev. George Whitefield.* 1837. Reprint, Spartanburg, S.C., 1972.

———. *The Works of the Rev. George Whitefield, M.A. Late of Pembroke College, Oxford, and Chaplain to the Rt. Hon. the Countess of Huntingdon, Containing All His Sermons and Tracts Which Have Been Already Published With a Selected Collection of Letters.* 6 vols. London, 1771.

The Glasgow-Weekly-History Relating to the Late Progress of the Gospel at Home and Abroad; Being a Collection of Letters partly reprinted from the London-Weekly-History. . . . December 1741–December 1742.

Goen, C. C., ed. *Jonathan Edwards: The Great Awakening.* Vol. 4 of *The Works of Jonathan Edwards.* Edited by John E. Smith et al. New Haven, 1972.

Hawks, Francis L., and William S. Perry, eds. *Documentary History of the Protestant Episcopal Church in the United States of America, Containing Numerous Hitherto Unpublished Documents Concerning the Church in Connecticut.* 2 vols. New York, 1863.

Heimert, Alan, and Perry Miller, eds. *The Great Awakening: Documents Illustrating the Crisis and Its Consequences.* New York, 1967.

Hooker, Richard J., ed. *The Carolina Backcountry on the Eve of the Revolution: The Journal and Other Writings of Charles Woodmason, Anglican Itinerant.* Chapel Hill, N.C., 1953.

Lemay, J. A. Leo, and P. M. Zall. *The Autobiography of Benjamin Franklin: A Genetic Text.* Knoxville, Tenn., 1981.

Matthews, Albert, ed. "Diary of Rev. Thomas Prince." *Publications of the Colonial Society of Massachusetts* 19 (1917): 331–364.

M'Clure, David, and Elijah Parish, eds. *Memoirs of the Rev. Eleazar Wheelock, D. D. Founder and President of Dartmouth College and Moor's Charity School; With a Summary History of the College and School. To Which Are Added, Copious Extracts from Dr. Wheelock's Correspondence.* Newburyport, Mass., 1911. Reprint, New York, 1972.

Minkema, Kenneth, ed. "The Lynn End 'Earthquake' Relations of 1727." *New England Quarterly* 59 (September 1996): 473–499.

Perry, William S., ed. *Historical Collections Relating to the American Colonial Church.* 5 vols. 1870. Reprint, New York, 1969.

Prince, Thomas. *A Chronological History of New England.* Boston, 1736.

———. *The Salvation of God in 1746.* Boston, 1746.

A Protestation Presented to the Synod of Philadelphia. Philadelphia, 1741.

Rutman, Darrett, ed. *The Great Awakening: Event and Exegesis.* New York, 1970.

Seward, William. *Journal of a Voyage From Savannah to Philadelphia and From Phildelphia to England.* London, 1740.

Smith, Josiah. *The Character, Preaching, etc. Of the Reverend Mr. George Whitefield, Impartially Represented and Supported, in a Sermon.* Boston, 1740.

Stoddard, Solomon. *The Efficacy of the Fear of Hell to Restrain Men from Sin.* Boston, 1713.

Tappert, Theodore, and John Doberstein, trans. *The Journals of Henry Melchior Muhlenberg.* 3 vols. Philadelphia, 1942.

Tennent, Gilbert. *The Danger of Forgetting God, Describ'd and the Duty of Considering Our Ways Explain'd.* New York, 1735.

———. *The Danger of an Unconverted Ministry, Considered in a Sermon on Mark VI.34. . . .* Boston, 1742.

———. *The Necessity of Religious Violence in Order to Obtain Durable Happiness.* New York, 1735.

———. *Sermons on Sacramental Occasions by Divers Ministers.* Boston, 1739.

Testimony of the President, Professors, Tutors, and Hebrew Instructor of Harvard College, against George Whitefield. Boston, 1744.

Turell, Ebenezer. *Mr. Turell's Dialogue Between a Minister and his Neighbour about the Times.* Boston, 1742.

Walettt, Francis G. "The Diary of Ebenezer Parkman, 1739–1744." *Proceedings of the American Antiquarian Society* 72 (April 1962): 31–233.

Watts, Isaac. *An Humble Attempt Towards the Revival of Practical Christians.* 3d ed. London, 1742.

———. *Logick: Or, the Right Use of Reason in the Enquiry After Truth.* 4th ed. London, 1731.

Webster, Alexander. *Divine Influence: The True Spring of the Extraordinary Work at Cambuslang and Other Places in the West of Scotland.* Boston, 1743.

The Weekly History; Or, An Account of the Most Remarkable Particulars Relating to the Present Progress of the Gospel. By the Encouragement of the Rev. Mr. Whitefield (London). April 1741–November 1742.

Wigglesworth, Samuel. *An Essay for Reviving Religion.* Boston, 1733.

Williams, William. *The Duty and Interest of a People.* Boston, 1736.

Secondary Sources

Ahlstrom, Sydney E. *A Religious History of the American People.* New Haven, 1972.

Beales, Ross W., Jr. "God and Man at Yale, 1742." *Connecticut Historical Society Bulletin* 41 (January 1976): 29–32.

———. "Harvard and Yale in the Great Awakening." *Historical Journal of Massachusetts* 14 (January 1986): 1–10.

Bebb, Evelyn D. *Nonconformity and Social and Economic Life, 1660–1800: Some Problems of the Present as They Appeared in the Past.* London, 1935.

Berens, John F. "Religion and Revolution Reconsidered: Recent Literature on Religion and Nationalism in Eighteenth-Century America." *Canadian Review of the Study of Nationalism* (Fall 1979): 233–245.

Bloch, Ruth H. *Visionary Republic: Millennial Themes in American Thought, 1756–1800.* Cambridge, England, 1985.

Bonomi, Patricia U. *Under the Cope of Heaven: Religion, Society, and Politics in Colonial America.* New York, 1986.

Bonomi, Patricia U., and Peter R. Eisenstadt. "Church Adherence in the Eighteenth-Century British American Colonies." *William and Mary Quarterly* 39 (April 1982): 245–286.

Brauer, Jerald C. *Protestantism in America: A Narrative History.* Philadelphia, 1953.

Bridenbaugh, Carl. *Mitre and Sceptre: Transatlantic Faiths, Ideas, Personalities, and Politics, 1689–1775.* New York, 1962.

Brooke, John L. *The Heart of the Commonwealth: Society and Political Culture in Worcester County, Massachusetts, 1713–1861.* Cambridge, England, 1989.

Brown, Anne S. "Visions of Community in Eighteenth-Century Essex County: Chebacco Parish and the Great Awakening." *Essex Institute Historical Collections* 125 (July 1989): 239–262.

Bumsted, John. "Religion, Finance, and Democracy in Massachusetts: The Town of Norton as a Case Study." *Journal of American History* 58 (March 1971): 817–831.

———. "Revivalism and Separatism in New England: The First Society of Norwich, Connecticut, as a Case Study." *William and Mary Quarterly* 24 (October 1967): 588–612.

———. "Sermon Literature and the Louisbourg Campaign." *Dalhousie Review* 62 (Summer 1983): 264–276.

———. "'What Must I Do To Be Saved?': A Consideration of Recent Writings on the Great Awakening in Colonial America." *Caas Bulletin* 5 (Spring–Summer 1969): 22–53.

Bumsted, J. M., and John E. Van de Wetering. *What Must I Do to Be Saved? The Great Awakening in Colonial America.* Hinsdale, Ill., 1976.

Bushman, Richard. *From Puritan to Yankee: Character and Social Order in Connecticut, 1690–1765.* Cambridge, Mass., 1967.

Butler, Jon. *Awash in a Sea of Faith: Christianizing the American People.* Cambridge, Mass., 1990.

———. "Enthusiasm Described and Decried: The Great Awakening as Interpretive Fiction." *Journal of American History* 69 (September 1982): 305–325.

Campbell, Ted A. *The Religion of the Heart: A Study of European Religious Life in the Seventeenth and Eighteenth Centuries.* Columbia, S.C., 1991.

Carwardine, Richard. "The Second Great Awakening in the Urban Centers: An Examination of Methodism and the New Measures." *Journal of American History* 59 (September 1972): 327–340.

Cherry, Conrad. "Promoting the Cause and Testing the Spirits: Jonathan Edwards on Revivals of Religion—A Review Article." *Journal of Presbyterian History* 51 (Fall 1973): 327–337.

Clark, J.C.D. *English Society, 1688–1832: Ideology, Social Structure and Political Practice during the Ancien Regime.* Cambridge, England, 1985.

Clarke, William K. L. *Eighteenth Century Piety.* London, 1944.

Coalter, Milton J. *Gilbert Tennent, Son of Thunder: A Case Study of Continental Pietism's Impact on the First Great Awakening in the Middle Colonies.* New York. 1986.

Cook, Edward M., Jr. "Social Behavior and Changing Values in Dedham, Massachusetts, 1700 to 1775." *William and Mary Quarterly* 27 (October 1970): 546–580.

Cowing, Cedric. *The Saving Remnant: Religion and the Settling of New England.* Urbana, Ill., 1995.

———. "Sex and Preaching in the Great Awakening." *American Quarterly* 20 (Fall 1968): 624–644.

Crawford, Michael J. "The Invention of the American Revival: The Beginnings of Anglo-American Religious Revivalism, 1690–1750." Ph.D. diss., Boston University, 1978.

———. "Origins of the Eighteenth-Century Evangelical Revival: England and New England Compared." *Journal of British Studies* 27 (October 1987): 361–397.

———. *Seasons of Grace: Colonial New England's Revival Tradition in Its British Context.* New York, 1991.

Currie, Robert, Alan Gilbert, and Lee Horsley. *Churches and Churchgoers: Patterns of Church Growth in the British Isles since 1700.* Oxford, 1977.

Dallimore, Arnold A. *George Whitefield: The Life and Times of the Great Evangelist of the Eighteenth-Century Revival.* 2 vols. London, 1980.

Davies, C.S.L. *Peace, Print and Protestantism, 1450–1558.* London, 1977.

Davis, Mollie C. "The Countess of Huntingdon and Whitefield's Bethesda." *Georgia Historical Quarterly* 56 (Spring 1972): 72–82.

———. "George Whitefield's Attempt to Establish a College in Georgia." *Georgia Historical Quarterly* 55 (Winter 1971): 459–470.

Denault, Patricia. "Jonathan Edwards, The Great Awakener." *American History Illustrated* 6 (January 1972): 28–36.

Diefendorf, Barbara B., and Carla Hesse. *Culture and Identity in Early Modern Europe (1500–1800).* Ann Arbor, Mich., 1993.

Dowd, Gregory E. *A Spirited Resistance: The North American Indian Struggle for Identity, 1745–1815.* Baltimore, 1992.

Downey, James. *The Eighteenth Century Pulpit: A Study of the Sermons of Butler, Bradley, Secker, Sterne, Whitefield, and Wesley.* Oxford, 1969.

Durden [O'Brien], Susan. "A Study of the First Evangelical Magazines, 1740–1748." *Journal of Ecclesiastical History* 27 (July 1976): 255–275.

———. "Transatlantic Communications and Influence during the Great Awakening: A Comparative Study of British and American Revivalism, 1730–1760." Ph.D. diss., Hull University, 1978.

———. "A Transatlantic Community of Saints: The Great Awakening and the First Evangelical Network, 1735–1755." *American Historical Review* 91 (December 1986): 811–832.

Endy, Melvin B., Jr. "Just War, Holy War, and Millennialism in Revolutionary America." *William and Mary Quarterly* 42 (January 1985): 3–25.

Fawcett, Arthur. *The Cambuslang Revival: The Scottish Evangelical Revival of the Eighteenth Century.* London, 1971.

Febvre, Lucien, and Henri-Jean Martin. *The Coming of the Book: The Impact of Printing, 1450–1800.* Translated by David Gerard. London, 1976.

Fiering, Norman. *Jonathan Edwards's Moral Thought and Its British Context.* Chapel Hill, N.C., 1981.

Finke, Roger. "Religious Deregulation: Origins and Consequences." *Journal of Church and State* 32 (Summer 1990): 609–626.

Finke, Roger, and Rodney Stark. *The Churching of America, 1776–1990: Winners and Losers in Our Religious Economy.* New Brunswick, N.J., 1992.

Frantz, John B. "The Awakening of Religion among the German Settlers in the Middle Colonies." *William and Mary Quarterly* 33 (April 1976): 266–288.

Fraser, James W. "The Great Awakening and New Patterns of Presbterian Theological Education." *Journal of Presbyterian History* 60 (Fall 1982): 189–208.

Gallay, Alan. "Jonathan Bryan's Plantation Empire: Land, Politics, and the Formation of a Ruling Class in Colonial Georgia." *William and Mary Quarterly* 45 (April 1988): 253–279.

———. "The Origins of Slaveholders' Paternalism: George Whitefield, the Bryan Family, and the Great Awakening in the South." *Journal of Southern History* 53 (August 1987): 369–394.

Gaustad, Edwin S. *The Great Awakening in New England.* New York, 1957.

Geertz, Clifford. *The Interpretation of Cultures.* New York, 1973.

Gewehr, Wesley. *The Great Awakening in Virginia, 1740–1790.* Durham, N.C., 1930.

Gilbert, Alan D. *Religion and Society in Industrial England: Church, Chapel, and Social Change, 1740–1914.* London, 1976.

Goen, Clarence C. *Revivalism and Separatism in New England: Strict Congregationalists and Separate Baptists in the Great Awakening.* New Haven, 1962.

Goodwin, Gerald. "The Anglican Reaction to the Great Awakening." *Historical Magazine of the Protestant Episcopal Church* 35 (December 1966): 343–371.

Green, Richard. *Anti-Methodist Publications Issued during the Eighteenth Century.* London, 1902.

Greene, Jack P. "Search for Identity: An Interpretation of the Meaning of Selected Patterns of Social Response in Eighteenth-Century America." *Journal of Social History* 4 (Spring 1970): 189–219.

Greven, Philip J., Jr. *The Protestant Temperament: Patterns of Child-Rearing, Religious Experience, and the Self in Early America.* New York, 1977.

———. "Youth, Maturity, and Religious Conversion: A Note on the Ages of Converts in Andover, Massachusetts, 1711–1749." *Essex Institute Historical Collections* 108 (April 1972): 119–134.

Grossbart, Stephen R. "Seeking the Divine Favor: Conversion and Church Admission in Eastern Connecticut, 1711–1832." *William and Mary Quarterly* 46 (October 1989): 696–740.

Gura, Philip F. "Sowing for the Harvest: William Williams and the Great Awakening." *Journal of Presbyterian History* 56 (Winter 1978): 326–341.

Hall, David D. *Worlds of Wonder, Days of Judgment: Popular Religious Belief in Early New England.* New York, 1989.

Hall, Timothy D. *Contested Boundaries: Itinerancy and the Reshaping of the Colonial America1 Religious World.* Durham, N.C., 1994.

Harlan, David C. "The Travail of Religious Moderation: Jonathan Dickinson and the Great Awakening." *Journal of Presbyterian History* 61 (Winter 1983): 411–426.

Hatch, Nathan O. *The Democratization of American Christianity.* New Haven, 1989.

———. "The Origins of Civil Millennialism in America: New England Clergymen, War with France, and the Revolution." *William and Mary Quarterly* 31 (July 1974): 407–430.

Hawes, Clement. *Mania and Literary Style: The Rhetoric of Enthusiasm from the Ranters to Christopher Smart.* Cambridge, England, 1996.

Hawes, Lilla. "A Description of Whitefield's Bethesda: Samuel Fayrweather to Thomas Prince and Thomas Foxcroft." *Georgia Historical Quarterly* 45 (December 1961): 363–366.

Heimert, Alan. *Religion and the American Mind: From the Great Awakening to the Revolution.* Cambridge, Mass., 1966.

Heitzenrater, Richard P. "The Oxford Diaries and the First Rise of Methodism." *Methodist History* 7 (July 1974): 110–135.

Henretta, James A. *The Evolution of American Society, 1700–1815: An Interdisciplinary Study.* Lexington, Mass., 1973.

Henry, Stuart. *George Whitefield: Wayfaring Witness.* Nashville, Tenn., 1957.

Heyrman, Christine. *Commerce and Culture: The Maritime Communities of Colonial Massachusetts, 1690–1750.* New York, 1984.

Hiner, N. Ray. "Preparing for the Harvest: the Concept of New Birth and the Theory of Religious Education on the Eve of the First Awakening." *Fides et History* (Fall 1976): 8–25.

Holifield, E. Brooks. *The Covenant Sealed: The Development of Puritan Sacramental Theology, in Old and New England, 1570–1720.* New Haven, 1974.

Holstun, James, ed. *Pamphlet Wars: Prose in the English Revolution.* London, 1992.

Hoopes, James. "Jonathan Edwards' Religious Psychology." *Journal of American History* 70 (March 1983): 849–865.

Housley, Donald D. "The Response of Conservative Presbyterians to the Great Awakening in the Middle Colonies." *Susquehanna University Studies* 8 (June 1970): 301–314.

Ignatieff, Michael. *The Needs of Strangers.* New York, 1984.

Isaac, Rhys. "Dramatizing the Ideology of Revolution: Popular Mobilization in Virginia, 1774–1776." *William and Mary Quarterly* 33 (July 1976): 357–385.

———. "Religion and Authority: Problem of the Anglican Establishment in Virginia in the Era of the Great Awakening and the Parson's Cause." *William and Mary Quarterly* 30 (January 1973): 3–36.

———. *The Transformation of Virginia, 1740–1790.* Chapel Hill, N.C., 1982.

Jackson, Harvey. "Hugh Bryan and the Evangelical Movement in Colonial South Carolina." *William and Mary Quarterly* 43 (October 1986): 594–614.

Jones, George F., and Don Savell, eds. "The Fourth Transport of Georgia Salzburgers: Diary of Mr. Vigera from London to Ebenezer in Georgia, London, the 18th Sept. st. v. 1741." *Concordia Historical Institute Quarterly* 56 (Summer 1983): 52–64.

Kendall, R. T. *Calvin and English Calvinism to 1649.* New York, 1979.

Kenney, William H. "Alexander Garden and George Whitefield: The Significance of Revivalism in South Carolina, 1738–1741." *South Carolina Historical Magazine* 71 (January 1970): 1–16.

———. "George Whitefield, Dissenter Priest of the Great Awakening," *William and Mary Quarterly* 26 (January 1969): 75–93.

Lambert, Frank. "The Great Awakening as Artifact: George Whitefield and the Construction of Intercolonial Revival, 1739–1745." *Church History* 60 (June 1991): 223–246.

———. "'Pedlar in Divinity': George Whitefield and the Great Awakening, 1737–1745." *Journal of American History* 77 (December 1990): 812–837.

———. *"Pedlar in Divinity": George Whitefield and the Transatlantic Revivals, 1737–1770.* Princeton, 1994.

———. "Subscribing for Piety and Profits: The Friendship of Benjamin Franklin and George Whitefield ." *William and Mary Quarterly* 50 (July 1993): 529–554.

Landsman, Ned. "Revivalism and Nativism in the Middle Colonies: The Great Awakening and the Scots Community in East New Jersey." *American Quarterly* 34 (Summer 1982): 149–164.

Lemay, J.A.L. "Franklin's 'Dr. Spence': The Reverend Archibald Spencer (1698?–1760)." *Maryland Historical Magazine* 59 (June 1964): 199–216.

Lodge, Martin E. "The Crisis of the Churches in the Middle Colonies, 1720–1750." *Pennsylvania Magazine of History and Biography* 95 (April 1971): 195–220.

Lovejoy, David S. *Religious Enthusiasm in the New World: Heresy to Revolution.* Cambridge, Mass., 1985.

Lucas, Paul. *Valley of Discord: Church and Society along the Connecticut River, 1636–1725.* Hanover, N.H., 1976

McLoughlin, William G. *Billy Graham: Revivalist in a Secular Age.* New York, 1960.

———. "'Enthusiam for Liberty': The Great Awakening as the Key to the Revolution." *Proceedings of the American Antiquarian Society* 87 (April 1977): 69–95.

———. *Modern Revivalism: Charles Grandison Finney to Billy Graham.* New York, 1959.

———. *Revivals, Awakenings, and Reform: An Essay on Religion and Social Change in America, 1607–1977.* Chicago, 1978.

Marty, Martin. *Religion and Republic: The American Circumstance.* Boston, 1987.

Maxson, Charles H. *The Great Awakening in the Middle Colonies.* Chicago, 1920.

May, Henry. *The Enlightenment in America.* Cambridge, Mass., 1976.

Mead, Sidney. *The Lively Experiment: The Shaping of Christianity in America.* 1963. Reprint, New York, 1976.

Milburn, Geoffrey E. "Piety, Profit and Paternalism: Methodists in Business in the North-East of England, c.1760–1920." *Proceedings of the Wesley Historical Society* 43 (December 1983): 45–92.

Miller, John C. "Religion, Finance, and Democracy in Massachusetts." *New England Quarterly* 6 (1933): 29–58.

Miller, Perry. "Jonathan Edwards' Sociology of the Great Awakening." *New England Quarterly* 21 (1948): 50–78.

Miller, Perry. *Jonathan Edwards.* New York, 1949.

———. *The New England Mind: From Colony to Province.* Cambridge, Mass., 1953.

Minkema, Kenneth P. "A Great Awakening Conversion: The Relation of Samuel Belcher." *William and Mary Quarterly* 44 (January 1987): 121–126.

Moore, R. Laurence. *Religious Outsiders and the Making of Americans.* New York, 1986.

Moran, Gerald F. "Conditions of Religious Conversion in the First Society of Norwich, Connecticut, 1718–1744." *Journal of Social History* 6 (Spring 1972): 331–341.

Morgan, David T. "The Consequences of George Whitefield's Ministry in Georgia and the Carolinas." *Georgia Historical Quarterly* 55 (Spring 1971): 62–82.

———. "The Great Awakening in South Carolina, 1740–1755." *South Atlantic Quarterly* 70 (Autumn 1971): 595–606.

Morgan, Edmund. *Inventing the People: The Rise of Popular Sovereignty in England and America.* New York, 1988.

———. *Visible Saints: The History of a Puritan Idea.* New York, 1963.

Nash, Gary B. *Forging Freedom: The Formation of Philadelphia's Black Community, 1720–1840.* Cambridge, Mass., 1988.

———. *The Urban Crucible: Social Change, Political Consciousness and the Origins of the American Revolution.* Cambridge, Mass., 1979.

Niebuhr, H. Richard. *The Social Sources of Denominationalism.* 1929. Reprint, Hamden, Conn., 1954.

Nobles, Gregory H. *Divisions throughout the Whole: Politics and Society in Hampshire County, Massachusetts, 1740–1775.* Cambridge, England, 1983.

Noll, Mark A., David W. Bebbington,, and George A. Rawlyk, eds. *Evangelicalism: Comparative Studies of Popular Protestantism in North America, the British Isles, and Beyond, 1700–1990.* New York, 1994.

Nordbeck, Elizabeth. "Almost Awakened: The Great Revival in New Hampshire and Maine, 1727–1748." *History of New Hampshire* 35 (Spring 1980): 23–58.

Nybakken, Elizabeth J. "New Light on the Old Side: Irish Influences on Colonial Presbyterianism." *Journal of American History* 69 (March 1982): 813–832.

O'Connell, Neil J. "George Whitefield and Bethesda Orphan-House." *Georgia Historical Quarterly* 54 (Spring 1970): 40–62.

Onuf, Peter S. "New Lights in New London: A Group Portrait of the Separatists." *William and Mary Quarterly* 37 (October 1980): 627–643.

Payne, Rodger M. "New Light in Hanover County: Evangelical Dissent in Piedmont Virginia, 1740–1755." *Journal of Southern History* 61 (November 1995): 665–694.

Pears, Thomas, ed. "William Tennent's Sacramental Sermon." *Journal of the Department of History of the Presbyterian Church in the U.S.A.* 19 (June 1940): 76–84.

Pears, Thomas, and Guy Klett, eds. "Documentary History of William Tennent and the Log College." *Journal of the Department of History of the Presbyterian Historical Society* 28 (March 1950): 37–64.

Probert, John C. C. *The Sociology of Cornish Methodism to the Present Day.* Redruth, England, 1971.

Raboteau, Albert. *Slave Religion: The "Invisible Institution" in the Antebellum South.* Oxford, 1978.

Raimo, John W. "Spiritual Harvest: The Anglo-American Revival in Boston, Massachusetts, and Bristol, England, 1739–1742." Ph.D. diss., University of Wisconsin, 1974.

Ramsey, David A., and R. Craig Koedel. "The Communion Season—An Eighteenth-Century Model." *Journal of Presbyterian History* 54 (Summer 1976): 203–216.

Rawlyk, George. *Ravished by the Spirit: Religious Revivals, Baptists, and Henry Alline.* Montreal, 1984.

———. *Wrapped Up in God: A Study of Several Canadian Revivals and Revivalists.* Burlington, Ontario, 1988.

Rawlyk, George, and Gordon Stewart. *A People Highly Favoured of God: The Nova Scotia Yankees and the American Revolution.* Hamden, Conn., 1972.

Remer, Rosalind. "Old Lights and New Money: A Note on Religion, Economics, and the Social Order in 1740 Boston." *William and Mary Quarterly* 47 (October 1990): 566–573.

Richey, Russell E. *Early American Methodism.* Bloomington, Ind., 1991.

Roberts, R. Phillip. *Continuity and Change: London Calvinistic Baptists and the Evangelical Revivals, 1760–1820.* Wheaton, Ill., 1989.

Rutter, Robert S. "The New Birth: Evangelicalism in the Transatlantic Community during the Great Awakening, 1739–1745." Ph.D. diss., Rutgers University, 1982.

Sargent, Mark l. "Plymouth Rock and the Great Awakening." *Journal of American Studies* 22 (August 1988): 249–254.

Schmidt, Leigh E. *Holy Fairs: Scottish Communions and American Revivals in the Early Modern Period.* Princeton, 1989.

———. "'A Second and Glorious Reformation': The New Light Extremism of Andrew Croswell." *William and Mary Quarterly* 43 (April 1986): 214–244.

Scribner, R. W. *Popular Culture and Popular Movements in Reformation Germany.* London, 1987.

Semmel, Bernard. *The Methodist Revolution.* New York, 1973.

Seymour, A.C.H. *The Life and Times of Selina Countess of Huntingdon.* 2 vols. London, 1840.

Shea, Daniel B., Jr. *Spiritual Autobiography in Early America.* Princeton, 1968.

Shute, Michael N. "A Little Great Awakening: An Episode in the American Enlightenment." *Journal of the History of Ideas* 37 (October–December 1976): 589–602.

Sklar, Robert. "The Great Awakening and Colonial Politics: Connecticut's Revolution in the Minds of Men." *Connecticut Historical Society Bulletin* 28 (July 1963): 81–95.

Smith, Timothy L., ed. *Whitefield and Wesley on the New Birth.* Grand Rapids, Mich., 1986.

Smout, T. C. "Born Again at Cambuslang: New Evidence on Popular Religion and Literacy in Eighteenth-Century Scotland." *Past and Present* 97 (November 1982): 114–127.

Stein, Stephen. "George Whitefield on Slavery: Some New Evidence." *Church History* 42 (June 1973): 243–256.

Stoeffler, F. Ernst. *The Rise of Evangelical Pietism.* Leiden, 1971.

———, ed. *Continental Pietism and Early American Christianity.* Grand Rapids, Mich., 1976.

Stout, Harry S. *The Divine Dramatist: George Whitefield and the Rise of Modern Evangelicalism.* Grand Rapids, Mich., 1991.

———. *The New England Soul: Preaching and Religious Culture in Colonial New England.* New York, 1986.

———. "Religion, Communications, and the Ideological Origins of the American Revolution." *William and Mary Quarterly* 34 (October 1977): 519–541.

Stout, Harry S., and Peter S. Onuf. "James Davenport and the Great Awakening in New London." *Journal of American History* 70 (December 1983): 556–578.

Sweet, William W. *The Story of Religion in America.* 1930. Reprint, New York, 1950.

Thomas, Isaiah. *The History of Printing in America.* 2 vols. Worcester, Mass., 1810.

Tracy, Joseph. *The Great Awakening: A History of the Revival of Religion in the Time of Edwards and Whitefield.* Boston, 1841.

Tracy, Patricia J. *Jonathan Edwards, Pastor: Religion and Society in Eighteenth-Century Northampton.* New York, 1980.

Tyerman, Luke. *The Life of George Whitefield.* 2 vols. New York, 1877.

———. *The Life and Times of the Rev. John Wesley, M.A.: Founder of the Methodists.* 3 vols. London, 1872–1875.

Valeri, Mark. "The New Divinity and the American Revolution." *William and Mary Quarterly* 46 (October 1989): 741–769.

Vandermeer, Philip R., and Robert P. Swierengs, eds. *Belief and Behavior: Essays in the New Religious History.* New Brunswick, N.J., 1991.

Walsh, James. "The Great Awakening in the First Congregation of Woodbury, Connecticut." *William and Mary Quarterly* 28 (October 1971): 543–562.

Walsh, John. "Religious Societies: Methodist and Evangelical, 1738–1800." In *Voluntary Religion*, ed. W. J. Shields and Diana Wood, 279–302. Worcester, England, 1986.

Warch, Richard. "The Shepherd's Tent: Education and Enthusiasm in the Great Awakening." *American Quarterly* 30 (Summer 1978): 177–198.

Ward, W. R. "Power and Piety: The Origins of Religious Revival in the Early Eighteenth Century." *Bulletin of the John Rylands University Library* 63 (1980): 231–252.

——. *The Protestant Evangelical Awakening.* Cambridge, England, 1992.

Weber, Donald. *Rhetoric and History in Revolutionary New England.* New York, 1988.

Westerkamp, Marilyn J. *Triumph of the Laity: Scots-Irish Piety and the Great Awakening, 1625–1760.* New York, 1988.

White, Eugene E. "The Decline of the Great Awakening in New England, 1741–1746." *New England Quarterly* 34 (1961): 35–52.

Willingham, William F. "Religious Conversions in the Second Society of Windham, Connecticut." *Societas* 6 (1976): 109–119.

Wolfe, Don M., ed., *Leveller Manifestoes of the Puritan Revolution.* London, 1944.

——. *Milton in the Puritan Revolution.* London, 1941.

Yodelis, M. A. "Boston's First Newspaper War: A 'Great Awakening' of Freedom." *Journalism Quarterly* 51 (Summer 1974): 207–212.

Index